The publisher gratefully acknowledges the generous contribution to this book provided by the Philip E. Lilienthal Asian Studies Endowment Fund of the University of California Press Associates, which is supported by a major gift from Sally Lilienthal.

MODERN MONGOLIA

A

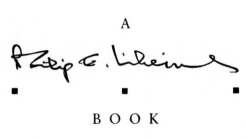

■   ■   ■

B O O K

MODERN MONGOLIA

From Khans to Commissars to Capitalists

Morris Rossabi

University of California Press   Berkeley   Los Angeles   London

FUP

Portions of chapter 1 derive from first-draft narratives of Peter Ackerman and
Jack DuVall, *A Force More Powerful: A Century of Nonviolent Conflict* (New
York: St. Martin's Press, 2000). Portions of chapter 5 appeared in different form
in the introduction to Tserendash Namkhainyambuu, *Bounty from the Sheep:
Autobiography of a Herdsman*, trans. Mary Rossabi (Cambridge: White Horse
Press, 2000). Portions of chapters 8 and 9 appeared in different form in "A New
Mongolia in a New World," in *Mongolian Political and Social Development dur-
ing the Past Ten Years and Future Prospect* (Taipei: Mongolian and Tibetan Affairs
Commission, 2000).

University of California Press
Berkeley and Los Angeles, California

University of California Press, Ltd.
London, England

Library of Congress Cataloging-in-Publication Data
Rossabi, Morris.
    Modern Mongolia : from khans to commissars to capitalists / Morris
Rossabi.
        p.   cm.
    Includes bibliographical references and index.
    ISBN 0-520-24399-4 (cloth : alk. paper) — ISBN 0-520-24419-2 (pbk. : alk.
paper)
    1. Mongolia—History—1990– I. Title: From khans to commissars to capi-
talists. II. Title.
    DS798.84.r67   2005
    951.7'3—dc22   2004017992

13 12 11 10 09 08 07 06 05
10 9 8 7 6 5 4 3 2 1

CONTENTS

Illustrations follow page 113.

This book has turned out to be the most challenging and most personally involving of all my writings. It is based in part on interviews and on-site observations: I visited slaughterhouses and cashmere processing factories, attended rock, folk, and classical music concerts, was guided by Mongolian herdsmen on a horse-riding journey through pristine, beautiful, and sparsely populated terrain, sat in on meetings of herders' cooperatives and women's NGOS, ate at pseudo-Italian, French, and Japanese restaurants in Ulaanbaatar, and, after terrifying jeep rides through the Mongolian steppelands and deserts, drank swamp water and milk vodka and ate fried bread, noodle soup, and boiled mutton.

I also interviewed stalwart officials from the communist era, herdsmen, members of the Khural, or parliament, and the president of Mongolia, film directors, surveyors of public opinion, scientists, politicians, students, health care workers, teachers, journalists, and Western advisors and consultants. Most of the interviewees could be classified as members of the elite, or at least those who have generally prospered as a result of the postcommunist transition. I talked with unemployed workers and professionals and poor herdsmen as well, but not as frequently as with the elite. Nor were they generally as articulate as the latter. Interviews are, moreover, often principally anecdotal, and interviewees may exaggerate or either intentionally or unintentionally falsify information, and I have sought to correct for the resulting biases by referring to written sources and statistical data and cross-checking among interviews.

My research and publications have, until recently, centered on traditional China and Central Asia and on the Mongolian Empire. The most consuming such project was my 1988 biography of Khubilai Khan, who sought to govern rather than plunder the lands subjugated by the Mongols. Like Khubilai Khan, the leaders who have come to power in Mongolia since the fall of communism in 1990 have attempted to develop institutions of governance. They themselves have esteemed the unifier and conqueror Chinggis Khan as the father of the Mongolians, a view that has some merit, but their true model should be Chinggis's grandson Khubilai, who went beyond unification and conquest to establish a government. Thus I have chosen to dub them the heirs of Khubilai Khan.

This book had its genesis in an invitation from Anthony Richter of the Open Society Institute (OSI, a part of the Soros Foundations) to accompany him to Mongolia in May 1994 to ascertain whether the Foundation could fill a niche in fostering democracy, basic freedoms, and transparency in the country. We interviewed a remarkable array of Mongolians and foreigners in Mongolia. From early morning until way past supper, we met with representative figures of a new Mongolia. Our host Dashiin Byambasüren, the first prime minister in post-communist Mongolia, and his assistants Perenlei Erdenejargal (later to be assistant director of the Mongolian Foundation for Open Society, the Soros Foundation office in Mongolia) and Chuluuny Ganbold (later the founder of the E-Mail Daily News or EDN, an important source for this book) facilitated our meetings with everyone from the president to directors of women's NGO, members of the Khural, university officials, foreign advisors, and foreign representatives of philanthropic organizations. On my return to the United States, I wrote a report proposing that OSI open a branch in Mongolia and suggesting specific program initiatives.

A year and a half later, Anthony Richter informed me that OSI would open an office in Mongolia and invited me to serve on an advisory board for the Foundation's Project on Open Society in Central Eurasia, which supervised activities in Armenia, Azerbaijan, Mongolia, Tajikistan, and Uzbekistan. As a member of the advisory board, I subsequently recommended Christopher Finch, who had taken my course in Mongolian history at Columbia University, to OSI as the first executive director of the Mongolian office, a position he assumed in the fall of 1996.

The advisory board of the Project on Central Eurasia, concerned about the paucity of materials on postcommunist Mongolia, commissioned me to write a pamphlet on developments in Mongolia since 1990, together with a brief introduction on traditional Mongolian society. I accordingly returned to Mongolia in January 1997 to conduct interviews and to seek research materials for the pamphlet entitled *Mongolia in the 1990s: From Commissars to Capitalists?* which was issued in the Open Society in Central Eurasia Occasional Paper Series in August 1997. By then, I had become intrigued by the changes, both positive and negative, in postcommunist Mongolia

Recognizing that my work with OSI and my studies of Mongolian history and culture gave me remarkable access to the subject, I conceived of a book on Mongolia since the collapse of communism. No other comprehensive work had appeared, and no specialist on Mongolia had explained why the country, despite its rank as the fifth largest per capita recipient of foreign aid in the world, had very high rates of poverty and unemployment, weak growth of gross domestic product (GDP), and declining state services. This work seeks possible explanations and simultaneously focuses on the principal Mongolian actors and their foreign advisors.

I applied for and received a fellowship from OSI to pursue such a study, and in the following year, I obtained a grant from the Smith Richardson Foundation to spend additional time on research. In 1998, I spent two months in Mongolia. Every year since then, I have visited Mongolia at least once a year for periods of from three weeks to several months. I have conducted my own research but have also served, on occasion, as an advisor to the Mongolian Foundation for an Open Society (Soros Foundation) on the Culture and Arts and Higher Education programs and on the development of an open forum as a means of fostering public discussion and debate on issues of public policy. I also went several times simply to familiarize myself with the various regions of this beautiful country and some of its remarkable people.

It is easier to observe the influence of globalization, the market economy, unemployment, poverty, and identity crises in Mongolia, with its population of only some 2.5 million, as opposed to China, with its population of 1.3 billion. I have been able to meet Mongolian educators, officials, clerics, film directors, and pastoralists with less difficulty than in a more populated country. Diverse views have been more readily available, and trends and developments have been somewhat easier to spot. Corruption, the influences of both Mongolians and foreigners, and the motives underlying particular policies are more readily apparent. I do not wish to imply that a study of modern Mongolia is not daunting. But it has been my good fortune to have had access to a wide variety of perceptive Mongolians and foreigners to complement my own research in written sources.

I have frequently mentioned OSI, another agency that facilitated my research and writing. Its representatives prompted my initial interest and research on modern Mongolia. Its fellowship program provided the opportunity for a year of research in both Mongolia and the United States, and I have learned a great deal about Mongolia from evaluations of some of its projects. However, this book reflects my own views and not those of OSI. I would not expect OSI or its Mongolian Foundation to concur with all of my own findings, although we obviously share a desire to foster democracy and a better life, with decent health, educational, and welfare facilities, for the Mongolian people.

A significant part of this book deals with the activities in Mongolia of international donor agencies such as the International Monetary Fund, the World Bank, the Asian Development Bank, the Japanese International Cooperation Agency, and the U.S. Agency for International Development and some of their contractors and consultants, although I should add that their views are not unanimous. With the collapse of communism in 1990, these agencies had an opportunity to foster an equitable and productive economy if they took into account Mongolia's unique heritage and society. Instead, they advised Mongolian officials to adopt the so-called Washington Consensus—an economic plan that was proposed throughout the former communist world. This book is, in some ways, a case study of attempts by true believers in a market economy, both foreigners and Mongolians, to reshape the political, economic, social, and cultural life of Mongolia by means of a market economy, with which most Mongolians had had limited experience. The ensuing shock therapy menu of privatization, minimal government, and sale of state enterprises has resulted in some political benefits (stability, peaceful transfer of power from one political party to another) but has also led to unemployment, poverty, growing disparities in income, declining educational, medical, and social welfare facilities, and reduced support for the arts, culture, and environmental protection. The advocates of these economic changes have not come up with sufficient funding to cope with the negative consequences of their advice. This book describes some of both the positive and negative consequences of the policies they championed. I ought to add that many representatives of these international donor agencies were honorable and presumed that their activities were helping Mongolia. When this book describes some of the negative results of their policies, it is critical of the underlying philosophies of the agencies but not of their often dedicated personnel.

I have, over the past few years, studied the broad theoretical issues of globalization, neoliberalism, or the so-called Washington Consensus, and pure market fundamentalism, and I trust that this book will contribute to the discussion. However, in focusing on Mongolia, a test case in the policy debates concerning these vital and contentious issues, I have refrained from speculation in this respect. I believe that empirical evidence will prove useful in these discussions, and I have offered such data and analysis in this book. Likewise, I have generally not attempted to compare Mongolia to the other postcommunist countries undergoing transformation, because the transitions in each of these have differed considerably and such comparisons would have diverted me from my own central concerns here.

I have incurred numerous debts in the writing of this book. For financial support, I am indebted to the Individual Fellows Program of the Open Society Institute and to the Smith Richardson Foundation. Both provided fellowships that offered time to conduct research and to write, and neither has sought to influence me in any way. The Mongolian and Tibetan Affairs Commission in Taiwan twice invited me to present papers at conferences on Mongolia, which formed first drafts of two chapters in this book. I wrote a draft of a third chapter for a conference organized by Professors Ole Bruun and Li Narangoa titled "Mongolians from Country to City," held in Copenhagen in October 1999. The discussions at these conferences were invaluable in helping me to revise these chapters.

The late Michel Oksenberg arranged a three-months' stay for me at Stanford University in the winter quarter of 1999 to continue my research. Several speeches to faculty and students helped me clarify my views. Like many others in the field of East Asian studies, I am indebted to Mike for his support of research on modern East Asia. I am also grateful to him for his and his wife's hospitality during my stay in Palo Alto.

I presented parts of this book in speeches at the Council of Foreign Relations, the University of Toronto, the Modern China Seminar at Columbia University, the Woodrow Wilson Center, Florida Atlantic University, the Smithsonian Institution, an informal symposium on Inner Asia funded by Harvard University, the China Institute, and the annual meeting of the Association for Asian Studies at San Diego. The audiences at each of these meetings offered useful and much appreciated criticism of my ideas.

I should like to thank all of the Mongolians and foreigners who permitted me to interview them. Even if I eventually arrived at conclusions that differ from their assessments, their contributions to this work were notable.

I should like as well to cite some friends and colleagues whose assistance was critical: Anthony Richter (of OSI); Jenny Lawrence (formerly of *Natural History* magazine) and John Snyder; Chris Finch (formerly of the Mongolian Foundation for Open Society, or MFOS); Perenlei Erdenejargal (of MFOS); the freelance journalist Lkhagvasüren Nomin; Luvsandendev Sumati of the Sant Maral Foundation; Jargalsaikhany Enkhsaikhan, the former ambassador of Mongolia to the United Nations; Foreign Minister Luvsangiin Erdenechuulun; Robin Mearns of the World Bank; Professor Carl Riskin of Queens College and Columbia University; Professors Thomas Bernstein and Andrew Nathan of Columbia University; Tserenpil Ariunaa, executive director of the Arts Council of Mongolia; Professor Ole Bruun of the Nordic Institute of Asian Studies; Professor Steven Fish of the University of California at Berkeley; Professor Steven Kotkin of Princeton University; Professor Caroline Humphrey of Cambridge University; and Dr. Sanjaasüregiin Oyun and Hashbat Hulan, present and former members of the Khural respectively.

My brother Mayer became quite ill while I was in Mongolia. Knowing that he was dying, he still insisted that I finish my studies before returning to the United States, and he died a month after I came back. We had planned to grow old together on the Upper West Side of Manhattan. Sadly, that is not to be. I trust that this book will be a fitting memorial to his concerns for social justice and equity.

This is the third book that I have published with the University of California Press. On two of them, I have had the good fortune to work with Sheila Levine. She has added immeasurably to this book by asking the right questions, which required rethinking and rewriting parts of the manuscript. I am grateful for her assistance.

My children Amy and Tony were rightly involved with their families and work, but they encouraged, even prodded, me to complete the book. My wife Mary, who participated in many of the interviews and who translated *Bounty from the Sheep,* the autobiography of a Mongolian shepherd, which proved useful for this work, could almost be a co-author of this book. She traveled with me to Mongolia and discussed and analyzed my ideas, contributing a great deal to the final work. If I wrote any more about her contributions, I would embarrass her. So let me stop here.

ABBREVIATIONS AND ACRONYMS

ADB	Asian Development Bank
ADRA	Adventist Development and Relief Agency
AI	Amnesty International
ALA [European Union]	program to assist Asian and Latin American developing countries
DANIDA	Danish International Development Assistance
EDN	E-Mail Daily News, Mongolia
EIU, *Mongolia*	Economist Intelligence Unit Country Report, Mongolia
FBIS	Foreign Broadcast Information Service
IMF	International Monetary Fund
IRI	International Republican Institute
JICA	Japanese International Cooperation Agency
MDU	Mongolian Democratic Union
MFOS	Mongolian Foundation for Open Society
MNA	Montsame Mongolian News Agency
MNDP	Mongolian National Democratic Party
MPR	Mongolian People's Republic
MPRP	Mongolian People's Revolutionary Party
MSDP	Mongolian Social Democratic Party

NGO	nongovernmental organization
NORAD	Norwegian Agency for International Development Cooperation
OSI	Open Society Institute, part of the Soros Foundations
TACIS	[European Union] Technical Assistance to the Confederation of Independent States
UNDP	United Nations Development Programme
USAID	United States Agency for International Development
WHO	World Health Organization

PROMINENT MONGOLIANS IN THE NARRATIVE

Mongolians generally use only their personal names, although they retain their patronymics as their surnames. I generally give both names on first mention and thereafter follow the Mongolian practice and refer to them only by their personal names. In this list, full Mongolian names are presented in the following order: first name, followed by a comma, followed by the surname.

Amarjargal, Rinchinnyamyn
Leading advocate of the pure market economy; director of the College of Economics and Finance, 1991–96; minister of external relations, 1998–99; prime minister, 1999–2000

Bagabandi, Natsagiin
Member of the Central Committee of MPRP, 1990–92; member and Speaker of the Khural, 1992–97; president of Mongolia, 1997–present

Bat-Uul, Erdenii
March 1990 hunger striker; one of the founders of the Mongolian Democratic Union and the Mongolian Democratic Party in 1990; member of the Khural, 1996–2000

Batbayar, Bat-Erdeniin ("Baabar")
Founding member and chair of the Mongolian Social Democratic Party, 1990–96; has written popular versions of Mongolian history; minister of finance, 1998

Batmünkh, Jambyn
MPRP general secretary and MPR premier, 1984–90

Bold, Luvsanvandangiin — Reputedly Mongolia's first millionaire; founder of Bodi International and director of the Golomt Bank; member of the Khural, 1996–2000

Byambasüren, Dashiin — First prime minister after the first multiparty elections in Mongolian history, 1990–92; member of the Khural, 1992–96

Elbegdorj, Tsakhiagiin — Military journalist active in the 1989–90 demonstrations; member of the Khural, 1990–2000; head of the Mongolian Democratic Union, 1990–96; prime minister, April–July, 1998; forced to resign owing to bank scandal; prime minister, 2004–

Enkhbayar, Nambaryn — Member of the Khural and minister of culture, 1992– 96; general secretary of the MPRP, 1996–2000; prime minister, 2000–2004; Speaker of the Khural, 2004–

Enkhsaikhan, Mendsaikhany — Economist supportive of pure market economy; leader of Mongolian democrats; member of the Khural, 1990–96; first prime minister during era of Democratic Union, 1996–98

Erdenebat, Badarchyn — President of Erel Mining Company; founder of the Motherland Democratic Party; member of the Khural, 2000–2004

Erdenebileg, Tömör-öchiryn — Grandson of Tömör-öchir, a leading Communist official purged in 1962; prominent democratic reformer, brother-in-law of Hulan Hashbat, member of the Khural, 1996–2000

Ganbold, Davaadorjiin — Principal exponent of shock therapy and the pure market economy; founder of the National Progressive Party in 1990; first deputy premier, 1990–92; member of the Khural, 1990–2000

Hulan, Hashbat — Leader among the democratic reformers; member of the Khural, 1996–2000; chair of the Social Welfare Subcommittee of the Khural, 1996–2000

Idshinnorov, Sunduyn — Historian purged in 1962; director of National Museum of Mongolian History, 1995–2003; died 2003

Jargalsaikhan, Bazarsadyn	President of the Buyan Cashmere Company; ardent supporter of the pure market economy; founder of the Republican Party
Jasrai, Puntsagiin	Leader of the old guard communists; member of MPRP Central Committee; prime minister, 1992–96
Narantsatsralt, Janlavyn	Mayor of Ulaanbaatar, 1996–98; prime minister, 1998–99; ousted owing to Erdenet scandal of 1999
Nomin, Lkhagvasüren	Leading journalist; granddaughter of the military hero and minister of defense Jamyangiin Lkhag-vasüren
Ochirbat, Punsalmaagiin	Chair of the Khural, 1990–92; first elected president of Mongolia, 1992–97
Odjargal, Jambaljamtsyn	Founder and president of the MCS International Company; strong links with international financial organizations
Oyun, Sanjaasürengiin	Member of the Khural, 1998–present; founder of the Civil Will Party; Cambridge University Ph.D. in geology; Deputy Speaker of the Khural, 2004–
Sumati, Luvsandendev	Founder of the Sant Maral Foundation; leading pollster in Mongolia
Tsagaan, Puntsagiin	Promoter of the pure market economy; director of Golomt Bank, 1995–96; minister of finance, 1996–98
Tuya, Nyam-Osoryn	Member of the General Council of the Mongolian National Democratic Party; first woman to serve as minister of foreign relations, 1999–2000
Ulaan, Chultemiin	Member of the Khural, 1996–2004; minister of finance, 2000–2004
Unenbat, Jigjidiin	Director of the Mongol Central Bank, 1996–2000; one of architects of the abortive and scandal-tarnished merger of the Reconstruction and Golomt Banks in 1998

Zoljargal, Naidansürengiin Ardent advocate of the pure market economy; director of the Stock Exchange, 1990–96; senior advisor to Prime Minister Elbegdorj, 1998

Zorig, Sanjaasürengiin Leader of the democratic movement in 1990; member of the Khural, 1990–98; minister of infrastructure in 1998; murdered October 1998

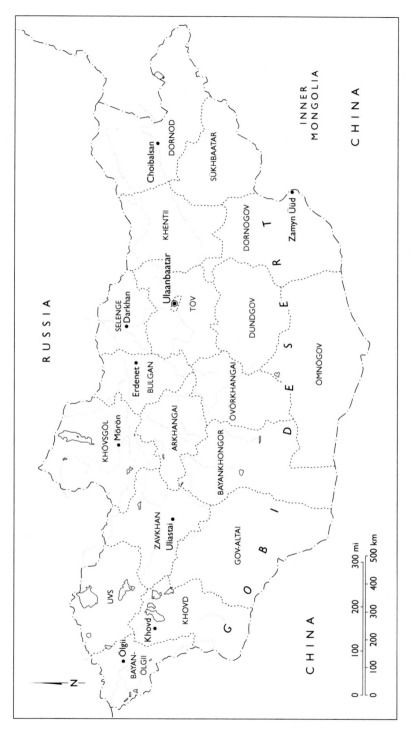

RUSSIA

INNER MONGOLIA

CHINA

Choibalsan
DORNOD

SÜKHBAATAR

Zamyn Üüd

KHENTII

DORNOGOV

SELENGE
Darkhan

Ulaanbaatar

TÖV

DUNDGOV

Erdenet

BULGAN

ÖVÖRKHANGAI

ÖMNÖGOV

KHÖVSGÖL
Mörön

ARKHANGAI

BAYANKHONGOR

ZAVKHAN
Uliastai

GOV-ALTAI

UVS

KHOVD

Khovd

BAYAN-ÖLGII
Ölgii

N

CHINA

T R E S D I B O G

300 mi
500 km

0   100   200   300 mi
0   100   200   300   400   500 km

Mongolia

The December 10, 1989, Mongolian celebrations of International Human Rights Day did not proceed as planned. The authoritarian communist government that had ruled Mongolia since 1921 had in the past orchestrated numerous demonstrations, as well as so-called spontaneous mass movements, to commemorate important events or personalities in its history or launch new policies or programs. Military pageants, lengthy speeches by leaders of the Mongolian People's Revolutionary Party (MPRP), the only legal political party, and snippets of patriotic and communist songs and folk dances, performed by resplendently costumed professionals, characterized these ceremonies, as did the ever-present security guards, who kept close tabs on the crowds. Competitions in the three traditional Mongolian sports of archery, wrestling, and horse-racing highlighted highlighted the Naadam festival.[1] The rulers of the Mongolian People's Republic (MPR), the name of the country since 1924, had had abundant experience in managing such spectacles, but they would be unable to manage the events of December 10, 1989.

Like their counterparts in the USSR and the People's Republic of China, Mongolian government officials and MPRP leaders had access to an ideal public space for some of these celebrations. The Soviet Union had Red Square in Moscow, the PRC had Tiananmen Square in Beijing, and Mongolia had Sükhbaatar Square in Ulaanbaatar, named for Sükhbaatar, who in July 1921 proclaimed the country's independence from China, confirming the victory of communism in the country. Like the main squares in Moscow and Beijing, Sükhbaatar Square is in the center of the capital. A large statue of Sükhbaatar on his horse is one of the two principal features of the square, which is otherwise mainly vacant. Government House, where the Khural, or parliament, meets and in which government and MPRP leaders have offices, is situated behind the second structure, a mausoleum in which repose the remains of Sükh-baatar and his successor, Choibalsan, often referred to as Mongolia's Stalin. Government House overlooks the square, permitting officials to observe and hear public events. Other buildings around the square include the Palace of Culture, which houses the National Modern Art Gallery, and the State Opera and Ballet Theater.

The scene observers in Government House witnessed on December 10, 1989, both surprised and shocked them. As snow drifted down gently, two hundred people marched around with banners and signs calling for the elimination of "bureaucratic oppression" as well as a promise to implement perestroika (in Mongolian, *uurchlun baiguulalt,* or "restructuring of the economy") and glasnost (*il tod,* or "openness and greater freedom of expression"). The demonstrators were mostly young, well-dressed, polite, and in no way obstreperous, but officials in Government House surely heard them articulate their demands, as the rock band Khonkh ("Bell") provided musical accompaniment.[2] Neither the government nor its security guards made any moves to disperse the small crowd, but officials must have been relieved when the demonstrators left the square.

They were concerned about the makeup of the crowd, which included some of their own well-educated and sophisticated adult children. The ensuing conflict could be interpreted as an intergenerational struggle for power. Most of the officials were in their fifties and sixties, and most of the demonstrators were in their twenties or early thirties. Many of these scions of privileged families had received their educations in the USSR or Eastern Europe and had been exposed to the new ideas swirling around in the freer Soviet era of the 1980s. All knew one or another of the Slavic languages, and several were comfortable in English and German, offering them exposure to Western newspapers, radio, and television.

Born in 1962 to an elite family, Sanjaasürengiin Zorig, later known as the "Golden Magpie of Democracy" and commonly accepted as the leader of the democratic movement, was in many ways typical of this group. His father was a Buryat—that is, from a minority Mongolian group—and his mother, a physician, was half-Russian and half-Mongolian. His paternal grandfather, a distinguished Russian scientist and explorer, had died in a Siberian prison camp. His maternal grandfather, a Buryat herdsman, had met the same fate as many Buryats in his generation: owing probably to a directive from the USSR, the Mongolian government had executed him.[3] Although Zorig had received his elementary and secondary education in Mongolia, he had attended Moscow State University, graduating in 1985 with degrees in philosophy and the social sciences. Moscow State University introduced him to the excitement of student groups calling for an end to communist repression.[4]

Returning to Mongolia, Zorig found few reverberations of the concept of political diversity, which was gaining ground in the USSR. By 1986, he had become a lecturer in the Faculty of Social Sciences at the Mongolian National University and had started to broach the new ideas with students and faculty. Shortly thereafter, he began to meet with like-minded young people, some of whom had also studied in the USSR, to discuss political reforms and the elimination of the oppressive communist bureaucracy. In 1988, he organized a so-called New Generation group that often met in his apartment and also secretly pasted placards in Ulaanbaatar challenging the autocratic government. Recognized as "one of the promising young theoreticians in his field" and "very educated" compared to others in the group, Zorig won the respect of his contemporaries, in part because he espoused nonviolence.[5]

Zorig's younger sister Sanjaasürengiin Oyun, who attended many of these meetings, modestly says that she was "in the background . . . taking care of all the housework . . . in the apartment . . . and cooking for Zorig's friends." However, her fluency in English meant that she was invaluable in translating declarations and, later, in interpreting for foreign journalists who wished to interview her brother. She had her first taste of politics in 1989–90, although she maintains that she was "not in the forefront of events." After receiving bachelor's and master's degrees in geochemistry from Karlova University in Prague, she had spent two years as a field geologist in Mongolia. Called to the capital by her family after the December 10 demonstration, she loyally stayed on for almost a year to help her brother. But she was determined to return to her first love, geology, and she would do so.[6]

Zorig was one of the planners of the demonstration on December 10, and his scholarly appearance and gentle demeanor had quieted the crowd, which heard three speakers—the journalists Tsakhiagiin Elbegdorj and Sükhbaatariin Amarsanaa and the scientist Erdenii Bat-Uul—announce the formation of a democratic movement.

Hashbat Hulan keenly observed the December demonstrations. A member of a prominent family (of the Khalkha Mongolians, the dominant group in the country, constituting about 85 percent of the population), she was perhaps even more cosmopolitan than Zorig, if only because she was fluent in English. The oldest of three daughters of a career diplomat, she had as a child lived in Yugoslavia, where her father was ambassador, and in the USSR, where he had also been stationed. In 1964, when she was three years old, her father had been selected to study at Leeds University and was thus among the first Mongolian students at a Western academic institution. However, she had studied in the USSR, graduating from the Institute of International Relations in Moscow. During her student days at the institute in the 1980s, she engaged in heated discussions and debates about the possibility of reforming the Communist Party and of progressing toward democracy.[7]

This flurry of intellectual excitement and political involvement was not matched on Hulan's 1986 return to Mongolia, her native land, but a place in which she had scarcely resided. In an interview, she expressed her dismay: "I was amazed at the ignorance and seclusion in my homeland."[8] Ulaanbaatar seemed to her a provincial town, hardly in touch with the intellectual currents sweeping across the Soviet bloc. Frustrated by what she perceived to be the backwardness of Mongolia, she took a job at the Mongolian Academy of Sciences, where she translated works from English into Mongolian and vice versa, edited publications, and compiled bibliographies. After two years, she took a job at the Oriental Institute to study and analyze trends toward regional cooperation in East Asia.[9] Simultaneously, she came across proponents of democratic reform, a number of whom had studied in the USSR or Eastern Europe. By September 1989, she had begun to attend clandestine meetings, whose members hoped to initiate the transformation of Mongolia. On December 10, she and her sister Minjin hurried to Sükhbaatar Square, only minutes away from their offices, where they heard speeches proclaiming the establishment of the Mongolian Democratic Union, "the first popular mass movement organization,"[10] with Zorig as its general coordinator. "I did not like the views of some of the reformers," Hulan said later. "They were too supportive of the market economy and not enough concerned about the welfare of the people."[11] Hulan's observation revealed the differences among the reformers, which remained concealed in their initial struggles against the government but would later lead to serious rifts. Some supported democracy, while others advocated the establishment of a market economy, and still others were eager to maintain the communist-era advances in health, education, and social welfare but eliminate the MPRP's monopoly on power. Still another group was composed of opportunists who simply sought to profit from the turbulence.

In their education and careers, Hulan and Zorig were in some sense typical of the democratic reformers. Most of the original Mongolian reformers had been educated in the USSR. Paradoxically, the authoritarian Soviet system, which had helped to curb democracy and basic human rights in Mongolia, turned out to be the inspiration for openness and reform in Mongolia. Mongolian students learned about perestroika and glasnost in the USSR and brought these ideas back to their native land. In addition, many reformers were not members of Mongolia's major ethnic group, the Khalkha Mongolians. Both Erdenii Bat-Uul, who later became chair of the Mongolian Democratic Party, and Dashiin Byambasüren, who later was the first prime minister in a reform government, were Buryats; and Davaadorjiin Ganbold, an ardent supporter of privatization and an advocate of a market economy, had a Chinese grandfather. In late 1990, Nick Middleton, a British writer with scant knowledge of Mongolia, noted: "Several of the leading members of the Mongolian Democratic Party, the first opposition party to rise from the fledgling democracy movement, were . . . half-castes, either half Russian / half Mongolian or half Chinese / half Mongolian."[12] Although the Khalkha Mongolians tolerated the presence of so many "half-castes," or minorities, as leaders in the early reform movement, ethnic tensions mounted throughout the 1990s, weakening the reform movement and parties.

Hulan and Zorig knew that a few urban intellectuals could not, by themselves, generate a successful movement toward democracy. They needed to enlist herders and laborers throughout the country. Nonetheless, the reformers' demonstrations in the center of Ulaanbaatar reflected a more widespread dissatisfaction with the regime.

The two Hashbat sisters, Zorig, and the other demonstrators knew that the authorities were watching and listening to them. A few steps away, the officials in Government House were observing the extraordinary spectacle below from their windows. Yet they did not call on troops to disperse the crowd that had mounted this singular challenge to authoritarianism. Did the demonstrators represent themselves alone? Would government repression draw even greater attention to the agitators? Rumors also persisted that Mikhail Gorbachev, first secretary of the Soviet Communist party, had cautioned the Mongolian government to avoid violence.

THE GOVERNMENT FALTERS

What forces prompted a previously tyrannical government to waver, thus giving the reformers an opening? It had hardly hesitated in the past. The MPR had had counterparts to Lenin (Damdiny Sükhbaatar, d. 1923) and Stalin (Khorloogiin Choibalsan, d. 1952). From 1924 on, its policies echoed those of its patron and protector, the USSR. New mass movements or programs announced in the USSR would shortly thereafter be introduced in Mongolia, prompting the view that the second communist country in world history was merely a Soviet satellite.[13] Soviet influence was certainly dominant in Mongolia, and the MPRP and the authoritarian Mongolian government often unhesitatingly enforced policies devised in the USSR. In the late 1920s, herders had opposed collectivization of their animals, as had the kulaks under Stalin. Both the Russian and Mongolian governments dealt with these groups severely.[14] Like the Kremlin, the Mongolian communists were quick to purge former Party officials and the army. The wealthy Buddhist monasteries were singled out for harsh treatment. Estimates of lives lost during this repression vary considerably, but the most reliable figure hovers around 25,000. The number of executed Buddhist monks within that figure is also in dispute, but specialists concur that of the 100,000 or so monks in the early twentieth century, fewer than a thousand continued to serve in the monasteries by mid-century. Most were defrocked, but some were killed, and the vast majority of the monasteries were either destroyed or severely damaged.[15]

The death of Choibalsan in 1952 and the rise of his successor Yumjaagiin Tsedenbal modified this authoritarian system. However, the MPRP continued to dominate Mongolia and violate human rights. It continued to purge dissidents, but the offenders were imprisoned or exiled, not executed. In 1962, Tsedenbal turned against one of his closest associates Tömör-öchir (whose grandson Tömör-öchiryn Erdenebileg would marry one of Hulan's sisters), accusing him of antiparty activities. Yet, despite a barrage of denunciations in the media, he simply exiled Tömör-öchir to the industrial city of Darkhan.[16] Similarly, he either jailed or dismissed scholars and artists whom he perceived as dissidents.

However, the early 1980s witnessed changes that would eventually shape the government's response to the December 10 demonstrations and their aftermath. Tsedenbal and his Russian wife, who had considerable influence over her husband, had adhered to policies enunciated in the USSR, but they ignored the changes signified by perestroika and glasnost. They also persisted in denunciations of the PRC, verbal attacks that had started two decades earlier with the onset of the Sino-Soviet conflict, while the USSR now was inching toward reconciliation with the Beijing leadership. Economic problems had also arisen. Introduction of agriculture in so-called virgin lands (this reflected one of Nikita Khrushchev's famous "hare-brained schemes" in the USSR, the "virgin lands" policy), a risky venture in a country with such a short growing season, had not met expectations. Lack of variety in foodstuffs and shortages of consumer goods contributed to dissatisfaction. Tsedenbal's continued use of purges to oust potential rivals for leadership also generated hostility. At least twice in the late 1970s and early 1980s, he had removed or reassigned younger officials who ranked just below him in the MPRP or government hierarchy and who had been viewed as possible successors.[17]

Tsedenbal's own dismissal in August 1984 thus did not generate much protest. While he was on a visit to the USSR for medical treatment, his opponents overthrew him with Moscow's collusion, announcing that poor health prevented his continuance as general secretary of the MPRP and premier of the MPR, and that Jambyn Batmünkh, a university administrator and stolid apparatchik, would succeed to those positions. Batmünkh and the new leadership appeared ready to introduce some changes in government and the economy, although they differed in their assessment of the pace and comprehensiveness of such restructuring. Most of the old guard grudgingly accepted the need for some transformations, but relatively few were enthusiastic advocates of reform.

Nonetheless, in the years following Batmünkh's accession, changes seeped into government pronouncements and programs. In 1986, Batmünkh first confronted the country's economic problems, attributing some of the failures to overly centralized planning. He explained that individual enterprises and localities required greater flexibility and autonomy in order to increase efficiency and production. Batmünkh's pronouncements echoed Gorbachev's program of perestroika, set out in the official MPRP daily paper, *Unen,* which published a full translation of Gorbachev's speech to the 1986 Congress of the Communist Party of the Soviet Union demanding a liberalization of the economy.[18]

In the same year, Batmünkh advocated reforms in the bureaucracy, but he took few steps to replace the old leadership or lesser officials who resisted change. In a speech in July 1987, he noted that it would be difficult to alter the communist influence on popular attitudes and behavior.[19] He proposed that the bureaucracy embrace openness or, to use a word now fashionable, "transparency." Highlighting the role of the mass media in this, he entrusted journalists with the tasks of fostering greater openness and criticizing bureaucratic highhandedness, ineptness, or inefficiency. Mongolian newspapers were soon permitting publication of letters from readers critical of government officials.

External events, which lay beyond the control of the Mongolian leadership, were fueling changes and placing pressure on the Batmünkh regime. The USSR faced its own difficulties in the mid to late 1980s, owing in part to vast military expenditures to counter the perceived Western threat, to mismanagement and inefficiencies in the economy, and to the rise of wealthy and unscrupulous entrepreneurs. These economic reversals affected Mongolia, which was dependent on Soviet trade and aid. Soviet technical assistance was also invaluable, and many experts from the communist bloc assisted in managing the Mongolian economy. Roughly 100,000 Soviet troops had been stationed in Mongolia in the mid 1960s, after the onset of the Sino-Soviet conflict, and this force was still deployed throughout the country. Naturally, expenditures on these troops imposed additional burdens on the increasingly fragile Soviet economy, which seemed excessive in an era when the USSR was trying to cement better relations with China.

In 1987, the USSR started to shift course, which compelled changes in Mongolia's foreign and domestic policies. Even earlier, in a speech in

Vladivostok in July 1986, Gorbachev asserted that tensions in Northeast Asia had eased considerably. By April 1987, he had withdrawn about a quarter of the total Soviet force stationed in Mongolia. He thus signaled his perception of the reduction of the threat of a Sino-Soviet war and his desire for closer relations with China. Mongolia quickly adopted the same policy, seeking to heal the wounds of more than two decades of hostility. In June 1987, the MPR and China signed agreements concerning the peaceful resolution of border disputes. They also agreed to promote trade, as well as to develop joint technological and scientific cooperation on livestock production and energy.[20] Perhaps as important, with the USSR starting to limit its commitment to Mongolia, Batmünkh and his MPRP associates had no choice but to cultivate relations with previously hostile states. Moreover, Gorbachev's increasing links with the West, particularly America, paved the way for the other communist states to pursue similar initiatives, and Mongolia established formal relations with the United States in 1987.[21] Representatives of the two countries planned for the exchange of ambassadors and for the development of cultural, educational, and economic links.

By 1988, key government leaders had started to challenge past policies. A Politburo member actually broached the subject of democracy as part of a ringing endorsement of greater openness and of governmental institutions responsive to the people. Several scholars and officials condemned the secrecy of the past, which had prevented an honest assessment of the authoritarianism that had bedeviled communist Mongolia.[22] One scholar dared to suggest that the MPRP allow several candidates to stand for each office.[23]

In the same year as the December 10 demonstrations, the government and the MPRP initiated a number of changes. The purges instigated by Choibalsan in the 1930s and 1940s had been condemned from the mid 1950s on, but in 1989, a commission appointed by the Politburo analyzed this repression and asserted that at least 20,000 Mongolians whom the state had put to death should have their names cleared. At the same time, Batmünkh charged Tsedenbal with creating a cult of personality and incarcerating people unjustly.[24] The report, as well as additional commentaries after its release, provided the first serious critique of the leader who had ruled during the recent so-called thaw in the MPR's history. The Party rehabilitated Jamyangiin Lkhagvasüren, whom Tsedenbal had dismissed as minister of defense, and proclaimed him a hero for having defeated the Japanese in the battle of Nomonhan, on the Mongolian-Manchurian border, in 1939. His son became the director of the country's national civilian airline, and his daughter became a prominent radio journalist.[25] His granddaughter Lkhagvasüren Nomin (about whom more will be said in later chapters), who was studying in the USSR, would become one of the ablest journalists in the country in the 1990s.

Relations with foreign countries also spurred changes in the government. The USSR brought home 8,000 troops from Mongolia and planned to recall most of its military contingent by 1990. Meanwhile, trade with China increased at a rapid clip, and the Mongolian foreign minister and his Chinese counterpart exchanged visits and signed agreements to promote additional trade, facilitate transport and communications, and increase cultural and educational ties.[26] Finally, the foreign minister asserted that the MPR should increase its ties with Western countries, which would, of necessity, lead to greater openness and to exposure to new ideas and beliefs.[27] Western radio broadcasts and magazines now began to reach Mongolia, and Western television would soon be available too, with a potentially great influence, particularly on young people.

In short, by the time of the December 10 demonstrations, an indeterminate number of leaders in the MPRP and government hierarchy supported reforms designed to promote democracy and accountability in government. Yet MPRP and government support for some changes had not translated into reforms by December 1989. The MPR was the only legal party. The government still violated human rights and still had not loosened its grip on the mass media. The secret police, security guards, and army had remained intact, and repression continued. For example, officials attempted to capture the reformers who, throughout the late 1980s, posted signs and pasted placards all over Ulaanbaatar demanding changes in the one-party system.

The MPRP and the government were divided on reform. Some officials acknowledged the need for democratic changes, while others tried to check any deviations from the status quo. This split resulted in a slow pace of reform, causing "young Mongolians . . . [to show] signs of impatience at the conservative leadership's seeming inability to move more quickly and radically."[28] The young people also had an advantage: the divisions within the MPRP and the government promoted indecisiveness, from which the would-be reformers could profit.

Having openly challenged the authorities, the young reformers now had to articulate a program, attract others living outside the capital, and develop coherent strategies and tactics. Before the December 10 demonstration, the meetings of the reformers had been sporadic and somewhat amorphous. As early as the end of 1988, they had founded a "Club of Young Economists," whose leading lights were Mendsaikhany Enkhsaikhan, a Soviet-trained economist who worked at the Ministry of Foreign Economic Relations and Supply, and who would eventually serve as prime minister from July 1996 to April 1998, and Davaadorjiin Ganbold, also a Soviet-trained economist, who had taught at the Mongolian National University.[29] The authorities clearly knew about these meetings and those of other groups, because government agents attended them and reported on the discussions to their supervisors. Yet the growing influence of perestroika and glasnost prevented the authorities from banning the meetings. The club was the venue for discussions but had not taken specific action. In short, the efforts of the reformers now needed to be organized, and their slogans had to be welded into a program. They also had to counter the perception that unity would prove elusive, as it had for Mongolian political movements in the past. To succeed in dealings with an apparently divided government and MPRP, the reformers had to maintain a united front.

Their first undertaking was a statement of the changes they proposed. The placards carried by the demonstrators on December 10 revealed their basic program: "A Multiparty System Is Essential," "Honor Human Rights Above All," and "Freedom of the Press."[30] Days after the December 10 demonstrations, the Mongolian Democratic Union began to meet, and by December 17, its leaders had proffered their demands to government authorities. After a rally attended by two thousand people, they delivered a petition that incorporated the reforms they proposed to the MPRP authorities. This submission was in and of itself remarkable, because it was the first such citizens' manifesto publicly presented to the communist leadership.

The principal goal of the reformers was to convene a multiparty election for the Khural by early 1990, an election in which voters freely chose representatives. The Khural would be accountable to the people, not the communist hierarchy, and a record of its meetings ought to be available to the public. Changes in the organization of the economy were also vital for the new Mongolia that some of the reformers wished to foster. Influenced by the West, part of the reform group proposed that a market economy be installed in place of the centrally planned economy. They also sought official respect for basic human rights. The government had to protect freedom of the press, freedom of speech, freedom of travel, and freedom of religion and to publicize these rights to the people. "Finally, the government had to acknowledge and publicize crimes against citizens and monks during Choibalsan's terror. And the reformers insisted that all these rights be incorporated into a newly amended constitution."[31]

After some discussion and initial hesitation, the Politburo responded positively to the demands of the reformers. At a meeting of the Seventh Plenum of the Nineteenth Congress of the MPRP convened on December 11 and 12, just a day after the reformers' demonstrations in Sükhbaatar Square, officials supported glasnost and perestroika and, theoretically, demands for change.[32] It seemed clear in the first place that the USSR, still Mongolia's most important patron and protector at that time, would not endorse a harsh repression of the dissidents. Gorbachev had disapproved of the Chinese attack on demonstrators at Tiananmen six months earlier and was not eager for a repetition in the communist world. In addition, the Mongolian government recognized that such a crackdown would constitute evidence of instability, which China might try to exploit. Despite gradually improving relations, Mongolia's communist leaders feared interference by their neighbor in the event of a domestic crisis, and to prevent this, they therefore sought to compromise with the reformers. Mongolians remembered that China had ruled their country as a colony for more than two centuries and were unwilling to provide a pretext for the Chinese either to send in troops or insinuate themselves into Mongolian domestic politics again.[33]

Yet the compromise proved disappointing to the reformers. Officials pledged that they would implement reforms but were vague about a timetable. They appeared to support the concepts of a multiparty system, free elections, and civil liberties, but were in no hurry and said that they were willing to introduce these reforms within five years.[34] The young reformers whose principal banner when they handed their petition to officials on December 17 had read "Democracy Is Our Goal" did not want to wait. They were gratified that between December 10 and 17, the government had undertaken a reshuffling in which a few opponents of change had been demoted, but they could not accept a delay of five years for the implementation of reforms. Irrespective of this, however, the reformers in the Mongolian Democratic Union had succeeded in drawing up a program to which they all could agree, a major accomplishment.[35]

THE REFORMERS EXPAND THEIR BASE

The reformers needed to incorporate a broader cross-section of the population into their political endeavors. Naturally, they continued to stage meetings in Sükhbaatar Square on weekends, generating public interest and publicity. After repeated calls at these meetings for access to the mass media, they finally received permission to present their views on a state radio program on December 28.[36] Meanwhile, they tried to reach like-minded individuals outside Ulaanbaatar, and eventually some workers and engineers at the copper mine in Erdenet became their staunch allies. Founded in the mid 1970s as a joint venture of the USSR and Mongolia, the copper mine recruited a large number of Russian engineers and workers. Mongolian employees at the mines were infuriated that the Russians received higher salaries and better benefits for the same work. As one Mongolian engineer said, "We Mongolians noticed daily that we played second fiddle, that we were the underdogs. This deeply wounded our pride and national feelings."[37] The reformers attempted to find common cause with these workers. They tried to focus the workers' hostility toward Russia on dissatisfaction with the MPRP and the Mongolian government, which still perceived the USSR as patron and protector. Having common foes, the two groups were able to forge a mutually beneficial alliance. Erdenet employees had convened a protest meeting early in December, during which one speaker vowed: "We want no longer to be led by the hand of the USSR. We want the same wages for the same work. We've had enough of the Russians' being paid twice as much as we Mongolians are for the same work."[38]

Learning of the meeting in Erdenet from one of the participants, the Mongolian Democratic Union decided to make contact with the dissident employees. On December 22, it sent the scientist Bat-Uul, a fine orator despite his image as a ruffian (rumors about his rudeness and obstreperousness were quite common), to Erdenet to negotiate with representatives of the mine workers and engineers. He met with them in a small room in the House of Culture and described the objectives of the Mongolian Democratic Union, emphasizing that the workers' concerns could be allayed and their economic goals met only by a movement that encouraged changes in the MPRP and the government. The movement organized in the capital city by the Mongolian Democratic Union could succeed, he noted, only if it aroused similar protests elsewhere. The assembled participants assured Bat-Uul of their support.[39] He returned to Ulaanbaatar with such solid evidence of an agreement that the Mongolian Democratic Union dispatched representatives to different parts of the country to explain its program and objectives and elicit support.

By the end of 1989, the reformers had achieved two of their goals and started on their third. They had a clear, well-devised program of reforms, and they had cultivated allies outside of Ulaanbaatar who represented workers, technicians, and herdsmen. However, they now required a clear plan, as well as carefully defined tactics, rather than demonstrations and reactions to events; they had to shape events to their own schedule and to their own advantage. Effective control and planning of strategy and tactics required organization and leadership, and the Mongolian Democratic Union was too large an umbrella group to decide upon policy and activities. By the end of December, therefore, it selected a coordinating committee, with Elbegdorj as head, to deal with day-to-day activities.[40] Elbegdorj, a military man who had been trained as a journalist in the USSR and worked for a military newspaper, was an outspoken critic of the government and an advocate of confrontation with the regime. Although lacking the education and polish of many of the other reformers, he nonetheless proved to be charismatic and an excellent speaker, with an ability to relate to ordinary people. Despite his occasional awkwardness in relations with fellow reformers from elite families, he appealed to a wider cross-section of the population than most reformers could.

With the onset of the New Year, the coordinating committee began to define and tailor its activities for maximum results, organizing meetings of the Mongolian Democratic Union that allowed for full discussion and debate. On January 14, approximately 1,000 people convened in the Lenin Museum, a short distance from Sükhbaatar Square. Although most were intellectuals, representatives of workers and technicians also participated in the discussions, which were designed to build up the movement and to explain its objectives to newcomers. The symbolism of an alternative to the Khural, in which discussion and dissent were permitted and indeed welcomed, offered a sharp contrast to the official parliament, which most often simply rubber-stamped decisions made by its leaders. Such meetings of the Mongolian Democratic Union were significant because they entailed an implicit challenge to the official Khural. The authorities did not ban these meetings, and the union continued to meet sporadically over the next two months, constituting a thorn in the government's side. The coordinating committee then helped to organize a meeting of the Mongolian Journalists' Union on January 19.[41] With guidance from the committee, the assembled reporters renamed their organization the "Mongolian Democratic Journalists' Union." This one act did not, of course, translate immediately into a free press or a more aggressive brand of investigative journalism. Yet the use of the word "democratic" marked an important step, indicating that some journalists had begun to acknowledge the need for reforms and for alignment with the Mongolian Democratic Union.

The most remarkable event the coordinating committee planned was a demonstration on January 21 to hasten the implementation of reform. The contrasts between the demonstrations on December 10 and January 21, just a little over a month apart, reveal the progress the reformers had made. December 10 attracted a crowd of about two hundred people and was relatively spontaneous, and the demonstrators were uncertain about the reactions of the government and its security forces.[42] In spite of the frigid weather (−30°C), the January 21 demonstrations were well organized and drew thousands of participants. The crowd was no longer limited to intellectuals from Ulaanbaatar. Judging from the size and composition, the reformers had succeeded in broadening their base. Representatives of a variety of social groups from the smaller towns and the countryside participated. Unlike the December 10 demonstrators, the coordinating committee could be fairly confident that the government would not disperse or attack the marchers. In addition, its demands for change were more sharply defined than those of the December 10 demonstrations. It identified specific institutional and constitutional reforms that it advocated, rather than general condemnations of the existing system.

The January 21 demonstration, however, resembled the earlier one in two respects. It was held in Sükhbaatar Square, and January 21 was the date of Lenin's death in 1924, an anniversary that had been marked throughout the communist period.[43] The coordinating committee thus capitalized on an already existing event to organize its own protest. It also attracted more celebrities, including Dogmidyn Sosorbaram, an actor-singer who would eventually be awarded the title of Meritorious Artist of Mongolia. Sosorbaram and others gathered around the statue of Sükhbaatar and led the assembled crowd in singing traditional folk melodies lauding Chinggis Khan.[44] Such acclaim for Chinggis Khan could be seen as a challenge to the MPRP and the USSR, which had denigrated the Mongolian hero, portraying him as a barbarian pillager.[45]

The young reformers continued their campaign against the government by convening weekend demonstrations in January and February. The self-interest of the reformers did not necessarily shape their activism. Nearly all were employed and had good opportunities for additional training and education.[46] Neither deprivation nor poor career prospects dictated their protests. The democrats among them objected to insufficient guarantees of free expression, to human rights abuses, and to the influence wielded by the USSR in Mongolia.

The government itself had not been inactive. Members of the Khural continued to meet, despite their concerns about the disruptions precipitated by the activities of the young reformers, allied with workers, professionals, and other segments of the population. The Khural and the MPRP could not agree on a policy for dealing with the reformers. Neither the traditionalists who wished to crush the reformers nor the more conciliatory members of the MPRP and government elites who sought compromise emerged victorious. The MPRP and the Khural thus deadlocked and claimed that they would support moderate reforms. Their less savory and ultimately ineffective response was to cast aspersions on the reformers, who were described as alcoholics, corrupt, or self-serving. Such gossip did nothing to tarnish the images of the principal figures in the reform movement, although a few of these accusations did turn out to be accurate.[47]

Diverse reform groups took advantage of the inaction of the MPRP and the government to organize into opposition forces. On February 16, under the direction of Davaadorjiin Ganbold, one faction founded the National Progressive Party, which backed democratic government and privatization of state assets, including industries and banks, as means of fostering the introduction of a market economy.[48] Many reformers regarded Ganbold as an extraordinarily brilliant economist and indeed a brilliant man in general, but were concerned about his coldness and rigidity. He focused on the market economy and insisted that the main task of government was to generate a favorable environment for business. He also discounted government health, education, and social welfare programs. On February 18, Bat-Uul founded the Mongolian Democratic Party, inviting 200 observers as well as journalists to his party's convention. However, the government did not provide the requisite permission for foreigners, particularly journalists, to accept Bat-Uul's invitation to attend.[49] Two political parties had now materialized to challenge Article 82 of the Constitution, which had required one-party rule. Both demanded legalization of a multiparty system and an end to the MPRP monopoly. The issuance of *Shin Tol* ("New Mirror"), the first journal since 1921 that did not have government approval, also disturbed the government. As the reformers developed ever more sophisticated tactics, they defied ever more fundamental linchpins of the authoritarian system in Mongolia. The pace of change quickened.

The reformers were now ready for an assault on actual artifacts of the communist era. Ulaanbaatar and the smaller cities and towns were awash with representations of socialist and communist so-called heroes. A statue of Sükhbaatar dominated the central square in Ulaanbaatar. A sizable likeness of Choibalsan could be seen at the entrance of the Mongolian National University. One of the principal streets in the capital was named after Sükhbaatar, as was one of the country's *aimag*s, or provinces. Choibalsan in the *aimag* of Dornod was the fourth largest city in Mongolia.[50] However, the reformers did not initially focus on depictions of Mongolian communists. Instead, they sought to galvanize Mongolian resentment at the virtual deification of Russian communists. An enormous placard with Lenin's image greeted the visitor on the road from the airport to the city of Ulaanbaatar proper. The same visitor who stayed at the Ulaanbaatar Hotel, which along with the Bayangol Hotel provided the principal lodging facilities for foreigners in Ulaanbaatar, would discover a colossal statue of Lenin as he or she walked to the small garden in front of the hotel. However, the Mongolian reformers found the imposing statue of Joseph Stalin in front of the Mongolian State Library particularly offensive. They were horrified at the placement of an image of the dreaded Soviet dictator in front of one of the main treasuries of Mongolian culture. In their criticisms of the placement of the statue, reformers could harp on patriotism and anti-Russian sentiments. Having secured popular approval, they went to the State Library on the night of February 22 and dismantled Stalin's statue.[51]

A meeting organized two days later, on February 24, bolstered the position of the reformers. Representatives of the Mongolian Youth Union gathered together at the Mongolian National University. Although the young people knew that agents of the Ministry of Public Security were spying on them, they nonetheless passionately supported the program of the Mongolian Democratic Union: a multiparty political system, an affirmation of basic human rights, and elimination of restraints on private businesses. The reformers thus appeared to be gaining support from diverse segments of the population.

THE REFORMERS APPEAR TO WIN

Yet the reformers, as represented in the Mongolian Democratic Union, had not made substantive gains. They had not elicited concessions from the MPRP and the government concerning their program. Although individual reformers had founded political parties, the government had not altered the Constitution to legalize parties other than the MPRP. The government had not guaranteed freedom of speech, press, or religion. The Politburo meeting to be convened on March 4 thus offered scant hope to the reformers. Submission of petitions, demonstrations in Sükhbaatar Square, and public and private meetings with members of the Khural had not been sufficient. The reformers needed new tactics and ideas to achieve their objectives.

The most potent tactic they came up with was the hunger strike, a tactic unfamiliar to most Mongolians. From what source did the inspiration for such a remarkable demonstration come? One author attributes it to the reformers' knowledge of a hunger strike conducted in front of the White House by an American scientist who had opposed the Vietnam War.[52] But many of the reformers were aware of hunger strikes by Gandhi in India, by Irish Republican Army prisoners in Ireland, and, closer to home, by Chinese students in Tiananmen less than a year earlier. A number of the reformers were well informed about the Tiananmen events.

Erdenebileg, Hulan's brother-in-law, who later became a member of the Khural, could read and speak Chinese and knew about the Chinese demonstrations in Tiananmen.[53] A few also knew that hunger strikes did not always produce the desired results.

At 2 P.M. on Wednesday, March 7, the temperature in Sükhbaatar Square stood at −15°C when ten men defied the government's disapproval of traditional dress by wearing their *dels*, or traditional robes, and initiating a hunger strike. Bat-Uul was the most familiar of the ten, but others, including Gongorjavyn Boshigt (later the head of a political movement), Dambyn Dorligjav (who eventually became minister of defense), and Damdinsürengiin Enkhbaatar (later chair of the Khural's Subcommittee on National Security), would shortly thereafter achieve renown.[54]

The hunger strikers, with backing from the Mongolian Democratic Union, expanded the scope of their demands, challenging the legality of MPRP and government institutions. They not only advocated their traditional goals of democratic reforms, greater openness to foreigners and foreign trade, and a respect for Mongolian history and heritage but also added a direct attack on the authorities. Arguing that the Politburo was an appointed and not an elected body, they challenged its legitimacy. Similarly, they challenged the legality of the Khural, because its members faced no opposition in elections.[55] They submitted a manifesto in which they elaborated their views to the concurrent meeting of the Politburo. The Politburo responded that the Constitution granted full sovereignty to the Khural, which was indeed an elected body. This intractable response prompted the hunger strikers to be ever more resolute in continuing their fast until the collapse of the government.[56] The Mongolian Democratic Union now insisted on the abolition of the Politburo and the election of a multiparty Khural.

The hunger strikers at first drew a puzzled crowd, but within hours a large number of people had reached the square either to support or to debate the strikers or the leaders of the Mongolian Democratic Union, who stood nearby. Some passersby could not understand the reasons for the fast. Why refrain from food in a time when it was plentiful?[57] Most of the onlookers, however, quickly grasped the significance of the hunger strike. Some walked around the square to show sympathy for the strikers; others stopped to discuss the issues with representatives of the Mongolian

Democratic Union; and, by nightfall, still others, a small but significant group, had joined the hunger strikers. The crowd grew throughout the afternoon and reached well into the thousands by early evening. As darkness covered the city, the strikers allowed themselves to drink a mixture of water and glucose. Perhaps they took comfort in the sight of a Mongolian Red Cross ambulance parked not far from where they sat by Sükhbaatar's statue.

On March 7, Sükhbaatar Square was the principal, though not the exclusive, venue for expressions of dissatisfaction with the regime. The coordinating committee of the Mongolian Democratic Union had devoted considerable time and effort over the past month to informing the Mongolian population of the significance of the hunger strike and soliciting nationwide demonstrations. The workers at Erdenet with whom the MDU had cooperated in the past participated in a sympathy strike. On the afternoon of March 7, several hundred workers stopped work for an hour to express solidarity with the strikers in Sükhbaatar Square. Their leader gleefully reported: "We crippled the mine totally for one hour. That was an unreal feeling."[58] Simultaneously, workers in Darkhan, Mörön, and other towns followed the lead of the Erdenet miners and organized strikes. Back in the capital city, the Union of Mongolian Students called upon its members temporarily to ignore their schoolwork and to form committees to support the hunger strikers in any way possible.[59] The Gandan Monastery, the only operating monastery in Mongolia, sent monks to the square as a gesture of support, despite the reservations of the head of the monastery.[60]

Meanwhile the Politburo met throughout the day of March 7. Its agents spying on the hunger strikers and the growing number of sympathizers in Sükhbaatar Square relayed information about events, and MPRP loyalists and government officials provided reports about conditions in the country. From their meeting place in Government House, Politburo members could see and hear the ruckus in the square. They knew that this hunger strike and the attendant demonstrations were a grave threat to their authority. Members were divided about their response to the rapidly developing and seemingly uncontrollable events that jeopardized their positions. Hard-liners were eager to call upon the police and the military to disband the demonstrators, while others, wary of engulfing the country in chaos, sought a peaceful resolution of the crisis. Who the advocates were for each of the two points of view is not known, but surely many of those who had served in both the Choibalsan and Tsedenbal regimes sought to revert to the repressive policies of those times. A strong leader such as Demchigiin Molomjamts, who had started to climb the bureaucratic ladder during the Choibalsan period and had filled a variety of positions including those of minister of finance, chair of the State Planning Committee, and secretary of the Politburo, would not have hesitated to use force.[61] A sufficient number of such surviving hardliners still served in the Politburo or the Khural, preventing immediate concessions to the reformers.

As evidenced by their actions that evening, the authorities were indecisive on the first day of the hunger strike. They sent two representatives to persuade the strikers to abandon their fast, feigning concern for their health. The reformers rejected any such capitulation. All the hunger strikers were adamant in their desire to compel the government to resign. They politely refused the request of the two Politburo members, and the large, increasingly unruly crowd of sympathizers appeared to intimidate the two men.[62]

The stalemate persisted until the following day, when Dashiin Byambasüren, a moderate who was first deputy chair of the Council of Ministers, came out of Government House around 4 P.M. to meet with the reform leaders in the square. Byambasüren was an excellent choice as a negotiator, partly because, according to well-informed sources, he was related to Bat-Uul, a hunger striker and one of the two or three most important leaders of the reformers.[63] Byambasüren arranged a meeting with the reformers, which was aired live on radio and television. Byambasüren's dialogue with the reformers failed to reach a compromise, and the hunger strike continued. The reformers responded to the meeting with Byambasüren with a petition to the Politburo, explaining the need for dramatic changes. They pointed out that whereas the vast majority of the population was less than thirty years of age, about 50 percent of the Politburo qualified for pensions. In addition, thirty-one members of the Khural had served at least five terms. The Politburo and the Khural, from their standpoint, were thus unrepresentative of the general population.[64]

Meanwhile, the crowds at Sükhbaatar Square increased dramatically. March 8 was International Women's Day, an important holiday in communist Mongolia, which enabled more people to reach the square. Some rowdy individuals, who were not as committed to nonviolence as the Mongolian Democratic Union leaders, were now mixed in with the demonstrators. They laid claim to a slew of taxis and city buses and went to the Soviet Embassy and then to the official residence of Batmünkh, the head of the government. They drove around the two buildings and shouted anti-Soviet and anti-MPRP epithets.[65] The authorities and their Soviet patrons certainly realized that the demonstrators were unrelenting. But these obstreperous individuals, who may not have been as dedicated to reform as the original founders of the Mongolian Democratic Union, seemed to be co-opting the course of the reform movement. During those chaotic days, approximately seventy people incurred injuries, and one was killed. The MDU, which had advocated a policy of nonviolence, was losing its grip on the demonstrators. Mistakenly, the reformers had scarcely planned or prepared for crowd control. They had hoped to galvanize thousands of people and perhaps generate unrest, but not chaos. The hunger strike would surely attract some unstable individuals or a few reckless or alcoholic Mongolians, who could contribute to great disorder. The creation of an effective security force might have prevented any potential violence.

The resulting turbulence may, in fact, have prodded the Politburo to acquiesce. Aware of the growing unrest, Politburo members recognized the need for decisive action. Estimates of the number of demonstrators are notoriously difficult to verify, and in this case they vary from the vague "tens of thousands" to the perhaps too definitive "ninety thousand." No matter the tally, the authorities were concerned about the growth in the numbers. Yet it appears that the Minister of Public Security did not call upon the army to pacify the demonstrators because he feared that soldiers would not heed the commands to shoot at or even disperse the crowds, and that specific divisions might align themselves with the demonstrators.[66] The USSR urged Mongolian leaders to compromise and to avoid any further difficulties. The hard-liners knew they were on the defensive in light of the fall in 1989 of the former Soviet bloc regimes in Eastern Europe. In addition, they started to acknowledge that a belligerent Tiananmen-like policy would be too costly and that they could lose in such a violent confrontation. Lacking support from the USSR, moderate officials, and striking workers, the hard-liners finally backed down on March 9. Some Politburo and MPRP members viewed their concession as temporary. They believed that they would still have strong advantages even in a free election. They had support throughout the countryside, and the reformers did not have the advantage of that kind of political network.[67] Having considered this political situation, Batmünkh announced that he, along with the entire Politburo, would step down. The announcement was broadcast on radio and television, and shortly thereafter, the hunger strikers abandoned their fast, and the MDU leaders urged the demonstrators to leave the square. Security guards and the police moved into the square and other central locations in the capital to disperse or arrest unruly members of the crowd.[68]

After a relatively quiet weekend, the Khural convened on Monday, March 12. Three hundred and seventy delegates from all over the country streamed into Sükhbaatar Square to see, for themselves, the place where the hunger strikers had initiated the process of civil disobedience that had culminated in the resignation of the Politburo. These delegates, who represented the most diverse social groups, from trade unions to cooperatives to teachers' organizations, first focused on Article 82 of the Constitution, which had mandated a one-party system. The Khural rescinded Article 82, paving the way for a multiparty system.[69] Shortly thereafter, a Mongolian Green Party, a Union of Mongolian Believers, and a Mongolian Free Labor Committee, organizations that would have been unimaginable during the communist era, sent messages with an assortment of suggestions to promote democracy.[70] While the Khural considered these proposals, the leading reformers met with MPRP eminences in the protocol room of Government House to discuss the details of potential reforms. The Khural recessed on March 14, but negotiators from the MPRP and the MDU continued the dialogue. Amid these discussions, the MPRP began to reinvent itself, selecting a new leadership with greater representation of those advocating change. On March 15, it chose a new and younger Politburo to guide it in the new multiparty system.[71]

On March 21, the Khural reconvened. First, it accepted the resignation of Batmünkh as chair of the Khural and elected Punsalmaagiin Ochirbat, an engineer who had served as minister of foreign economic relations, as its new chair.[72] Within a few days, the Khural allowed political parties other than the MPRP to register their own slate of candidates. The assembled delegates decided to reconvene on May 10 to ratify and supplement these regulations. On that day, they gathered together and decreed that a free election for a totally representative Khural would be held in July.[73] They assured all other parties that the MPRP would not receive any special advantages.

Despite the government's concessions, the reformers remained suspicious. They were particularly concerned that the MPRP would still be favored in an election because of its greater monetary resources and the government's control of the mass media. Lacking the same access to the media and to funds and believing such disparities to be unfair, the reformers resorted to demonstrations to protest the MPRP's control over these assets. By late April 1990, these demonstrations were drawing tens of thousands of people both in Sükhbaatar Square and in other locations. Violence erupted on occasion, even though demonstrators had been warned to stay peaceful. At one point, Zorig was hoisted aloft and urged an angry crowd to avoid violence. His fellow reformer Bat-Uul was amazed that "Zorig succeeded in calming the violent crowd and [in] settl[ing] the situation in a peaceful way."[74] Zorig's quick-wittedness and fearlessness prevented injuries and possibly even more serious consequences, but he could not be everywhere. The reformers' abilities to control crowds and to impress upon them the value of nonviolence were tested and occasionally found wanting. As a result, the government was impelled to call upon the military to quell disturbances. The reformers responded with civil disobedience. In Khövsgöl *aimag,* they convened a meeting in early April without a permit from the government. The authorities immediately arrested four people who attended the meeting and abused them during their incarceration. On April 7, thirteen men and women initiated a hunger strike to protest what they perceived to be the illegal detention of their fellow reformers. Finally, on April 30, the two sides, both of whom had vested interests in averting violence, met to negotiate issues of freedom of assembly and electoral reform. On May 7, they concluded that official approval was unnecessary for legal assembly, and the hunger strike was terminated. Once the May 10 Khural promised a reputedly free and fair election in July, the demonstrations ended throughout the country, and both sides focused on the forthcoming elections.[75]

THE REFORMERS IN TROUBLE

Although the reformers had access to some funds, the MPRP, which had control over the levers of power, had distinct advantages. It could shape policy over the next two months in order to ingratiate itself with specific constituencies. For example, it mandated lower rates to be paid for heating in state-owned residences. Then it increased the wages for some relatively poorly paid workers, enhanced student benefits, and offered economic relief to agricultural cooperatives. The only consolation for the reformers was the MPRP's pledge not to electioneer among the military and the police.[76]

However, the reformers inflicted the greatest damage on themselves, and their actions over the next two months validated the views of government officials who as early as December 10 had questioned their ability to remain united. Having elicited the concessions of free elections for the government and of protection of basic human rights, the reform movement began to fragment. Until early May, the reformers had focused on institutions, policies, and individuals they opposed. They knew what they were against, but they had not defined their own positive political visions. Their initial goal had been to eliminate the old regime, and they were probably caught off guard by the relative ease with which they had succeeded. Surprised at the rapidity of their "victory," they scarcely had time to articulate a new program. Having celebrated their success, they faced the daunting tasks of defining their objectives, of changing from a movement into a political party, and of preparing for elections to be held in ten weeks. The leading reformers, who had cooperated during the protests against the MPRP and the government, now became adversaries. Each had his own views as to what would be best for the country. After almost seventy years of one-party rule, many reformers wanted to affirm and to implement their own visions. Unity, which had in part guided them to "victory," would now prove to be elusive, and disunity would damage their hopes of defeating the MPRP. The reformers, in any case, represented a broad spectrum of views, ranging from democratic socialists to pure market economy fundamentalists.

The champions of the market economy and the democratic reformers emerged as the principal groups in the postcommunist era. Except for Ganbold, the leading market fundamentalists, including Enkhsaikhan and Elbegdorj, to be joined later by the economist Rinchinnyamyn Amarjargal, were not descended from the old elites and were relative newcomers to Ulaanbaatar. Their principal objectives were to promote a market economy, to eliminate vestiges of a planned economy, and to limit government involvement in and regulation of the economy. They saw social policy, in particular, health, education, and a social safety net, as secondary to the creation of a market economy and the promotion of economic growth. They appeared less concerned about the distribution of income. On the other hand, the leading democratic reformers were often the children of the old elites and were generally well educated and cosmopolitan. The parents and close relatives of Zorig, Oyun, Hulan, and Erdenebileg had been influential figures in politics, diplomacy, and the academy in the communist period. The principal objectives of these sons and daughters of the old elites were to foster democracy and combat authoritarianism and one-party rule (and eventually corruption) and yet retain the best features of the communist system. Hulan and Oyun feared that if the market economists gained power, they would slight social welfare, with attendant declines in health and education and increases in unemployment, poverty, domestic abuse, and crime. They were also concerned about the potential for increasing inequality in income with a barely regulated market economy.

From as early as February, both reform groups had started to found political parties, but these did not initially subvert the unity of the principal leaders. Bat-Uul had founded the Mongolian Democratic Party, and Ganbold had established the National Progressive Party. It is difficult to discern the differences between the two parties except that the National Progressive Party tended to be a stauncher advocate of the market economy. The Mongolian Social Democratic Party, which was also established at the time, offered an alternative. Its founder Bat-Erdeniin Batbayar (popularly known as "Baabar"), a scientist who had spent almost a year conducting research in the United Kingdom, supported the democratic reformers and did not wish to dispense with the social welfare provisions of the communist era.[77] Seeking to dissociate his brand of social democracy from the authoritarian forms of the MPRP and the USSR, this rather garrulous figure, who was also a poet and an amateur historian and apparently loved the spotlight, sought legitimacy through an appeal to Mongolian patriotism by placing a smiling portrait of Chinggis Khan on his election posters.[78]

Aside from the cracks in the previously united reform movement, the reformers also confronted difficulties in attracting support in the countryside. Most of the reformers had urban roots. Their strength lay in Ulaanbaatar, the industrial cities of Darkhan and Erdenet, and the capitals of the *aimags*. They had not energetically sought members among the 35 to 40 percent of the population who earned their livelihoods as herders. For example, at the first Congress of the Mongolian Democratic Party, 53 percent were intellectuals, 40 percent were workers, and only 7 percent were herders; about 45 percent were university educated.[79] In part, their failure was due to the limited time they had had to organize in opposition to the MPRP and the government; a focus on the cities and towns was more effective and efficient than to spread out over the vast territory of Mongolia to reach the herders. Yet another reason for their failure was their social distance from the herders. Here the MPRP had significant advantages, with almost seventy years of experience in dealing with herders and the rural areas. Moreover, every *aimag* governor endorsed the MPRP, which influenced the herders to follow suit.[80]

The reformers' political naiveté contributed to their difficulties. Less than a dozen were experienced politicians. Moreover, the reformers did not have the organization to mount a winning campaign against the MPRP. Even more humiliating, they found themselves unable to proffer a complete field of candidates for the Khural elections to be held in July. The MPRP ran 430 candidates for the 430 seats in the Khural. The three reform parties together could offer only 346 candidates, so 84 MPRP members would be unopposed.[81] Despite their obvious weaknesses, the three major opposition parties did not cooperate or share expenses during the campaigns. Their efforts lacked spirit; the parties believed that most Mongolians were hostile to the MPRP and that this would translate into victory for their candidates. However, the reform candidates were not well known, and they had scant resources for posters, advertisements, and the other accouterments of a successful campaign.

The July elections proved to be disappointing for the reformers. With all their disadvantages and self-inflicted harm, they must have known that they could not count on overwhelming victories. Yet their showing was worse than expected. The ensuing results were predictable: the MPRP had 357 seats, the Mongolian Democratic Party 16 seats, the National Progressive Party 6, and the Mongolian Social Democratic Party 4. About 8 percent of the seats were temporarily vacant because of errors or uncertainties about specific ballots. The popular vote was actually less unbalanced. The MPRP received only 60 percent of the vote, while the reform parties got about 30 percent. Despite protests by the reformers, votes were weighted in favor of the countryside, where the MPRP had its strongest support. The countryside received one representative for every 2,500 people, while the urban areas required 10,000 people for each representative.

In the first free election in modern Mongolian history, the MPRP had emerged victorious. The new Khural convened in September 1990, with the MPRP in charge. Yet the reformers had made great strides. MPRP advocates of change had replaced many of the older leaders. The moderate Punsalmagiin Ochirbat became president, and Dashiin Byambasüren, who had helped to end the hunger strike in Sükhbaatar Square, was elected prime minister. Shortly thereafter, Byambasüren had attempted to appease the reformers by offering Ganbold, a leader of the reform movement, the position of first deputy premier, a vital role in the new cabinet.

THE AFTERMATH

Within the year, a few changes were discernible. Nick Middleton, who visited Mongolia in 1990, wrote: "The simple fact that it was apparently possible for me to visit any part of the country was a transformation from my first trip when travel outside the capital had been well-nigh impossible."[82] Tim Severin, a renowned foreign travel writer, observed: "I suspect that I was at a crucial moment in modern Mongol history. . . . [T]he Mongols themselves were being given unparalleled freedom . . . and ordinary Mongols were responding by trying to find their true national identity."[83] Yet the transition to a new system has proved to be fraught with difficulties.

The sons and daughters of the privileged Mongolian elite initiated the nonviolent movement that led to the breakdown of an authoritarian system. The reformers, who derived mostly from the intellectual and professional classes, had no military forces at their command and resisted the use of violence. The movement for change thus originated at the top of the social hierarchy and then gradually evolved into a mass organization to appeal to and attract those at the bottom of the social pyramid. The authorities did not take repressive measures partly because the protesters belonged to the elite. Partly, too, the USSR, the principal patron and protector of communist Mongolia for almost seven decades, did not sanction violence. Throughout the 1980s, moderates had slowly filled positions in the Mongolian government, and they argued against the violent tactics proposed by hard-liners. The result was a deadlock. Fearful of Chinese involvement if violence erupted between government forces and the protesters, the authorities also permitted the reformers great leeway.

The reformers took advantage of the government's indecisiveness to make effective use of nonviolence. They first developed a clearer system of organization—from a disparate group of intellectuals, they evolved into a mass movement; they created a more coherent strategy and sought to contact and appeal to workers, youth, religious leaders, and others beyond the intellectual and professional classes; and they used nonviolent tactics such as demonstrations, hunger strikes, and work stoppages to prod the authorities into negotiations. In addition, they developed a clear and accessible program that could be readily expressed in a few slogans. As they began to extract concessions from the government, they also emphasized ethnic traditions (Buddhism, Chinggis Khan, customary dress, etc.) that had been portrayed negatively in the communist era, and patriotism, which often verged on anti-Russian attitudes.

The so-called reformers erred in two ways. One was that they did not develop a proper system of crowd control in the demonstrations and strikes they organized. Had the minor outbreaks among the crowds erupted into confrontations with the police or security guards, the reformers would have been vulnerable to the charge of having provoked violence. Their second weakness was their inability to maintain unity even before they had extracted the most important concessions from the government. They founded a large number of political parties, which ultimately led to their defeat in the first free elections in Mongolian history.

The MPRP old guard was still powerful but now faced the first challenges to its dominance in about seventy years. Many in the old communist hierarchy, as well as their younger supporters, acknowledged that they needed to compromise with both the democratic reformers and the advocates of the pure market economy. They also recognized that their power was gradually eroding. Nonetheless, they sought to retain their political authority and to preserve the cooperatives, the state enterprises, and the social welfare policies of the communist era. Throughout the 1990s, they would be fighting a losing battle: they could not stave off privatization and retrenchment of the state's commitment to education, health, and social programs. However, as of 2004, they remained a significant minority, which was ready to take advantage if the democratic reformers or the supporters of a pure market policy faltered.[84]

Chapter 2 | FROM RUSSIAN TO
WESTERN INFLUENCE

Despite the anticommunist demonstrations of 1989–90, many reformers had ambivalent feelings about the USSR. Sanjaasürengiin Zorig and his sister Oyun, for example, had a Russian grandfather; Hashbat Hulan had attended schools and university in the USSR; and the father of Davaador-jiin Ganbold, one of the most resolute advocates of a pure market economy, had been Mongolia's chief representative in the Soviet-sponsored trade association known as the Council of Mutual Economic Assistance (COMECON). Each of them resented the authoritarian USSR government but at the same time recognized the benefits that had accrued to Mongolia through the assistance of the Soviet Union.

The reformer Tömör-öchiryn Erdenebileg, whose grandfather had been purged and exiled in 1962, and who had majored in Chinese studies at university, believed that the USSR had saved Mongolia from continued Chinese rule. In the late seventeenth century, under the Qing dynasty (1644–1911), the Chinese had invaded and brought Mongolia under their control, he pointed out. With the support of the Buddhist hierarchy and elements of the Mongolian nobility, China had ruled and exploited the Mongolians until 1911. Mongolia had become increasingly dependent on Chinese products, and many Mongolians had become increasingly indebted to Chinese merchants, bankers, and officials.[1]

Erdenebileg also knew that the collapse of the Qing in 1911 had offered Mongolians the opportunity to regain their independence, but their own internal divisions, as well as the intervention of Chinese warlords, White Russian commanders, Japanese agents, and Mongolian noblemen, undermined such efforts. Chaos afflicted the country from 1915 to 1921, permitting the bizarre, murderous, and anti-Semitic White Russian leader Roman Nikolaus Fyodirovich von Ungern-Sternberg to occupy the capital city of Urga (the old name for Ulaanbaatar) for several months in 1921. In turn, the hostility he engendered through his brutal policies prompted a small group of patriots, with diverse political views, to seek assistance from the successful Bolshevik leaders who had assumed power in Russia.[2] Receiving such aid, they ousted and killed Ungern-Sternberg. By July 1921, Mongolia, under the tutelage of the Bolsheviks, had become the second communist state in world history. In 1924, the Mongolian revolutionaries established the Mongolian People's Republic (hereafter MPR), modeling it on the USSR, which had been founded two years earlier.

COMMUNIST MONGOLIA AND THE USSR

For the following seven decades, the MPR pursued policies in imitation of those devised by the USSR. During this period, the MPR was described as a Soviet satellite. It generally abided by Soviet policies, although several of its leaders attempted to deviate from rigid adherence to their neighbor's dictates. Scholars may quibble about the exact degree of Soviet control, but it is unquestionable that policies and programs instituted by its neighbor would often be implemented in the MPR as well.

The primary goals of the MPR and its Soviet patrons included collectivization of the herds, industrialization, and urbanization. After a disastrous failure at collectivization in the 1920s and early 1930s, the government adopted a more cautious strategy from 1956 to 1959, culminating in collective ownership of most of the herds. Herders became workers, with stipends provided by the collectives, and no longer privately owned large numbers of animals.

At the same time, the government, with the strong support of the USSR, unveiled major efforts at industrial development and urbanization. With Soviet assistance, the Mongolians constructed an industrial complex in the new city of Darkhan, with flour mills and leather, poultry-processing, and construction industries.[3] Erdenebileg remembers visiting Darkhan as a child to see his exiled and purged grandfather. He was amused that the communist hierarchy, which had intended to send his grandfather to a remote location, inadvertently wound up exiling him to what became the second most populous city in the country. Another large new city was built at Erdenet. Discovery of molybdenum, copper, and fluorspar in the region prompted the Mongolian government, with Soviet guidance, to develop a major industrial complex there. Fuel for the industries in Darkhan and Erdenet required extensive development of coal mining, still another growing industry.

The government needed to encourage a rural-to-urban migration to supply the labor force and the support services for these enterprises, an effort that would have wide-ranging ramifications on the activists of the 1990s who did not derive from elite backgrounds. Many of the reformers moved to Ulaanbaatar as part of this migration. To be sure, Zorig, Hulan, Ganbold, and Oyun had been born into elite families and lived either in Ulaanbaatar or abroad. However, many of the activists who actually gained power moved, with their families, to Ulaanbaatar at this time. Tsakhiagiin Elbegdorj was born in Khovd; Dambyn Dorligjav, one of the hunger strikers in the 1990 demonstrations, hailed from Uvs; Randaasumbereliin Gonchigorj, the first vice president in the first democratic election, was a native of Arkhangai; and Natsagiin Bagabandi, who became the second president, was born in Zavkhan. More and more people flocked to Ulaanbaatar, Erdenet, Darkhan, and the centers of the country's *aimags*. In 1956, less than a quarter of the population resided in towns and cities, but by 1978, the number had soared to more than 50 percent. Nonetheless, the government also initiated a natalist policy to provide the laborers for industry and infrastructure projects. The population almost tripled from 1950 to 1989.[4] Even so, the largest factories and mines and the major infrastructure projects suffered from severe shortages of labor.

Soviet influence extended to Mongolian culture as well. The National University (founded in 1942) and the country's primary and secondary schools heavily emphasized Marxism-Leninism and used authoritarian teaching methods based on those of the Soviet Union.[5] Russian was the second language in the schools, and the capital had several specifically Russian schools, primarily for the children of the elite. The political and technocratic elites, including nearly every important activist so far mentioned in this book, attended college or graduate school in the USSR or Eastern Europe. Russian literature, art, theater, and films influenced Mongolians, and many Mongolian writers, artists, musicians, ballet dancers, and film directors studied in the USSR. In my interviews with them, Hulan, Oyun, and others repeatedly referred to Russian novels and to Russian history to bolster some particular point they wished to make. Even more dramatic, in 1941, the Mongolian government mandated the substitution of the Cyrillic alphabet for the Uyghur script in the transcription of the Mongolian language (although five years elapsed before it actually implemented the change).[6]

On the other hand, the Mongolian elite questioned aspects of USSR influence. Soviet archeologists excavated sites in Mongolia and often sent artifacts to museums and institutes in the USSR. For example, they dispatched many objects from Khara Khorum, the first capital of the Mongolian empire, to the Hermitage Museum in Leningrad.[7] Until Gorbachev's withdrawal of Soviet troops in the late 1980s, the elite had been concerned too about the large Soviet military force based in Mongolia. The Sino-Soviet dispute had offered the USSR a perfect rationale for stationing troops in Mongolia, as both the Mongolian and Soviet governments asserted that Chinese soldiers across the border engaged in provocations and were poised to make incursions in Mongolia. A sizable Russian military presence appeared to transgress on Mongolian sovereignty and grated on Mongolian nationalist sensitivities.

Special privileges accruing to Soviet citizens also contributed to the hostility of the Mongolian elite. Russians and other Eastern Europeans shopped in special stores, lived in what appeared to be better residential areas, earned higher salaries and wages than Mongolians for comparable work, and were entitled to more lavish benefits than their Mongolian counterparts. However, Mongolians, fearful of government retaliation, could not complain of these disparities. Nor could they grumble about the insularity of the Russian community or its resemblance to a "culture of colonialism." Some, including Ganbold, were perturbed that the USSR had access to Mongolia's mineral and natural resources at fire-sale prices and did environmental damage in exploiting them.

These tensions and animosities festered beneath the surface and occasionally erupted into unpleasant incidents. Altercations between Russians and Mongolians occurred, but the media reportedly concealed many of these disputes. Chinese sources, which were naturally hostile to the USSR during this time, mentioned a few incidents that had been hushed up. They pointed to a traffic accident in which a Russian bus had caused injuries to Mongolian citizens but that had not been reported publicly, "for fear of portraying the Soviets in a bad light."[8] Probably exaggerated rumors that Russians had been advised to stay indoors at night to avoid assaults by hostile Mongolians surfaced repeatedly throughout this time.

However, when questioned about Mongolian fears concerning preservation of Mongolian identity during the Soviet era, Hulan, Erdenebileg, and other activists said that they did not have a visceral fear that the Soviet government would transfer large numbers of Russians into Mongolia. They were much more concerned about such a scenario in the case of China, their other powerful neighbor, which had already colonized Inner Mongolia, where the Mongolians were now vastly outnumbered and under great pressure to assimilate. Hulan and Erdenebileg (who could speak Chinese and had studied China's annexation of Inner Mongolia, Tibet, and Xinjiang in the seventeenth and eighteenth centuries) feared that with China's population continuing to grow at a rapid clip from the 1950s to the 1970s, the Chinese would seek lebensraum in Mongolia, one of the most thinly populated countries in the world.

Moreover, Hulan and Erdenebileg said that collectivization, urbanization, and industrialization, all supported by the USSR and Eastern Europe, had translated into economic progress by the 1980s. They noted that the size of the herds remained stable, but industry and trade experienced substantial expansion.[9] Industry accounted for 7 percent of Mongolia's Net Material Product (NMP) in 1950, but for 35 percent of the total by 1985, and trade increased from 10 percent in 1950 to 26 percent by 1985. Agriculture, including herding, which accounted for 68 percent of NMP in 1950, had declined to 20 percent by 1985.[10] Employment patterns followed a similar trajectory. In 1960, 61 percent of the employed worked in the agricultural sector, but by 1985 only 33 percent earned their livelihoods in that sector. Industry gained workers during that time, but education and health employment more than doubled. Education employed 4 percent of the labor force in 1960, but this had jumped to 10 percent by 1985, and the number of health workers had increased from 3 to 6 percent.[11] These gains in the service sector jibe with the greater emphasis on the social development of the population. GDP figures for Mongolia, which are not calculated in the same way as those for other countries, also record growth throughout the 1980s. As late as 1988, the annual increase in GDP amounted to 5.1 percent. At 46 percent of GDP, the rate of investment, mostly Soviet and Eastern European, but some from the Mongolian government itself, was likewise impressive.[12]

Erdenebileg, who spent most of the 1980s in Mongolia, mentioned that the standard of living was relatively low, but few Mongolians experienced abject poverty or lacked the basic necessities, a view confirmed by the later reports of international donor agencies. Rent, utilities, food, and other consumer needs were subsidized.[13]

However, the Mongolian economy was not obstacle-free. Its reliance on trade and investment from the Soviet bloc made it vulnerable to the economic and political convulsions plaguing the USSR in the late 1980s and the early 1990s. Mongolia's minerals were processed in the USSR, from which it also imported most of its petroleum and petroleum products. The Soviet grid provided most of its power needs, especially in Western Mongolia.[14] The rate of economic growth was adequate, but technology in most enterprises was dated.[15]

The gradual disintegration of the Soviet bloc in the late 1980s and the collapse of one-party rule in Mongolia in 1990 resulted in considerable economic turbulence. When Ganbold became first deputy premier in the first democratically elected government in Mongolian history in 1990, he found disruptions in trade, reductions in investment, and a wedge in the previously close relationship between Mongolia and the Soviet bloc. Mongolia's former communist partners now demanded payment in hard currency, which the Mongolians could generally not provide. This new policy, as well as the interruptions in the reliable transport of goods within the Soviet bloc, led to shortages of fuel, materials, and spare parts. Repeated suspensions of fuel deliveries idled factories and disrupted the planting and harvesting of crops. Some factories closed, leading to the first serious levels of unemployment since the advent of the communist state. In the urban areas, such staples as sugar and butter were unavailable, and meat, rice, and matches, among other goods, were rationed. The countryside had meat and dairy products but often could not obtain flour, sugar, candy, and other goods. One foreign journalist who passed through Ulaanbaatar noticed that "many of the shelves in the markets are empty."[16]

MONGOLIA AND THE INTERNATIONAL DONOR AGENCIES

Ganbold and his fellow economists acknowledged that they needed a substitute, at least temporarily, for the Soviet assistance that had helped to sustain their economy. On the other hand, Zorig, Oyun, and other reformers who favored democracy but not necessarily a pure market economy, believed that long-term dependence on foreign aid would hamper the development of a self-sustaining and productive economy. Among both groups, exhilaration over the departure of Soviet officials and troops was muted. They all recognized that the virtual termination of Soviet aid and the decline of trade with the USSR had generated a crisis, which compelled Mongolia immediately to request aid from different countries and to seek other trading partners.

Having moved away from Soviet influence or domination, the newly elected Mongolian officials sought to chart a foreign policy that emphasized greater contact with the capitalist world. They knew that they had a receptive audience in the Western countries (including Japan), whose leaders could not help but gloat over the collapse of the Soviet bloc. From their perspective, capitalism had bested communism, an indication that the market economy was superior and unassailable. Proponents of a market economy branded the planned economies as inefficient, unproductive, and authoritarian. Emphasizing the need for economic growth, they called for structural reform of the planned economies, which in practice meant privatization of public assets, elimination of state subsidies, and in general minimal government involvement in the economy. Their trickle-down theory dictated that economic policy take precedence over social concerns. They assumed that pure market forces would lead to a strong economy, which would solve social welfare problems. As important, they emphasized a transition from the previously authoritarian communist system. For many of them, in fact, democracy equated with a market economy.[17] Mongolia offered the pure market advocates a laboratory in which to experiment. If their theories fostered economic growth in land-locked, sparsely populated Mongolia, they would presumably be effective in other underdeveloped regions with more promising potential.[18]

Under these circumstances, the visit of U.S. Secretary of State James Baker in August 1990 assumed great significance for Mongolia's future. Three years earlier, Mongolia and the United States had initiated diplomatic relations, and by 1990, U.S. officials certainly knew of Mongolia's economic difficulties. At the same time, Mongolia began to regard the West as its principal defense against possible Chinese economic domination. Baker's trip led to the first significant face-to-face meetings between a major U.S. official and the leaders of a new multiparty government in Mongolia. Baker was particularly impressed that a month before his arrival, Mongolia had had its first free multiparty elections, "with a voter turnout of more than 90 per cent," and he called it the first Asian Communist country to move toward democracy.[19] In his view, Mongolia's relatively uncomplicated economy and ethnically homogeneous population would facilitate establishing a market-based system. He met with Ganbold and Prime Minister Byambasüren and promised economic assistance and support in gaining admission to the international donor agencies.

Within the next two years, a variety of international organizations, including a few at the instigation of Secretary Baker, began to arrive in Mongolia to complement the United Nations Development Programme and other agencies already in the country.[20] Both donor agencies and politically oriented organizations and foundations established offices in Ulaanbaatar to promote change in Mongolia. Resident representatives of these agencies and consultants streamed into the country.

The stage was set for closer cooperation with the international donor agencies. The new Mongolian government began to take a few steps toward a market economy, a requirement for attracting support from donors. These agencies would eventually demand more steps, but they were sufficiently satisfied to entertain applications from the Mongolian government. In February 1991, the International Monetary Fund, the Asian Development Bank, and the World Bank all admitted Mongolia to membership, qualifying the country for loans and grants.[21]

These financial organizations were the dominant Western forces in Mongolia. They had the most money and provided the most aid, and they thus had substantial leverage with the Mongolians. This aid, in the form of grants and loans, would not be unrestricted. Laying out a program of macroeconomic reforms, the donor agencies conditioned aid on adherence to and implementation of such dramatic changes. As noted earlier, this package of reforms necessitated liberalization of prices and elimination of government subsidies, a balanced government budget, privatization of state assets and of banking, local money linked to a convertible currency, tight credit policies to preclude what these agencies considered to be the great evil of inflation, and elimination or reduction of restrictions on foreign trade. Private entrepreneurs would replace government-managed industries, and the planned economy would be dismantled. The donor agencies emphasized economic growth and export-growth industries but scarcely focused on equitable distribution of income. Under these guidelines, government would divest itself of ownership of such enterprises as airlines, factories, and stores. Elimination of subsidies from the USSR and diminution of the state's role in the economy would require the government to scale back on what the donor agencies believed to be overly generous social welfare entitlements, which could not be sustained by the Mongolian economy.[22]

In addition to the international donor agencies, other agencies introduced Western influences and supported democracy and the market economy, which they tended to equate. The Konrad Adenauer Foundation, which was sponsored by the Christian Democratic Party of Germany, was perhaps the most overtly political of these agencies. Werner Prohl, its resident representative in Mongolia from 1993 to 1998, explained to me that it sought to support Mongolian leaders who shared "its fundamental convictions." As early as 1991, the foundation had been in touch with several of the Mongolian participants in the movement to topple the communist system, and the following year, it had invited them to Germany for a study tour. In August 1993, Prohl became the resident representative of the foundation, with a mandate to assist the factions opposed to the MPRP. Bringing in consultants from Europe, he and his underlings initially worked with the non-MPRP members of the Khural, offering specific advice on party organization and on how to appeal to the electorate. They founded a Political Academy to train such leaders as Hulan, Zorig, Elbedgdorj, and the economist Mendsaikhany Enkhsaikhan (who would be the first non-MPRP prime minister). These training programs, which included study tours and workshops, set the stage for the foundation's plans to foster a coalition among the dissident parties against the MPRP. Prohl also funded the Sant Maral Foundation, founded by Luvsavdendev Sumati, who had had a Mongolian father and a Russian Jewish mother, to conduct polls about the preferences of the electorate.[23]

The Adenauer Foundation did not conceal its activities in support of advocates of the pure market. Its program of assistance may be regarded as a contribution to democracy or as interference in the domestic politics of Mongolia. To be sure, seminars and training sessions on the principles and practice of democracy were valuable, but help on tactics and strategy to one anti-MPRP faction and assistance in developing an anti-MPRP political party smacks of partisanship and intrusion in the political process. It seems unlikely that a Western country such as Germany would tolerate foreign support for a specific political party. Indeed, in the United States, foreign monetary contributions to a political party are illegal. Yet, in his interviews with me, Prohl did not hesitate to say that his foundation had supported the anti-MPRP political coalition.

Similarly, the International Republican Institute (hereafter IRI), a U.S.-sponsored organization, also played a role in domestic politics in Mongolia, after initiating contacts there in September 1991. The IRI is not associated with the Republican Party in the United States, but prominent Republicans as Senator John McCain and former National Security Advisor Brent Scowcroft serve on its board.[24] As noted earlier, Secretary Baker had revisited Mongolia earlier in 1991, promising aid. His cordial reception in Ulaanbaatar certainly encouraged the IRI to dispatch staff members to Mongolia.

Like the Adenauer Foundation in the early 1990s, the IRI assisted the non-MPRP parties. It offered training in founding a political party, developing a message, grassroots organization, campaign management, and communications. With $450,000 (a considerable sum in Mongolia), the IRI sent staff and consultants on twenty trips to Mongolia, eventually set up an office in Ulaanbaatar, and provided equipment such as computers and technical advice to the so-called democratic opposition. One of its principal Mongolian employees was Zorig and Oyun's brother, whose views appear to have differed from those of his siblings. In any event, the IRI, like the Adenauer Foundation, played an active role in Mongolian politics.

The Asia Foundation, an American NGO funded by the U.S. Congress, as well as by corporations, individuals, and other foundations (and that in the 1960s received funds from U.S. intelligence agencies), also opened an office in Ulaanbaatar in the early 1990s, locating it in the Log Cabin adjacent to Freedom Square. Its mandate was to promote the development of civil society through technical and material support for judicial and legal changes, including assistance in the drafting of a new constitution in 1992, and for education about democracy—for example, donating 25,000 books to Mongolian NGOs, libraries, and universities. It eventually formulated a Voter Education Project, which among other efforts funded media programs designed to inform the public about the electoral process and representative institutions; it funded NGOs, particularly those dealing with women's issues; and it supported transparency in government, calling for publication of transcripts of Khural discussions and of the voting records of its members. Among its earliest projects was training for potential politicians, mostly from the anti-MPRP political parties, and staff members would eventually point out, with great pride, that 22 percent of those elected to the Khural in 1996 (or about 40 percent of the non-MPRP members elected) had received Asia Foundation grants, as would three of the five chairs of the standing committees in the Khural. The question is, did the Asia Foundation intrude in Mongolian domestic politics? Unlike the IRI, it did not deliberately aim to support the anti-MPRP candidates for the Khural, but its programs, according to its own promotional literature, initially appeared to benefit them.[25]

THE ARRIVAL OF WESTERN
PHILANTHROPIC ORGANIZATIONS

Christian missionary organizations were still another group that began to arrive in Mongolia after the collapse of communism. Because the Communist government had attacked and devastated Buddhism in the 1920s and 1930s, Christianity faced less resistance than it might otherwise have done. It also profited because Buddhism is not a sole truth religion and does not seek absolute loyalty to the exclusion of all other views. In addition, the excesses and exploitation of the Buddhist monasteries in the precommunist era had alienated some Mongolians, and the antireligious propaganda during the communist period contributed to the vulnerability of Buddhism. As early as 1992, the Mormon Church started to send missionaries, and by the late 1990s, Mormon services in Ulaanbaatar were conducted in a sizable hall, located less than fifty feet away from the museum that houses the finest collection of Buddhist art in the country. The Mormon Church held services in five other locations in Ulaanbaatar as well and had branches in Darkhan, Erdenet, and Khovd. Teaching English gave the Mormons a foothold in many communities, and they proselytized in small towns and in the steppelands and deserts. I attended several of their meetings in Ulaanbaatar and found that more than 80 per-

cent of the worshippers were women. Because women have arguably suffered more than any other group as a result of the collapse of communism, they may be more responsive to Christianity. Cynics among the
reformers I interviewed suggested that the young converts had another
motivation: to seek marital partners among the strait-laced young Cau-
casian Mormon missionaries, who were more responsible than the growing number of unemployed and sometimes alcoholic and abusive Mongolian men. They noted that the possibility of trips to the United States
for study or other programs lured some to convert. Motivations aside, the
Mormons and other Christians made some impressive inroads. However,
statistics on the number of Christians are hard to come by.

Nonetheless, the increased activity of Christian groups and the growing number of converts concerned some in government and among the
general population. One Christian denomination set up a television station, Eagle TV, which broadcast entertainment and news programs but
also scheduled children's cartoons with a religious message, as well as
shows for adults that described Christian tenets. Some Western Christians registered as educators, not as missionaries, and illegally proselytized
for Christianity.[26] Hulan and other reformers resented this subterfuge,
resentments that may have prompted the Mongolian government to
impose limitations on Christianity. For example, Mongolian Customs
officials confiscated Bibles—10,000 of them, according to one source—
and 600 videos that one denomination sought to import. Almost a year
elapsed before officials released the Bibles, and even then they retained
the videos. However, reflecting the official view, the Speaker of the Khural
insisted that the Mongolian government would not prevent Christians
from proselytizing.[27] The missionaries continue to spread the Christian
message, although some observers occasionally challenge their reputed
successes.

Other foreign nonpolitical and nonreligious agencies streamed into
Mongolia in the 1990s. Some attempted to alleviate the hardships that
befell the population after the collapse of socialism and the adoption of
austerity measures. Typical was Save the Children–UK, which sought to
help the growing number of abused, working, and street children and
school dropouts. Aside from providing shelter, summer camps, and educational and vocational training for those among the children who had no
links with their parents, Save the Children produced valuable reports on

the economic and social status of Mongolia and on international donor agencies' policies contributing to disarray. A few Christian organizations, including the Adventist Development and Relief Agency (ADRA) and World Vision International, which focused on schools, health, and the construction of straw-bale housing, also initiated projects for vulnerable groups. When I talked with their executive directors, they said that they deemphasized efforts to proselytize for Christianity, and that their organizations were principally interested in contributing to social welfare.[28]

Still other organizations attempted to promote the development of new institutions or new modes of thinking. They organized a wide variety of programs, including English-language instruction, civics education, scholarships to foreign universities, reform of school curricula, and public health initiatives. It is still too early to evaluate the results of these programs, although some, such as scholarships for graduate study abroad, appear to be successful. Competitions for most such fellowships have been based on merit, a welcome corrective to the favoritism and nepotism that have plagued Mongolia for generations. Yet these agencies employed numerous consultants who knew very little about Mongolia to conduct workshops and seminars on subjects ranging from civics to alcohol and sex education. They appear to send the same consultants to many of the countries in which they operate, lending a "cookie-cutter" approach to their programs and leading to ignorance and lack of concern for the uniqueness of each culture. Having attended some of their seminars for Mongolian professionals, I was repeatedly surprised by their lack of knowledge of Mongolian heritage and history and wondered how effective they could be. Oyun and Hulan, among many other Mongolians I interviewed, were critical of this kind of foreign technical assistance.

Also detracting from the contributions of these agencies was duplication. Because there were scarcely any efforts to coordinate the activities of these diverse groups, several of them undertook the same kinds of programs or conducted similar needs assessments. Numerous reports on energy needs, prospects for tourism, and strategies for protection of the environment were prepared, and most were simply reiterations of earlier reports. Such duplication squandered resources designed to aid Mongolia.

Chapter 3 | PRESSURE FOR A MARKET ECONOMY, 1990–1997

As an economist and first deputy minister, Davaadorjiin Ganbold was eager for the involvement of the IMF, the ADB, and the World Bank. Although he had a "limited exposure to market economics," he would seek to implement an economic program that, "he recalls proudly, was exactly according to Milton Friedman's ideology."[1]

The IMF and the ADB sent groups to study the Mongolian economy and to interview Ganbold and other, like-minded economists. An IMF research team conducted an official visit in August 1990 and produced a report entitled *The Mongolian People's Republic: Toward a Market Economy,* and ADB staff arrived in Mongolia in late May 1991 for three weeks to complete a more comprehensive analysis entitled *Mongolia: A Centrally Planned Economy in Transition.* The subtitles reveal the objectives of both agencies: to promote a market economy, which they identified in terms of "reforms." Two of the four chapters in the IMF report include "reform" in their titles. The foreword to the ADB volume is also liberally sprinkled with the term "reform" and labels privatization "the centerpiece of reform." Both the IMF and ADB teams believed that government ought to play only a limited role in the economy. One way of reducing the government role was to restrict the revenues at its command, which in practice meant considerable reductions in taxation and sharp cutbacks in the size of its bureaucracy. Ganbold and his fellow market economists subscribed to all of these principles.

However, this agenda seemed at odds with the policies that had proved successful in postwar East Asia. The Four Tigers—Hong Kong, Japan, South Korea, and Singapore—had fostered economic growth through active government involvement and supervision of their economies. Their experiences indicated a need for a strong government that promoted the rule of law, the legitimacy of contracts, a stable banking system, and a social safety net to protect the vulnerable. The governments in these burgeoning economies had invested in infrastructure, technology, and human capital and had used tariffs to protect a few industries until they became strong enough to compete, a policy abhorred by the proponents of free trade and an unfettered market economy in the IMF and ADB, and by Ganbold as well. In addition, these governments had also supported education and devoted an increased share of their budgets to schools and universities, which emphasized the sciences, mathematics, and engineering.[2] However, the austerity budgets that Ganbold and his fellow economists and the IMF and ADB supported would translate into reduced investments in education.

In their recommendations, the two reports scarcely took into account the historical characteristics of Mongolian society. A market economy, with privatization at its core, would be their principal remedy for Mongolia's economic ills, a prescription they had applied to all the so-called transition economies of the former Soviet bloc. Knowledge of the Mongolian heritage might have prompted them to reconsider their support for privatization of the pastoral economy, which had traditionally been based on cooperation in an often harsh environment. Nonetheless, whatever their ideological agenda, their survey of the Mongolian economy is useful and interesting.

After a preliminary sketch of Mongolia's resources (and very little on its society and culture), the ADB report assesses the changes introduced during the communist era. Planners had, from the 1960s on, transformed a pastoral economy into a mixed herding, agricultural, and industrial one. However, the ADB team did not share the communist planners' objectives. They disapproved of Mongolia's excessive reliance on the Soviet bloc and its pricing system, which was "distorted" by government subsidies. They also criticized Mongolia's treatment of capital, because "investments were not subject to efficiency tests" and instead bolstered inefficient state industries and enterprises. A new development strategy required "dismantling of the commanded planned economy, privatization of public assets, and rapid introduction of market-oriented systems." This prescription is repeated throughout the report.[3]

Turning to the financial sector, the ADB team decried, in addition, the state-run banking system, which offered credit to enterprises based upon the decisions of planners rather than upon analyses of creditworthiness. They noted that individual savings deposits did not determine the funds available for capital investment and that interest rates on loans bore little relation to evaluation of risk and of collateral. The ADB team suggested the establishment of commercial banks and a reduction in the influence of the State Bank, which would henceforth regulate other banks rather than accepting savings or providing loans. However, they recognized that the development of this new financial system would necessitate considerable changes. Bank officers required proper training as regards evaluation of loans, policies concerning nonperforming loans, and means of attracting deposits. The State Bank had to foster expertise to supervise the practices of the new commercial banks and to maintain a check on the money supply to avert inflation. Yet until these standards were established and an effective banking system created, the market system that ADB championed would encounter serious obstacles. A gradual approach would be more likely to ensure success. Considerable time would be required to build institutions, such as a banking system, for a market structure. However, Ganbold and the international donors, including ADB, were soon encouraging shock therapy, which would appear to conflict with the magnitude of the changes they proposed.

Integral to shock therapy was a reduction in the state budget. The ADB team decried the sizable state budget, which, they insisted, comprised too large a portion of GDP. Government revenues derived principally from a turnover tax, produced from the difference between state-determined, fixed domestic prices and the contract prices for either exports or imports. The other main source of revenues had been a tax on the profits of enterprises. Income taxes had been a negligible source. Recommending a liberalization of prices, the ADB team would virtually eliminate the turnover tax. In addition, in line with their advocacy of free trade, they suggested only a very limited use of tariffs and export duties. Instead, they approved of the Personal Income Tax and Corporate Income Tax Laws enacted in 1991. They also acknowledged that the "Government taxation machinery" needed to be "strengthened because it was not used to the new concepts and modes of taxation."[4] Yet the shock therapy they proposed failed to allow the time required to train enough revenue agents, let alone to explain the new income tax system to those who needed to understand it. Under these circumstances, the question was, would the government secure sufficient revenues to undertake investment in infrastructure, education, transport, environment, public enterprises (e.g., energy), and other public services?

The ADB team, supported by Ganbold and his group of market economists, proposed other sources of revenue as well. One was a sales tax, a readily collectible levy. The ADB economists failed to mention that this tax was regressive and would impose an additional burden on ordinary and lower-income Mongolians, who would in any case face higher prices for essential goods because of the team's proposal to eliminate government subsidies. Another source of income proposed was sale of public assets. The government would not only gain an immediate inflow of funds but would also secure taxes from the newly privatized enterprises. Ganbold and the ADB team assumed that privatization would result in greater efficiency and productivity in such new enterprises.

According to the ADB, less revenue necessitated a reduction in state expenditures. The state had provided export subsidies (about 7 to 8 percent of the budget) and consumer subsidies, the latter in the form of free food and medical care for children, and fixed, low prices for staples such as meat, milk, clothing, heat, and electricity. Such state regulation of prices translated into low rates of inflation, but the ADB team emphasized the need to deregulate these prices. Ganbold also viewed such subsidies as untenable and, in addition, supported the devaluation of the Mongolian currency unit, the tugrik, from 3 to 5.6 per U.S. dollar, and the resulting so-called price adjustments, an euphemism for price increases and, possibly, inflation.

Ganbold and the ADB team deplored subsidies to producers and free services and support, such as fodder, construction and maintenance of wells, and the services of veterinarians, which, they claimed, further entangled government in the economy. Moreover, the privatization of state enterprises would reduce the size of the government bureaucracy that supervised them. This would lower the amount spent on wages and subsidies, which constituted about 10 percent of the state budget.[5] The ADB team, supported by Ganbold, also maintained that expenses on education, health, welfare, and culture should be cut back, because they contributed to the budget deficit, which in the past had necessitated loans from the Soviet bloc countries, principally the USSR.

Ganbold recognized that foreign investment from outside the Soviet bloc was limited and that the nonconvertible Mongolian currency hindered economic relations with noncommunist countries. He and the ADB team recommended promotion of exports to foster greater links with the world community and enable Mongolia to import a larger variety of goods. They also proposed a regimen of free trade. Limited or no tariffs would result in greater trade turnover and lead to elimination of tariffs by Mongolia's natural trading partners. Mongolia ought also to devalue its currency to make its products more competitive in international trade.

Yet the ADB economists were aware of some of the potentially harmful effects of such policies. Devaluation meant that imported goods and probably goods in general would be costlier, a further burden on lower- and middle-income Mongolians. Rapid integration into the convertible currency zone and continued currency devaluation could cause even greater distress. Gradual elimination of the state trading companies, as well as other state enterprises, could lead to substantial unemployment and a higher incidence of poverty. Recognizing these hazards, the ADB team conceded that "the medium-term economic outlook for Mongolia is not bright," but it concluded that "these are the costs of adjustment and restructuring that must be borne by the country during the transition to a market-oriented economy."[6] Ganbold seemed willing to accept the human costs of shock therapy. On the other hand, the Mongolian democratic reformers feared the social dislocations of this pure market economy program. For example, Hashbat Hulan, who would become the chair of a social policy committee in the Khural in 1996, correctly predicted that the unemployment and poverty and attendant social pathologies resulting from shock therapy would be far more serious than the market economists foresaw.

Ganbold and the ADB economists assumed that privatization would "improve the efficiency of resource allocation," an assumption questioned by several Western economic advisors to Mongolia.[7] Nonetheless, that assumption governed the policy of the ADB and the country's first democratically elected government toward the Mongolian economy.

The ADB team also focused on exports by the private sector, because the domestic market was small. At the same time, the new private companies needed to cultivate foreign investment, because domestic sources such as commercial banks were just beginning to develop. To attract foreign investment, the government needed to remove restrictions on the free flow of capital.[8]

The ADB team and the new government's economists then assessed the transport, communications, and energy infrastructure and found them deficient. They noted that only 1,247 kilometers of the country's roads were paved, and that the remaining dirt roads could be impassable after heavy rains. I can attest to the paucity of roads in the countryside and the unfortunate consequences, having witnessed many vehicles passing through and degrading valuable pasture and arable lands. In addition, the state, which owned nearly all the buses and trucks, faced shortages of vehicles, spare parts, and fuel because of the collapse of the Soviet bloc. The ADB team suggested privatization, user fees (taxes on fuel, payments for licenses, etc.), and large infrastructure construction to cope with these problems. They also recommended a market orientation and user fees for railways and air transport, which were also bedeviled by shortages of spare parts and fuel and by aging fleets and inadequate radar and airport facilities.

In sum, Ganbold and the ADB economists offered a useful description of Mongolia's economic problems as of 1991 and had a specific prescription for its ills: commercialization and privatization, which, they believed, would yield a more efficient system than a planned economy. And the more rapid the privatization, the better for the economy.

By the time the ADB report was issued late in 1991, some foreign and domestic support for privatization had been created. Jeffrey Sachs, the Harvard University architect of shock therapy for the communist economies, visited Mongolia in March 1991, giving moral support to Ganbold and the other Mongolian advocates of a market economy. He did caution that in the short term, Mongolia would suffer a worse downturn than that experienced in Eastern Europe.[9] Nonetheless, his ideas about shock therapy prevailed. Prime Minister Dashiin Byambasüren and his newly appointed group of ardent believers in the market economy, including Ganbold, were about to initiate "one of the fastest privatization programs in the reforming socialist countries."[10]

Some Western economists and Mongolian reformers cautioned against the use of shock therapy. Frederick Nixson, a professor of economics at

Manchester University, who served briefly as an advisor to the World Bank, proposed a gradual and sequenced development toward a market economy, which required an effective banking system, a proper legal structure, and a well-conceived plan for privatization of state assets. He and his colleagues at Manchester University feared that shock therapy would lead to corruption, unfair division of state property, and poor prospects for economic growth.[11] Several of the most prominent Mongolian democratic reformers were also wary, but the MPRP victory in the July 1990 elections and Prime Minister Byambasüren's appointment of Ganbold and other advocates of the market economy to major positions in government left them without much power. Distressed by this, some turned away from politics. Sanjaasürengiin Oyun won admission to study for a doctorate in geochemistry at Cambridge University; Hulan received a fellowship to conduct research in Maine; and although Baabar remained as chair of the Mongolian Social Democratic Party, he devoted most of his time to research and writing of books on Mongolian history. They were all apprehensive that the policies advocated by the market economists would result in abuses, growing inequality, and damage to the health, educational, and social welfare systems of the communist era.

PRIVATIZATION AND SHOCK THERAPY, 1990–1992

Ganbold and his fellow economists in Byambasüren's government ignored these concerns, administered shock therapy, and thus ingratiated themselves with the international donor agencies. They first fostered the privatization of approximately 25 million animals in the country, with the leaders of the cooperatives, or *negdels*, promptly parceling out animals to their members. This process of privatization resulted in serious abuses, because the former managers and their families and friends laid claim to more animals than the ordinary herders.[12]

Ganbold and the economists then turned their attention to the privatization of enterprises, which they divided into two separate categories: "large" privatization, designed for substantial enterprises and companies valued at more than $50,000, and "small" privatization, focused mostly on trade and service operations. Because money was scarce, the privatization would be conducted through vouchers. Each citizen born before May 1991 would receive, for a nominal payment, seven vouchers to be used for the large privatization and three vouchers for the small privati-zation.[13] By the middle of 1992, approximately one year after its incep-tion, the small privatization had resulted in the conversion of most trade and service outlets and retail stores from state-owned to private property. A few accusations of corruption and favoritism were leveled at the process, but workers in these enterprises sometimes banded together to become the joint owners. In theory, those with the greatest number of vouchers would have become the owners of the property.

The market economists in government sought to speed up the large privatization (which in theory included the *negdels*) as well. As soon as they proposed the sale of all but the few state-managed operations deemed to be of great strategic value, they quickly encountered opposi-tion from some MPRP members in the Khural, and the more radical visions had to be abandoned. Nonetheless, within two years, the state retained ownership mostly of the major enterprises (the national airlines, the largest cashmere factory, the Erdenet copper mines, etc.). The sale of the enterprise usually began with the use of the vouchers to purchase shares in the new company on the Stock Exchange (which had been established on January 1, 1991, but barely operated). The scheme's sup-porters exultantly proclaimed that "this country-wide network gives every citizen the opportunity to invest in any of the country's enterprises."[14] Such observations by the many consultants who had poured into Mon-golia ignored the country's past. For seventy years, it had been under a communist system, and before that it had been dominated by the Manchus and the Chinese for more than two hundred years. The vast majority of Mongolia's citizens had almost no conception of the value of their shares or of what the Stock Exchange was. As a result, "people with private capital bought the vouchers [for little money] from those people trading them in the market who needed the money to buy consumer goods."[15]

A market economy was beyond the experience of ordinary Mongo-lians, who had had almost no exposure to the outside world and were allowed no time to learn about these very new institutions.[16] The scheme was therefore ripe for exploitation and abuse. The solution proposed by its champions was that "those citizens overwhelmed by the complexity of such information have an easy alternative: the brokerages run mutual funds that invest in a portfolio of firms."[17] They failed to consider the likelihood of the brokerage firms and other entrepreneurs taking advantage of ill-informed and credulous citizens by offering them a pittance for their vouchers.

One important study stated that "the sum effect of these [efforts at privatization] was to have the programme substantially discredited in the public view."[18] Many citizens who were not conversant with a market economy sold their vouchers at depressed prices and thus gained very little from the redistribution of public assets. The politically and economically well-connected profited enormously, frequently gaining partial or complete control of enterprises. As Oyun wrote later: "330 shareholding companies were created [out of state-owned enterprises]. Currently [i.e., in 2003], no more than 1,500 individuals, representing 0.5 per cent of the population, own over 70 per cent of the shares of these 330 companies."[19] Moreover, the new owners of the enterprises had received public assets without much expenditure. They had not been compelled to save or gather funds to pay for these assets, which they had gained as a bonanza; they therefore had no particular incentive to save or to invest additional capital in the enterprise.

The lack of a proper legal tradition also undermined privatization. The market economists in government instituted laws concerning property only after privatization had been initiated. The 1992 Constitution mandated the protection of property rights, but the Securities Law was enacted only in 1994, three years after the establishment of the Stock Exchange and one or two years after the privatization of many large enterprises. Implementation of the existing laws was haphazard. As a recent study of Mongolian privatization reports, "the late or non-payment of commercial debts and State taxes puts great strains upon creditors and merits stricter enforcement."[20] The lax implementation of the existing contractual regulations and laws undermined privatization.

There were also problems for the banking system owing to the rapidity of the changes required by the policy of shock therapy. By 1991, six commercial banks had been carved out of the old State Bank, and in 1992, nine smaller banks had been established. They had few qualified assessors of loans and faced a tradition in which loans had been granted to comply with the planned economy and with the demands of policy-makers. Lacking the requisite skills and controls, the banks incurred numerous bad debts because of poor assessments of risks and of insider loans, either government-directed or nepotistic. With massive inflation from 1991 to 1993, the banks faced an adverse lending rate, because their interest on loans lagged behind the rate of inflation. Seeking to compensate, they raised the interest rate dramatically, but the rate paid to depositors did not increase as rapidly. Both depositing funds in banks and borrowing from them became less attractive. In addition, high-risk loans to friends and the well-connected constituted a substantial segment of some bank portfolios, jeopardizing their liquidity and financial soundness. By 1994, the government had no choice but to compel two troubled smaller banks to merge with larger ones.[21] Worried depositors started to withdraw their funds. However, it was not until 1996 that a major crisis occurred.

Liberalization of prices, the second part of the pure market agenda championed by Ganbold and the market economists, also took place at a rapid rate. The government eliminated many price controls and reduced subsidies to enterprises and individuals. Prices increased dramatically, and production declined, contributing to an inflation of 325 percent in 1992 and 183 percent in 1993.[22] With sharp rises in prices and without government support, many industries became unprofitable and thus went bankrupt, leading to a drop in production and an increase in unemployment.

A reduction in the budget and in the size of government, the third pillar of the pure market approach, meant a hasty renunciation of seventy years of communism. The state had been intimately involved in the country's economy, and government officials shaped the annual plans for production and distribution.[23] Immediate shifts toward a balanced budget translated into reductions in government services and investment, which Ganbold and the advocates of privatization also approved. In addition, as state enterprises were privatized, the state's assets declined. Had such privatization been undertaken gradually and in an orderly way, the government might have had the time and opportunity to devise a regular system to fulfill its myriad obligations in the social sector, make investments, and build infrastructure.[24] This weakened government championed by the advocates of the market economy would be more likely to accept deregulation of the economy. Agencies that regulated health and safety in the workplace and protected the natural environment would be shorn of much of their resources, authority, and power.

Meanwhile, the government sought to reduce its budget deficit by cutting back on education, health, social welfare, and environmental protection. At the same time, newly privatized companies dismissed employees, claiming that the previous communist enterprises had hired too many workers.[25] Yet, as one commentator noted, "In spite of all these rapid steps toward a market economy, the general economic situation remained in a critical state." In 1992, industrial production declined 23.7 percent from the previous year.

Investment, which had amounted to 46 percent of GDP in 1989, had fallen dramatically to 29.3 percent by 1992.[26] Although the Stock Exchange had been established in January 1991, secondary trading had not developed until August 1995 because of lack of demand and fear of foreigners dominating.[27] Despite the grandiose claims of Naidansürengiin Zoljargal, the very young (b. 1963) director of the Stock Exchange from 1990 to 1996, it did not generate much activity. This self-publicizing "free-market messianist,"[28] who had visited the United States briefly in 1989 on a scholarship and was captivated by Jeffrey Sachs's ideas, was unable to create a robust Stock Exchange, and his brother's involvement in a Mongol Central Bank scandal in the early 1990s tarnished his image as well. Thus the Stock Exchange failed to provide a flow of capital. Hyperinflation wracked the economy with the floating and devaluation of the currency and the elimination of price controls and subsidies, resulting in the closing of additional enterprises.[29] Trade, which was no longer in state hands, fell into disarray, and many products were unavailable, leading to rationing. Even when goods became available by the mid 1990s, many Mongolians did not have the money to pay for them.[30] The conditions that characterized the USSR and postcommunist Russia also prevailed in Mongolia. Consumers in the communist era had suffered shortages of goods and long lines, but prices were low; after the mid 1990s, products were available, mostly from abroad, but prices were so high and salaries so low that most consumers could only look longingly at store window displays.

However, the first two or so years after the collapse of communism also witnessed some positive developments. In January 1991, a Small Khural of fifty members had been assigned the responsibility of writing a new constitution. The International Commission of Jurists, Amnesty International, and the Asia Foundation all offered advice to the drafters, who included some of the leading reformers.[31] The structure eventually mandated in the 1992 Constitution consisted of a 76-member, popularly elected parliament, known as the Khural, with a prime minister and a cabinet to implement policy. Whether the prime Minister and the cabinet could concurrently serve as members of the Khural was left unclear, and this lack of clarity would create difficulties in the mid to late 1990s. Also somewhat vague was the extent of the president's power as head of state. The two presidents who have to date been elected to the office have attempted to assert their powers. The second president rejected several candidates for the position of prime minister, creating a deadlock in government. It appears likely that the Mongolian and foreign drafters of the Constitution devised a system with two executives, the president and the prime minister, to avoid the risk of a strong central government, and this cumbersome and somewhat ill-defined structure has led to difficulties in governance.[32]

The Constitution, with its seventy articles, was the first important statement in Mongolian history of the basic political freedoms of speech, press, assembly, and movement, of protection of minority rights, and of separation between religion and the state, and it also guaranteed economic rights. The state was obliged to provide education, medical care, employment, and a clean environment for its citizens. The Constitution mandated that the official name of the country be changed from "Mongolian People's Republic" to simply "Mongolia" so as to avoid association with the communist era, but its affirmation of economic rights dovetailed with the country's previous seventy-year history. However, the 1992 Constitution differed from the constitutions of the communist era (in 1924, 1940, and 1960) in protecting the political rights of individuals.

Despite the Constitution and free elections for the Khural in 1990, the economy appeared to be in free fall, which required foreign aid to avert even more dire consequences.[33] President Punsalmagiin Ochirbat traveled to Tokyo in September 1991 to seek assistance at the first meeting of international donors that was convened to consider Mongolia's problems. Organized by the Japanese government and the World Bank, the meetings were also attended by the ADB, IMF, UNDP, and government representatives from Japan, the United States, and Europe. The conference set the stage for subsequent donor meetings that have been convened at intervals of from one and a half to two years. The donor agencies and the individual governments offered Mongolia a package about equally divided between grants and loans. The allocations presaged the direction of foreign aid. Some of the funds were devoted to emergency assistance, including supplies of food; to the balance of payments; and to unspecified social welfare needs. However, fully one-third of the money was for what was euphemistically described as economic management improvement or structural adjustments—in other words, promotion of a market economy. These funds were designed to foster privatization, liberalization, and foreign investment, a vital part of the international donor agencies' agenda and of Ganbold's policies, which would remain so for the rest of the decade. About 25 percent of the aid was devoted to energy, transport, telecommunications, and other infrastructure projects.[34] Yet, again, the international donors continued to support these enterprises throughout the 1990s. Such sizable support contrasts sharply with the rather meager amounts offered to deal with the increasing rate of poverty.

Despite foreign aid, the economic crisis persisted as the next Khural election rolled around, and the voters responded to the uncertainty and the declining economy. The electorate blamed Ganbold and the pure market economists in government for the hyperinflation, the economic decline, and the growing pauperization of the country.[35] Meanwhile, the economists and their allies in government reinforced their own negative image by a considerable amount of infighting and mismanagement. For example, a group of traders at the Mongol Central Bank, including Zoljargal's brother, who according to several sources had the support of some high officials in government, perhaps including Ganbold, lost about $82 million, or most of the country's foreign currency reserves, in international currency speculation. Lacking experience, but emboldened by their faith in the pure market philosophy, they gambled away much of the hard currency required to pay for such imports as food and fuel that Mongolia needed.[36]

MODERATION OF SHOCK THERAPY, 1992–1996: STABILITY AND CORRUPTION

In June 1992, these unsettling conditions prompted the electorate to repudiate the shock therapy that had been prescribed for the economy and to elect MPRP leaders, including members of the old guard, who were pledged to moderation. The MPRP faction, which had a more cautious approach to the pure market economy and professed an interest in maintaining a social safety net, won the election in part by capitalizing on the disunity and proliferation of political parties among the opposition. Although Ganbold himself was reelected to the Khural, he lost much of his power, and he and the other young advocates of shock therapy, who were mostly in their twenties and thirties, found themselves in disfavor. Several were accused of improprieties, and the traders in the foreign currency debacle were subject to prosecution. Sanjaasürengiin Zorig and Tsakhiagiin Elbegdorj, renowned leaders of the 1990 demonstrations, were likewise elected to the Khural, but the old generation of MPRP leaders was in charge.

Yet the new government, with Prime Minister Puntsagiin Jasrai at its head, faced the same economic problems as the previous administration and the same philosophy on the part of the international donors. The Economist Intelligence Unit referred to the economy as in a "continuing depression."[37] Moreover, the government itself suffered splits within its own ranks. Jasrai, a member of the MPRP old guard, sought to preserve some of the social welfare benefits of the old system and perhaps also some of the authoritarianism of the communist structure, and he had some support from the old MPRP members who now took charge. However, they were increasingly on the defensive, as even President Ochirbat disapproved of the new government's economic moderation and supported the shock therapy economists. A representative of the older generation of MPRP leaders therefore opposed him in the June 1993 elections. But Ochirbat defeated the MPRP candidate, fostering a division between the MPRP-dominated Khural and the president.

The period between 1992 and 1996 witnessed some amelioration of the country's economic problems. Severe disruptions in transport and energy supplies began to be remedied. The power stations in Ulaanbaatar operated better by the mid 1990s, with fewer concerns about breakdowns of equipment and supplies of coal. Queues for food, particularly bread, disappeared, and the attendant mini-riots among those waiting in long lines declined. By early 1993, one report noted: "There are now goods in shops which were bare a year ago—if one has the money to buy them."[38] Trade began to be restored, first with Russia, but increasingly also with China, and shortages and rationing gradually receded. After declines of 9.5 percent in 1992 and 3 percent in 1993, GDP slowly grew, registering a 2.3 percent gain in 1994 and a 6.3 percent increase in 1995.[39]

However, these gains were somewhat misleading. State farms had collapsed because the government no longer supplied seeds, equipment, transport, or advice. Lacking such support, individual farmers produced fewer goods, leading to disappointing harvests of potatoes, wheat, onions, carrots, and cabbage, and to the need for food imports, principally from China.[40] The increase in industrial production was largely owing to a rise in natural resource and mineral extraction, much of which was dispatched to foreign countries. Export of such nonrenewable resources as copper, molybdenum, and, increasingly, gold, did not contribute much to long-term economic prosperity. Nor did it compensate for the closing of so many industries of the communist era. In Dundgov province, for example, only 15 of 83 industries had survived by 1994,[41] and this was typical of much of the country. In addition, the dependence on exports of raw materials held the country hostage to the vagaries of world commodity prices. Unemployment and poverty increased.

The Jasrai government was increasingly bereft of resources. Many state-owned enterprises had been sold relatively cheaply, and much of the income had been used for operating expenses rather than for long-term investment. "Below-target tax receipts" exacerbated the government's financial problems.[42] Some enterprises evaded taxes; others, which had not prospered under private ownership, could not afford them; while still others, which were not accustomed to paying taxes, simply neglected their obligations. As a result, government became smaller. Its role in preserving a social safety net, in regulating health and safety in commercial enterprises, and in protecting the environment was diminished. At the same time, the government faced requirements from the international donors to balance its budget, necessitating further reductions in services. It increasingly depended upon loans from the international donors merely to maintain essential services.[43]

Inflation, which had devastated the economy in the early 1990s, had diminished considerably by the mid 1990s, partly as a result of government policies but also partly because of lower demand. The rate of inflation dropped from 325 percent in 1992 to 66 percent in 1994 and 53 percent in 1995. Part of this decline was due to the government's policy of tight credit, which the international donors supported. However, growing unemployment and increased poverty meant that much of the population could not afford the more abundant consumer goods, reducing demand-pulled inflation.[44] Although the favorable balance of trade in 1994 and 1995 indicated success in exporting nonferrous metals, it also signified that few Mongolians could pay for foreign products.[45]

Under pressure from the IMF, the Jasrai government continued the tight credit regimen, with extraordinarily high rates of interest, even as inflation declined. This deprived small businesses in particular of the capital they needed.[46] With scant options, they therefore turned to pawnbrokers, who also demanded high rates of interest but, unlike banks, were willing to provide loans to small and occasionally risky enterprises. However, borrowers who lapsed in their payments did not realize that they faced tenacious creditors who had no compunction about repossessing not only business-related assets but also such personal belongings as their apartments.[47]

Meanwhile, banks approved substantial loans principally to borrowers who had strong links with government officials or with the bankers themselves. Nepotism, which had traditionally been acceptable in Mongolian society, often played a more important role in credit decisions than assessment of ability to repay and quality of collateral. Advocates of shock therapy like Ganbold and the international donors were, in part, responsible for these difficulties. They had promoted the rapid development of commercial banks without taking into account the pattern of favoritism that was integral to the Mongolian past.[48]

With its own economy and institutions not providing sufficient capital for development, the state increasingly counted on foreign aid. As the Economist Intelligence Unit stated late in 1995, "the government's chief solution for all the country's problems is external aid." The state's increasing dependence on foreign aid naturally offered greater leverage for the international donors, particularly the IMF. Yet, according to one source, "Outside the government there is still widespread suspicion of the IMF's economic reforms [because] in view of declining living standards and increased social problems, some critics see the reform programme as an ideological experiment conducted by the IMF . . . to the benefit of external interests."[49] The IMF countered with the argument that inflation had been reduced and that production was beginning to rise. Yet former Prime Minister Byambasüren, who generally shared the IMF's advocacy of the market economy, disagreed in this case and responded that the vast majority of such production increases were in natural resource extraction, and that the manufacturing industries (including food processing and textiles) continued to decline.[50]

In retrospect, both Oyun and Hulan said the donors of foreign aid did not offer much support for the alleviation of poverty.[51] Although a Poverty Alleviation Program was established in 1994, the funding for this effort was minimal as compared to the total of donated funds.[52] Moreover, the international donors did not appear as concerned about the "remorseless growth of inequality" in Mongolian society, a development that resulted by the mid 1990s in the wealthiest 20 percent of the population having eighteen times the income of the poorest 20 percent.[53]

In interviews, Oyun complained about the leverage foreign aid offered to the donors. She noted that funding always centered around projects that the representatives of the donor agencies helped to select. Mongolian officials did not by themselves determine the uses of grant money. They negotiated with donors about the projects to be chosen. Moreover, the donor agencies capitalized on their influence to shape unrelated economic policies. For example, the ADB threatened to withhold a pledged payment of $15 million, which was essential to balance the budget, if the government did not rescind its ban on the export of raw cashmere.[54] Also, the international donors frequently focused on large-scale construction projects such as renovation of airports and roads, on economic restructuring toward a market economy, and on communications and energy, all of which, according to Oyun, inadvertently offered optimal opportunities for embezzlement and bribery.[55]

The state also relied on foreign investment, not foreign aid alone, to foster economic development. Prime Minister Jasrai and President Ochirbat repeatedly traveled abroad to attract foreign investors.[56] Yet foreign investors were not confident about the banking system, the somewhat capricious customs and tariff structure, poor transport, and irregular implementation of contracts. Several complained that they were forced to renegotiate contracts after they had been agreed to and signed.[57] As a result, foreign investment did not grow rapidly.

The democratic reformers, particularly Zorig, were appalled at the corruption and scandals bedeviling the economy. Under the communist system, the threat of severe punishments for embezzlers, disapproval of bourgeois materialism, the impossibility of owning land, apartments, and vehicles, the fear of arousing suspicion by high living, and the paucity of consumer goods had all served to limit corruption. After 1990, a weak government, the rise of private property in the forms of factories, vehicles, and herds, and the disappearance of the ideal of economic equality all paved the way for corruption. According to the reformers, the poor salaries of government officials made some of them vulnerable to gifts and bribes in return for preferential treatment, and the failure to implement anticorruption laws also contributed to the freewheeling environment.[58]

The disruptions following the collapse of communism offered the unscrupulous opportunities for enrichment. Equipment, machinery, and other assets had been left behind with the precipitous withdrawal of 100,000 Russian soldiers and thousands of Russian advisors and technicians. The state itself relinquished considerable property when it privatized enterprises. Ownership of or access to the country's plentiful mineral and natural resources was another prize. The sizable packages of foreign aid were still another source of funds that could be pilfered or misused. And then there was preferential access to bank loans, which might not be repaid.

Sumati, the leading poll taker, a sardonic observer of the political scene, and Hulan and Oyun claimed that in promoting rapid privatization and a weaker government, the international donors had not taken into consideration Mongolia's history of nepotism and favoritism.[59] Such associations had been held in check during the communist era. With a less powerful government, the restraints were eliminated. The nexus of close relations, family or otherwise, among the small, generally well-educated, and comfortable elite in Ulaanbaatar also contributed to an environment of favoritism in which corruption flourished.[60]

The 1991 foreign exchange speculation, which resulted in the loss of much of Mongolia's foreign currency reserves, has already been mentioned. However, more damaging was the fact that the speculators were not punished. None received a prison sentence, partly because they were well connected. One, for example, was the grandson of Sükhbaatar, "Mongolia's George Washington."[61] More shocking still was the negotiation of an agreement in April 1993 with IBEX Group, a mysterious American corporation. This ninety-nine-year contract, signed by Vice Premier Choyjilsürengiin Purevdorj, provided IBEX with an extraordinary monopoly on extraction of mineral resources, telecommunications, tourism, and cashmere. Any domestic or foreign entity seeking to invest in these fields would require IBEX's permission. In March 1995, the National Security Council cancelled the agreement, proclaiming it to be a threat to national security.[62] Only a leak to the media by two dissident politicians averted this potential squandering of the country's principal assets. Similarly, exposure to the media and a strike by employees aborted the privatization of the State Department Store, at a woefully low price, to a company that still owed taxes to the government.[63]

Accusations of corruption and abuses of power reached to the highest levels of the government and the economy. In 1994, the state procurator cleared Prime Minister Jasrai of charges of "undeclared and illegal business interests with China through his son and daughter" and of unauthorized granting of false Mongolian passports to Chinese citizens.[64] Yet rumors persisted of chicanery, bribery, and graft in Government House. The successful prosecution of some of the leaders of the most important banks and one of the leading cashmere-processing companies confirmed the "extent of economic crime."[65] These influential figures had misappropriated funds to provide loans to a former physical education teacher named Ms. Tsolmon, who had founded her own company. Under such circumstances, tax evasion and inadequate collection of taxes were common.[66] Petty chiseling, such as misuse of foreign aid for the buying of private mobile phones, cars, and computers, scarcely attracted attention, and favoritism by government officials raised few eyebrows.

The distinctions between public duties and private gain became increasingly blurred. Officials would leave government posts and then start consulting companies that dealt with the agencies they had previously supervised. One example of such blurring involves MCS, a leading company that had become a successful conglomerate. In the late 1990s, Jambaljamtsyn Od, the brother of its president, Jambaljamtsyn Odjargal, became foreign policy advisor to the prime minister, offering the company a myriad of potential advantages. Because the company was subject to government regulations and required state licenses and approvals, a highly placed and influential government official could be of immense value to it.[67] After leaving government, the brother became a vice president in MCS. Even if no preferential treatment was extended to the company, the appearance of favoritism was troubling. Moreover, the company's record of cultivating and winning favor with U.S. companies and USAID lent some credence to critics' accusations of influence peddling and to the assertion that international donors favored specific individuals and companies. I attended several dinners at which Odjargal and an employee who had only a few months earlier been a government regulator entertained consultants for USAID, another of his contacts with foreign dispensers of funds.

It is no wonder then that both the highest official in the land and the largest foreign donor expressed dissatisfaction. President Ochirbat complained that officials "gave preferential treatment to friends and acquaintances in the disposal of state assets," and that the Khural had delayed the enactment of an anticorruption law. A year later, officials in the Japanese government were dismayed by the apparent failures of some projects, and by the Mongolian government's illegal plan to sell shares in industries established with Japanese financial support.[68]

No wonder, either, that the general public expressed cynicism about privatization and foreign aid. A survey conducted later in the 1990s, but reflecting earlier perceptions as well, found that 52.9 percent of the population believed that state officials benefited most from privatization, and 25.4 percent claimed that businessmen were the greatest beneficiaries. Most said that ordinary people had scarcely profited.[69]

CRITIQUES OF FOREIGN AID

By 1996, despite some gains in GDP, based in large part on extraction of natural resources, the economy remained weak, and unemployment was high, prompting renewed criticisms of the agendas of the international donors among many Mongolians and, in particular, the democratic reformers. Mongolian democrats also singled out the IMF for its advocacy of price liberalization, which they described as inflationary and as contributing to the weakening of the tugrik. They also objected to the IMF's demand that the ban on the export of raw cashmere be rescinded.[70]

By 1996, many Mongolian democrats, including Hulan and Erdenebileg, had expressed concern about the policies of the IMF and other international donors in Mongolia. They complained of the foreigners' linking of democracy with a market economy and privatization and argued that a market economy was not a prerequisite for democracy. They also objected to the international donors' call for a weaker government because they believed that the development of a dynamic private sector might well require the existence of a strong and dynamic state sector. The state was considered vital in protecting citizens adversely affected by the gyrations of the market, in safeguarding the country's environment and resources, and in fostering a more equitable distribution of income.[71] Thus the IMF's emphasis on reducing taxes was judged counterproductive because it deprived the government of the ability to perform these functions. A consultant who advised Save the Children–UK challenged the IMF's characterization of the Mongolian government's bloated bureaucracy. He asserted that the civil service constituted only 17.6 percent of total employment, a percentage that was not out of line with other governments. In some fields, particularly regulation and environment, the government was, in fact, woefully understaffed, undermining its ability to function properly.[72]

The democratic reformers' most impassioned criticisms were leveled at the IMF's concerns to rein in inflation, budget deficits, and the rate of exchange, and its relative lack of concern for labor and the poor. Its own publication confirmed an apparent indifference to the fate of workers. Its 1996 *Economic Review of Mongolia* notes approvingly that "wage controls were eliminated in the private sector, and the minimum wage was reduced in real terms so as not to hamper job creation," evincing little concern for poorly paid workers, whose income had fallen 50 percent from 1990 to 1992 and continued to fall from 1992 to 1996, although at a slower rate.[73] The *Economic Review* advocated limiting wages to less than the rate of inflation. Its supply side emphasis, which was shared by Mongolian advocates of the pure market in the government, contributed to the "remorseless growth of inequality" in Mongolia.[74] The *Economic Review* does not mention the increasing disparity in income between rich and poor, giving credence to critics' claims that the IMF hardly concerned itself with social inequality and increasing poverty among the Mongolians.

Oyun and Erdenebileg were critical of some of the representatives of the donor agencies. They asserted that many knew little of Mongolian culture, society, and history. While conducting interviews with resident representatives of the IMF and the World Bank, I too was surprised that they did not know about the Mongolians' strong family, tribal, and regional identifications and the implications this might have for aid programs. The possibility of nepotism would certainly come to mind under such circumstances.[75] However, because these representatives had a specific agenda, which was the same for all countries, they did not need to be experts or even particularly well informed about Mongolia's heritage. Oyun and other democratic reformers accused these representatives of thinking they knew what was best for the country, every so often overriding the views of Mongolian officials, and of ignoring or rejecting both domestic and foreign criticism. The Mongolian critics believed that these foreigners' ideas revealed a victory of ideology over reality and an attempt to impose an economic system that was not applicable to Mongolia.

They were also concerned that the representatives of these supranational organizations appeared to be unaccountable to any specific country or public. Elected government officials from the United States and other nations had scant leverage and oversight over these agencies, their employees, and the private contractors they employed, permitting the latter to introduce pure market policies and programs that would have been controversial in America or other Western industrial economies. Oyun and other Mongolians asserted that the lack of rigorous oversight offered extraordinary power to the donor agencies and their representatives.

Many consultants on specific projects who stayed in Mongolia for a month or less knew little about the country's heritage and society, but seemed intent on changing Mongolia to fit a specific model. International donors called on dozens, if not hundreds, of these consultants to write reports and make recommendations on everything from the banking system to pensions to structural reforms. After only a short mission, an international consultant would "draft a proposal for a project, including funding to be obtained from international donors," a Mongolian economist associated with the democratic reformers observed. He suggested that aid projects instead shift from a donor-driven approach to "mutually-driven and executed schemes."[76] In other words, the aid projects ought not to be imposed by foreign advisors and ought to take into account serious Mongolian criticisms.

The lifestyles of the resident representatives of the international donor agencies also raised some eyebrows. A few, although certainly not all, lived in gated, guarded communities in Ulaanbaatar, while a tiny group were in even more lavish surroundings, guarded by the military, in an area where the president and the prime minister resided, which was closed to the public. Visitors had to have invitations; otherwise, the military would not permit them to enter this compound. The spacious quarters, well-appointed furnishings, and the latest appliances, contrasted sharply with the lifestyles of all but the very highest officials with whom the foreign representatives dealt. Numbers of them also attended the coyly labeled Friday evening "Steppe-in" cocktail party at the British Embassy, which had initially excluded Mongolians. Even when Mongolians were formally admitted, few came. The expatriate community had its own jogging groups, restaurants, bars, markets, theatrical productions, and night-clubs, which a few Mongolians, either wealthy or employed in an international organization, also patronized. To many Mongolians, some foreigners representing the international donors appeared to live a colonial lifestyle.[77] To be sure, conditions in Mongolia are demanding. Winters are long and severe, and the early 1990s witnessed electrical brownouts and blackouts and suspensions in delivery of heat (from coal-fired plants). However, by the mid 1990s, electricity and heat were more reliable. The consultants could have followed the example of Westerners who worked in philanthropic organizations or taught in schools and universities or served in NGOs and foundations (and some among the representatives of the international donors), who lived comfortably, but not luxuriously, in middle- or upper-middle-class neighborhoods.

Perhaps as important, the democratic reformers were concerned about the changes in foreign aid after 1994. From 1991 to 1994, 60 percent of the funds had been allocated for emergency assistance. However, from 1994 to 1996, such assistance diminished considerably and aid began to center on large projects.[78] Japan provided aid for roads, energy, and export industries; the World Bank supported macroeconomic stability, "private sector"–led growth, and reforms in finance and enterprises; USAID emphasized privatization and the market economy (together with democratic institutions); and the ADB offered funds for the Ulaanbaatar airport, roads, and educational reforms.[79] As noted earlier, Oyun has pointed out that large-scale infrastructure and energy projects are ripe for cost overruns and for graft and corruption, and she has repeatedly called for an investigation of these projects. In open letters addressed to the president and other leaders, she has advocated the establishment of "a Parliament working group to inspect foreign assisted projects, especially projects in the energy sector."[80] There were also other democratic reformers who questioned the need for foreign aid in specific fields.[81] For example, the communist educational system had succeeded in achieving a high rate of literacy and in fostering good basic skills for primary school students. Ironically, some of the international donors promoted the U.S. model of education, which had not succeeded as widely as communist Mongolian education in developing basic literacy and other skills.

Foreign assistance had been essential in the initial period of transition, but it had its costs. The disruption of the economic relationship with the USSR and Eastern Europe left Mongolia vulnerable in the early 1990s, and foreign aid prevented even more severe shortages of food and medicines. However, the donors did not simply provide funds to the Mongolians. Together with selected government officials, they determined the specific projects they would support. Moreover, because more than 50 percent of the aid consisted of loans, the government became increasingly indebted to the donors, who thus had the leverage to promote their own objectives.[82]

As annual economic growth did not fulfill the optimistic projections of the representatives of some of the international donors, particularly the IMF, Mongolia became increasingly dependent on foreign aid. Although the loans were long-term and did not require payment for some years, their very existence shaped Mongolian policy. In his final speech to the Mongolian people, outgoing U.S. Ambassador Don Johnson asserted that "[h]istorically Mongolia has been too dependent on foreign aid. Mongolia can and should stand on its own two feet."[83]

Some Westerners also questioned the value of foreign aid. A Foreign Service officer I interviewed at the U.S. Embassy in Ulaanbaatar, who shall remain anonymous, was even more pessimistic about foreign aid. Concerned about a lack of oversight in and the viability of some of the projects, the officer suggested sarcastically that the annual foreign aid be divided equally and given directly to individual Mongolians (it would amount to $125–150 each), which would increase their income by about 30 percent, would develop a domestic market for food, energy, medicines, and other necessities, and would revive domestic industries. This person did not believe that the cafes, restaurants, kiosks, and other service enterprises touted by some foreign advisors as evidence of an entrepreneurial spirit, many of which catered principally to foreigners, either had a future or had created wealth for the country. Most foreign aid, the officer said, did not reach ordinary people.

By 1996, these nagging economic difficulties had given rise to disillusionment with the government and the MPRP. Unemployment, poverty, and rising consumer prices were blamed on state policies, and the government's delay in paying civil servants, teachers, and medical professionals alienated many. Corruption and the apparent involvement of government officials in such scandals eroded trust in the bureaucracy and the administration. In addition, the MPRP appeared complacent. Having ruled the country for seven decades, its leaders could not imagine being voted out of office.

FOREIGN ORGANIZATIONS
AND THE 1996 ELECTIONS

Most observers confidently predicted that the MPRP would emerge victorious in the Khural elections. However, the Sant Maral Foundation, a private polling organization, had discovered a slippage of confidence in the MPRP. Only about 30–35 percent of those surveyed believed that the MPRP was the most competent of the parties to cope with unemployment and the decline in living standards. The survey concluded that "practically all the parties have lost a substantial part of their former electorate but in absolute figures MPRP has suffered the heaviest losses since 1992."[84]

Moreover, the opposition parties received considerable foreign support. The Konrad Adenauer Foundation's Werner Prohl had organized seminars for the leaders of the main opposition parties, the Mongolian National Democratic Party (MNDP), which represented the market economy advocates, including Ganbold, and the Mongolian Social Democratic Party (MSDP), including Baabar, which sought to preserve the social welfare gains of the communist era, and for representatives of women's NGOs.[85] The trainers and the trained included a number of future members of the Khural and several prominent activists in women's NGOs.

In addition, on February 14, 1996, the International Republican Institute staff persuaded the MNDP and the MSDP to form a coalition known as the Democratic Union, which they then helped to "develop a campaign strategy based on the 1994 Republican strategy" in the United States. The "Contract with the Mongolian Voter" that they helped to devise included political and governmental reforms, strengthening of local government, and an independent judiciary, and calls for a free press, but the specifics related to a market economy—privatization, a 20–30 percent tax cut, a better climate for investment, membership in the World Trade Organization, reductions in the central government's budget, curbing of inflation, and tax exemptions for charitable contributions. Figures for the cost of the 1996 elections are unavailable, but the total for the 2000 Khural election amounted to $333,000. Assuming that the expenditures for the 1996 elections were approximately the same, the support of the International Republican Institute for the Democratic Union in Mongolia, which totaled $450,000 up to 1996, was surely significant. Before the important Khural elections of 1996, the IRI proclaimed its primary objective: a Mongolia that "will become a truly free, market-oriented society, "for "without continued economic liberalization, Mongolia will slide from a potentially politically and economically dynamic country into [a] stagnant, underdeveloped nation." In its promotional material, for example, the IRI highlighted Luvsanvandangiin Bold, a budding tycoon and Mongolia's first millionaire, who became a member of the Khural in 1996. His success in creating the Bodi International Group, a $10,000,000 corporation, and in organizing the private Golomt Bank impressed the IRI and made him the "darling" of the international donors, which apparently did not consider potential conflicts of interest between his commercial holdings and his duties as a legislator.[86]

The IRI showed scant reluctance to take considerable credit for the electoral victory in 1996 of the Democratic Union, which elected forty-seven members to the Khural, while independents allied with it won three seats, and the MPRP wound up with twenty-five members. IRI staff members repeatedly emphasized their contributions to the creation of the Democratic Union coalition and cited praise for their efforts by Mongolian political leaders. Ganbold, who had become the chair of the MNDP, was quoted in their promotional material as saying: "[C]ontinued support from IRI will allow us to gain control of parliament in the 1996 election." Even more extraordinary were the words of Elbegdorj, co-chair of the Democratic Union: "[T]he victory is as much IRI's victory as it is ours." The IRI's leaders apparently did not consider whether such partisan involvement in the domestic politics of a foreign country was appropriate. And they continued to reward favored political leaders with foreign study tours, banquets during visits to the United States, and support for international conferences.[87]

One other organization from the United States also championed the mostly young opponents of the MPRP. The Asia Foundation, among other projects, provided grants for the training of political leaders. Although both it and the IRI proclaimed that they were nonpartisan, the leaders of the anti-MPRP groups were the principal beneficiaries of these efforts. The Asia Foundation's assistance paid off: 36 percent of the members elected to the Khural in the 1996 election defeat of the MPRP had been Asia Foundation Fellows. However, the foundation did not wish to be portrayed as overtly political, and indeed many of its activities (donations of books, promotion of transparency in government, etc.) had no particular political overtones.

The IRI advisors would eventually be surprised by the rapid fragmentation of the Democratic Union into regional, personal, and tribal cliques.[88] Moreover, although the MPRP was now the minority party in the Khural, it still had sufficient numbers to block the two-thirds majority required to override a presidential veto and to convene a quorum.[89]

In any event, the 1996 election was not a ringing endorsement of the Democratic Union. Many political analysts thought that the electorate was reacting to the corruption, unemployment, poverty, and eroded social safety net associated with the MPRP's reign from 1992 to 1996. It had shown its disapproval by, in the words of the Economist Intelligence Unit, opting "for a motley collection of young and inexperienced people."[90] However, several of the leaders were the sons and daughters of the old "nomenklatura . . . who reached agreements with the international agencies, which have the mandate to . . . advise countries on their way to a 'free market economy' and 'democracy.' "[91]

The new leaders were ardent advocates of the pure market economy, with a smattering of democratic reformers such as Hulan, Zorig, and Erdenebileg, who were more skeptical of such an economy. The Khural for the first time included a sizable contingent of businessmen, and most members, whether businessmen or politicians, had extraordinary faith in the pure market economy. Interviews I conducted in 1997 and 1998 attested to their single-minded devotion to this form of capitalism. Randaasumbereliin Gonchigdorj, the chair of the MSDP and then the new Speaker of the Khural, told me that the main task of government was to generate a favorable environment for business. A wealthy businessman named Zandaakhuugiin Enkhbold, the chair of the State Property Committee, which was entrusted with privatization of state assets, used almost the same words in describing the responsibility of government. Former First Deputy Minister Ganbold, now a prominent member of the Khural, told me that the government needed to focus on the economy, probably to the detriment of the social sector.[92] In a speech to the Khural, Prime Minister Mendsaikhany Enkhsaikhan echoed Ganbold's views, saying that the "best economic policy is the best social policy"—that is, economic growth would "automatically take care of the country's social development problems through the . . . trickle-down effect."[93] In a highly revealing interview with me, Tserenpuntsag Batbold, the prime minister's chief economic advisor, said that unemployment and recession were valuable in disciplining labor, in curbing absenteeism, and in promoting productivity. He added that Mongolia could not afford Western European–style social assistance programs and thus had to depend on economic growth and foreign investment for social benefits for its population. His underlying implication that Mongolian workers were lazy and undisciplined, and that the unemployed could find work if they chose, and the Social Darwinism evident in his approval of occasional bouts of recession and unemployment, reflected the attitudes of many influential officials in the new government.[94]

The Western advisors to the new government reinforced these attitudes. A Western economic advisor to the new prime minister, whose assignment was funded by the USAID, presented his views in an essay in an edited volume published in the United States. He criticized some government officials, noting that "there are still many people, some in high government positions, who are unwilling to accept that markets generally work and that central planning generally does not."[95] He was also critical of donors who, attempting to gain influence and friends in Mongolia, had not vigorously promoted what he referred to as reforms—that is, a shift to a market economy. He emphasized specific "reforms"—a foreign-owned bank, a better environment for foreign investment, a decentralized government that was accountable to its constituencies, acceleration of privatization, construction of roads, and tapping of energy resources.

The influence of these Western advisors can, in part, be gauged by the locations of their offices. The IMF representative and a Western economic advisor to the prime minister had offices in Government House, the building where the Khural met and where Khural members had *their* offices. This would be equivalent to a foreigner, representing a foreign government, having an office in the U.S. Capitol or the Senate Office Building. It would be difficult to imagine the U.S. government accepting such a foreign presence in the building housing its legislature. More important, did the Western advisors' proximity to the top government officials not perhaps translate into considerable influence?

Whatever their influence, Prime Minister Enkhsaikhan's first major letters to international donors and to U.S. foundations described a program that embodied the pure market agenda. He wrote that accelerated privatization of state enterprises was to be a major component, because such efforts had "ground to a halt from mid-1992." Reduction in "the size of government in the economy" and a decrease of taxes by about 30 percent were to be critical features of the new prime minister's program. He also signaled that price liberalization and the elimination of subsidies were crucial, and alluding to the nonperforming loans and the liquidity crisis in several banks, he intimated that they would need to be closed. Like the foreign advocates of the market economy, he said that Mongolia should focus on an export- rather than an import-substitution policy. His program mentions alleviation of poverty, but no details are provided. It is unclear how poverty could be reduced if the government and its resources were to be cut back. In addition, his stated plan to remove 100,000 people from the pension rolls must surely be expected to increase the rate of poverty.[96]

The prime minister's confidence in the market economy mirrored the views and aspirations of the international donors. The Tokyo Donors' Conference of 1996, for example, revealed their objectives, proclaiming that "the challenge is to . . . rapidly complete the transition process to a market economy."[97] "Rapidly" became the key word for the new government. The so-called Democratic Union acted as "swashbucklers," quickly promoting the switch to a market economy. Recognizing that their policies would cause great pain, they implemented them regardless, counting on improvement in the economy by the time of the election of 2000. If conditions did not improve as rapidly as they anticipated, they professed to being willing to admit defeat and be simply a one-term majority party. They believed they were doing the "right thing" and had the same self-assurance as some of their Western pure market advisors.

The democratic reformers elected to the Khural as part of the Democratic Union were concerned about the strong pure market views of the new government but had limited power. Although Zorig was popular because of his important role in the peaceful revolution of 1990, he was not in the cabinet or in a leadership position in the Khural. Hulan became chair of the standing committee on social welfare, but, as I saw when she graciously granted me permission to attend meetings of the committee in May 1998, she faced considerable opposition from the mostly pure market members. Meanwhile, Oyun had earned her Ph.D. at Cambridge University, was working as a geologist, and appeared to have no political aspirations.

THE DEMOCRATIC UNION IN POWER

The new government moved expeditiously to implement its program and to reduce the government. The thirteen ministries and three departments were consolidated into nine ministries. Six standing committees were newly established in the Khural, and their chairs were mainly the young leaders of the so-called Democratic movement of 1989–90. This new leadership soon dismissed senior and mid-level officials, either abolishing their positions or replacing them with members of their own party.[98] In the process, the Khural lost experience and, in addition, representation from the rural areas, because nearly all the Democratic Union leaders were urbanites. Although the Democratic Union was principally based in the urban areas, it had, within a few months, reduced the availability of government services, which seriously affected herders and all those living in the countryside.[99]

Simultaneously, the new government adopted policies that dramatically affected urbanites. Two months after the elections, it increased energy prices, reducing the communist regime's subsidies for this vital "commodity" in the often bitterly cold Mongolian winters. This so-called liberalization of prices, which resulted in a 48 percent increase in the cost of coal, a 60 percent increase for electricity, and a 40 percent increase for heating, would naturally harm the vulnerable, the poor, and those on fixed incomes in the towns and cities, as well as small and medium-sized enterprises.[100] The new leaders justified their decision by stating first that the mines and power stations were indebted and had to be subsidized, placing a severe strain on government resources. Parenthetically, they also mentioned that the IMF and the ADB would not provide a $50 million loan unless energy prices were liberalized. Yet again, the international donor agencies had used their leverage to dictate government policy, a policy that Zorig and the other democratic reformers believed entailed an overly rapid liberalization of prices and would push an indeterminate number of families below the poverty line.[101]

The Democratic Union's next radical actions concerned banks. The international donors had already indicated their displeasure at the highly risky loans made by banks and their serious liquidity problems. In July 1996, the Central Asian Bank, a private commercial bank, went into bankruptcy because of poor lending practices. One of the bank's directors had just been elected to the Khural, so depositors demonstrated around Government House. This proved the harbinger of a series of bank scandals engulfing the Democratic Union. In October, yet another controversy erupted when the director of the Mongol Central Bank dismissed the chair of the Ardyn or People's Bank, one of the largest banks in the country. After a protest about the government's interference with the bank and a threat to sue, his dismissal was rescinded. Rumors spread, rightly or wrongly, that the Mongol Central Bank sought to gain control over Ardyn Bank's new fourteen-story building, which lay within two blocks of the Mongol Central Bank headquarters.[102] Whatever the accuracy of these rumors, it seems clear that Ardyn Bank had made numerous risky loans, at least 40 percent of which were nonperforming. On December 13, 1996, in cooperation with several international donor agencies, 900 government officials swooped down on and closed 153 branches of the Ardyn Bank and the Mongol Daatgal Bank, which had a combined total of more than 60 percent of the deposits in the country's banks. Some of the representatives of the international donor agencies hailed this radical step as a triumph.[103] A year later, a Western economic advisor to the prime minister wrote: "Mongolia's get-tough approach has restored confidence in the country's banks and may offer a model for addressing the region's financial woes."[104] Within a year, however, this confident prediction would be challenged.

Even before a second banking crisis erupted in 1998, the Democratic Union faced difficulties. One was the apparent favoritism by both the government and the international donors toward the Golomt Bank, a private commercial bank. The minister of finance, Puntsagiin Tsagaan, had been director general of the bank, and Luvsanvandangiin Bold, a favorite of the IRI and the founder of the bank, had just been elected to the

Khural.[105] Two important executives from one specific commercial bank holding such lofty positions in the government gave the appearance of conflict of interest, and developments over the next year tended to affirm the privileged position of the bank.

Both government officials and private citizens continued to criticize the banking system. The democratic reformers complained about the Mongol Central Bank for following IMF dictates by tightening credit and limiting liquidity.[106] Small and medium-sized enterprises could not afford to borrow money, particularly as, by 1997, the Mongol Central Bank was charging annual rates of 48 to 66 percent to other banks, and the banks themselves charged customers interest of 5 to 10 percent a month.[107] Economic growth would surely be stifled with such high rates of interest. Yet the IMF focused on inflation and proposed a tight credit fiscal policy. Its representatives were convinced that a stable currency would translate into higher purchasing power for ordinary people and thus be a means of alleviating poverty and other social problems. However, the democratic reformers insisted that greater access to credit would promote economic growth, and they were less worried about mild inflation.[108]

Prime Minister Enkhsaikhan and Khural member Ganbold first took on and hoped to accelerate privatization in response to what they perceived to be abandonment or at least delays in the process under the previous government. Ganbold, given a second chance on the political stage after his loss of status when the MPRP moderates regained power in 1992, was determined to press forward with privatization of state assets.[109] Shortly thereafter, however, a trade union official complained that 16,000 salespeople, mostly women, had been fired, with little if any compensation, after privatization of state-run retail stores.[110] It appears that the governments since 1990 (and their international advisors) had either not devised or not implemented plans for those dismissed from state enterprises. Because of the emphasis on more limited government, the state did not have the resources to offer services for the increasingly large number of unemployed.

Zorig, Hulan, and other democratic reformers questioned the fairness of privatization. Moreover, the head of the State Privatization Committee was dismissed for revealing that state assets had been sold at ridiculously low prices—one for as little as 10 percent of the value of the enterprise.[111] He also accused government officials and private entrepreneurs of collaborating to undervalue state enterprises. His successor at the State Privatization Committee, in conducting an inventory, discovered numerous instances of misappropriation or theft of state assets.[112]

The major success involved housing privatization. After considerable debate and a plan for selling apartments that aroused tremendous opposition, the state had simply turned over most residences to their inhabitants in 1996 at little or no cost; 68,000 apartments in Ulaanbaatar and 120,000 throughout the country were quickly privatized by a law enacted on October 25, 1996.

Accelerated privatization in turn led to reduced government revenues, because many enterprises simply did not pay taxes. Many of the tax evaders were privatized companies.[113] But with funds now limited, the state did not have the resources to monitor enterprises and individuals and enforce tax provisions.

The elimination of virtually all tariffs, yet another tenet of the pure market philosophy, was a further element in revenue shortfalls. On May 1, 1997, with Ganbold's support, the prime minister abolished all customs taxes on imported goods except for oil products, alcohol, tobacco, and motor vehicles.[114] This policy dovetailed with the liberalization of trade or free trade program advocated by the international donor agencies. Representatives of these agencies justified this dramatic step, which would place Mongolia in the forefront of the free trade countries in the world, as a means of stimulating foreign and domestic enterprises to import new technologies and machinery, which Mongolia desperately needed. The lack of tariffs on technology transfer would presumably reduce the costs for superior domestic and foreign businesses, which would encourage them to invest in Mongolia. The reduced prices resulting from the lack of tariffs would benefit not only Mongolian consumers and producers but also foreign companies and investors. Without the artificial imposition of tariffs, Mongolia would, it was hoped, discover the economic sectors where it had comparative advantages.

The democratic reformers responded that free trade would not create equality in such unequal circumstances. A country with infant industries could not compete with another country's well-developed industries without some initial protection. As Oyun would later note, industries such as wool, leather, and cashmere "in which Mongolia can compete with its neighbors should be protected until they are strong enough to be competitive."[115] They required protection until they were strong enough to be on an equal footing with China's industries, which often received government subsidies and interest-free loans, further tipping the scales in their favor. Oyun argued that the rigid application of the pure market tenet of liberalization of trade made Mongolian industries vulnerable, and indeed many would not survive. It did not result in a significant increase in foreign investment in the introduction of new technology, except in mining and a few processing enterprises, which secured loans or established joint ventures with foreign companies. A successful foreign investors' conference within a month of tariff reduction attested to foreign investors' interest, principally in mining.[116] As, if not more, serious, the government would, according to Oyun and other democratic reformers, have less money to pay teachers, medical personnel, and providers of social services.

The sizable reduction in revenue meant that the state faced serious financial problems. It coped first by removing 103,000 pensioners who had retired early from the rolls, a policy that the Democratic Union had announced that it would undertake almost as soon as it took power. It also rejected pay increases for state medical and educational personnel.

The government, with limited resources, did not adequately provide even for the military or other essential personnel. Its failure to supply sufficient food, clothing, or fuel resulted in serious cases of malnutrition and frostbite among the soldiers.[117] Seeking additional revenue, it was, however, unwilling to impose a higher and effectively implemented income tax particularly on businessmen and other nouveaux riches, who were among its principal supporters and were strongly represented in the Khural. It resolutely followed the pure market dictum of lower company and income taxes.

Prime Minister Enkhsaikhan, Ganbold, and the other pure market advocates focused on user fees and value-added taxes, the most regressive of taxes, to obtain needed funds. For example, on April 24, 1997, they initiated an ill-conceived twelvefold increase in the annual vehicle tax on trucks, from TG 13,000 to TG 160,000.[118] Truck drivers and transport companies had the power and the leverage—that is, by suspending the delivery of vital supplies to Ulaanbaatar and other towns—to resist this sizable increase. Two hundred truckers drove their vehicles into Ulaanbaatar, deliberately tying up traffic and eventually occupying Sükhbaatar

Square where demonstrations were supposedly banned. President Ochirbat thereupon quickly vetoed the law imposing this tax. Still desperate for funds, the government then resorted to leasing space in state buildings. I was surprised to find that the Museum of National History rented office space to NGOs and that some of the government ministries leased space to shops and restaurants.[119]

A single year of the Democratic Union's economic policies had led to considerable dislocation for the population. Enkhsaikhan and Ganbold had acknowledged that these policies would result in difficulties for Mongolians for two or three years but claimed that they would lead to a stronger country. However, as a correspondent for the *Far Eastern Economic Review* wrote, "This is cold comfort for those who must suffer the pain of the present."[120] Prices of consumer goods rose 32.6 percent and inflation increased 66 percent in the first four months of Democratic Union rule (as compared to 16 percent in the first six months of 1996). At the same time, real income declined by 30 percent, and the annual rate of growth in GDP decreased from 6.3 percent in 1995 to about 3 percent in 1996. The tugrik fell in value from about 550 to the dollar in July 1996 to 700 to the dollar by December, owing partly to liberalization of fuel prices, but also to a growing foreign trade imbalance.[121] Unemployment was conservatively estimated at 20 percent of the population.

The local elections in the fall of 1996, which took place right after a substantial increase in heating and electricity prices, indicated the first real stirrings of concern about the Democratic Union's policies. On October 6, the MPRP won a majority in *khurals* at the city, provincial, and *soum* levels.[122] The MPRP victory in these local elections presaged more difficulties ahead for the Democratic Union as it pressed to implement its pure market program.

The economy remained a cause for concern by the time of the presidential election in 1997. Copper and cashmere were the Mongolians' principal products and foreign exports, and dependence on these two commodities made Mongolia a hostage to their vagaries in price on the world market.[123] In 1997, the price of both had declined considerably. To be sure, these economic problems and the attendant increase in unemployment preceded the accession to power of the Democratic Union. Yet Batbold, the chief economic advisor to the prime minister, appeared callous when he told me, in an interview, that the government should not create jobs for the unemployed; the private sector would provide employment more efficiently, and the government should not intervene in the economy.[124] This laissez-faire philosophy signaled that the government would only do the minimum for the vulnerable and for infant or ailing industries.

Neither the international donor agencies nor the Democratic Union government offered more than token programs to alleviate the pain caused by the liberalization of fuel prices and the increase in consumer prices. The international donors focused on support for large projects involving coal mines, energy, heating, roads, and airports.[125] Meanwhile Prime Minister Enkhsaikhan and Ganbold still proclaimed creating a good environment for investors to be their principal priority.[126]

The Democratic Union was harmed by the self-indulgence of its members and by the corruption among officials and the general perception of such malfeasance, behavioral patterns it inherited from the previous government, which would be even more pervasive after 1997. Complaints abounded about the expenses and uselessness of the frequent overseas trips of Khural members. On several occasions, the Khural could not convene because it lacked a quorum.[127] Critics also objected to Khural members' participation in so-called study tours funded by international donor agencies, some of which were labeled boondoggles and described as shopping expeditions.[128] Having spent a couple of days following a Khural member, I observed that the honest and capable members were appalled by the excesses of others who accepted gifts or possibly bribes, failed to attend meetings, and so on.

Hulan and other democratic reformers complained of increased corruption under the Democratic Union. Bearing in mind the earlier privatizations, they were thus apprehensive of the Democratic Union's intention, spelled out in the spring of 1997, to sell the national airline MIAT, the post office, the Ulaanbaatar railway, Gobi Cashmere, and large coal mines.[129] They also accused some customs officials, judges, local government officials, and university educators of accepting bribes. An investigation discovered that even the military sold government-issued weapons and clothing illegally. Perhaps the most telling indication of the pervasiveness of corruption was the case brought against the chair of the Association for the Disabled for the embezzlement of funds and for the sale of donated wheelchairs for his own profit.[130]

Further criticism was reserved for the administration of foreign aid both before and after the accession of the Democratic Union. The State Audit Commission revealed a failure by organizations receiving aid to maintain required and accurate records.[131] One critic leveled charges about the misuse of ADB loans for heating counters for enterprises. He demanded: "How come that a single counter costs about $10,000 while Russians can supply similar equipment for only about $1,000?"[132] Whatever the validity of this particular accusation, some foreign aid money was surely diverted to other uses. Surprisingly, the ADB, one of the largest donor agencies, did not have a resident representative in Mongolia to ensure accountability. Some of the foreign NGOs, such as the Save the Children–UK and the Mongolian Foundation for an Open Society, which emphasized social welfare or development of democratic institutions, monitored their programs carefully, but their budgets were miniscule compared to the large international donor agencies, where possibilities for corruption and embezzlement were plentiful.

The 1997 presidential election signaled doubts about the economic policies of the Democratic Union, which supported Punsalmagiin Ochirbat, the incumbent president, so far the only postcommunist occupant of the office. Ochirbat had the unenviable task of defending policies that had created considerable hardships for the population and had led to demonstrations and strikes. The MPRP chose as its candidate Natsagiin Bagabandi, a rather colorless MPRP politician who had been Speaker of the Khural from 1992 to 1996. The election results on May 28, 1997, showed a rejection of Democratic Union policies, as the uninspiring Bagabandi readily defeated Ochirbat. One observer wrote: "Mr. Ochirbat's defeat reflects widespread public concern about high poverty levels, continued high inflation, and declining real wages."[133] Would the Democratic Union modify its policies in light of this electoral defeat?

Chapter 4 | POLITICAL AND ECONOMIC DISLOCATIONS, 1997–2004

Even after the defeat of its candidate for president in May 1997, the Democratic Union did not revise its policies. Prime Minister Mendsaikhany Enkhsaikhan and Davaadorjiin Ganbold, the most enthusiastic advocates of the market economy, pressed forward with privatization for the remainder of their years in power. This espousal of privatization conformed to a curious association and conflation of democracy with a market economy. Many in the Democratic Union agreed with the view that "the advance of democracy . . . depends . . . on the achievements of privatization."[1] They talked about business, the GDP, inflation, and privatization, but not about poverty, the social sector, and the growing disparity between the rich and the poor.[2]

Despite indications of abuses in earlier privatizations, the international donor agencies lobbied hard to continue the process. The IMF pressed for the privatization of what it referred to as the Most Valuable Companies and threatened to withhold pledged loans if the Gobi Cashmere Company and NIC, an oil company, were not sold. Both the IMF and the Democratic Union government asserted that such privatization of NIC, in particular, would result in greater employment, improvements in technology, and funds for the state budget, a view at odds with the previous experiences in most privatizations, which had resulted in layoffs, little new employment, the decline of many industries, and state budget deficits.[3]

The process of privatization continued to be criticized. Many Mongolians believed that foreigners, particularly Chinese investors, paid Mongolians to bid for them in privatization auctions, which could result in valuable and strategic enterprises being turned over to outsiders. After leaving the post of prime minister, Enkhsaikhan himself lambasted the State Property Committee, which supervised privatization, for a lack of transparency and a lack of respect for the law and demanded that the money obtained from privatization be used for investment rather than for immediate operating expenses. The MPRP described the Democratic Union's efforts as "corrupt and deliberate mismanagement of the previous privatization."[4]

The privatization of the power plants, which supplied 70 percent of Ulaanbaatar's heat and electricity, gave rise to the most intense lobbying. U.S. Assistant Secretary of State Thomas Pickering traveled to Mongolia to press the government to sell the plants to Applied Energy Services Corporation (AES), a U.S. energy company. Vice President Al Gore wrote to President Natsagiin Bagabandi urging the sale. Many Mongolians feared that this lobbying was designed to enable AES to buy the plants cheaply. Some were concerned that foreign control of 70 percent of the heating and electricity of the capital might be a security problem.[5] Yet the international donor agencies, particularly the IMF and USAID, strongly supported the sale. The Mongolians faced the ever-present threat of a suspension of aid if they refused to sell the plants. Yet as the Economist Intelligence Unit discovered, "privatization of state energy is widely opposed."[6] Despite additional lobbying by two former prime ministers of the Democratic Union to sell the power plants to AES (which has been accused of serious transgressions in energy problems in California and Brazil), the opposition prevented the Democratic Union from doing so.[7]

A large number of privatized companies also failed to pay taxes. One survey found that only 68 percent of corporations paid taxes. The official government media revealed that only four commercial banks paid taxes.[8] The growth of the informal sector, which the international donor agencies and their Mongolian pure market allies, including Enkhsaikhan and Ganbold, viewed as valuable entrepreneurship, led to further fiscal problems, as many in the so-called underground economy evaded taxation.[9]

Without a reliable flow of corporate and income taxes, the Democratic Union turned increasingly to sales taxes and user fees. Under pressure from the IMF, the government raised excise taxes on tobacco, alcohol, and other products, as well as the previously limited VAT, which by 2002 was producing more revenue than income taxes. Even though some organizations were accused of not turning over the VAT they collected to the government, it still constituted a substantial part of state revenues.[10] Even with the increased VAT, however, the government faced revenue shortfalls. Rinchinnyamyn Amarjargal, the last of the four Democratic Union prime ministers, who had earlier founded an economics college with a market economy philosophy, responded by proposing that the salaries of civil servants be based on the profit they earned for the state and the amount of tax they collected, a proposal that was too radical even for the staunchest proponents of the market economy in the Democratic Union.[11] Amarjargal, whose father had been a chauffeur for the minister of foreign relations, became one of the most ardent advocates of the market economy and a staunch supporter of the erection of a statue of Milton Friedman in Ulaanbaatar.[12]

The Democratic Union resorted to other means of raising revenue. World Bank representatives urged the government to install water meters and charge individual households for their water consumption. They were apparently not aware of the government's experience with installation of electric meters, many of which were repeatedly stolen.[13] Concerned about budget deficits, the IMF pushed for a 13 percent gold export tax, although this contravened the Minerals Law of 1997, which had pledged free trade in minerals. President Bagabandi opposed the tax, but IMF pressure resulted in its imposition, leading several foreign gold companies temporarily to abandon their operations in Mongolia.[14] The president himself sought additional funds through privatization but demanded, to little avail, that the money be used for investment, not operating expenses.[15] Very little appears to have been used for state investment, and the government, in general, had few resources for investment in public works and creating jobs for the large number of unemployed.

Still another source of revenue was the issuance of government bonds, which the Democratic Union did extensively. From 1996 through 1999, it issued bonds worth TG 52 billion, of which TG 18 billion was not, as required, approved in advance by the Khural. It turned out that the authorities could not account for some of the substantial sums and the projects that ought to have been constructed with these funds.[16]

With the government not providing vast sums for investment, credit institutions assumed greater importance in the era of the Democratic

Union. However, the major credit institutions, the banks, remained unstable throughout the Democratic Union domination of the government. A foreign advisor to the prime minister who had predicted that the "get tough" approach in closing two banks in December 1996 would translate into more responsible banks proved mistaken. Of the twenty-five banks opened from 1991 on, twelve had been forced to close by the end of 1999; eight of these closings occurred during the era of the Democratic Union government. The interest rates the banks charged for loans were still exceptionally high, reaching 50 percent or more annually.[17]

Moreover, the banks had not overcome the disarray of the pre-Democratic Union period. Less than a year and a half after the Reconstruction Bank was founded in the wake of the closing down of the two principal Mongolian banks, a crisis arose in the new bank. In its brief history, the Reconstruction Bank issued an astonishing number of unsecured and high-risk loans, several to friends and relatives of bank officials.

The historian Baabar, who had been appointed minister of finance, and the American-trained Jigjidiin Unenbat, head of the Mongol Central Bank, acted over a long holiday weekend on June 1 to deal with this problem. They forced through the ill-considered Resolution Number 80, which merged the state-owned Reconstruction Bank with the commercial Golomt Bank. By acting over a holiday weekend, they clearly hoped that few would notice and that the merger could be presented as a fait accompli. The resolution was cleared with the IMF and the World Bank, but the Khural was neither consulted nor its approval sought.[18] Resolution 80 simply transferred a state bank's assets to a favored commercial bank without issuing a tender or calling for an auction. No other bank had been contacted or allowed to bid for the failing bank.

The opposition was not deflected. The new MPRP leader Nambaryn Enkhbayar, formerly the minister of culture from 1992 to 1996, a fine translator of Russian literature into Mongolian, and a fluent speaker of English, quickly labeled the merger illegal and boycotted the Khural, preventing it from having a quorum. He declared that the Democratic Union "wanted the two banks to merge because they and their supporters owed money to the Reconstruction Bank"; additionally accusing members of the MNDP of having close links with Golomt.[19] The millionaire director of the Golomt Bank was a Democratic Union member of the Khural, raising suspicions of favoritism. The Golomt Bank, which had almost no branches outside of the capital, would absorb the

Reconstruction Bank's elaborate network of rural branches, a potentially lucrative bonanza for this commercial bank.

The media questioned the integrity of the process, and a Canadian journalist who had lived in Mongolia for two years wrote: "[M]ost Mongolians . . . noted the suspiciously high proportion of Mercedes drivers and Italian-suit wearers among the MPs who earn less than $100 a month. They . . . read of the businesses registered to brothers and husbands and wives, of the children sent to college in the United States or Britain. The bank merger [gave] focus to their resentment and envy and discontent."[20] By July 10, the Democratic Union began to retreat, explaining that the merged bank would be largely state-owned. However, by this time, Enkhbayar and a growing number of democratic reformers who were members of the Democratic Union distrusted the government and rejected this new pledge.[21] On July 23, the MPRP, assured of victory, returned to the Khural and on the very next day, it joined dissidents from the Democratic Union to vote no confidence in the government, which then resigned.[22] The planned merger was derailed, and Resolution Number 80 was revoked.

The international donor agencies were distressed that their efforts had been thwarted. They did not acknowledge that the MPRP had raised serious concerns about transparency, corruption, and democracy and reacted by withholding loans and grants from the government. The IMF suspended a $45 million loan, and the World Bank and the ADB followed suit.[23] These punitive policies angered some Mongolians, who recommended that "Parliament should stop the wrong practice of passing laws in pursuit of money from foreign donors."[24] Meanwhile, the underlying problems with the banks had not been resolved. The politicians and bank officers in the Reconstruction Bank fiasco were not jailed; instead, bank officers received pardons, which hardly inspired confidence in the banking system or in the political and judicial process. A year after the debacle, local governors were criticizing the Mongol Central Bank for selling the branches of the Reconstruction Bank "at low prices without public announcement," still another stain on the banking system.[25]

As of February 1999, an informed observer estimated that 41 percent of bank loans were nonperforming. Also in 1999, only nine of fifteen commercial banks submitted required annual reports on time. Small and medium-sized enterprises still could not obtain affordable loans, which they desperately needed.[26] The inability of the government to regulate the banks and other parts of the economy revealed the state's incapacity to protect the property rights of owners and creditors. Ironically, the weak state championed by such advocates of the pure market as Ganbold and Amarjargal actually harmed individuals by its inability to protect their rights.

All of these disruptions undermined economic growth and prevented the development of policies to stem increasing inequality of incomes. "Mongolia is in economic free fall," a journalist from the conservative U.S. *Washington Times* declared after visiting the country; "few would have predicted that the next generation would be poorer than their parents," he added.[27] Richard Tomlinson, another American journalist, writing in *Fortune* magazine, published an article entitled "Mongolia: Wild Ride to Capitalism."[28]

Herding, the traditional basis of the economy, was devastated, particularly in the last years of Democratic Union rule. In the mid 1990s, the head of DANIDA, the Danish development aid agency, had stated that "privatization of animal husbandry has worsened the impact of natural disasters," a view and a prediction that would be confirmed at the end of the decade.[29] In the meantime, agriculture continued its downward slide. The abandonment of the state farms and the inequitable distribution of their assets, including vehicles, seeds, and equipment, meant that many small farmers had scant prospects.[30]

Industries dependent on animal husbandry and agriculture suffered as a result of the turbulence in those sectors and the removal of nearly all tariffs in May 1997. Mongolia had exported 336,000 woolen blankets in 1990, but by 2000, the figure had decreased to 4,500. Nearly all woolen products experienced similar declines. Exports of carpets went from seven million square meters in 1990 to less than 100,000 square meters in 2002. Leather and leather products industries virtually collapsed: 87,000 leather garments were exported in 1990 but almost none in 2000; 4,800,000 pairs of shoes were produced in 1989 but fewer than 4,000 in 2000.[31] All of these industries had lost state support and could not readily obtain affordable loans from banks or credit-raising institutions. The elimination of tariffs compounded their difficulties, because they faced competition from cheap Chinese and Inner Mongolian goods, which were produced by companies with access to low-interest or credit-free loans or state subsidies. The departing U.S. ambassador nonetheless contended in 1999 that Mongolia must not succumb to "protectionism." President Bagabandi apparently disagreed; he advocated state involvement in the economy in the form of export loans to native industries, tax assistance to such industries, and the development of industrial zones.[32] However, few of these policies were actually implemented before 2000.

Mongolian industrial production thus centered on exploitation of mineral and natural resources. The international donor agencies encouraged this emphasis, and the World Bank partially funded the first foreign investors' conference in 1997, which focused on mining.[33] Coal continued to be a vital source of energy in the often devastatingly cold winters in urban areas. Although coal production declined from about eight million tons in 1989 to about 5.5 million tons in 2002, the total amount remained relatively stable throughout the 1990s. Copper production also decreased from a high in 1989, but it slowly stabilized, and copper became Mongolia's most important export. However, Russia and China had the closest and the most economically feasible plants for smelting it, an exceptionally profitable business for the smelters.[34]

In the mid 1990s, after prospecting for several years, SOCO International struck oil in Mongolia, but as of 2001, the highest output had been about 73,000 barrels in one year, not a substantial amount.[35] Prospects for a sharp increase in oil production remained uncertain.[36] Capital for the pipelines required to bring the limited reserves so far discovered to market has been limited, partly because of the known oil and gas fields and deposits in Russia, Kazakhstan, Azerbaijan, and Turkmenistan. Transport costs undermine Mongolia's efforts to compete. Thus, as of 2004, Mongolia still imported petrol, jet fuel, and diesel fuel, mostly from Russia.[37]

Mongolia also has untapped reserves of uranium, but when President Bagabandi supported its exploitation, he encountered stiff resistance from herders in the province of Dundgov.[38] As of 2004, the protests appeared to stall prospecting and mining.

The greatest success story, gold mining, had slowly increased from extraction of 640 kilograms of gold in 1980 to about 3,360 in 1989. The arrival of Canadian, U.S., and other foreign firms and the granting of licenses to Mongolian firms led to such an explosion of output that 2002 saw 12,097 kilograms mined. Rumors of favoritism in awarding rights to specific Mongolians were rife throughout the 1990s. There were also complaints about the environmental depredations wrought by generally un-regulated companies.[39] As noted in chapter 7, with 130 entities involved in gold mining, the government could not regulate them.[40] Moreover, San-jaasüregiin Oyun, a trained geologist, and other democratic reformers crit-icized this dependence on a nonrenewable resource for the economy and for the government's budget.[41]

Seeking to avert dependence on Russia for power, Enkhsaikhan and the pure market economists hastily devised a plan, with Czech advisors and economic support, to build a hydroelectric plant in the western province of Bulgan. There was little consideration of the environmental impact or of the possible destruction of major archeological sites, however, so it has thus far remained on the drawing board.[42]

Transportation witnessed some, although not extraordinary, growth after 1995. The international donor agencies, particularly the ADB, pro-moted this sector of the economy. In 1999 alone, the ADB provided $160 million in loans and grants for transport and energy and another $25 mil-lion for road building.[43] The principal beneficiary of the emphasis on bet-ter roads was the passenger car. The number spiraled from 6,660 in 1990 to about 70,000 in 2002, mostly used vehicles, about half of them in Ulaanbaatar. Moreover, the number of such vehicles in Ulaanbaatar exceeded the world level by 300 percent in relation to available roads. The opening of a Mercedes-Benz service center in the capital attests to the fact that many of these vehicles were luxuries, served as status symbols, and served to confirm the growing gap between rich and poor.[44]

Communications experienced similar patterns of growth and decline. The number of telephones doubled from 1990 to 2002, with three-quarters of them in Ulaanbaatar, including many mobile phones. French and Korean companies played an important role in the market and secured much of the profit. The number of television sets also increased, mostly in the capital, although not dramatically. Again, they were produced abroad. The increase in television sets was more than matched by a substantial decrease in radios. Television replaced radio in many homes in Ulaan-baatar, but the sharpest decrease in radios was in the countryside, where increasingly impoverished herders could not afford to buy batteries, pro-vided at low cost or free during the communist era. On balance, urbanites benefited from changes in telecommunications, but the herders, by and large, did not and were increasingly isolated. The potentially most important innovation in telecommunications was Internet access. By 2004, there were half a dozen Internet service providers and dozens of Internet cafes in Ulaanbaatar. Yet access to computers remains limited to a small percentage of the population. The Internet has the potential to promote communications and transmission of information, at least for urbanites. The question is whether the government will be able to regulate it to prevent excessive profiteering, to foster better service, and to promote its use as a means to facilitate growth, rather than as an end in itself.[45]

Tourism was another sector of the economy with great potential, but the downsized Mongolian government did not have the resources to improve the country's tourist infrastructure or advertise in foreign countries, which it generally left to private enterprise. However, except for "Festivals of Mongolia" in various countries, most of the smaller tourist companies could not afford to pay for promotion in the West or in East Asia, the likeliest sources of tourists, and neither could they undertake the necessary infrastructural improvement (e.g., improving hotels, restaurants, and *ger* [tent] facilities, training guides, and creating "user-friendly" museums, monasteries, etc.), or prevent pollution or degradation of the environment at beautiful locations that would appeal to ecotourists. Thus tourism has declined. In 1998, about 42,000 tourists, more than half from East Asia and the Pacific, visited Mongolia. By 1999, the figure had slipped to about 36,500, and in 2001, it decreased further to approximately 32,000. Even so, according to unofficial figures, tourism pumped $100 million into the Mongolian economy in 2002. The SARS epidemic in 2003 led to a further decrease in tourism, but the Mongolian Tourism Board has generated some publicity and hopes for a better tourist season in 2004. Nonetheless, a solid government policy and government support would be beneficial for this potentially lucrative enterprise.[46]

CONTINUED MISSTEPS
OF THE DEMOCRATIC UNION

Despite these economic difficulties, the Democratic Union leadership remained optimistic and even made grandiose predictions about the future. In an interview in June 1998, the minister of foreign relations, Rinchinnyamyn Amarjargal, one of the two leading advocates of the pure market in the Democratic Union, predicted an 8 percent annual growth rate in GDP if Mongolia facilitated foreign investment and guaranteed property rights. He contended that the government should stay out of the economy and allow private entrepreneurs to create jobs and eliminate poverty. The remaining unemployed could be sent to Korea or Japan as laborers for private companies. Privatization of the health and educational systems, he asserted, would also contribute to the strong growth that he anticipated.[47]

Meanwhile an economic consultant employed by Save the Children–UK challenged Amarjargal and the other Democratic Union economists, arguing that the government needed to play an active, not a minimal, role in the economy and questioning the policy of austerity that the IMF recommended. In a Human Development Report published in 2000, the UNDP echoed his views, noting that "a blind push for small government can be very damaging."[48] The financier George Soros also supported this view, telling the BBC: "The new market fundamentalism is more dangerous to the world now than Communism."[49]

The Save the Children consultant argued that the government ought to focus on human development, not just economic growth, which meant restoring the cutbacks imposed on health, education, and social welfare. An economic plan should be directed at fostering animal husbandry and agriculture through state support for cooperatives, and such infrastructure as wells and transport, as well as access to veterinarians. He continued that state support for infrastructure and an emphasis on social services and education should be accompanied by an increase in wages and pensions, which would seek not only to reduce the growing gap between the wealthy and the poor but also to broaden the purchasing power of the population: the greater the purchasing power, the greater the stimulus to domestic manufacturing, as consumer demand and ability to pay increased. Small manufacturing enterprises, which generally employed more people than larger and more mechanized factories, were more valuable in the long run than those exploiting nonrenewable resources such as gold, copper, and oil. A sustainable domestic manufacturing sector that paid its workers well would generate more purchasing power and more savings, contributing to a larger pool of domestic investment, which was preferable to foreign investment.[50]

Neither Amarjargal nor the consultant for Save the Children–UK focused on corruption, which appears to have accelerated after the tri-

umph of the Democratic Union. Poor salaries for many government officials made them susceptible to accepting bribes and gifts. The process of
privatization, which the Democratic Union sought to promote at a faster
clip, also lent itself to illegal activities. As one UNDP consultant noted,
"During the first five years of privatization in Mongolia, no external audit-
ing system was in place." A survey conducted in 1999 found that 93 percent
of the population believed that corruption was increasing, attributing the
increase to poor accountability, privatization, poor law enforcement, and
deteriorating morality.[51] Judges were poorly paid, and charges of their cor-
ruptibility were rampant. Students complained that they had to pay teachers and administrators in order to receive their degrees and diplomas.[52] It
is difficult to ascertain how widespread these practices were.

Government officials, in particular, were accused of improprieties.
Many Mongolians viewed Khural members as self-serving and corrupt.
Hashbat Hulan, now a Khural member herself, concurred with this
assessment, saying to a *New York Times* reporter: "This is a very small
country. People have eyes and ears, they can see how much their leaders
are spending and how much they earn in their public jobs."[53] Convening
a press conference with Tömör-öchiryn Erdenebileg, another member of
the Khural, she contended that "transparency and accountability in the
highest echelons of government are essential to combat corruption in
society." Implying that some funds for big projects and from foreign aid
had been misused, they asserted that a "personal income declaration
should be a must at all levels of government." She and several of her colleagues eventually founded an NGO to combat corruption, but apparently to no avail.[54] A year later, a major newspaper reported that many
officials complained of corruption in government but had done little to
bring it under control.

Scandals wracked the government. Some of the funds from the sale of
U.S.-donated wheat that were supposed to help farmers to buy seed and
to foster a Green Revolution were embezzled. The government agreed to
guarantee foreign loans to certain Mongolian companies, a policy fraught
with potential abuses. And the State Property Committee sought repeatedly to privatize what the IMF called the Most Valuable Companies,
reportedly sometimes falsely announcing that one or another of these
enterprises was not prospering in order to justify its sale.[55]

Even more ominous was the unsolved murder of Sanjaasürengiin
Zorig, one of the fathers of Mongolian democracy and a leading light

among the democratic reformers. Zorig had served in the Khural from 1990 but was a member of the minority until 1996. In the first two years of Democratic Union rule, the market economists overshadowed him. After the failure of Resolution 80 and the proposed merger of the Reconstruction and Golomt Banks and the subsequent dismissal of Prime Minister Tsakhiagiin Elbegdorj, Zorig became a principal candidate for the prime ministership. It was rumored that he was concerned about the misuse of foreign aid and about the corruption in infrastructure projects and was determined to mount a serious campaign against such crime. Some sources indicate that he would have been offered the position of prime minister in the second week of October 1998, a clear threat to malefactors. However, on October 2, 1998, he was killed as he walked into his apartment. Within a few months, his sister Oyun abandoned her career in geology to replace him in the Khural and to persevere in his advocacy of democratic reform. She would become a major figure in Mongolian political circles. Nonetheless, almost six years after his death, the circumstances surrounding his murder remain murky. The authorities have made little progress with the investigation.[56]

The behavior of some of the Democratic Union Khural members also contributed to the general public's lack of respect. Three of the seventy-six members received prison sentences for corruption in a major scandal relating to the establishment of a gambling casino in Ulaanbaatar. Khural members were accused of excessive spending on transport and receptions, using money that could have gone to hire assistants and researchers to help them with their official duties. A Khural subcommittee on ethics reported that "the discipline and responsibility of parliamentarians does [sic] not live up to . . . standards."[57]

Hulan and Erdenebileg asserted that "millions of dollars worth of foreign loans to Mongolia [had] disappeared into thin air." The State Audit Commission found that $190 million of $650 million in foreign loans could not be accounted for. It pointed to lack of documentation, "unclear receipts," unmade transfer-of-loan agreements, and wastage of funds and noted that the Ministry of Finance could not, for example, provide details about a substantial loan from Russia, additional evidence of a weak government. Poor record keeping was certainly one element, but embezzlement was surely another. In the words of one journalist: "An audit had found that millions of dollars' worth of Mongolia's lifeline of foreign aid had been misappropriated or was simply missing."[58] The auditors were able to confirm that "at least $10 million in loans was misused" and that "the sum could be higher if information on the missing millions was available."

Critics also questioned the priorities of foreign aid. Most of the funds were for large-scale projects, often focused on energy and mining. For example, of the money pledged by international donors in 1998, 30 percent was for mining, 27 percent for energy, 19 percent for transport, 8 percent for telecommunications, and only 3 percent for social services.[59] USAID was typical of the nonphilanthropic agencies, inasmuch as it emphasized technical assistance in privatization, rural development, energy, pensions, macroeconomic stability, and restructuring of the financial sector.[60]

Many Mongolians agreed with Oyun in fearing the country's growing indebtedness. Anywhere from 70 percent (provided at the Tokyo Donors' Conference in October 1997) to 80 percent (at a donors' meeting in November 1994) of the foreign aid consisted of soft loans, which required repayment.

In the world outside Mongolia, some of the agencies themselves started to question the aid priorities and the so-called Washington Consensus, or pure market policies. James Wolfensohn, president of the World Bank, contended that the donor agencies had overly emphasized macroeconomic stability and the taming of inflation and had relegated health, education, environment, and social welfare to secondary positions. "[T]oo often we have focused too much on the economics, without a sufficient under-standing of the social, the political, the environmental and cultural aspects of society," Wolfensohn said, and he acknowledged that the World Bank, IMF, and other agencies had favored large projects at the possible expense of programs that assisted ordinary people. The emphasis on financial sta-bility, he argued, was insufficient. Moreover, privatization and reductions of state subsidies were no answers for the developing countries. The World Bank needed to provide safety nets and to emphasize greater equity and social justice, not merely economic growth. It ought to help empower pop-ulations, write and enact laws, protect the environment, reduce corrup-tion, and support women's rights. Wolfensohn ended with a critique of the trickle-down theory, noting that "the poor cannot wait on our delibera-tions. The poor cannot wait until we debate a new architecture."[61]

New guidelines from the central offices of the donor agencies prompted some reorientations of aid policies in Mongolia. In April 2000, the ADB announced a shift from sizable projects to emphasis on eradication of poverty. Similarly, the IMF made what appeared to be an about-face by allocating $18 million to poverty reduction. The UNDP had cautioned that grants of money were insufficient for this purpose; the vulnerable needed assistance to overcome poverty—to start businesses, to find employment, and to acquire new skills.[62] In addition, a decade of social disarray had fostered a culture of poverty. The poor needed not only money but also assistance with coping in society.

Did the World Bank, ADB, and IMF pronouncements and actions signal a true shift in policy? It is still difficult to tell, but as we shall see later, events immediately after 2000 were not encouraging. The continuation of overly optimistic and inaccurate predictions by the international donor agencies and the government, moreover, did not bode well. In the case of Mongolia, the projections and predictions of the international donor agencies have often been askew. The IMF, for example, has repeatedly overstated the rate of growth of the GDP in its predictions. In 1995, it predicted that the rate of growth would be 4.5 percent; the actual figure turned out to be 2.6 percent. In 1997, it posited a growth rate of 6 percent for each year from 1997 to 2000, but real growth in 1997 amounted to 3.3 percent. Undaunted, early in 1998, it forecast a 5.5 percent rate, but the real figure turned out to be 3.5 percent. The IMF and the government persisted and forecast 3.5 percent growth in 1999 and 6 percent by 2002.[63] The actual figure for both 2000 and 2001 was 1.1 percent, not a good augury.

Meanwhile, foreign investment did not increase as rapidly as foreign grants and loans. From 1990 to 1999, foreign investment amounted to $284 million, meager for a developing economy. By 1999, foreign investment amounted to less than 4 percent of GDP, whereas the average for developing countries was 11 percent. One foreign advisor asserted that Mongolia should have $250 million a year in foreign investment, an amount that would certainly dwarf indigenous investment but might also give foreigners great leverage over the economy.[64] Foreign investors, feeling that the Mongolian legal and banking environments were not stable, were reluctant to invest substantial amounts given the country's remote location and undeveloped infrastructure. In addition, some of the foreign enterprises, especially the Chinese ones, did not have a good reputation in Mongolia. In 1999, inspectors found that 80 percent of joint venture businesses violated health and labor laws. Another survey discovered that only 30 percent of such enterprises abided by safety standards.[65]

No wonder that economic conditions gave rise to considerable pessimism. A survey conducted by the World Bank confirmed that many Mongolian households believed that economic conditions had worsened throughout the 1990s and that the period from 1995–2000 had witnessed a greater increase in poverty than the period from 1992 to 1995. A foreign journalist living in Mongolia added that there was "growing public opposition to capitalist-style economic reforms that have caused unemployment and hardship in the poor country sandwiched between China and Russia."[66]

Turmoil within the Democratic Union government also contributed to disarray. Nearly all its leaders lacked political experience, and a few, it later turned out, were corrupt opportunists. Although they professed to be democrats, some among the market economists did not believe in transparency and the proper legislative process. The first hurdle they faced was a constitutional provision that appeared to prohibit Khural members from serving in the cabinet. The Constitutional Court had "found that parliamentary deputies could not hold cabinet posts."[67] Because most of the top leaders had been elected to the Khural, the cabinet and the prime minister who took power in the summer of 1996 were not the most prominent members of the Democratic Union. The ambitious Khural members who had been denied executive positions were disappointed and sought to reverse the constitutional taboo. In April 1998, they seized the opportunity to displace the government and chose Elbegdorj, a good orator but a man whom many Mongolians did not consider sufficiently capable to head the government, as the new prime minister. Some of his critics portrayed this as a naked grab for power. Elbegdorj's nomination of inexperienced and reputedly incompetent candidates for ministerial appointments was his first gaffe.[68] The Khural and the president rejected several of these candidates, causing delays in setting up a government. Elbegdorj's second major error was to support the questionable merger of the Reconstruction and Golomt Banks. The Khural's censure of this projected merger led to his resignation in July and a five-month interlude before a successor was appointed.[69] The president rejected several of the Democratic Union's candidates, accusing one of having been arrested for drunk driving. On at least five separate occasions, he also refused to confirm the appointment of Ganbold, the principal architect of the Democratic Union's pure market policies, because of the latter's support of the "scandalous" bank merger. Finally, in December, Janlavyn Narantsatsralt, the mayor of Ulaanbaatar and a compromise candidate, became prime minister.

Meanwhile the coalition that composed the Democratic Union was splintering rapidly. By late 1998, the MNDP and the MSDP no longer trusted each other. Several MSDP members had voted no confidence in Elbegdorj, helping to bring about his downfall. In January 2000, Hulan, Erdenebileg, Oyun, and a Khural spokesman for the rural areas named Tserendorjiin Gankhuyag, who were concerned about corruption in government, broke away from the Democratic Union. Two successful businessmen, also disillusioned with the Democratic Union, founded their own political parties. Badarchyn Erdenebat, the flamboyant and shrewd owner of one of the largest gold-mining enterprises, established the Mongolian New Socialist Party (later the title "Motherland" was added to the party's name), and Bazarsadyn Jargalsaikhan, the egotistical owner of a large cashmere-processing factory, who would himself eventually be accused of unethical and perhaps illegal activities, started the Republican Party.[70]

Slightly earlier, on July 22, 1999, the third prime minister in the Democratic Union's four-year rule was ousted, having lasted less than a year. Janlavyn Narantsatsralt was accused of acquiescing to a Russian government sale of its share of the Russo-Mongolian joint copper venture in Erdenet to Zarubezhtsvetmet, a private company, for a pittance. He was compelled to resign. According to the Economist Intelligence Unit, "The shares were later purchased . . . , according to Mongolian MPs, [for] less than $240,000. They regarded this price as scandalously low, although Zarubezhtsvetmet denies that this was the price. Mr. Narantsatsralt was attacked for signing this letter without prior consultation with parliament and ministers, who argued that in any sale of Erdenet the other partner (i.e., Mongolia) must have first refusal." This time the search for a new prime minister was not lengthy. Rinchinnyamyn Amarjargal, the former foreign minister and a strong supporter of the pure market, served out the remainder of the term, but he had little time to introduce major new policies before the July 2000 elections. With all this turbulence, no wonder that 87 percent of respondents in a well-respected poll asserted that the Khural did not reflect public opinion.[71] By June 2000, the public had grown weary of the political infighting and corruption, and poll takers predicted that the Democratic Union would lose in the July elections.

The resurgent MPRP was a potent challenger in the elections. Capitalizing on the Democratic Union's failures and pledging to focus on social problems and to devote more resources to health and education, the MPRP won an impressive victory. Of the seventy-six seats in the Khural, seventy-two went to the MPRP, and Nambaryn Enkhbayar, the former minister of culture, became prime minister.[72]

MPRP WINS BUT LITTLE CHANGES

Although the MPRP pledged to increase wages and pensions substantially and to repair the social safety net, during its first three years, it had, in fact, devoted considerable effort to the privatization policy championed by the Democratic Union government. Despite the criticism leveled at the unfairness and corruption that accompanied the earlier privatization, Finance Minister Chultemiin Ulaan insisted on its primacy and on the importance of lower taxes for private enterprises. The democratic reformers had complained that between 1998 and 2000, the Democratic Union government had sold twelve companies at very low prices. There have been similar accusations about the MPRP's privatization policies. However, the government went ahead with the privatization of APU, the state-run liquor and soft drinks company, which led to complaints about considerable pillaging of its assets by the old and new directors. Another potential problem arose when it was revealed that the discredited U.S. accounting firm Arthur Andersen had been an advisor to the government on privatization and had been accused of not paying debts it had incurred in Mongolia.[73] Yet the United States, in particular, exerted considerable pressure on the government to privatize. In a widely reported speech, U.S. Ambassador John Dinger said that private sector growth was the key to poverty reduction. Shortly thereafter, USAID offered an $11 million loan through the Golomt and other commercial banks for "developing the private sector."[74]

Acquiescing to this pressure, Prime Minister Enkhbayar, who had never previously been identified with the advocates of the pure market economy, but who now clearly felt pressure from the international donors, embarked on the privatization of arguably the most successful bank in the country. The state-run Trade and Development Bank had avoided the rash of high risk and thus nonperforming loans that had afflicted most banks in the 1990s. It had a net profit of $6 million in 2000 and almost $5 million in 2001, and in the latter year, it contributed just under $4 million to the Mongolian treasury. Given the high rate of return on investment and its contribution to taxes, its sale seems strange. Even stranger, only two groups bid for the bank. In spring of 2002, Gerald Metals, a firm based in Connecticut, and Banco Lugano Commerciale, a relatively small operation, bought the 76 percent government share of the Trade and Development Bank for approximately $12 million, which many Mongolians found to be a sizable undervaluation of the bank in light of its net profits in 2000 and 2001. The new buyers pledged to invest funds in the bank, but a sizable percentage of this amount would be allocated to the American firm that consulted on the privatization. Moreover, Gerald Metals had reportedly had no involvement in Mongolia until 2000, when it started to buy copper from Erdenet. It remains to be seen whether the sale will benefit Mongolia, but the sale price seems, on the face of it, to have been a bargain for Gerald Metals and its partner. The individual shareholders who owned 24 percent of the bank also believed that the price paid by Gerald Metals was an undervaluation, reducing the price of their own shares. They are currently contesting the sale in the courts, arguing that they were not consulted.[75] The sale has also been controversial because it has resulted in a considerable decline in tax revenue from the Trade and Development Bank. In 2001, the bank contributed TG 10.2 billion in taxes, but the new owners, possibly through underreporting of income or through capitalizing on tax loopholes, had paid only TG 321 million in the first nine months of 2003.[76]

Later, the Agricultural, or Khaan, Bank, still another successful bank, was sold to a Japanese securities firm that appeared to have scarcely any experience in banking. As of November 2003, it was, nonetheless, doing well (with higher net profits, 257 new employees, and fourteen new branches), perhaps partly because it retained the old management.[77] Another important privatization effort did not work out as well. In July 2003, NIC, the state petroleum company, was privatized to a consortium composed of Russians, Cypriots, and Mongolians, but within a few months the government canceled the deal, claiming that the would-be buyers sought ownership for purposes of money laundering.[78] Several months later, the government also canceled the privatization of Gobi, the state cashmere-processing enterprise, because of "irregularities."[79] MIAT, the national airline, experienced similar difficulties when the government turned to an Irish consulting company to manage it. The new managers were accused of reducing the number of international flights, overloading some flights (which raised safety concerns), arranging flights at inconvenient hours, and delaying cargo deliveries to cut costs, and of creating poor morale among employees. The Irish managers have disputed these claims, although earnings have clearly declined.[80]

The assistance of earlier governments to private enterprises resulted in yet more problems. One newspaper reported that from 1991 to 2001, state agencies had either granted funds or guaranteed foreign loans for specific Mongolian companies. The $278 million figure cited in this account cannot be verified, but one crisis that erupted in 2002 may be a precursor of others. The Marubeni Corporation of Japan sued the Mongolian government in a British court for payment of a $20 million loan granted to Buyan, a large cashmere-processing company in Mongolia, which the government had reputedly guaranteed. Jargalsaikhan, the owner of Buyan and the founder of the Republican Party, who was regarded by many Mongolians as aggressive and arrogant, had used the loans to purchase new machinery and to build a brand-new factory, which I visited in the late 1990s and found impressive. Disputes have erupted between the MPRP leadership of 1992–96 and the first prime minister of the Democratic Union (1996–2000) concerning which of the two governments offered the guarantees. Much remains murky: was the government acting legally in providing the guarantees? If so, did it require any collateral?[81] An even more important question is whether other defaults of this kind are on the horizon. The government must surely be concerned about such possibilities and the obligations they may entail.

These difficulties notwithstanding, encouraged in part by the foreign and indigenous advocates of the pure market, the government went further and began to discuss privatization of the so-called social sector. Prime Minister Enkhbayar advocated this for some educational and health organizations and for institutions offering social services. Some Khural leaders met with President Bagabandi to press for his support for such a policy. Within a short time, however, there were complaints about such privatization. For example, the faculty and staff of the Trade and Industry Institute expressed concern that they had not been consulted with regard to the privatization of their institution.[82]

James Wolfensohn, the president of the World Bank, who had criticized international donor policies that emphasized privatization and unrestrained economic growth, visited Mongolia in May 2002 and seemed to change his views.[83] Reiterating the ideas of the pure market advocates, he supported privatization of the social sector, dependence on privatized companies, and reduction of the state budget, the same policies that the World Bank and the IMF had pursued in Mongolia since 1991 as solutions to the country's problems. These views on Mongolia were at odds with his analysis a few years earlier of what he described as the misplaced IMF and World Bank emphasis on privatization and macroeconomic stability, and decreased spending on health, education, and the social sector.

Abiding by the pure market approach, the MPRP government attempted to avoid overinvolvement in the economy, a policy that elicited criticism from manufacturers and unions. Apart from the mining companies, which benefited from international donor support and from foreign investment, and a few favored companies and joint ventures, most industrial concerns did not receive much state support. Indeed, the limited state revenues precluded substantial state investment in the economy, investment that could be invaluable in promoting job growth. MCS, which became the agent in Mongolia for Coca-Cola and for Siemens in energy and medical equipment, was an exception because of its links with the government and aid agencies. For example, it received government commissions, such as providing hydroelectric power in two major *aimags*. Other industries, lacking state assistance, did not fare as well.[84] Interest rates on loans and access to credit remained prohibitive for most small and medium-sized enterprises.

The Stock Exchange also provided little capital for these enterprises either. By 1998, it had become eerily quiet. Of the 400 or so companies listed at that time, only one-fifth offered dividends, and most had no stockholder meetings.[85] Supervision was lax; although there were regulations banning insider trading and concealment or distortion of information by brokers, dealers, and other officials, enforcement of these provisions was minimal. Thus investors lacked confidence, and small and medium-sized enterprises could not rely on the Stock Exchange for much needed capital.[86]

In addition to the lax government regulation of banks and the lack of affordable credit, native enterprises did not receive the kind of MPRP support in the form of favorable policies that they yearned for in seeking to grow. The government's inaction was owing, in part, to the policies of the international donor agencies. For example, the IMF threatened to withdraw aid if the government imposed an export tax on raw cashmere in order to help native processors. Thus, despite the repeated pleas by processors for such protection, the government did not act. Processors' demands for interest-free or low-interest loans, which the IMF described as subsidies, were also denied.[87] Many enterprises that processed animal products, including cowhide, leather, and cashmere, could not obtain sufficient raw material because itinerant Chinese or Mongolians from Inner Mongolia could outbid them.

Under these circumstances, many industries simply could not survive. Reports of such failing industries often appear in the press. The metallurgical industry at Darkhan, perhaps the country's most important industrial center, was operating at 20 percent capacity because 4,000 to 5,000 tons of scrap metal a year were sold to China, which paid higher prices for the unprocessed metal. Another plant in Darkhan, built in 1994 with Japanese aid, could not obtain sufficient iron ore and was idle much of the time.[88] Many enterprises in Dornod *aimag* had collapsed, resulting in considerable unemployment.

Prime Minister Enkhbayar, who had majored in literature at university and had little knowledge of economics, faced the seemingly intractable problem of vast unemployment. A reliable and independent Mongolian economist estimated that Mongolia required 48,000 new jobs annually for those entering the labor force and for the officially unemployed, not to mention the much larger number of unregistered unemployed. With a GDP that in 2000 was about 20 percent below that of 1989, and processing industries that had declined even further, the new government faced severe difficulties.[89]

With the livestock sector faltering, with industry not growing at a healthy rate, and with increasing dependence on mining, Enkhbayar sought to foster economic growth through a major infrastructure project known as the Millennium Road, a 2,700-kilometer highway linking east to west Mongolia, conservatively estimated to cost $350 million. Towns and settlements would be established along the road, and each would also be connected by an upgrade of information technology (e.g., the Internet).[90] The advocates of the road pointed out that the transport nexus, including trains and roads, tilted in favor of north-south connections, and that a new east-west link would benefit the country.[91]

The democratic reformers criticized Enkhbayar's Millennium Road project, claiming that Mongolia would need to borrow vast sums and issue bonds to build it, adding to the state's heavy debt burden. Moreover, they pointed out that the existing roads, even those in the capital, were not well maintained, and that such a development would create only impassable and degraded roads that could not be maintained because of lack of resources. Nonetheless, some foreigners and international donor agencies endorsed the project.[92]

INFORMAL SECTOR
AND FOREIGN INVESTMENT AND AID

The representatives of the international donor agencies championed the informal sector, which had burgeoned from the mid 1990s on, as an important engine for economic growth. A report prepared by consultants for USAID lavished praise on the informal sector, which they defined as "small-scale, usually family-based economic activities that may be uncounted by official statistics and may not be subject, in practice, to the same set of regulations and taxation as formal enterprises." The study surveyed retail trade (which consisted of kiosks, counters, and drugstores), financial services (pawnshops and money changing), transport (taxis, minibuses, tracks, and car parking), services (shoe repair, canteens, barbershops, games, and catering), and manufacturing (baked goods and soft drinks), mostly in Ulaanbaatar and in representative *aimags*. It estimated that the total annual value added by the informal sector amounted to about 13.3 percent of GDP, with retail trade providing the bulk of the increase. About two-fifths of the sector's workers were between the ages of 20 and 40 and a notable number were well educated—46 percent had university, college, or vocational training, and another 37 percent had completed at least ten years of secondary schools. The authors of the report point out that informal sector enterprises in Mongolia differed from such enterprises in other countries because they were subject to a so-called informal sector income tax. The report concluded by specifying the advantages of the informal sector: (1) reduced labor costs, because the enterprises were not compelled to pay for social or health insurance; (2) limited start-up costs—capital expenses except for transport were low, and state licensing was easier to obtain; (3) there was no need for assistance from the weak formal sector—unlike larger enterprises, most of these informal enterprises did not require loans from banks (which in any case charged interest rates that they could not afford); and (4) there were fewer difficulties with corruption, in part because they were smaller operations.[93]

Bernard Walters, a professor of Economics at Manchester University and a consultant for the UNDP, noted that this rosy report made little of the fact that recourse to the informal sector was, for many, an act of desperation. Workers with no regular means of earning a living took these jobs as a last resort. The surveyors and writers apparently did not wonder why educated Mongolians would wish to drive minibuses or to open kiosks or bakeries or start pawnshops. Neither did they take into account the loss to the economy and society, not to mention the individuals themselves, of trained and educated citizens undertaking work not at all commensurate with their abilities and skills. Walters acknowledged that the enterprises had reduced costs, but at the expense of workers who lacked social and health insurance protection, which meant no paid vacations, no sick days, no limits on hours at work, and so on. The USAID survey also failed to indicate the threats to health and safety posed by these informal and often unregulated enterprises.[94] Those working as caterers or operating kiosks and drugstores sometimes sold dated and defective products, while unregulated taxis and minibuses were fraught with potential dangers to the population. Moreover, pawnshops could not for long substitute for banks. Although the report stated that the informal sector was liable for taxation, it did not cite the amount of tax paid. Other sources question whether the government could elicit a fair share of taxes from this shadow economy. A World Bank survey two years later, noting that the shadow economy's share of GDP had risen from 13.3 percent in 1999 to about 20 percent in 2002, expressed concern about links between corruption and the informal sector. In short, the rise of the informal sector revealed weaknesses in the overall economy. The informal sector was working, but the economy was not operating properly.[95]

It is true that in 2002, the country's economic growth rebounded, in part, from the puny increases in 1999, 2000, and 2001. It reached about 3.7 percent, though the 3.1 percent rate of inflation eroded some of the gains. In 2003, it increased to about 5 percent, but much of the gain was based on mining (which constituted 55 percent of industrial production and about 60 percent of exports), the Millennium Road, and construction of retail stores and office buildings in Ulaanbaatar, which often used foreign laborers or employed relatively few workers.[96] A much higher rate, probably 7 to 8 percent, will be required to accommodate young people entering the labor market and the previously unemployed.

In 2002 and 2003, foreign investment increased, largely owing to a Canadian investment in gold and copper mines and to Chinese investment in mines, construction, and textile factories. However, most of the Chinese textile factories are pulling out, because China has joined the World Trade Organization and no longer faces restrictions on exports to the United States and Canada. (The Chinese had set up these factories in Mongolia to circumvent these restrictions.) Moreover, mining, which comprised the largest percentage of this investment, provided work for only about 16,000 workers and used up a nonrenewable resource, and much of the profit went to foreigners.[97]

Despite this caveat, the government has granted exploration rights over 46,000 square miles in the Gobi desert (at a site known as Oyu Tolgoi, or Turquoise Hill) to a controversial American named Robert M. Friedland, called "Toxic Bob" because of an environmental disaster his gold mining company apparently inflicted in Colorado (which was cleaned up by the Environmental Protection Agency at a cost of $200 million). Friedland claims to have spent $60 million in his exploration of Oyu Tolgoi and to have discovered one of the world's largest deposits of gold and copper. It is difficult to gauge the exact size of these deposits, the costs of extracting them, and the expenses likely to be involved in transporting them out of the country. Moreover, the government's dependence on such a controversial figure has aroused concern among some Mongolian and American residents of Mongolia.[98] In any event, analysts found the report on the Oyu Tolgoi deposits, which he commissioned, to be based on overly optimistic assumptions, estimates, and assessments, and shares in his company, Ivanhoe Mines, plunged dramatically after the issuance of the report.[99]

These difficulties prompted the government increasingly to rely on foreign aid. A telling indication of the power of the international donors is that the Khural delayed consideration of the state budget for a week in 2002 until representatives of the IMF and the World Bank arrived in Mongolia. Moreover, in late 2002, the IMF representative in Mongolia offered the same prescriptions of a reduced state budget, tight credit and monetary policy, anti-inflationary policy (despite low inflation for three years), a strong exchange rate, opposition to wage increases, and auster-ity—conditions that a Mongolian journalist called "too harsh on Mon-golia." Like his predecessors, the IMF representative implicitly threatened the Mongolian government, observing that "the international commu-nity looks to the Fund [IMF] for an evaluation of a country's economic management and outlook. In effect, it is looking for a seal of approval. In countries where the Fund is unable to provide such approval, donors become more reluctant to commit funds as aid in the context of inap-propriate macroeconomic management."[100]

Between 1991 and 2002, donors had provided $2.9 billion in grants and loans. In 2002, they supplied more than 30 percent of the annual GDP, or about the same percentage the USSR had offered in the communist era. They and the government could no longer assert that the continuing eco-nomic stagnation and the declining social services were owing to the loss of massive Soviet aid. The donors now provided the same level of assis-tance as the USSR had, yet the results were no better and arguably worse. From 1990 to 2000, infrastructure consumed 37 percent of the total (and the percentage increased throughout the period), agriculture and industry got 10 percent, and other spheres, including the social sector, received 15 percent. Structural reform, or "fiscal and economic management," which comprised efforts to reduce the size of the government and to foster a mar-ket economy, amounted to 23 percent, a seemingly high rate for technical assistance that would not necessarily contribute to economic growth.[101]

Opposition to the pure market policies apparently endorsed by Enkhbayar and the international donors began to be expressed more openly. In October 2002, the head of the Mongol Bank, frustrated by the IMF's demands and by what he perceived as its interference in Mongo-lia's domestic affairs, argued: "The country should not develop at the instructions of others and blindly follow their instructions. First of all, the interests of the Mongolian state and the people should guide the nation." In February 2002, the Civil Will Party, founded in the late 1990s by Oyun and a few colleagues, which was widely regarded as one of the most hon-est of the political parties, if not the most honest, convened a meeting to discuss foreign loans, at which Oyun expressed her concern that Mongo-lia, "whose foreign debt about equals 90 percent of GDP," would be unable to pay back the $848 million in loans, thus "endangering the national security and independence."[102] She suggested a moratorium on the acceptance of loans and later an annual limit to loan taking. Her Civil

Will Party issued a declaration, demanding that a "working group be set up to investigate and monitor the exploitative procedures of internationally funded projects and tender." The former head of the Council of Ministers of the MPRP echoed her views: "The Mongols . . . should employ their own wisdom and common sense. . . . The demands of the IMF, imposed in three directions, namely, to open the economy without limit, reduce the regulating role of the state almost to zero, then to balance the already poor budget has [sic] been not effective in creation of a market economy."[103] In sum, there was growing resentment against the policies and style of the IMF and the other international donor agencies.

The democratic reformers and a few Western agents of the philanthropic organizations were often specific in their critiques of the international donor agencies. An employee of Save the Children–UK pointed out that the ADB, which had supplied about 40 percent of the loans since 1991, had no resident representative in Mongolia to oversee the distribution of funds and to prevent abuses. Only in mid 2001 did it finally establish an office in Ulaanbaatar. Several journalists showed that the ADB and other donor agencies funneled their grants through intermediaries—banks or other financial institutions—which either deducted a percentage or lent funds at a high rate of interest, enjoying a profit while reducing the amount originally intended for a designated purpose. For example, ADB loans for the construction of new housing were granted to the Golomt, Mongol Shuudan, Zoos, and Savings Banks, which charged 16 percent interest for ten years. This tended to limit access to such apartments to the elite.

In short, critics, and Oyun in particular, emphasized that Mongolia needed to make better use of foreign grants and loans. Even the first ADB resident representative reported that since the international donor agencies had been involved in Mongolia, "we haven't seen the level of poverty reduced." Jeffrey Sachs, the architect of the "shock therapy" policy, reversed his position and now lamented his earlier prescriptions for cutbacks in the state budget and for education, health, and the environment and urged the IMF and the World Bank to halt their austerity campaigns and their fixation on inflation.[104]

Criticism of the priorities of foreign aid continued after 2000. Many Mongolians whom I interviewed (but who requested anonymity) questioned the fees, including overhead costs and fringe benefits, paid to the consulting firms. The technical assistance these firms provided was part of the foreign aid and loans granted to Mongolians, which would have to be repaid. In addition, a few challenged the changes in Ulaanbaatar, which the advisors took credit for and paraded as progress—for example, the proliferation of stores and restaurants. Critics pointed out that most of these establishments catered either to the Mongolian nouveaux riches or to the expatriate community, and many had foreign owners. The owner of one of the new restaurants confirmed the critics' view, observing that "our business is mostly dependent on a small number of expatriates and foreign tourists in the summer." A journalist who lived in Mongolia for two years reported that "these restaurants, though cheap by Western standards, were outrageously expensive to most Mongolians. They existed to serve a small, affluent, and desperate crowd of development workers."[105]

The growing criticisms prompted the international donor agencies to rethink some of their policies yet again. Perhaps embarrassed that massive aid and a special poverty alleviation program had failed to lower the poverty rate, they announced new programs. The International Donors' Conference in the summer of 2002 proposed a program to achieve a 25 percent reduction in the poverty rate by 2005, and 50 percent by 2015.[106] However, neither of these programs was comprehensive, and, as a UNDP study observed, none was integrated into Mongolia's economic plan. The IMF continued not only to insist that macroeconomic reforms were essential to reduce the rate of poverty but also to emphasize tight credit, antiinflationary efforts, a balanced budget, and reliance on the private sector to spur employment and fight poverty. However, its advice to the government contradicted its commitment to poverty reduction. Its opposition to higher wages, salaries, and pensions belied such commitment, while its support for such regressive taxes as VAT and for user fees scarcely contributed to the alleviation of poverty. The UNDP team asserted that a successful poverty reduction program had to be an integral part of Mongolia's and the international donor agencies' economic development plans.[107]

The international donors' aid programs sometimes failed to fulfill expectations owing to their specific economic agendas. Ulaanbaatar needed housing, particularly for the poor who had moved from provincial centers or from the countryside either because of the closing of state enterprises or because herding could no longer sustain them and their families. In December 2000, the ADB provided loans for construction of private homes but required property as collateral, limiting access to such funds to the elite. A Mongolian economist complained in the press that a project designed for "families with low and middle incomes" turned out to be a "Project for Housing Families with High Incomes."[108] In addition, newspapers reported that a few entrepreneurs who took these loans simply placed them in savings accounts paying higher interest, reaped the profits, and did not build the housing. It is difficult to gauge the level of profiteering, but to an unknown extent, corruption certainly undercut the effectiveness of some of these programs.[109]

On the other hand, some of the international donors' other programs were successful. The ADB supplied funds for the renovation of forty school buildings in the countryside, for five to twelve computers apiece for 140 secondary schools, for teacher training workshops, for helping to develop new textbooks, and for building science laboratories at several universities. Nonetheless, the question of monitoring the use of the funds is vital. For example, in 2003, the press reported that several Ministry of Health officials had embezzled World Bank funds.[110]

Inasmuch as tax revenues did not meet the government's needs, it turned to other sources, increasingly relying on the VAT and reduced corporate and income taxes.[111] Under pressure from the World Bank, ADB, and IMF, it also relied on user fees, increasing the price of electricity, heating, and hot water in 2000 and in 2002. Trade unions objected to these increases and demanded wage adjustments, particularly since the government had reneged on its preelection pledge to increase wages and pensions to a much higher level. Oyun, the principal dissenting member in the Khural, wondered why the government increased these prices when the largest segment of foreign aid was devoted to energy.

The sale of assets such as the state liquor company, APU, the Trade and Development Bank, and the Agricultural Bank offered an additional way for the government to cope with revenue shortfalls, although some members of the Khural charged that these privatizations lacked transparency. Some well-informed Mongolians declared that the government was privatizing state enterprises to repay its foreign loans.[112]

Corruption further contributed to problems for the government. Former Prime Minister Amarjargal, a staunch supporter of the market economy, charged his own political party, the Democratic Party (a new coalition that included the old Democratic Union), with corrupt and undemocratic policies, and its leader was accused of misappropriating funds when he had been director of the Erdenet copper complex. Investigators proved that the Ministry of Finance had misappropriated funds in 1998 and 1999. Rumors persisted that Former Prime Minister Elbegdorj had used government money to build a private house.[113] The governors of several *aimags* spent public funds on luxury cars, receptions, and functions. A survey by the Mongolian Employers' Confederation revealed that 66 percent of its members had offered bribes of money, cars, and lesser gifts to officials.[114] No wonder that the police official designated to ferret out corruption observed that "everybody is aware that corruption is present everywhere." And Oyun's Civil Will Party added that "democracy has become a mechanism for making a few people rich."[115]

Many accused the government of not launching a war against corruption. Oyun complained that the new anticorruption law that she championed had not been passed in the Khural. She publicly released information on her own income and assets and demanded that the other Khural members follow suit, but only one did so.[116] Toward the end of 2002, a headline in one of the English-language newspapers in Ulaanbaatar asked: "Is This Why the Anti-Corruption Law Has Been Shelved for Two Years?" The article raised questions about potentially illegal acts by former prime minister Puntsagiin Jasrai of the MPRP (1992–96), the current prime minister, and the ministers of education, culture and science, social welfare and labor, and infrastructure.[117]

The privatization of urban real estate and farmland, which began in 2003, also proved to be controversial and possibly marked by corruption. Foreigners were forbidden to own land, but critics questioned whether they might not buy land through Mongolian agents. Oyun, an expert in the field as a result of her training in geology, contended that the lack of cadastral maps and of a survey of land quality offered advantages to the well-connected and harmed the middle and poor classes in what might be a corrupt land registration process. Complaints from poor families that the local government in Ulaanbaatar had evicted them from land they expected to receive in order to benefit commercial enterprises appeared to confirm Oyun's fears.[118] The director of a teacher's college echoed these complaints, saying that "two years have passed since [I] had requested permission for a plot of land to extend the school. Meanwhile, a private company has obtained within a month the permission to possess the land."[119] Several hundred such incidents (some labeled "illegal acts" in the press) were reported in the year following the onset of land privatization. In the capital alone, ninety such disputes arose within the first six months of privatization.[120] In November 2002, farmers protested the new law by driving tractors into Sükhbaatar Square, because arable land would be sold and "ordinary farm workers [could not] afford to buy the land on which they work and [were] concerned that it will be bought by large farming companies." They feared that the abuses in the privatization of the herds would be replicated in this privatization. Police arrested forty-nine people, and, as of mid 2004, privatization of urban real estate and farmland was progressing very slowly, amid continuing controversy.[121] A Japanese academic specialist on Mongolia asserted that the World Bank, the IMF, and the ADB, lacking knowledge of Mongolia, were promoting privatization of urban real estate and farmland, hoping that it would lead to privatization of pastureland, a policy that he believed ran counter to Mongolian historical experience and would harm the interests of the majority of herders.[122]

The lack of public confidence in the Khural added to the disarray. Polls repeatedly showed public distrust of the Khural. Oyun's Civil Will Party was one of the few parties that the public regarded favorably.[123]

In sum, by 2004, despite thirteen years of one of the highest per capita levels of foreign aid to any country in the world, the Mongolian economy still faced considerable difficulties. GDP was lower than the international donor agencies perennially predicted, although it increased in 2003 and the first half of 2004. This limited growth could not, however, accommodate the annual influx of young people into the labor force. The result was substantial unemployment, higher than 20 percent in the urban areas. Moreover, the high percentage of Mongolians living below the poverty line, which the World Bank estimated at 36 percent in 1994, had not changed.[124]

Industrial production has been largely based on mining, left mostly unregulated, which harmed the environment and made the country vulnerable to the volatile world prices for minerals.[125] Processing industries, which had great value-added effects, declined with the lack of state support. Abiding by the dictates of the international donor agencies, the government had adopted perhaps the freest trade policy of any country in the world and failed to impose tariffs in order to protect its fledgling native industries. Again following the advice of the international donors, the state mandated tight credit, and the high interest rate charged to borrowers—with a considerable spread between that rate and the interest paid to depositors—limited the access of enterprises to credit. In addition to high interest rates, the banking system had been riddled with favoritism, nepotism, and corruption, resulting in high-risk and nonperforming loans. No banks collapsed after 1998, but several remained weak. In late 2002 and early 2003, the two most successful banks, both state-owned, were sold to foreigners, one to a U.S. metals dealer and a Swiss bank and the other to a Japanese securities firm. The democratic reformers questioned whether these two banks would foster economic growth, although the Agricultural Bank has increased the amount of its loans and has pledged assistance to small enterprises in rural areas and poor districts in the capital. It is too soon to tell how effective such an effort may be.

The private sector has thus far been unable to make a substantial dent in unemployment or poverty, and much more state involvement is clearly required. The chief of the Government Employment Board acknowledged that after three years of MPRP rule, the number of unemployed actually increased from 220,000 in 2000 to 265,800 by early 2004.[126] The credit squeeze has generated the development of nonbanking financial institutions such as pawnshops and other lending enterprises. Most have remained unsupervised, and there have been increasing calls for regulation of these informal sector operations.[127]

The declines in herding, farming, and many industries, owing in part to the withdrawal of state support, resulted in a gradually diminishing ratio of exports to imports. By 2003, the annual trade deficit reached $167 million, or about 17 percent of GDP. With only limited import duties or effective import controls, the deficit threatened to increase and to reduce the funds available for domestic savings and investment.[128]

Foreign aid compensated for much of the shortfall, but it also drove the country into increased debt.[129] Part of the foreign aid itself seems to have been misappropriated owing to mismanagement and the corruption that afflicted segments of local government, the highest levels of the central government, the Customs Service, the courts, the police, and the banks. The amount of foreign aid diverted from its intended purposes is a matter of dispute, but the Civil Will Party, many NGOs, and even USAID conceded that corruption and misuse of foreign funds were serious problems.[130] To be sure, some of the foreign aid was invaluable. It created jobs, offered assistance to the vulnerable, and provided funds for education and health, but the biggest donors focused on fostering a market economy and devoted most of their aid to promoting that agenda. When they disagreed with a particular policy, they withheld the desperately needed assistance, limiting the government's authority to develop decision-making skills and to take responsibility for the consequences, as well as undermining the principles of democracy.

Some entrepreneurs prospered, whether through their own talents or through their connections with influential officials or their links with foreigners, but most of the population fared worse than under the communist system.[131] Disparities in income between rich and poor widened considerably throughout the 1990s and early 2000s. Even discounting some hyperbole, the number of poverty-stricken households was sizable. Half the population lived on less than $2 a day, leading to predictable declines in health and education.[132] Hard pressed for funds and encouraged by the international donor agencies to be less involved in the economy, the government failed to maintain the social safety net that had existed during the communist era. Foreign aid and foreign philanthropic assistance provided relief for some of the vulnerable, but street children, unemployment, and single-parent households, which had scarcely existed during the communist period, were serious problems.

Western observers and many Mongolians have argued that, despite the economic failures, the political system has been liberalized. Four Khural elections and three presidential elections have been generally fair and open, and independent foreign observers have certified their honesty. Khural meetings have, on occasion, been televised, and minority parties, although somewhat disadvantaged because of lack of extensive coverage in the media, have survived. However, as the educational system and the literacy rates decline, the foundations of a stable and democratic political system may erode.

By 2004, the democratic reformers, who had played pivotal roles in the 1990 collapse of the communist system, were no longer influential. The pure market economists had superseded them in 1990 and had dominated the government. Distressed by economic and social disarray and by corruption, the reformers frequently opposed the government but rarely influenced policy. Their leadership ranks had been depleted. Zorig had been murdered; Hulan's husband had been named ambassador to Russia, and she dropped out of politics, until she put forward her candidacy in the 2004 Khural elections; and Erdenebileg had been defeated in the 2000 elections. Zorig's sister Oyun remained a lone voice in the Khural.

Readying herself for the 2004 Khural elections, Oyun sought partners for her Civil Will party. In February 2002, she joined together with the Republican Party, virtually the personal bailiwick of Bazarsadyn Jargalsaikhan, the capricious owner of the troubled and debt-ridden Buyan cashmere mills. This bizarre coalition, a ragged mismatch, fell apart in December 2003.[133] She then cooperated with the Democratic Party, a new coalition designed to reinvigorate the old Democratic Union, but clashes between the partners persisted.[134] Further complicating matters was the fact that Erdenebat, the leader of the Motherland Socialist Party and an important member of the coalition (partly owing to his wealth and his willingness to spend vast sums to support his political career) was accused of evading income taxes.[135] Nonetheless, the Motherland Socialist Party and the Democratic Party, joined by Oyun's Civil Will Party, constituted the main opposition to the MPRP in the elections.

The survival of the communist old guard and their younger adherents further complicates the political equation. Many former communist leaders, including former Prime Minister Jasrai, have remained relatively quiescent, partly because of the influence and leverage of the pure market advocates in the government and in the international donor agencies. However, if poverty, unemployment, and corruption persist and are met with ineffective state responses, the old guard may revive, and the former communist leaders may seek to reintroduce their old agenda of a very powerful state and a command economy.

The June 27, 2004, Khural elections revealed the considerable popular dissatisfaction with the programs and policies of the Enkhbayar government. Despite the evident disarray of the Motherland Democratic Party coalition and the government's own extraordinary leverage over the media, its massive expenditures on advertising, and the support of Russian advisors, the MPRP suffered stunning reversals. Its nearly total control of the Khural was shattered. The 72 to 4 majority it had enjoyed was reduced to the point where it could be sure of only 36 members. Although it could justifiably accuse the opposition of fraud, buying votes, and illegal transportation of voters to several closely contested districts (the opposition, in turn, complained of MPRP irregularities), it could not explain away its losses. Neither of the two parties emerged victorious.

Some observers conceived of the results as a protest vote, because many of the Motherland Democratic Party candidates had been members of the

Democratic Union who had been voted out of office in 2000. The 2004 Khural elections did not appear to be a ringing affirmation of the opposition, although the Motherland Democratic Party's pledge to provide 10,000 tugriks a month to each child (a pledge that seemed difficult to believe in light of the country's economic problems and of the power of the international financial organizations) may have proved attractive to some voters. It seemed to represent a protest against the corruption and the pure market economic policies of privatization of state assets, private sector economic growth, liberalization of prices and trade, minimal government, and dependence on massive foreign aid (with its restrictions on government and society), which had not benefited much of the population and had not stemmed growing income inequality, unemployment, and other serious social problems. As one journalist wrote, "Mongolia remains mired in a social crisis with jobs, poverty, and education the main concerns of voters."[136] Another attributed the election results and the post-1990 migration of at least 50,000 Mongolians to foreign countries to "growing poverty, social apathy, unviable programs, and weak development plans."[137] Although Hulan lost in a close election, Oyun and several other democratic reformers were elected; but it seemed unlikely that they had the power to shape new policies.

After almost two months of negotiations, the MPRP and the Motherland Democratic Party formed a coalition government. Elbegdorj, who had been compelled to resign as prime minister owing to the Reconstruction Bank scandal of 1998, would become prime minister for two years, and Enkhbayar would assume the title of Speaker of the Khural for two years. Leadership after these initial two years until the next Khural elections in 2008 would revert to the MPRP, with Deputy Prime Minister Chultemiin Ulaan becoming prime minister. Judging from the previous relations between the MPRP and the Democratic Party, this compromise would appear to be problematic. In any event, negotiators chose Elbegdorj because of his links with Western organizations and his ardent espousal of a market economy. His selection signaled continuation of policies that had not prevented significant unemployment and poverty, and his choice of Ganbold and Tsagaan as advisors indicated his faith in the market economy. Oyun would become the Deputy Speaker of the Khural, but it was unclear how influential she would be.

Tsakhiagiin Elbegdorj (with headband) at a demonstration in 1990. He would later be prime minister. Courtesy of the Democratic Union Archives.

Demonstrators in Sükhbaatar Square, Ulaanbaatar, 1990. Courtesy of the Democratic Union Archives.

Davaadorjiin Ganbold (with briefcase) negotiating with the MPRP government, 1990. He would later be first deputy minister. Courtesy of the Democratic Union Archives.

Hunger strikers in Sükhbaatar Square, Ulaanbaatar, March 1990. Courtesy of the Democratic Union Archives.

Randaasumbereliin Gonchigdorj (later Speaker of the Khural) on
hunger strike, March 1990. Courtesy of the Democratic Union Archives.

Sanjaasürengiin Zorig (with glasses) calming a crowd of demonstrators, 1990. Courtesy of the Democratic Union Archives.

Bat-Erdeniin Batbayar ("Baabar"), the founder of the Mongolian Social Democratic Party, at a demonstration, 1990. Courtesy of the Democratic Union Archives.

Sanjaasürengiin Zorig (with glasses) and foreign observers at a polling place during the Khural election of 1992. Courtesy of the Democratic Union Archives.

Poll taker
Luvsandendev
Sumati on holiday,
2003. Courtesy of
Luvsandendev
Sumati.

Statue of murdered
leader Sanjaasürengiin
Zorig in central
Ulaanbaatar.
Courtesy of San-
jaasürengiin Oyun.

Sanjaasürengiin Oyun, founder of the Civil Will Party, at her desk in 2003. Courtesy of San-jaasürengiin Oyun.

The herder and former Khural member Tserendash Namkhainyambuu (left) and his mother, a Buddhist nun (center), with an unidentified man in 1999. Courtesy of Mary Rossabi.

Tserendash Namkhainyambuu, his wife, and several of their children in Gachuurt, 1999. Courtesy of Mary Rossabi.

The journalist Lkhagvasüren Nomin on a hike in the Gobi desert. Courtesy of Lkhagvasüren Nomin.

Statue of Lkhagvasüren, Lkhagvasüren Nomin's grandfather, in central Ulaanbaatar, 2002. Courtesy of Lkhagvasüren Nomin.

Ovoo (shamanic symbol) near the town of Mörön. Courtesy of Mary Rossabi.

From left: the author with the Mongolian ambassador to the United States, Jalbuu Choinhor; an interpreter; and President Natsagiin Bagabandi at the Asia Society, New York, 2003. Photo by Elsa Ruiz, courtesy of the Asia Society.

Hashbat Hulan at Columbia University, 2004.

Chapter 5 | HERDERS AND THE NEW ECONOMY

In his life and writings, the democratic reformer Tserendash Nam-khainyambuu, the only herder so far elected to the Khural in the post-communist era, reflects the tumultuousness and substantial difficulties in Mongolian pastoralism over the past half century. In his early childhood in Zavkhan *aimag* in the western part of Mongolia, many herders persisted in an independent lifestyle, migrating in search of grass and water for their animals. By the time he was ten years old, in 1958, the government had either forced or cajoled herders to join *negdels*, or collectives. As a member of a collective, Namkhainyambuu achieved remarkable renown for his expertise in herding. He also witnessed the decollectivization and then privatization of the animals in 1991–92 and observed, with great concern, the ensuing difficulties in the pastoral economy, problems that still plague his fellow herders. In six lengthy interviews that my wife and I conducted with him between April 1999 and June 2002, as well as in his book *Khonini khishig (Bounty from the Sheep)*, he came across as witty, engaging, and shrewd.

He was aware that for more than two centuries the Qing Empire had ruled Mongolian lands and organized Mongolians into "banners" governed by Mongolian princes. Under this hierarchical system, the leading princes, in alliance with Buddhist monasteries, had controlled sizable numbers of animals and the best pastures, moving their animals frequently to secure access to the best lands. Ordinary herders barely eked out a living on pastureland of mediocre quality. Without shelter for their animals and without fodder, they suffered great losses in their herds during the climatic disasters that befell parts of Mongolia on the average of at least once every decade.[1]

The communist leadership that took power in Mongolia in 1921 was ambivalent about the herders, a fact reflected in its policies. The MPRP considered itself the vanguard of the proletariat; it was thus not, first and foremost, the party of the herders. However, because Mongolia's economy was based on pastoralism and most of its people were herders, the MPRP recognized its dependence on what it perceived to be a nonrevolutionary and perhaps "backward" class. Its early leaders were determined to turn the herders into semi-proletarians—that is, wage earners. In the late 1920s and early 1930s, their poorly planned and brutal effort at collectivization failed. Having learned its lesson from this fiasco, in the 1950s, the government used economic incentives, persuasion, education, and propaganda to foster the development of cooperatives, or *negdels*, which by 1960 managed about 75 percent of the country's livestock.

Around this time, Namkhainyambuu quit school and started his career in a *negdel*, an institution that he cherished and praised. He claimed that the *negdels* fostered innovations that improved and promoted herding, for example, the introduction of trucks to facilitate movement. Because trucks were more efficient and could carry more weight than camels, which were the previous means of transport, many herders quickly switched to them. With this boost to mobility, the herders could, in his words, "just follow the pastures." The government's and the *negdels'* authoritarianism notwithstanding, they appear to have permitted herders leeway in managing their animals. In particularly arid years, Namkhainyambuu noted, he and other herders even moved their animals to neighboring *aimags*, which certainly lay beyond the grazing area assigned by government officials.[2]

Namkhainyambuu also revealed that the *negdels* encouraged training for herders. He himself could identify an astonishing range of plants, grasses, mountain ranges, and rivers and was well versed in traditional herding practices. The government sought to foster such knowledge by publishing a guide to herding by Jamsrangyn Sambuu, chair of the presidium of the Khural, in the very same year that the second collectivization effort began.[3] This compilation by such an important state official indicates that the government sought to encourage pastoral productivity.

Namkhainyambuu himself compiled a manual of detailed instructions on the proper care of sheep.[4] The Mongolian government also sent a number of students to conduct research on agronomy in Soviet institutes of higher learning.[5] They returned to Mongolia and worked in agricultural institutes to disseminate innovations in herding to individual herders. In addition, newly trained veterinarians, many of whom had been educated in the USSR or Eastern Europe, passed on these innovations on the local level. By 1989, there were 839 specialized veterinarians, 2,179 veterinary technicians, and 456 animal health workers in the country.

The *negdels,* according to Namkhainyambuu, also promoted the livestock economy through new and better facilities. They encouraged the construction of temporary animal shelters in the herders' winter quarters. However, Namkhainyambuu sternly instructed herders not to "fence in the sheep. Let them be free and strong." He was less ambivalent about the *negdels'* support for the digging of wells, writing that "water is everywhere a jewel," and also recommended production of hay and other forage. The *negdels'* provision of fodder saved many animals and reduced the herders' helplessness in facing a demanding winter environment.

Namkhainyambuu's book (really an autobiography) attests to increased mechanization, also meant to promote productivity and to reduce the risks confronting herders. He saw his first tractor as a young boy. Although his encampment initially was suspicious of and derided what Namkhainyambuu refers to as the "red ant," most soon adopted the machines offered by the authorities. Such equipment helped them to increase the production and the harvesting of the hay, enabling their animals to survive harsh winters. The new equipment also assisted in reaping harvests from potato fields and vegetable gardens. In fact, however, most of the fodder, grain, and vegetables were produced on large state farms. By 1960, there were only 25 state farms but more than 350 *negdels.*[6] These huge mechanized farms, with substantial storage facilities and sheds, were not only responsible for fodder and agricultural production, but also cross-bred animals, experimented with seeds, and opened up new lands. In addition, they developed subsidiary activities such as the raising of poultry and pigs and the making of felt and leather. Although the state farms increased labor productivity and made the country self-sufficient in flour, they often damaged the semi-arid plains.[7]

The state organized the marketing and distribution of the meat, wool, and other animal products produced by herders. The Central Procurement Co-operative Union dispatched trucks to collect animals and animal products and transport them to slaughterhouses and processing plants.[8] In return for these products, it provided consumer goods that herders could buy with the wages paid to them by their *negdels*. The herders received 80 percent of their projected wages on a monthly basis and the balance, plus bonuses, at the end of the year.

The state had reached its objective of turning the herders into wage earners—that is, semi-proletarians. As more animals became collectivized, herders became employees of the *negdels* and resembled workers in other enterprises. Because money held no special attraction for herders, the state used other incentives, such as titles and awards, to encourage industriousness and productivity. Namkhainyambuu told me that he had worked very hard to be awarded the titles of "Champion" or "Hero of Labor" and to receive the "Star of Sükhbaatar" and the "Golden Soyombo" medals. He mentioned with pride that his wife, Jargal, had earned a "Best Herder" gold medal and a "Champion Youth" silver medal. He himself became possibly the most renowned herdsman, partly for fulfilling his pledge to raise 10,000 white sheep in twenty years and for his advice to herders in newspapers, and partly because of his appearances in films and at important public events.

Local government and *negdel* leaders decided on the incentives and assumed even more consequential responsibilities in the economy and society. Often themselves either experienced herdsmen or trusted members of the MPRP, they assigned water and pasture land to the herders in the *negdels*, organized labor for the cutting of hay and other collective pursuits, and fostered new technologies and techniques that increased production. A recent study accords such leaders a central role in the fate of the collectives, concluding that "the success of intensified specialized pastoralism was based on direction by central leadership."[9] Namkhainyambuu wrote that their success in averting problems and settling potential conflicts meant that "there were no disputes over pasture lands," again perhaps too rosy an assessment. He was candid in noting that the authoritarianism of the system prevented "openness [because] people were frightened that their careers might be in jeopardy if they disagreed with the administration."

The *negdels* undoubtedly allayed some of the risks faced by ordinary herders. Nomadic pastoralism is inherently precarious. Herders face numerous threats, such as successive years of heavy snowstorms. Different hazards afflict different parts of the country. Some contend with drought, others with floods, and still others with blizzards and frost that deny pasture to their animals. The state and the *negdels* provided insurance against such risks and potential losses. They helped to replenish livestock, transported hay for starving animals, and dispatched veterinarians to care for the ailing herds. In short, they attempted to minimize the risks associated with the nomadic pastoral economy.

Perhaps as important as the state's and the *negdels'* boost to the herders' households were their innovations in medicine and social welfare. The establishment of the *negdels*, which often had centers that developed into small towns, facilitated state efforts to deliver medical care, at no cost, to the herders. The small towns would have clinics or hospitals, and doctors could, if necessary, travel to encampments in distant locations in case of emergency. The state provided medicines, although one anthropologist writes that "the range of what was available was inadequate by our standards."[10] Nearly all had access to maternity rest homes, where pregnant women stayed in the last weeks before giving birth, and where they could be assured of good medical care. Such facilities underscored the state's pronatal policies.

Other social benefits provided by the *negdels* and the state also appealed to Namkhainyambuu and other herders. Clothing allowances, paid vacations, and payments for child support served as means of retaining the loyalty of *negdel* members. Palaces of culture, libraries, a basic mail service, and newspapers and radio (which included a heavy dose of political propaganda but also offered valuable details about weather conditions) were also provided. The state recruited or compelled students or urbanites to serve as so-called volunteers to help herders during busy times. Perhaps the most appreciated benefit was pensions. Most Asian and African countries do not offer pensions to their rural inhabitants, but the Mongolian state did so during the *negdel* era. Women could retire at the age of fifty-five, although they could start to receive their pensions earlier if they had four or more children. Men received their pensions at sixty. With such pensions, other subsidies, cash income, and their private animals, it is no wonder that "these benefits and services placed Mongolia far ahead of other Third World nations such as China and India."[11]

The herders' children benefited from the state-sponsored educational system. The government set up schools in *soum* (district) centers, providing relatively good salaries to teachers. It emphasized schools in part because better-educated herders might be less hostile to new techniques and machinery that would promote productivity. Children whose parents migrated with the herds lived in school dormitories, and the state covered all expenses for room and board. The success of this system may be gauged by the extraordinarily high rate of literacy in the countryside. Although Namkhainyambuu left school after the fourth class, he praised his teachers for teaching him to read and for "introducing [him] to art and culture." He attributed his voracious appetite for learning, and for reading everything from Mongolian classics to Daniel Defoe, to his teachers.

Despite many attractive features, the *negdels* had drawbacks, some of which Namkhainyambuu alluded to. Lazy herders neglected their animals, scarcely performed their work properly, and did not fulfill their quotas for animals and animal products. Yet the *negdels* rarely punished or fined the lazy and the incompetent, and the state continued to provide them with wages and did not offer sufficient incentives to increase productivity.

Namkhainyambuu's observations about indolent and unskilled herders coincided with evidence about productivity during the *negdel* period. Although the number of animals increased, the livestock quotas for the Five-Year Plans were on occasion not fulfilled, or were set so low that the herders could meet them. Part of the difficulty lay in a number of years of abominable weather, with snows, frost, and wind storms, which resulted in depletion of the livestock. Another problem was that the yield of the pastures decreased because of overgrazing, drought, and soil degradation.[12] Still another problem was the growing disparity between the city and the countryside and the consequent lure of urban life for some herders. Increasing urbanization, including the growth of the capital at Ulaanbaatar and the establishment of industrial centers in Darkhan and Erdenet, offered the amenities of city life, which attracted some herders. Namkhainyambuu's sister commented that "it's better to live in city dust than in sheep dung."

THE MARKET ECONOMY AND THE HERDER

Many herders suffered during the transition after the collapse of communism in 1990. As noted earlier, the Western advisors to whom the Mongolian government appealed for aid sought to develop a market economy as rapidly as possible and promoted a policy of shock therapy as the best and most expeditious means of creating such an economy.[13]

Such a market economy model had been developed and applied to sedentary agricultural or industrial economies but had not been tested in a society in which about one-third of the population sustained itself by pastoral nomadism. Several economists and officials questioned its validity, declaring that "such tenets of economic theory as wealth accumulation, [and] the innate desire of individuals to acquire material goods" were not necessarily true of Mongolia.[14] Western advisors initially focused principally on industries and the urban areas, paying less attention to and having little contact with the herder population. They cooperated with educated Mongolians, mostly descended from the old elites, who had scant links with the countryside, reflecting a growing separation of the urban and rural. Throughout the 1990s, the Khural generally represented the interests of the townsmen. The herders did not have a political party of their own to reflect their concerns and champion their rights.

The drive for privatization had a substantial impact on the herders. Within two years, in 1991 and 1992, the pastoral collectives had been abolished, and 224 joint stock companies emerged from the 255 negdels. Animals, not land, were privatized, but no individual or agency regulated rights to grazing land. Without institutions to regulate land usage and rights to water in wells, lakes, and rivers, disagreements have occurred, because some households have trespassed on the customary pasturelands of other herders.

The Khural lifted limits on the size of private herds, permitting entrepreneurs and some negdel and state leaders to amass large numbers of animals. The same privileged individuals divided up the trucks, the machinery, and the negdels' other tangible assets. A Danish anthropologist who conducted field research in the countryside wrote: "The final privatization process was frequently reported to be chaotic . . . enabling negdel leaders to maintain control over key assets."[15] On the other hand, some blamed lazy and incompetent herders for not breeding and maintaining sufficient animals, thus creating their own difficulties.[16]

Namkhainyambuu and many herders remained suspicious of privatization in 1991 and 1992 and counseled caution in its implementation. A herder on pension revealed his anxiety when he said: "Maybe the free market is better for Mongolia, but we cannot start it right away. We need time to learn about how the market system works and how we as nomads will operate under it. Things must be introduced gradually."[17] A young herder feared the growing disparity in wealth if privatization proceeded too rapidly and without some controls: "In the market system the more capable will do well and take advantage of it and become rich, and those who are less capable will become poor. We have to watch out that we don't return to the past feudal system."[18] He proved prescient. The overly rapid privatization left most herders with barely sufficient animals for their needs. Various authorities estimate that a household requires from 100 to 125 animals (and some offer a figure as high as 200) to survive and to market their products.[19] Families with fewer than 75 head have to slaughter animals for food, and they thus find it increasingly difficult to replenish their herds. By the mid 1990s, about one-third of herding families, hardly any of whom owned the requisite number of animals, lived below the poverty line.[20] Although many herders in the old communist *negdels* lived simply, there was little of the abject poverty that developed after privatization.

The gap between the rich and the poor widened considerably in the 1990s. As of 2002, 601 herding households, a tiny percentage of the population, owned more than 1,000 head apiece.[21] Out of the 243,000 households, 166,000 had fewer than 100 head, not a commercially viable number, meaning that many are limited to a barely self-sufficient herding style and do not produce for the market. The wealthy not only had more animals and a higher per capita number of animals but also had more vehicles and camels to facilitate mobility, access to lusher seasonal pastures, and transport to markets. In addition, they had more laborers in their households and greater access to spring shelters for the animals.[22]

Part of the difficulty stemmed from the large number of herders. The collapse of many industries and factories starting in 1990 generated significant unemployment, particularly in provincial centers, and many of the unemployed had returned to the countryside to take up herding just when the herds were about to be privatized. The herder population in 1990 amounted to about 147,000, but, because of the stresses in the Mongolian economy, it had more than doubled by 1993 and had tripled by 1998.[23] Many of the traditional herders resented the newcomers, fearing the additional burden on the pasture lands.[24] The two groups clashed over grazing and water rights, contributing to the problems in the countryside.[25] Compounding the difficulties, the newcomers had few of the skills necessary for herding, and most became a part of the one-third of herders who lived below the poverty line. Disastrous winters in 1999, 2000, and 2001 compelled many of these herders to abandon their pastoral existence and flee to the towns, and particularly to Ulaanbaatar, creating a tremendous burden on the economy, infrastructure, and social safety net in the capital. Preliminary figures indicate a 25 percent increase in Ulaanbaatar's population from 1997 to 2002.[26]

The insistent calls for minimal government with scant state involvement in the economy had had grave implications for herders. Before 1990, the state had paid the herders and the *negdels* for animals and had brought them to market. With privatization, herders were on their own, and the state no longer guaranteed purchases. In addition, the state did not transport animals and animal products to market. Herders who needed to sell sheep, goats, wool, cashmere, and other products to buy wheat, rice, tea, and other consumer goods were vulnerable. Those who herded in pasture lands far from towns often had to sell to middlemen (often Mongolians from Inner Mongolia or Chinese) who were aware that they had an advantage because herders could not, on their own, transport their products to market. They offered relatively low prices, and the herders, stymied by poor roads, bridges, and generally poor transport, as well as poor communications infrastructure, were often forced to accept.[27] Because the state did not provide information through the media about market prices to herders, they were at an even greater disadvantage; they could not readily bargain with the traders.[28]

Herders developed different strategies to cope with these difficulties. Quite a few, including Namkhainyambuu, moved their encampments closer to the cities or other settlements, the principal potential markets for their products, or at least close to roads. The greater the number of herders and the greater number of animals they brought with them, the more degradation of the land around the urban centers there was. A recent assessment rates 51 percent of the pasture land, particularly near population centers, as medium-degraded.[29] Herders were not, as a result, as mobile, a vital element in the sustainability of the pasturelands, and permitted their animals to graze year-round on what were meant to be seasonal pastures. At the same time, the abandonment of single-species herding, which had been emphasized in the *negdel* period but was regarded as too risky for the individual herder in the new market economy, meant that herders could not be specialists and lost the advantages associated with expertise. Namkhainyambuu continued to herd only sheep, but he was unique; most herders tended different species in their herds.

Another herder strategy entailed seeking loans from banks to purchase new machinery, to dig wells, and to buy vehicles to facilitate migrations with animals. Credit would also enable herders to purchase the consumer goods they needed during winter and spring, when they had scant incomes. However, a survey in 2003 reports that "access to credit is particularly difficult for rural residents. Herders and the rural poor are not attractive risks because their income is often seasonal and their only collateral is livestock, which is vulnerable to disease and weather."[30] In addition, as noted earlier, the banking system was in disarray, and herders had to barter with itinerant and often exploitative traders, who knew that they had little income at certain times of the year, and who thus charged high prices for their goods, which herders had to pay.[31] With little money available, herders have generally bartered animals for the goods they require. Such transactions naturally preclude taxation, which in turn reduces government revenues.

The collapse of the USSR and the subsequent problems faced by Russia have added to the herders' woes. The USSR had been the principal market for Mongolian meat.[32] In 1980, total meat exports amounted to 45,900 tons a year, but by 2003, that figure had been reduced to 14,000 tons. The economic downturn in their country meant that many Russians could not afford to pay for imported meat. In addition, the Russian government had imposed tariffs on imported meat and established standards of quality that the Mongolian herders could not attain, particularly with repeated outbreaks of hoof and mouth disease.[33] The Western European nations have similarly high standards, which prevent imports of Mongolian meat. Without a sizable export market, herders have had little choice but to hold on to their herds, which for a time resulted in a significant increase in the total number of the five principal animals (sheep, goats, yaks, camels, and horses) from about 25 million in 1990 to about 33 million in 1999. Such growth also placed an additional burden on the available pasture lands.

Still another herder strategy that has had mixed results is a dramatic increase in the number of goats in Mongolia, a response to what appeared to be market demand, but one that Namkhainyambuu repeatedly criticized in his conversations with us. Learning of the high prices being paid for cashmere in the early 1990s, pastoralists who were now on their own and dependent on the market increased the number of goats in their herds, and they have continued to do so, despite a sharp drop in prices. In 1990, Mongolia had approximately five million goats; by 1997, the number had risen to close to eleven million.[34] Because China, the other major producer of cashmere, also had not imposed limits on its herders, the market was glutted. Lacking guidance from the government, Mongolian herders have focused on quantity, not quality,[35] which further undercuts the prices they can command. Namkhainyambuu repeatedly complained that animal health, nutrition, and genetic quality had not received much attention. Herders have learned the hard way that "large numbers of goats are no guarantee of wealth."[36] In addition, increasing the number of goats in response to the market has placed an enormous burden on the land. As one writer notes, "Mongolia must remember that in some countries goats have destroyed pastures and left them as useless drybeds."[37] Adaptation to temporary market demands has not, in this case, served the herders well.

The collapse of the *negdels* affected children and women in particular. Households needed replacements for the "volunteers" of the collective era, who were now no longer available. Herders' sons were often recruited to perform the work, obliging them to drop out of school. Although Namkhainyambuu sought to keep all nine of his children in school, it has become difficult to do so. The burdens on women have also increased.[38] Without assistance from the other women in the *negdel*, individual women have had to undertake greater responsibilities. They not only cook; sew; wash; produce butter, yogurt, and cheese; and care for children but also milk animals, cure hides, and make boots, among other chores. The *negdels* had made these tasks communal, reducing the burdens on individual women.

The processing of animal products has languished, because in addition to the state farms and *negdels*, dairies; poultry, fish, and egg farms; and leather and boot factories closed down. The government could not or would not maintain subsidies and was forced or chose to abandon such processing plants. In 1990, Mongolia's output of butter amounted to 4,400 tons, but by 2002, the figure was negligible.[39] Before 1990, forty mechanized farms had produced fifty million liters of milk, but by 1999,

Mongolia imported about 875 tons of milk products, an extraordinary situation for a country with such a large number of dairy animals.[40]

Without state support and subsidies, agricultural production also declined. Although Mongolia had been self-sufficient in flour before 1990, it imported substantial quantities of wheat in the last few years of the 1990s.[41] The country as a whole has become increasingly dependent on imports of cereals and vegetables, which come mostly from China.[42] In 2004, the ADB, the World Bank, and the European Union aid agency TACIS announced plans for a $100,000 program in support of agriculture, but this is a tiny fraction of aid money as a whole and certainly insufficient for this sector of the economy.[43] Despite some calls for imposition of a tariff on imported foods and complaints of adulterated or insect-laden flour from China, Mongolia continues to rely on imported foods. Perhaps more significant for the herders, quotas for the preparation of hay have frequently not been met owing to lack of machinery, fuel, or government support.[44] Herders thus cannot always rely on hay as a supplement for their animals or in emergencies.

Privatization and the simultaneous decline in state support have heightened the risks faced by herders. Veterinarians now charge for their services, and fewer are being trained. Those veterinarians who are working prefer service near the urban centers.[45] Herders also cannot expect the state to help them restock if a bad winter or disease decimates their herds. For example, in the late 1980s, the local government of Bayan-Ölgii *aimag* spent TG 211–76 million (in 2003 currency) to prevent diseases in animals, but by 2003, the figure amounted to only TG 25 million.[46] Many herders supported the initial privatization, but, like Namkhainyambuu, a substantial number now wonder whether private ownership compensates for the loss of state support in the forms of digging of wells, provision of fodder, veterinary services, and trucks for transport, which previously reduced the risks in an exceptionally perilous occupation.

Many reports document the decline of medical care in the countryside. Quite a number of maternity rest homes, which housed women in the last days of pregnancy, have closed; medicines are in short supply; standards of sanitation in local clinics and hospitals are poor; and needles, blood supplies, and diagnostic tools, such as X-rays, are unavailable or dangerously ill maintained or tainted. Moreover, as of January 1, 1999, herders have had to pay for their own medical insurance. No wonder that a journalist traveling in the South Gobi wrote that "while wages had been low under the socialist system, no one had really been in want even in the remote regions because the state provided for the basics of life: health care, education, jobs and pensions."[47] In my own travels through the countryside, herders have asked me for medicines for ailing family members, and Mongolian and other travelers have quite frequently confirmed my experience. Surely there must have been some in communist days who did not have access to these "basics," but the number of such individuals was relatively small. In a recent interview, Dashiin Byambasüren, the first prime minister after the fall of communism, pointed to still another deficiency when he warned against the government's plans to reduce pensions for herders.[48]

Education, another state service, has likewise suffered from lack of funding. Government expenditures on education have decreased since the *negdel* period,[49] and the need for child labor in the privatized herding economy has led to a substantial increase in the number of school dropouts.[50] The minister of education estimated on August 25, 1998, that truancy rates for 1998–99 would increase to about 23 percent, and that most of the dropouts would be children of herders.[51] Western relief agencies, with the support of Ministry of Education officials, conceived of a plan of importing sheepdogs from New Zealand to replace the children who currently tend the animals, and ten dogs arrived in August 1997.[52] However, many more dogs will be required if the children are to be relieved of this task. State-mandated hikes in tuition and demands that herdsmen pay for the dormitories, food, and supplies for their children in boarding schools have contributed to the growing truancy rate, because some herders either cannot afford such costs or simply perceive scant value in education for their children.[53] In addition, adult herders' knowledge and education have been compromised by the virtual cessation of newspapers previously provided by the state.[54]

Several observers, including Namkhainyambuu, have had misgivings about the relative lack of state involvement in the pastoral economy. Although they reject the authoritarian, despotic model of pre-1990 Mongolia, they assert that the state has to play a greater role than it has done since 1990 if the vast majority of herders are to sustain their pastoral nomadic way of life and concurrently to have access to the veterinary, medical, educational, and cultural opportunities of the modern world.

They contend that the laissez-faire government envisioned by the pure market economists and the international donors cannot meet the needs of the herders. In his conversations with us, Namkhainyambuu repeatedly aligned himself with the democratic reformers in advocating state support for herders and provision for social welfare. He believed that the social welfare of the population ought not to be sacrificed to a drive for privatization. One anthropologist who studied the effects of privatization concluded that "the notion of pastoralists' independency is . . . but a romantization [sic] of Mongolian nomadism" and that "the present situation of a total 'rolling back of the state' exposes herders to conditions which will be unbearable in the long run."[55] A number of rangeland specialists have concluded that regulations by the state or by locally elected managers, perhaps the leaders of the *soums* or the heads of the four to seven *bags* that constitute a *soum,* are essential for sustainable management of Mongolian pastureland.[56]

Namkhainyambuu and many other herders had opposed the precipitous abandonment of the *negdels* partly because they believed that cooperatives were essential in the harsh conditions in Mongolia. They regretted that political pressures and attempts to please international financial organizations had prompted the government to promote privatization of herds at such a rapid pace. As Namkhainyambuu told me, "now in Mongolia there is no sense of caring for others so when a trader buys wool today, he thinks only of his own profit." He had cautioned against blindly following foreigners and accepting foreign models for Mongolia. Mongolia did not, according to him, need foreign teachers and counselors to advise on herding, for Mongolians had herded successfully for centuries. He had, in particular, been skeptical about foreign loans, claiming rightly or wrongly that much of the money had been siphoned off to the relatives of influential figures in the government or in business.[57]

The disastrous winters (known as *zuds*) of 1999, 2000, and 2001 revealed the perils of privatization. The herders found themselves having to cope with these devastating winters alone, without the support of cooperatives, and they lacked adequate sheds, wells, and sufficient fodder. The results were predictable. The *Guardian Weekly* reported in March 2000:

> Mongolia is on the brink of disaster with half a million people from herders'
> communities facing starvation. . . . Up to half the livestock in some areas

have died. . . . The sheep eat . . . stones in desperation. . . . Without horses to ride, pregnant women about to give birth have to walk miles to hospitals that lack essential equipment. . . . Schools have stayed shut because children cannot get to classes or because their families are trekking long distances in search of fresh pasture. . . . Welfare and health schemes run by the state have collapsed, and teachers are forced to raise their herds to supplement meager incomes. . . . *Experts have long warned that the crisis was waiting to happen, in a country where post-communist economic reforms worsened the position of Mongolia's already numerous poor.* [emphasis added][58]

The *Economist* asserted that "under collectivization, with fewer beasts, greater mobility, and the state delivery of supplementary feed, such a disaster would not have happened."[59] Many herders and rangeland experts, including Namkhainyambuu, believed that the impending disasters could have been predicted by the summer droughts that preceded the *zuds*.[60] Compounding the difficulties was the fact that only 6 percent of the herders had been able to afford insurance for their herds, a service earlier provided by the state.[61]

The livestock census declined from 33.5 million in 1999 to 30.2 million in 2000 and 23.5 million in 2002. Seventy percent of the herding households now owned fewer than one hundred animals—for most, not a sustainable number.[62] "Before we had a regular income," one herder complained. "Now we have to depend on the animals."[63] As one specialist wrote, "leaving the animal husbandry unregulated to the extent that only market forces impact herders' behavior is disastrous and counterproductive to any sustainable development of the country," and he noted that "a herder cannot dig a well alone."[64] Another specialist noted that "pastoralism has always depended upon a political authority to regulate pastures."[65]

The weak state that many of the international donor agencies and the Mongolian advocates of the pure market economy had demanded was unable to provide much relief for the areas and herders afflicted by the *zud*. Instead, it often relied on foreign philanthropic organizations and foreign countries to help herders who had lost many or, in some cases, all of their animals during the winters and early springs of 2000 to 2002. The Red Cross, the UNDP, World Vision, and foreign governments were solicited and did contribute. Private individuals, such as Mohammed al-Fayad, the owner of Harrods department store in London, offered money for the relief effort.[66] The government also called upon urban workers and bureaucrats to donate one or more days' pay to relief. Most revealing was the government's lack of resources to deal with the situation in a country prone to natural disasters. Reductions in taxes, the elimination of most tariffs, and the abandonment of many state industries restricted the government. As distressing was an article in a respected journal, *Mongolia This Week,* that asserted that some donors were reluctant to provide relief because of the pilferage and embezzlement in local relief agencies.[67]

Because of the severe winters of 1999–2001, the government and the international donor organizations have belatedly recognized that individual herders require assistance in Mongolia's harsh environment and have begun to support the establishment of cooperatives. However, such support for cooperatives has consisted of convening meetings, providing training for managers, some credit allocation through the Agricultural Bank (which, however, benefits mostly the well-off herders), insurance schemes (which many herders either cannot afford or cannot understand), and innovations in wind and solar power (which are too expensive for many herders, who have little cash to purchase spare parts and batteries, even if the equipment were donated). Much more effort and many more resources will be required to foster the development of such cooperatives.[68]

International donor organizations have devised piecemeal programs meant to assist herders. The World Bank has offered loans to build rural meteorological stations to provide weather forecasts for herders. It has also provided loans to dig wells, to encourage a Green Revolution, and to offer access to veterinarians in order to reduce rural poverty, but the interest rate of 2.8 percent per year will no doubt prevent the poorest herders from taking advantage of these.[69]

The government and the international donor agencies responded to this series of catastrophes with new solutions. Prime Minister Nambaryn Enkhbayar proposed the radical step of urbanizing 90 percent of the population and of establishing animal husbandry cooperatives for about 10 percent of the people, reducing the herding population from one-third to one-tenth. Under his plan, the mobility of the herders would be restricted; they would be settled near a new group of towns along an ambitious east-west Millennium Road construction project. In sum, herding would play a lesser role in the new economy, which is presumably to be based on high-tech enterprises. Foreign rangeland specialists, including Robin Mearns of the World Bank and Caroline Humphrey and David Sneath of Cambridge University, contradict the prime minister's view, asserting that mobility is essential to herding.[70] They contend that pastoralism could not readily survive in the mostly sedentary animal husbandry cooperatives that the prime minister advocates; movement to new pastures is essential. Moreover, they note that Enkhbayar did not carefully spell out what he means by this new economy. In addition, herding and agriculture constitute about 30 percent of GDP, not to mention their contribution to the manufacturing sector, and it is not clear how the new economy will compensate for this. Another proposal supported by some of the international donor agencies is to privatize pasture land. According to the same rangeland specialists cited above, the ensuing fencing of pasturelands would limit mobility, favor rich herders, who would be able to lay claim to the best lands, and result, as in the privatization of pasture in Inner Mongolia, in degradation of the land.[71] State authorities have asserted that they have not seriously considered privatization of pastureland. Some herders have thus continued their migrations without having to contend with private and perhaps fenced-in land.

Namkhainyambuu offered a different plan. He proposed more state involvement in the economy and disputed the view that democracy entails a limited role for government. The state, according to him, was needed (1) to provide and maintain roads and bridges to permit herders to reach their markets; (2) to prevent profiteers from raising the price of gasoline beyond the reach of herders; (3) to conduct research on plants, soils, and animals in order to promote productivity; (4) to supervise the constructions of wells and sheds and to make preparations for emergencies; and (5) to support herders when disasters strike in this fragile environment.

Namkhainyambuu remained optimistic, but in 1999, at the age of 51, he had contracted renal disease, and the devastating winters from 1999 to 2001 coincided with his own debilitating physical affliction. In 1992, he, his wife, and nine children had moved from the countryside in Zavkhan *aimag* to an area close to Ulaanbaatar because he had been elected to the Khural. When he left the Khural, he decided to remain near the capital because of the decline of the school system and of the herding economy in his native *aimag*. Based in an almost barren settlement about fifteen miles outside of Ulaanbaatar and possessing few animals, he was bedridden as of June 2002. His children were either in school or working in Ulaanbaatar; to his chagrin, none planned a career in herding. The breakdown of the health system meant that hospital facilities were inadequate for his care. Recognizing the failures of the system, government officials sent him briefly to South Korea for treatment. After he returned to Mongolia, he apparently needed dialysis, but he did not wish to burden his family with the expense of such treatment. In September 2003, this truly selfless and patriotic figure died at the age of fifty-five, depriving the democratic reformers of still another major advocate of their policies in opposition to the champions of the pure market economy.[72]

Many herders whose animals died in the *zuds* joined Namkhainyambuu in Ulaanbaatar and the surrounding countryside. As with Namkhainyambuu's children, it appears unlikely that they or their children will return to herding. They are now part of the increasing number of unemployed and poor barely scratching out a living around the capital. The questions are: Could this disaster have been avoided by a less pressured and pell-mell attempt to move toward privatization and a market economy? Could the Mongolian advocates of a market economy and their advisors in the international donor agencies have adopted different policies that would have better fostered the herding economy?

Preliminary figures for 2003 indicate an increase in the herds to 25.3 million. However, goats account for about 95 percent of the increase, a cause for alarm because of the damage caused to the grasslands by that animal. Moreover, such a sizable increase makes herders even more dependent on the volatile international market for cashmere.[73]

THE PURE MARKET AND THE SOCIAL SECTOR

From 1990 on, the repeated calls by international donor agencies and Mongolian advocates of the pure market such as Ganbold and Amarjargal for austerity and cutbacks in government spending had dramatic effects on social policy. Suspicion and denigration of the state impinged upon its ability to undertake its social welfare responsibilities.[1] The advocates of the pure market placed their faith in privatization of many social services, including education and health. They asserted that the state ought not to increase spending on social welfare without a guarantee of additional revenues. Yet they generally advocated reductions in taxes and privatization of most state assets. Under these circumstances, it was unclear how the state could secure the resources required to meet the social needs of the population.

The foreign advisors and the Mongolian supporters of the pure market suggested that economic growth and job creation would reduce the number of social welfare problems. Private enterprises, not the government, ought to be the source for new jobs because they were more effective producers of wealth. The state, which would have fewer assets and revenues than during the communist era, could not maintain the pre-1990 levels of support to the vulnerable.

The victory of the Democratic Union in the Khural elections of 1996 permitted the ruling coalition to implement its vision of economic growth and employment creation as panaceas for social welfare. At news of their success, "there was jubilation—especially in the camp of the foreign diplomats and advisors in Ulaanbaatar who had done so much to craft the outlook of the country's young new rulers."[2] The new government and the foreign groups who had helped it come to power asserted that Mongolia, with its small population of about 2.5 million, required no more than a handful of successful economic activities. They were confident that Mongolia's natural resources, especially its copper, cashmere, and vast herds of livestock, together with a revival of some efficient industries, could foster a productive economy that would eventually translate into improvements in social welfare.[3]

The Mongolian democratic reformers, including Erdenebileg and Oyun, and several Western agencies and individuals warned of the impact of shock therapy and of dependence on economic growth and job creation for the social welfare of the population. Frederick Nixson, the Manchester University professor of economics who served early in the 1990s as an economic advisor to the World Bank, cautioned that "there is no guarantee that the market alone can solve problems of poverty, inequality, and unemployment."[4]

The withdrawal of Soviet assistance in 1990–91 was a serious blow to the Mongolian economy and the first step in the downward spiral that generated a sizable pauper population. Lack of Soviet subsidies and the rapid erosion of the Russian market for Mongolian products were important setbacks, compelling the government to ration rice, sugar, tea, flour, and soap, among other commodities. The international donors' demand for privatization of large state enterprises and for the elimination of state subsidies dealt a second blow to the economy, as many of the newly privatized businesses fired workers and managers, while some government operations simply closed down. The repeated calls by the champions of the pure market for a smaller government led to the dismissal of civil servants.[5] Neither the Mongolian government nor the international agencies sponsoring these dramatic steps had prepared for the human costs of these reversals in the economy.

Unemployment rose markedly, although until July 2000, the government disingenuously issued statistics based on the minority of the jobless who registered with state agencies. Those who sought to enter the labor force for the first time could not register for unemployment benefits; only those with previous employment could do so. Thus the bulk of the unemployed could not register. Moreover, because the benefits were meager, some who were eligible did not take the time to register and apply. The more realistic MPRP government that took power in 2000 acknowledged that the figures for unemployment were much higher than previously acknowledged. The minister of finance and economics, Chultemiin Ulaan, said that the real number was 220,000, not the 40,000 or so registered as unemployed.[6]

Given that the majority of the Mongolians are under the age of twenty-five, and 75 percent are under thirty-five, economic growth is needed to create jobs. The International Labor Organization estimated in 1997 that a growth in GDP of 6 percent, or possibly 7 percent, was needed to absorb new entrants into the labor force.[7] The new government in 2000 also asserted that the country had to create 48,000 jobs annually to accommodate the 30,000 new workers, as well as to reduce current unemployment.[8] Such an increase in economic growth required investment. However, the insistance on minimal government by most international donors and Mongolian champions of the pure market meant that the state no longer had the resources for investment in job creation in the public sector. Moreover, as noted earlier, indigenous sources of investment have been limited, partly owing to the inadequacies of the banking system and Stock Exchange, and foreign investment was insufficient to compensate for the limited domestic sources.

Disparities in income, partly the result of the privatization process, contributed to the dissatisfaction of some of the unemployed. A few Mongolians emerged with big gains, but most suffered in the new market economy, and the income gap between rich and poor widened.[9] "During the period 1995–2002, the Gini coefficient of inequality increased from 0.31. to 0.37," Oyun lamented.[10] To be sure, the market economy resulted in the greater availability of goods. By 2002, markets displayed kiwis from New Zealand, apples from the United States, pickles from Vietnam, and bottled water from Indonesia and China, but such goods were too expensive for most Mongolians—for example, a kilogram of oranges from the State Department Store or the Merkuri market (one of the better-stocked markets) in Ulaanbaatar cost the equivalent of 5 percent of an average worker's monthly wages.

Only in 1994, three years into the transition, did the Mongolian government and the international donor agencies develop a program to assist the approximately 26.8 percent of the population who had fallen into poverty. Funded principally by the World Bank and the UNDP, this Poverty Alleviation Program sought to reduce those living below the poverty line to 10 percent of the population by the year 2000. "A UNDP spokesman . . . expressed confidence that poverty in Mongolia could be drastically reduced within five years," the Economist Intelligence Unit reported in 1994.[11] As with so many predictions of the international agencies, however, this was overoptimistic. The $10 million allocated for the program included $2.5 million for employment in public works and infrastructure, loans of $3.2 million for growing vegetables, and $2 million each for health and education. The total was a small percentage of foreign aid and barely scratched the surface of the serious problem of poverty. The program's staff consisted of ten people in Ulaanbaatar, thirty-one others in the *aimags*, and a small group of volunteers. The program emphasized job creation and public works programs. Market stratagems, such as providing microcredit to some of the poor and temporary jobs, were the core of the program. The principal strategy underlying the program was that the "private sector . . . step up its development," and an architect of the policy noted that "the government is trying to support businesses as best it can so that they can share the burden of social care." In 1994 and even more so after the Democratic Union victory in 1996, the government, spurred by foreign advisors and by Ganbold and its own pure market supporters, sought increasingly to rely on private businesses and the newly developing NGOs for resolution of social problems. It perceived welfare and support for the poor other than through employment as philanthropy rather than as its obligation and apparently did not conceive of a basic standard of living as an economic right guaranteed by the state. Typical of this philosophy are the assertions that "provisions such as clothing, food, and money for the poor are only gestures of charity" and "distributing gifts to the poor . . . is not considered effective as it makes them more consumption oriented." Such puritanical attitudes are also reflected in the government's efforts to "get rid of the 'feed me' attitude" and to stop the reputed payment of pensions without work. According to an advocate of this approach, the government intended to use "the bulk of foreign aid for [the] electricity, energy, fuel, transportation, and communication sectors . . . and the development of infrastructure." The trickle-down approach posited that jobs would be created in this way and the incidence of poverty reduced.[12]

Despite being relegated to a secondary position, the Poverty Alleviation Program did require measurement of the extent of poverty in Mongolia. In 1995, the State Statistical Office cooperated with the World Bank to conduct a Living Standard Measurement Survey to evaluate the level of poverty. Based on a so-called consumer basket of food, clothing and footwear, housing, fuel, and electricity, household items, medical care, cultural expenses, and miscellaneous items, the survey found that 36.3 percent of the population lived below the poverty line.

Although the Poverty Alleviation Program produced statistics on poverty, its policies, judged by its own standard of reducing the percentage of the poor from about 26 percent to 10 percent by the year 2000, failed. Many Mongolians had criticized the program. As early as 1996, a World Bank session that Prime Minister M. Enkhsaikhan attended "criticised the implementation of the Poverty Alleviation Programme . . . and recommended [the introduction of] more public scrutiny over the funds spending."[13]

Dr. Bernard Walters, a colleague of Frederick Nixson's at the University of Manchester, suggested that the growth emphasized by international donors would not necessarily address the problems of the poor. He argued that increased production did not guarantee a reduction in poverty and that a general poverty program that relied on market forces would not succeed. Believing that Mongolia's economic development program ought to be infused with consideration of the poor, he asserted that "poverty reduction has to be part of the development plan." Indeed, he contended, the economic policies of the government ought to tilt toward the poor. Given their vulnerability and lack of political power, they needed a protector, a role the government should assume. Keith Griffin, another student of poverty in Mongolia, insisted that poor countries ought to focus not merely on poverty but also on the increasing inequality of income distribution. Such inequality not only reduced the resources available to combat poverty but also compelled the state to impose regressive taxes (e.g., VAT) and user fees, which harmed the poor and vulnerable, to raise sufficient revenues.[14]

Several prominent foreigners and Mongolians were critical of the emphasis on job creation and lack of sufficient provision of immediate social welfare. On a visit to Mongolia, Carol Bellamy, the director of UNICEF, said: "It is important to concentrate on social problems in order to create economic stability." In an interview in April 1999, Oyun claimed that the focus on economic policy had not worked and had diverted attention from poverty and declines in social welfare.[15] "I am very doubtful that the considerable amount of foreign aid and credits coming to the Poverty Alleviation Program reaches the target group," S. Batbayar, a member of the Khural, told a newspaper in March 1998. "Mongolia has meetings and conferences on the subject of poverty alleviation all the time, the heads of Mongolian agencies take trips to foreign countries," an ordinary citizen said. "Little of it has any impact on women's lives."[16]

One group of statistics illustrates the problems the poor faced simply in obtaining food. In Ulaanbaatar, the tugrik equivalent of a U.S. dollar bought 3.3 kilograms of beef, 2.6 of mutton, 10 of flour, 16 loaves of bread, 10 liters of milk, or 5 kilograms of sugar in 1991. The equivalent amount of money bought 1.07 kilograms of beef, 1.2 of mutton, 1.9 of flour, 3.5 loaves of bread, 2 liters of milk, or 1.4 kilograms of sugar in 1998. The resulting decline in food consumption has been noticeable, because high prices and declines in vegetable and grain production have translated into lower calorie intake per capita.[17] In 1998, the Food and Agriculture Organization of the United Nations (FAO) reported that Mongolia faced food deficits. As late as 2002, there were widespread shortages of food and fuel in the countryside.[18]

It is therefore not surprising that by 2000, the Poverty Alleviation Program had not fulfilled the goals set forth, and the program could be considered a failure, despite much cosmetic publicity. Instead of bringing the number of those living below the poverty line down to 10 percent, the figure remained at more than one-third of the population. Microcredit loans produced a few jobs in the rural areas, but even the Democratic Union prime minister was forced to acknowledge that "not all of the funds allocated have been used properly and that one-third of the population is estimated to be still living below the poverty line."[19] Corruption consumed at least a portion of the funds; how much of the money was misused is difficult to gauge.

A second survey, sponsored by the World Bank and the UNDP in 1998, concluded that 35.6 percent of the Mongol population lived below the poverty line. Although the standards for assessing poverty differed somewhat from the 1995 study, the crux of the findings, which appeared to be unchallengeable, was that at least one-third of the population was poor.[20] The 1994 donor predictions concerning the Poverty Alleviation Program and the reduction of poverty were wide of the mark. The government, acknowledging that poverty had scarcely been reduced, reverted to the explanation that the limited economic growth had led to reduced job creation and thus to less progress in poverty alleviation. What it failed to acknowledge was (1) that the international donors' and the government's emphasis on privatization of state assets, reduction of taxes, and minimal government had left the state with few resources and limited tax revenues to tackle the problem of poverty and to provide a public works program; (2) that tax evasion (partly a product of the haste with which privatization had been carried out) and the continual pressure for tax reduction (a policy promoted by many champions of the pure market) precluded much state assistance for social welfare; and (3) that the growing disparity in income, a result in part of privatization and a weak state unable to protect the weak, contributed to poverty; and (4) that corruption and mismanagement in doling out of money impeded the program.[21]

Additional research confirmed the findings of the UNDP–World Bank field study and concluded that the poor spent about 74 percent of their income on food, leaving them with precious little for other necessities. Another report in early 1999 found that 60 percent of the 200,000 elderly lived below the poverty line.[22] The number of single-parent households, an important indicator of poverty, continued to grow from 1994 to 2003.[23] In addition, many in the *ger* households ringing the city of Ulaanbaatar had their electricity temporarily cut off because they could not afford the higher, "liberalized" prices imposed by the Democratic Union government in September 1996.[24]

The most withering critiques of the Poverty Alleviation Program were leveled at the government's underlying philosophy. Adopting the attitudes of many foreign advisors, Enkhsaikhan, Ganbold, and the Democratic Union government claimed that they did not want to make the poor dependent on handouts from the government and thus wished to pursue a policy of job training, microcredit, and employment to alleviate poverty. However, Bernard Walters of Manchester University noted that microcredit, even at a low rate of interest, was too expensive for the poor and entailed too many conditions. Moreover, before ensuring that jobs would be available, the government had pursued policies that led to the closing of many state economic enterprises and to much unemployment. "Investment which should [have been] made in health, education, and infrastructure was drastically reduced, social development indexes fell, and services failed," one critic noted. Confronted with such limited aid from the government, the poor often depended upon their families or relatives for assistance. Herders helped poor urban cousins with meat and animal products, while urbanites offered shelter to poor rural relatives who had been compelled to abandon herding. Perhaps reflecting a cultural trait, few of the poor actually complained about these conditions.[25]

After the second survey of poverty, in 1998, demonstrated that the Poverty Alleviation Program had accomplished little, international donor agencies began to pay attention, at least in their rhetoric, to the poor. The Asian Development Bank pledged to focus on poverty reduction and to emphasize discreet projects rather than the large infrastructure construction that did not yield tangible benefits to the poor. In October 2000, the IMF and World Bank organized a three-day seminar in Ulaanbaatar on poverty reduction.[26] The proposals that emerged from the seminar—a large road construction project to provide employment, supplying tools for vegetable gardening, and microcredit—appeared to be rehashes of previous policy and failed to consider immediate needs for social welfare, but the criticisms of previous policies and the attendant negative publicity compelled the international donors to focus not only on inflation, banks, and macroeconomic policy but also on the needs of the poor. Yet even with the depth of poverty and income inequality increasing, the 2003 donors' meeting in Tokyo continued to "stress the role of the private sector in poverty alleviation" and urged a "cap on public expenditures and promotion of the private sector" as the principal policies to reduce poverty.[27] A $17 million IMF poverty program initiated in the same year emphasized the same themes—changes in macroeconomic policies, restraints on public expenditures, and limits on wage and pension increases, particularly for civil servants. Critics asserted that it was difficult to understand how restraints on wages and pensions would reduce poverty.[28]

Some international donor agencies attempted to dispute the evidence about the incidence of poverty, but the reports from anthropologists who were actually out in the countryside challenged their views. Ole Bruun, a

Danish anthropologist who spent three months in a rural area in 1998 and another two months in 1999, was typical, declaring: "It is economic circumstance and government neglect through the 1990s that have driven Mongolian herders into a form of subsistence herding. . . . Today the town center leaves the impression of being ravaged by war or natural disaster . . . people speak of a time when there was secure employment and concern for everyone." The local school and the health clinic had closed, the power supply was irregular, and the terms of trade were poor. Bruun added that "medication for humans has become a heavy burden," and that there were no vegetables, candles, or batteries.[29] In 2003, the Ministry of Social Welfare and Labor itself acknowledged that 66 percent of the population in Zavkhan, a major province, could be classified as "very poor" or "poor."[30] In the same year, 70 percent of the reindeer herders in the province of Khövsgöl were classified as "very poor" or "poor" because of the reductions in state support (which translated into poor access to medical services and education) and the inbreeding of the herds.

POVERTY IN ULAANBAATAR

Poverty in the 1990s was observable in both rural and urban Mongolia, particularly in the unforgiving Gobi desert *aimags*, but other social problems may more readily be perceived in Ulaanbaatar and one or two other big cities. The Mongolians are dispersed over a large territory, and patterns may be more difficult to identify in areas of low population density than in Ulaanbaatar, now home to about 40 percent of the country's people. Although the difficulties in the rural areas may be as serious, if not more so, than those in Ulaanbaatar, the larger concentrations of people in the capital highlight the problems.[31]

Some problems in Ulaanbaatar derive from the increase in population from the mid 1990s through the present. From 1990 to 2000, the number of residents grew from about 555,000 to approximately 762,000, a 37 percent increase; 70,000 people migrated to Ulaanbaatar from the countryside and smaller towns.[32] As unemployment spread in the provincial centers, some Mongolians moved to the capital to seek work, most likely in the informal sector.[33] The disastrous winters from 1999 to 2002, which left many herders with few if any animals, accelerated migration into the capital.[34] A perception that rural schools and teachers were poor may also have influenced some in the countryside to move to Ulaanbaatar or other centers either permanently or for the school year.[35] The resulting growth in population imposed tremendous strains on the capital and on the government, which was squeezed by inadequate tax revenues.[36] Because the state did not have the resources to provide housing, and private construction companies could not afford the high interest rates charged by banks, many newcomers lived in the *ger* (or tent) districts (now home to more than 60 percent of the population) on the fringes of the city. Water had to be delivered to them in trucks, as most had no running water. The demands on water supply have increased so dramatically that the city's water table has declined precipitously over the past decade. A 1994 government study found that the wells in the *ger* areas contained an excessively high level of nitrates and that "levels of total dissolved solids, chrome, manganese, iron, copper, and *e. coli* exceeded standards in one or more wells" of each four tested.[37] Sanitation facilities in these instant communities were often inadequate, with few bathhouses and no drainage systems.[38] The *gers* had no central heat, and these areas had no street lights. Yet the inhabitants of the *gers* had a roof over their heads. Some of the unemployed were homeless and lived in the underground passages housing the city's hot water and heating pipes.[39]

Russia and China have recently committed themselves to assisting in the construction of new apartment houses, but the projected number of such buildings—360 units in the case of Russia and 1,000 in the case of China—is insufficient to meet the need for housing. Moreover, the projected cost of these apartments is prohibitive save for the tiny elite class.[40] There is indeed a housing construction boom in the city, but it consists principally of luxury housing for the nouveaux riches. Thus young adults, even those with families, often live with their parents, and apartments are continually being broken up into smaller units. Many of the apartment buildings require renovation. Hallways are dimly lit (the poor often steal the light bulbs) and often in need of painting, and the stairwells, where the homeless and street children sometimes sleep and live, are littered with used condoms, feces, beer cans, animal bones, and cigarette butts.

The UNDP and other relief organizations have promoted a cheap alternative to more elaborate and solid housing. They have encouraged the construction of straw-bale houses and public buildings, such as medical clinics. Touting them as inexpensive and energy-efficient, the UNDP and the Adventist Development and Relief Agency have built about thirty such houses, basically to demonstrate their feasibility. However, this demonstration project cannot substitute for large-scale government housing to accommodate the in-migration of the increasingly large numbers of herders who lost most of their animals in the winters of 1999 to 2002.[41]

Vast numbers of people in Ulaanbaatar, with scant government expenditures on facilities, have translated into high levels of air pollution. Stoves burning coal and wood in the *ger* districts, which include a minimum of 60,000 households, generate levels of carbon dioxide that can reach seven times higher than in the city center and can occasionally create sufficient smog to impede operations at the airport. Power plants use an estimated five million tons of coal annually, contributing to poor air quality.[42] Antiquated public buses and seventy thousand cars and vans belonging to foreigners and to the nouveaux riches, most of which are old models, emit vast quantities of noxious fumes. The resulting air pollution, particularly in winter, is four to five times above permissibly safe levels, not to mention the increasing number of traffic jams in a city not designed for an influx of automotive vehicles.[43] No wonder that an Australian advisor to WHO described the air in Ulaanbaatar as a danger to public health. With scant resources, the Ministry of Nature and the Environment has been unable to enforce emission levels in vehicles, power plants, industries, and stoves. The planting of trees, the creation of microgardens, and other minor palliatives are welcome but are insufficient solutions. Similarly, a so-called Green Revolution, with an emphasis on backyard vegetable gardens, has proved of little help.[44]

The combination of virtually uncontrolled in-migration and lack of state revenues, which the advocates of the pure market had in part contributed to by their emphasis on minimal government, resulted in problems in dealing with sanitation and clean streets. One statistic that attests to the insufficiency is that in 1980, 96 percent of all waste water was purified, but by 1995, the figure had fallen to 65.5 percent, and by 1999, to 50 percent, creating a potential public health hazard. In addition, the city, according to one estimate, required three hundred trucks to remove garbage, but as of 2001, it had only ninety.[45] The government imposed trash removal taxes on the *ger* districts that the inhabitants could not easily pay, and the lack of payment resulted in occasional suspension of such services and encouraged inhabitants simply to dump their garbage illegally; the children in the *ger* districts, lacking playgrounds, could be seen playing in the huge mounds of trash; the shortage of public toilets led to urination and defecation in public spaces; and public education campaigns seeking to change the attitudes of recently arrived immigrants from the countryside toward sanitation and clean streets had limited funds.[46] A German company and the Japanese government have expressed interest in promoting recycling as a means of dealing with the garbage problem, another indication of the Mongolian government's lack of revenue to undertake basic services.[47]

Still further evidence of the decline of government regulation is the construction of dachas in the suburbs. A few of the nouveaux riches have initiated an uncontrolled boom in the building of country homes, evading government licensing regulations. Such unregulated construction has potentially devastating environmental consequences. Pollution of pristine water and degradation of pastureland have been attributed to this indiscriminate building.[48] Building by the nouveaux riches and by refugees from the countryside in a nearby suburb threatened the city's drinking water.[49] As one of the leading English-language newspapers in Ulaanbaatar asked, "Will Ulaanbaatar's residents continue to drink polluted water or will the beautiful houses raised in Gachuurt [from which 60 percent of the city's drinking water is drawn] village be demolished?"[50]

As already noted, kiosks, which champions of the pure market touted as examples of the entrepreneurial spirit, constitute an additional hazard.[51] The government did not have the resources required to send health and safety inspectors to the large number of kiosks that had proliferated in the 1990s. It also could not keep health and safety tabs on the 245 restaurants (with faux Japanese, German, and Italian food), 66 cafes, 500 or so bars, 1,200 dining and tea rooms, and 580 nightclubs that had sprouted to cater to the foreign community and to Ulaanbaatar's nouveaux riches.[52] One local wag asserted that Mongolia had more "tigers" (the Mongolian word for "tiger" is *bar*) than Korea, Taiwan, or the other so-called "tiger" economies.

In contrast to the conspicuous consumption in these dining and drinking establishments for the foreigners and the local elite, most people have endured food shortages since 1990. Bangladesh, Cambodia, North Korea, and Mongolia were the four countries in Asia that faced the most severe threats of hunger, the director of the World Food Program said in 2000.[53] The terrible winters from 1999 to 2002 raised the price of meat, a staple of the Mongolian diet, and no doubt exacerbated the problem of hunger, but there had been food shortages prior to these three bad years.

The decline of agriculture in the 1990s and early 2000s has contributed to the dilemma of food security in Ulaanbaatar. Since the early 1990s, Mongolia has had to import many of the staples it previously produced. With no state farms, few greenhouses, and a harsh environment, the country has been unable to raise sufficient food. Shortages of good quality seeds and lack of machinery, fuel, and credit plagued farmers who were forced to rely on foreign governments and charitable organizations to secure such necessities. They could not depend totally on their own governments. The predictable result was that land acreage continued to shrink and that the inhabitants of Ulaanbaatar became dependent on imports of food.[54]

EMPLOYMENT AND PENSIONS

The state did not have the resources to police workplaces, and as a result, according to a government survey of employees and unions, "the labor protection level has drastically deteriorated," with a rising incidence of deaths and injuries in mining, light industry, energy, food-processing, and road construction. Another report noted that numerous workplaces did not abide by health and safety standards; poor lighting, deafening noise, handling of hazardous chemicals, and exposure to radiation and dust characterized many work environments. The Mongolian Federation of Trade Unions repeatedly complained about work conditions, particularly in foreign-owned enterprises. The U.S. government confirmed some abuses when it refused admittance to apparel produced in Mongolia in a Taiwanese-owned factory because it employed child labor.[55] Beyond actual abuses, many workers in the newly privatized enterprises feared, sometimes rightly, that the kindergartens, canteens, and other services previously provided in state enterprises would now be eliminated. Private entrepreneurs, seeking to curb costs, would be tempted to dispense with these social welfare amenities. Trade unions have objected to policies that have resulted in unemployment and unsafe conditions in workplaces and have even organized demonstrations in protest. However, the unions are weak and have received support neither from the state nor from international donors.[56]

The benefits accruing to retired employees or workers have also been jeopardized. Pensions, based upon a pay-as-you-go system during the communist era, were entitlements and were granted not only to workers but also to herders. The government made special provisions for particular groups. Workers in hazardous occupations (e.g., coal miners) and women with more than four children could retire early. The pensions were adequate but not lavish.

After the collapse of communism, several of the international donor agencies, which sought a smaller government and less public expenditures, wanted to limit the costs of pensions and to limit what they referred to as privileged pensions. Although an American consultant for USAID acknowledged "the absence of a crisis in the pension program," because it represented only 5 percent of GDP, he proposed a gradual shift from state-guaranteed pensions to individual accounts.

His and USAID's principal objectives appeared to be to endorse the view that pensions were not an entitlement and to ensure that pensions be self-financed. Under this plan, an individual would be responsible for his or her own pension. To use the consultant's language, he wanted gradually to shift from a "defined benefit" to a "defined contribution" plan, which limited pensions to the amount actually provided by the worker and his or her employer. He recommended ultimate privatization of the pension system, although he acknowledged that Mongolia was "not yet ready to privatize . . . its public pension plan." Fund managers would take charge of pension funds and would, in some cases, "allow pension funds to invest [in capital markets] in other countries." He also suggested that "some of the employer portion [of contributions to the workers' pensions] ought, over time, to be shifted to the employee," adding that this policy should be "effected in such a way that gross wages are increased proportionately." What he failed to explain was how the government would ensure that gross wages would be increased to compensate for the extra payments workers needed to make into their pension plans. Moreover, he assumed that all workers would be sufficiently knowledgeable to weigh the various financial options offered by pension funds and the serious risks in investment in capital markets. The fate of these workers in retirement would depend on proper investment of the contributions, and there would be no guaranteed income as in a defined benefit plan in which the government guaranteed a specific pension for the worker. To summarize, this consultant proposed a system to, in his own words, "directly link benefits to contributions, mitigate risk to the state, encourage individuals to take responsibility for themselves, improve payroll tax payment compliance, and facilitate an eventual transition to a funded system and privatization." He did not mention two other objectives—to reduce government expenditures and to move toward elimination of yet another of the Mongolian government's welfare obligations to the people, as mandated by the 1992 Constitution. He did mention, however, that some government assistance be provided for a specified minimum pension "to keep pensioners out of poverty."[57]

This USAID consultant to Mongolia proposed an emphasis on individual accounts, reliance on private financial managers, elimination of special arrangements for workers in hazardous occupations, and reduction of risks for the state, all of which are controversial policies in the United States itself. Many Americans contest such changes for their own Social Security system. Why then did USAID and its contractors propose only such schemes to the Mongolian government when many Americans appear to oppose them for their own pension system? It appears that this is another example of experimentation with a pure market economy policy and agenda by the donor agencies in Mongolia.[58]

In any event, the criticism of the pension system, as well as the Mongolian state's increasingly limited resources, generated service disruptions. As a result of inexpert tinkering with pensions in an effort to compensate for inflation, for a time pensioners who reached retirement age after 1995 received larger pensions than those retiring before 1995. However, the deliberate effort by the Democratic Union, which took power in 1996, and its Western advisors to remove recipients from the pension rolls was more important. Exact statistics on the numbers removed are difficult to verify, but a fairly reliable source gives a figure of 103,000. In addition, retirees repeatedly complained about substantial delays in the payment of pensions.[59] Even President Bagabandi vented his anger at such delays. Similarly, although inflation plagued the economy in the early and mid 1990s, and thus impinged upon retirees with fixed incomes, the government barely increased pension payments to keep pace with the rise in prices. When it took power, the MPRP raised pension payments slightly but not as much as it had promised during the elections of 2000.[60]

With new elections coming up in June 2004, the government suddenly determined to increase pensions and minimum wages in what seemed an obvious ploy to sway the electorate. Late in 2003, it sought to raise the minimum pensions from TG 20,000 to TG 30,000 (i.e., from about $18 to about $26) a month and to increase the salaries of doctors, teachers, and civil servants by about 20 percent. Even so, a government official reported that a "final decision [on such increases] will depend on the outcome of the donors' forum to be held in the middle of November in Tokyo."[61] Once again, the international donors would have a decisive role on a domestic policy issue. They apparently approved of some increases. Nonetheless, pensions would still hover around the poverty level, particularly in the urban areas.[62] In another election-year announcement, the government stated that it would provide free immunizations, treatment for some adolescents, AIDS prevention, and medical treatment for infants.[63] How extensive this program would be remained unclear. Would it, moreover, be curtailed after the elections of June 2004?

Unemployment, inadequate pensions, and a low standard of living translated into serious social dislocations. The rise in such social problems cannot be solely attributed to unemployment and poverty, but they were certainly factors. Antisocial behavior existed in the communist period, but it escalated in the 1990s.[64] Alcoholism reached almost epidemic proportions. According to one survey, 52 percent of Mongolian males were heavy drinkers, and the police annually picked up and transported 100,000 inebriated individuals to sobering-up or drying out stations.[65] It was no accident that cases of domestic abuse increased, leading in 1995 to the founding of a Centre against Violence, supported by an aid organization from Australia, which conducted research on domestic abuse, provided counseling for battered women, issued publications alerting women to their rights, established a safe house for battered wives, and lobbied for a domestic violence law.[66] Unemployment and poverty also resulted in increases in the crime rate. The total number of offenses rose from 9,060 in 1990 to 24,653 in 1997, and it fell only slightly, to 23,370, in 2001.[67] Cases of attempted murder and manslaughter tripled, and the number of thefts quadrupled, rising to about 40 percent of all criminal offenses.

Mongolians detained or actually convicted of criminal offenses were treated harshly, partly because the rising crime rate and the attendant arrests overwhelmed existing facilities. Several reports have documented the abuses inflicted on the accused during detention and pre-trial periods. According to an Amnesty International study, most prisons were notoriously overcrowded and had poor food, sanitation, and hygiene facilities, thus becoming breeding grounds for virulent strains of tuberculosis and other diseases. AI researchers considered the high rate of prison deaths to be the result of abominable conditions. Research for AI's report was concluded in 1994, but conditions have scarcely changed since then, in large part because the state does not have the resources to improve the situation.[68]

A DIFFERENT STRATEGY FOR POVERTY REDUCTION

A team of economic consultants for UNDP, under the leadership of Keith Griffin, formerly professor of economics at Oxford University, visited Mongolia in June and July of 2001 and advocated policies for reduction of poverty that differed from the pure market approach. They proposed that poverty alleviation be part of Mongolia's development strategy rather than merely the province of a single poverty program or a single government ministry.[69] They asserted that "after a decade of sacrifice, the economic reforms had failed to produce the promised improvement in the standard of living."[70] They suggested that the state needed to play an active role, and that the "state and the market are complementary," opposing the U.S. ambassador's view that "only a growing private sector can expand prosperity and reduce poverty."[71]

The team emphasized that a stronger state was required to tackle poverty. They included in their definition of poverty not only insufficient food but also illiteracy and inadequate health care, shelter, and clothing. They stated that policies implemented during the so-called transition had given rise to some of the problems of the poor. For example, the hurried privatization had harmed most herders, who received fewer animals, had lost marketing and veterinary facilities, and fought among themselves over land and water usage. Griffin and his colleagues recommended the reinstatement of cooperatives to restore these vital government services.

According to the UNDP economists, the government needed to intervene to reduce the rate of poverty by implementing investment strategies favoring the poor, fostering income equality, investing in public works to emphasize infrastructure, and supporting agriculture and industry. All of these programs would create employment. The informal sector, which accommodated some of the unemployed, created little new wealth. Investment in communications, transportation, housing, and extension of the public water and electricity supply systems would be more valuable, and the government ought to provide a true social safety net for the unemployed or those unable to work. Citing the experiences of other underdeveloped countries, Griffin and his UNDP team proposed reinstating tariffs on some imported products to help finance such projects. Similarly, they supported an import tax on luxury goods, such as cars, because they believed that foreign aid funds were diverted for such private purposes.

The team also diverged from the advocates of a pure market economy in affirming the need for controls on foreign aid and investment as a means of dealing with poverty. First, they declared that "the choice of direction for the country should be determined by the government, not by external donors."[72] From 1995 to 2000, the international donors had allocated what the team referred to as a measly 1.2 percent of all foreign aid to the Poverty Alleviation Program. Much more of this aid ought to have been provided for the government investment projects that could have reduced poverty. Mongolia had become the fifth most indebted nation in the world. Yet this high level of foreign aid, including loans that have to be repaid, had resulted in insufficient economic growth from 1990 to 2001. Similarly, although foreign investment had created some employment, it had been limited and relatively unregulated and had not substantially increased manufacturing or contributed to eradicating poverty. Indeed, Mongolia's balance of trade had become increasingly unfavorable. Without an import tax on luxuries and consumer items and some regulation of short-term capital, such an unfavorable balance would persist, reducing domestic savings, increasing debt, and siphoning off some foreign aid to cover consumption.

The UNDP team repeatedly emphasized the need for domestic savings and investment to create employment for the poor. They favored, in particular, immediate government investment in public works and promotion of human capital (education, health, etc.) and argued that unrestricted foreign aid (on projects that were often donor-driven) and investment had depressed domestic savings and investment.

In sum, they advocated a policy of growth favoring the poor that diverged from the advice of the international donor agencies. A UNDP report echoed their views, noting that "the Government's approach to securing macroeconomic balance is too strict and is potentially prolonging poverty and inequality. The pressure on the authorities to rigidly contain the fiscal deficit and pursue a tight monetary policy [is] stifling growth and employment . . . interpreting the budget deficit as evidence of fiscal mismanagement is forcing the state to further reduce core public expenditures [and] the cuts in social sector expenditures . . . also run the risk of further impoverishing people."[73] Griffin and his associates proposed greater state investment in rural infrastructure (e.g., wells, bridges) and support for cooperatives to boost productivity in animal husbandry, as well as investment in urban employment, housing, and infrastructure to counter unemployment and poverty. They concurred with the UNDP view that "there must be meaningful public participation"[74] rather than decision-making being done entirely by the state and the international donor agencies.[75]

Other critics have suggested that these economic deviations from the official Poverty Alleviation Program alone will not be sufficient for eradication of poverty. They have pointed out that many families and individuals, as much as 40 percent of the population, have lived below the poverty line for at least fourteen years. Numerous Mongolians have reached their teenage years or young adulthood mired in the culture of poverty. Poverty reduction programs that fail to address this culture of poverty may not succeed. Employment growth is essential, but compensatory education and other services will be required to help the poor develop the attitudes, skills, and values (e.g., arrival at work on time) they have not learned. These young people will need considerable support if and when they enter the labor force.

WOMEN AND THE MARKET ECONOMY

Cessation or reduction of many social services have especially affected women. In the earliest Mongolian history, women played such important economic roles in the pastoral households that they had more opportunities and rights than females in other East Asian societies.[76] However, by the early twentieth century, the status of women had eroded.[77]

Women, in general, profited from the communist era in Mongolia: a 1925 law abolished arranged marriages, and the government enacted other laws that guaranteed gender equality at work, in education, and in politics. By 1989, although equality in pay and benefits proved elusive, 86 percent of Mongolian women had joined the workforce, and 70 percent of doctors and teachers, about 64 percent of those in trade, and 67 percent of those in banking, finance, and insurance were women.[78] In addition, the state guaranteed employment to young women who graduated from secondary and vocational schools, and there was little unemployment. However, neither highly educated women nor ordinary female laborers reached the top levels or the most important positions in their professions or work very often.

Nonetheless, 96 percent of Mongolian women were literate (although some specialists have questioned this rather impressive figure), and 43 percent of university and technical college graduates were female.[79] Some rural parents valued education for their daughters because it offered the girls an avenue of escape from the demanding and difficult life led by women in a pastoral economy.[80]

The government had, in addition, emphasized health and welfare benefits for women. The communist government promoted the introduction of Western-style medicine. The ratio of doctors to the general population increased dramatically, so that in 1990, there were more than 6,000 physicians, three-quarters of whom were women.[81] The number of hospitals grew just as rapidly. The medical care system was accessible at little or no cost to women even in the most remote areas. State-sponsored maternity rest homes for pastoral women in the last stages of pregnancy helped to lower infant mortality from 109 per 1,000 live births in 1960 to 57.4 in 1990, and maternal mortality by about 25 percent from 1960 to 1990.[82] Women benefited from maternity leave guarantees, particularly with the development of a pronatal policy from 1970 to 1990. After their return to work, the state provided mothers with infant and child-care facilities, still another aspect of the pronatal policy. It also offered early retirement to women who gave birth to four or more children. Another important aid to women was the government's welfare program, which provided assistance to widows, pensions to the elderly, and care for the disabled. Because women were generally the primary caregivers, the government's support for such needy groups relieved females of some of these demanding responsibilities.

It should be noted that these policies were not always positive. The pronatal policy meant that abortion was illegal until 1989, potentially jeopardizing women's health. In addition, the drive for a larger population and the shortage of contraceptives caused women to have children at too early or too late an age (under eighteen or over forty) and to have inadequate spacing between births. Women considered pregnancies a civic duty rather than an individual family decision and thus had an inordinate number of births. The high fertility levels, which failed to take into account the health of individual women, led to high rates of maternal mortality.[83]

The collapse of communism in 1990 caused major disruptions for women. Though the 1992 Constitution emphasized health care as a right, the Mongolian advocates of the pure market and their supporters in the international donor organizations promoted privatization in medicine and fees for medical services. Yet a World Bank survey conducted in 1995 found that 40 percent of the poor could not pay the recently established medical fees.[84] General reductions in state expenditures on health no doubt also impinged upon women.

Maternal mortality rose, because the maternity rest homes in the countryside either closed or curtailed their services. By 1994, only 40 of the 392 rest homes in the *soums* were functioning. Some had reopened by the late 1990s, but with poor buildings and services, and "women are not happy with them," a UN study noted.[85] Medicines were expensive and in short supply; lack of fuel and transport often prevented rural women with high-risk pregnancies from traveling to clinics and ambulances from reaching them in emergencies. Nonetheless, by 2001, infant mortality rates had reputedly declined to 29.5 per 1,000 live births,[86] probably owing to the falling birthrate, particularly among older women with higher-risk pregnancies, and to underreporting of infant deaths, particularly in the countryside, where there are few doctors.

The young and the elderly, for whom women frequently had responsibility, experienced great difficulties because of state cutbacks. The government's reduction in the number of children's stations and nursery schools imposed burdens on working women, who now had to quit their jobs or pay for child care.[87] The state's late payment of pensions and its efforts to reduce its pension obligations and to eliminate early retirement for women with more than four children unsettled many of the elderly.

Women who had benefited from the previously advantageous pension system now faced difficulties. In addition, many women who cared for elderly parents or relatives discovered that their pensions did not cover basic living expenses. A considerable percentage of the elderly lived below the poverty line.[88] Such shortfalls caused some families to sink into poverty.

The high rate of unemployment also contributed to increasing economic difficulties of many women. Under pressure from international donors, the government reduced its budgets for health and education, two sectors of the economy that employed a significant number of women.[89] A few fortunate educated women, including the journalist Lkhagvasüren Nomin and several Mongolian students whom I either met or taught in the United States, secured positions with international financial organizations, foreign companies, or international humanitarian agencies, which found females more reliable and steadier workers, with a lower absentee rate, than men. However, such opportunities were limited. These organizations did not have sufficient positions for the many who had lost their jobs. Nor did most women have the skills required for these posts (e.g., fluency in English). Limited vocational opportunities, as well as chaotic social conditions, took a toll on women; for example, by 1994, female-headed households comprised approximately 25 percent of those living below the poverty line.[90] The number of such units increased throughout the 1990s and into the twenty-first century. In 1993, they amounted to about 37,800; by 1995, they had reached about 44,700, and by 2002, 61,765. As of 2002, they constituted more than 10.5 percent of all households, a 24 percent increase since 1995. The figures for single women with children under sixteen years of age witnessed similar increases. In 1989, the number was 16,500, but by 1995, it had just about doubled, to 32,300, and by 2002, it had climbed to 46,298. With unemployment, alcoholism, crime, and domestic abuse all on the rise, some women opted for divorce or were abandoned by their spouses. A survey in 1998 found that only one-half of the 180,000 people between the ages of sixteen and forty-nine were married.[91]

The increase in female-headed households reflected further social dislocation. Unemployed males frequently turned to alcohol, which sometimes translated into domestic abuse, to express their frustration. The resources of the Centre against Violence were limited, and it could make only a small dent in the problem of domestic abuse. Moreover, as one study notes, "there is a low level of awareness among staff of enforcement agencies such as . . . police officers to combat violence against women," and "the issue of violence against women has not made much headway within the mainstream institutions and organizations, whose decision-making instances are male-dominated."[92] Oidov Oyuntsetseg, a diminutive but dynamic woman, was the principal author of the study and had founded the Women's Information and Research Centre, which brought many of these problems to light. However, she now works at the United Nations in New York.

Facing such a large contingent of unstable men, a growing number of women either opted or were compelled to set up their own households. Divorce, usually initiated by women, increased somewhat, and some women chose to have children without marriage. Although divorce statistics remained relatively stable in the 1990s, the figures are misleading because "many marriages are not registered so they do not require divorce to end them."[93] Moreover, because assets often remained in the hands of husbands, divorce or separation was a greater hardship for women than for their spouses.

Having scant support from any state safety net, some poor women survived via the informal sector. They set up stalls in food markets and sold clothing, jewelry, household goods, and fresh milk at kiosks or on the black market. In this connection, the World Bank developed programs, in its own words, "to assist women in adjusting to the transition to a market economy" and to promote "private sector growth, economic efficiency, and development of small and medium scale industries."[94] This agenda of a private sector and market economy translated into programs particularly to provide credit for women entrepreneurs and to offer management training and commercial education. The World Bank chose to supply the credit through the newly developed banking system, which, as noted earlier, was riddled with nepotism and corruption. Thus the loan program did not fare as well, partly because the donors were determined to bypass the government and to foster a private sector, with which the population had had no experience.

Martha Avery's 1996 book *Women of Mongolia,* although anecdotal and impressionistic and not based on research, nonetheless shows some representative women's views of the postcommunist era. The first female ambassador in modern Mongolia criticized the Poverty Alleviation Program, noting that "the amount of money coming into Mongolia is enormous. And where indeed does it go?" Most of the women interviewed for Avery's book were either poor or refer to the devastating changes after 1990. "Before the market economy started . . . my salary was enough to get by on," a street sweeper explained. However, in the 1990s, her living conditions worsened, and she noted parenthetically that "[m]edical service is bad here. In fact there is really no medical treatment at all." A woman formerly employed in a government greenhouse raising vegetables survived on a daily diet of bread and tea and lived in a gutted, unheated building that used to be heated and had had running water. An enterprising beekeeper and doctor of science in apiculture living in a town north of Ulaanbaatar told the interviewer: "I must speak of our poverty. In this part of the country in particular it is very bad." A craftswoman lamented that "my husband and I had an apartment in one of the buildings in town. Both of us were salaried employees, but when the government changed, state enterprises stopped paying the salary. . . . Our old apartment was given to others." A physician trained in Irkutsk regretted that "with the change in government, the situation . . . has deteriorated. . . . There is no money and it is very disturbing to see people unable to get appropriate treatment."[95] The shock therapy and the decline in government services that the international agencies had advocated had resulted in poverty for many women, and the Poverty Alleviation Program had not reached any of the women interviewed for the book.

According to a survey conducted in 1999 by the Sant Maral Foundation, the most respected polling organization in the country, the first cause of concern for women was unemployment, which was followed by poverty and education. Their own economic conditions were their most pressing problems.[96] Unemployment often had devastating consequences; although gender breakdowns for the unregistered unemployed are difficult to obtain, collateral evidence suggests that joblessness had slightly more effects on women.[97] A report commissioned by one of the leading women's NGOs noted that because of "privatization and the selling off of government shares in pivotal enterprises, women in the labor force became far more vulnerable than before."[98]

The private sector industries that had sprouted in the 1990s employed some women but often under unfavorable circumstances. They occasionally hired women as temporary workers, thus eliminating most, if not all, benefits, including insurance. Even when they employed women full-time, they occasionally took advantage of them—for example, depriving them of overtime pay. Thus women working in the private sector had fewer benefits and less job security. Health and safety standards could be lax, and the government did not have the resources to enforce regulations. No wonder that about 43 percent of the workers in private sector employment preferred to return to state employment.[99]

Other impediments also bedeviled women in the private sector. Few had managerial executive positions and could participate in decision-making. Private and foreign capital was most frequently invested in mining, construction, and infrastructure, economic sectors that employed few women. Light industries (flour milling, dairies, and shoe- and bookmaking), which were often staffed by more women than men, received little private investment, leading to fewer employment prospects for women. Women have, in general, had less access to credit, partly owing to the badly managed and only sporadically regulated banking system and to the tight credit policies mandated by the international donor agencies.[100]

The need for cash exacerbated women's travails. They had to pay relatively high prices for rice and flour because the state no longer offered subsidies for these commodities. Women pastoralists also needed money to pay for their children's schooling, including food, lodging, and materials if they attended boarding schools. During the communist era, the government had not charged for any of these educational expenses, but since the early 1990s, such subsidies have been discontinued, partly at the behest of international donors.[101] Women in the countryside also required money to pay for health care, if any were available. Hunting, berry picking, and producing cashmere could have been valuable sources of supplementary income (and were for some large families), but each required transport and marketing, which was unavailable to most of these women. Without the state marketing apparatus, the women and their families were at the mercy of itinerant, mostly Chinese or Inner Mongolian, traders, which meant that the additional sources of income were neither steady nor lucrative.

To sustain themselves and their families in this era of economic distress, some girls and women living below the poverty line turned to prostitution. One survey, conducted in 1996, found 3,000 prostitutes in Ulaanbaatar, a figure that has surely risen with the decline in living standards since then.[102] Prostitutes serviced Mongolian men, but the influx of foreign consultants and experts provided new and often wealthier clients. It was no accident that a large number plied their trade within a block of the Ulaanbaatar Hotel, where many foreigners stayed. Ironically, some female college students became sex workers to cover the costs of their education, which the communist government had earlier offered gratis.[103] Others were vulnerable to confidence men who sold them into prostitution in foreign lands.[104] Still others were very young and part of the growing group labeled "street children."

Street children appeared in the 1990s. By 2000, in a country in which, according to one journalist, "no one was homeless ten years ago" (that is, in 1990), there were perhaps 6,000 such children in Ulaanbaatar alone.[105] "In a culture where children are traditionally treasured and to be childless is considered devastating, the existence of street children is a source of anguish," one foreign observer noted.[106] Some of these children lived on the streets full-time; others went home on occasion, particularly in winter; and still others, who lived at home but were neglected or abused, took to the streets to earn money for themselves and their families. By the late 1990s, Mongolian and foreign residents in Ulaanbaatar noticed "the voices of street children living underground among hot water pipes [that] echoed up through manholes."[107] They earned their livings in a variety of ways, including polishing shoes, carting heavy objects at the Black Market, selling cigarettes or chewing gum, washing cars, gathering wood or coal for sale, begging, and stealing. A few even sold their blood, while some of the girls became prostitutes. Some of these activities, such as collecting coal from abandoned mines, theft, and prostitution, were extraordinarily hazardous. Save the Children–UK and other foreign organizations, as well as domestic agencies, sought to help by providing shelters, teaching the children brick making and other skills, starting literacy classes, and founding summer camps, which also offered a rudimentary education and training for potential employment. World Vision, another philanthropic organization, has erected bathhouses and provided food for a few of the children.[108]

The Mongolian government was either bereft of resources or often relied on private philanthropies or foreign aid organizations to cope with the street children.[109] The Democratic Union government, champion of the pure market, appeared to assume few responsibilities for tackling the problem when it was in power from 1996 to 2000. Its bureaucrats rounded up street children to vaccinate them against cholera, and its police forces returned them to their households if their families were intact.[110] Some observers recognized the potential for street children to become asocial adults. "[W]hat is a country to do with unhygienic, potentially violent children who behave in socially unacceptable ways, steal from their friends, and wander the capital in increasingly aggressive district gangs[?]," one asked.[111]

Changes in education have also affected women, mostly adversely. Reductions in state expenditures on education have been as dramatic as those in health. Lacking state support, many crèches and kindergartens have closed, the literacy rate has decreased, and teachers have been poorly paid and have often faced significant delays in payments.[112] Attendance of girls at all levels of education has been greater than that of boys, who some-times drop out of school to help their families. Nonetheless, for both sexes, the market economy has meant that "a boy's or a girl's educational oppor-tunity becomes dependent on parents' ability and willingness to pay."[113]

Yet girls had a better chance of continuing with their education. Thus 62 percent of high school graduates and 70.7 percent of students in higher education were female. Women clearly will constitute a large seg-ment of the professional classes if and when a higher percentage of uni-versity and vocational school graduates secure employment in their cho-sen fields. Mate selection may be more problematic, because educated women may not be able to find husbands who are similarly well qualified and well educated.[114]

A few women sought to band together to protect their own and their gender's interests. Lacking confidence in the weak, cash-starved gov-ernment, they formed nongovernmental organizations. The Mongolian Women's Federation, a state agency during the communist era, had become too identified with the old regime. In addition, in the early to mid 1990s, reports surfaced that the foreign and state funds funneled through the Mongolian Women's Federation did not reach the needy and unem-ployed and instead were allocated to influential friends and associates. The rumors, whatever their accuracy, inspired ambitious and dynamic women to found other organizations, often with international support.

Some of these organizations, such as the Mongolian Business Women's Federation and the Mongolian Women Lawyers' Association, were professional groups, but others were more all-inclusive. The leaders of these nongovernmental organizations were determined and, recognizing their need for funds, sought to appeal to Western organizations for aid. By opportunistically emphasizing "democracy" and "free market principles," a few attracted support for their programs and for study tours and brief residences in the West. They tended to focus first on Ulaanbaatar, but they eventually started branches in the countryside. The Liberal Women's Brain Pool, one of these groups, emphasized support for women candidates for political office, but it was also concerned about women's health and education. Although not as well educated as many elite women, its founder was ambitious, was associated with the Democratic Union, and was elected to the Khural in 1996. Women for Social Progress initially promoted gender equality and economic rights for women, but grants from Western foundations resulted in a shift to the establishment of a voter education center and a concern with elections and so-called transparency in government. Its founder had a knack for attracting the support of such Western NGOs as the Asia Foundation and the Mongolian Foundation for an Open Society. A Women's Information and Research Centre, founded in 1995 with assistance from USAID, conducted studies and surveys on employment, family, prostitution, access to credit, and poverty. Although the statistics in the centre's reports were not always comprehensive, they revealed trends in the lives of Mongolian women. Leaders of each of these organizations were energetic and received perks from their involvement with Westerners. The organizations they headed no doubt assisted and were comprised principally of professional and educated women. It is difficult to gauge their success in bringing attention and helping to improve the lives of ordinary women.[115]

Most of these organizations asserted that fostering of women's rights and status required government action; nongovernmental organizations alone could not succeed. As a study commissioned by the Liberal Women's Brain Pool remarked, "there is a clear need for government policies and schemes to improve the position of women in the labor force and offer equal opportunities in the new business economy."[116]

The status of women in politics in the postcommunist era was ambiguous. In the communist era, the government mandated a quota by which women constituted about a quarter of the members of the Khural. Slightly more than a quarter of the deputies in local government were women, with about the same percentage of women as members of the MPRP, the only political party in the country. Despite these gains, no woman reached the top decision-making positions in government or in the party. Women have generally lost ground in the political arena since the collapse of communism. Quotas for female participation in the Khural have been discarded, resulting in a precipitous decline in the number of women in the legislature. After the 1992 elections, women constituted only 3.9 percent of the Khural. This figure increased to about 10 percent in 1996, and to 13 percent in the 2000 elections, but women have held almost no other major national positions. No woman has been elected president, prime minister, or Speaker of the Khural. The Democratic Union appointed only one woman to its cabinet. For about a year, that woman, Nyam-Osoryn Tuya, was the minister of external affairs. The MPRP victory in 2000 did not alter this pattern. All the members of the cabinet and all the chief executives were men. These patterns are all the more surprising in light of the important roles played by women promoting democracy throughout the 1990s and the early twenty-first century.

Even more discouraging has been the temporary or semi-permanent emigration of some of the most talented, intelligent, and energetic women. Some of the best and the brightest (and, in truth, a few opportunists), frustrated by the government's direction or policies, have moved abroad either for their own career advancement or for additional study. The first Mongolian woman to receive a Ph.D. in anthropology from an American (Ivy League) university has elected to remain in the United States; as noted earlier, the founder of the Women's Information and Research Centre has secured a position at the United Nations in New York; and Lkhagvasüren Nomin, one of the most astute journalists, was awarded a British Council grant to study in the United Kingdom in 2003–4, although she plans to return to her homeland. A few have married Westerners and have either moved or are planning to move to the West. In this connection, Oyun is unusual, having returned to assist in a new political course for Mongolia after receiving her Ph.D. at Cambridge.

EDUCATION IN POSTCOMMUNIST TIMES

Education had been one of the glories of the communist era, when the state devoted considerable resources to it. The first truly secular schools were established, and by 1990, nearly all children attended school for at least eight to ten years. Mongolians were proud of the resulting high rate of literacy. Education reached even to the countryside, and herders' children attended public boarding schools in district centers near the places where their households tended their animals. The curricula and styles of teaching were modeled on the Soviet system. There was a strong emphasis on Marxism-Leninism, Russian was the second language, and learning was teacher-directed and by rote, with high status and relatively good pay for teachers. The Mongolian National University was established in 1943, and the post–World War II drive to industrialize prompted the founding of numerous technical and vocational schools, mostly in Ulaanbaatar, the center of nearly all higher education in the country.[117] The Soviet Union and Eastern Europe provided advanced training for many Mongolian students, who in turn increasingly identified with Russian culture. As a result, Mongolian intellectuals and technocrats prized the literature, philosophical writings, and art of Russia and were introduced, through Russia, to Western civilizations.

The postcommunist era has been characterized by steady deterioration in the educational system. Encouraged by international donor agencies to play a lesser role in society and to charge user fees for social services, the government reduced its expenditures on education. Such declines in expenditures have affected the educational system. The percentage of the state budget allocated to education fell from 22.9 percent in 1991 to 17.6 percent in 1999 and then climbed to about 19 percent in 2000, but the budget itself shrank because of the increased emphasis on limited government.[118] Education's share of the weak growth of the GDP (which witnessed an actual decline in GDP per capita) during the 1990s also fell. The 11.5 percent figure in 1990 decreased to 6.9 percent by 1999. Despite an increase in dropouts, these financial cutbacks accompanied increases in the total number of students, resulting in a per capita decrease in expenditures. Nonetheless, as of 2002, schools continued to close because of lack of funds.[119]

These reductions have clearly had an impact on teachers. Because the total number of teachers fell, while the absolute number of students increased, the teacher-student ratio has similarly increased from 1 to 21.4 in 1990 to 1 to 25.4 in 2001 (and in the primary grades, the ratio was 1 to 31.8 in 2001).[120] In addition to larger class sizes, teachers encountered other results of the apparent downgrading of education. Reports accumulated throughout the 1990s of teachers not being paid for long stretches. One newspaper reported on May 14, 1999, that teachers in the second largest city in the country had not received their salaries in over two months. As of November 11, they had still not been paid.[121] As a result, teachers' strikes were not uncommon, with teachers complaining about poor salaries, lack of health insurance coverage, and inadequate heating and facilities in their schools. The strikes would persist, for, as one leader argued early in 1997, "despite nearly 60 percent inflation since January 1996 remuneration [has] not been increased."[122] Teachers claimed that "they could not survive on the present average wage of TG 26,000 ($33.10) per month because of the increase in inflation which followed last October's fuel price liberalization."[123] A salary increase was announced on May 1, 1997, but not all teachers would be covered by the rise in pay.[124]

Teachers began to resign in the mid to late 1990s, and strikes persisted, with a major one in Ulaanbaatar in 1999.[125] Meetings of teachers, which I attended at the Mongolian Foundation for Open Society in Ulaanbaatar, revealed low morale and frustration at a decline in their own status and at the lack of textbooks, copying equipment, computers, and even paper. Facing such hurdles even in Ulaanbaatar, many teachers were reluctant to move to schools in smaller towns or the countryside, posing substantial obstacles for proper education in the more remote regions.

The schools faced other problems as well. The government frequently did not provide sufficient funds for the printing and publication of textbooks. In some schools, two or three students had to share one text, and many of the texts were, in any event, dated.[126] The government often paid only for the sizable heating and electricity costs for schools and institutions; even so, some schools in the countryside had no electricity, heat, or hot water. Few resources remained for actual instruction.[127] Some institutes and universities received government funds for maintenance but no money for salaries and laboratories. Less public investment translated into the elimination of book, food, and clothing subsidies for students and to calls for the imposition of tuition.[128]

The financial squeeze on education took its toll on students, and the dropout rate, particularly among boys, increased throughout the mid 1990s before inching down somewhat in the late 1990s. The countryside and small towns witnessed the largest declines in attendance. One report attributes the dropout rate to "(i) increased direct and in-kind costs of schooling, (ii) increasing livestock herd sizes following privatisation and an ensuing need for family labour, and (iii) remoteness of schools and the closure and lack of heating of boarding schools."[129] Some herders complained that education did not relate to the work their sons would eventually do. Parents of boys living in the cities asserted that more education did not lead to better positions or higher wages. As a result, enrollment for eligible eight-to-fifteen-year-olds fell from 97.9 percent in 1990 to 81.5 percent in 1995 before gradually moving back to an estimated 89.7 percent in 2000. Almost 200,000 children dropped out between 1989 and 1998.[130]

Other problems, many stemming from inadequate financing, plagued education. The number of students in vocational schools declined from 26,400 in 1990 to 14,900 in 2001. The decrease in the number of vocational and technical schools challenged the government's oft-stated claim that it was training the unemployed for a role in the market economy. At the urging of international donors, private vocational and technical schools were founded, but as of 2001, they enrolled only about 100 students. Moreover, they frequently had poor supplies and equipment, unqualified instructors, and weak finances.[131] Many educators and the general public were critical of the private colleges and institutes that mushroomed in the mid to late 1990s, accusing them of hiring poor teachers and of not maintaining high standards. One critic wrote that the private institutions sought profit and their "main purpose . . . is to enroll as many students as possible." A recent survey discovered that 70.4 percent of the public preferred state institutions of higher learning.[132]

This instability in education offered optimal conditions for abuses. Corrupt local officials purloined money allocated for educational materials or teachers' salaries.[133] The media reported repeated cases of the sale of test questions from college entrance examinations, the purchase of admission into college, and payments to teachers for a passing grade. Scholarships for foreign study have, on occasion, been manipulated to the advantage of favored candidates.[134] A successful recipient of a scholarship for advanced study in China was displaced by the less qualified child of an employee in the Mongolian Embassy in Beijing.[135]

Lacking revenue, the government has been compelled to turn to foreigners for assistance with what used to be an effective educational system during communist times. Most foreign organizations did not have the resources for large-scale state projects but simply offered specific, not comprehensive, reforms or aid. The Mongolian Foundation for an Open Society, part of the Soros Foundations, is one such organization. Unlike other agencies, it did not have a specific political or economic agenda other than to promote an open society. Its education project focused on altering the old system by emphasizing student-centered and directed learning and downplaying rote memorization. It introduced a debate program, installed computers, and offered doses of progressive education to foster its reforms. Much of this effort was healthy, but the overlay of U.S. techniques, which substituted a so-called child-oriented version of progressive education for the rigors of the old academic programs, could lower standards.[136] A few other organizations, including the European Union's TACIS program of technical assistance to the countries of the old Soviet bloc in Eastern Europe and Central Asia, have offered assistance on specific projects in education (e.g., English-language instruction, new textbooks for the study of history), but there seems to be no overarching plan and little coordination among the various foreign aid agencies in the country. Some foreign agencies have focused on facilities, with Japan providing funds for the construction of six secondary schools and the Nordic Fund allocating $140,000 for dormitory repairs. Nonetheless, many schools are overcrowded. One school built in 1967 to accommodate 960 students had 1,800 in 2003.[137]

The ADB's "Education Sector Development Program" reflects the more typical policies of the international donor agencies. In 1996–97, the bank offered loans that emphasized privatization and lower costs. The bank focused on closing down "underutilized schools" (a policy labeled "restructuring education sector facilities") and reducing the number of teachers ("staff rationalization") in "overstaffed" schools. It also sought to strengthen the management in schools and universities, to equip laboratories and provide computers, and to retrain librarians and teachers, mostly teachers in economics, management, finance, and banking, and the sciences. Yet its stated objectives repeatedly referred to privatization. Its loans were designed to develop "a national policy on technical education and vocational education which promotes private sector participation," to promote "private sector provision of education and the privatization of higher education," and to provide "a role for the private sector in textbook publishing."[138] It sought to instill in students the skills required in a market economy and seemed primarily interested in privatization, administration, and equipment.

In addition, the ADB employed the technical assistance of the Institute for International Studies in Education of the University of Pittsburgh, which offered advice on educational management and supervision, management of higher education, and library and textbook publishing, and devised master plans that emphasized privatization and offered critiques of the overstaffing in schools.[139] The institute echoed the views of the ADB on these matters, but the basis of the bank's judgments about the "underutilization of schools" and the excessive number of teachers was unclear. An ADB survey had revealed that the ratio of teachers, administrators, and other professionals to students was higher than in most other developing countries, a finding that appears not to have considered the vast distances in Mongolia, which necessitated the dispatch of teachers and administrators to remote locations, where they taught relatively few children; yet these children would not otherwise be educated.[140] Shortly thereafter, the ADB would offer a $15 million loan for education, some of it to be used to pension off teachers and to increase the student-teacher ratio. But had the bank applied a formula for pupil-teacher ratios that had been developed in other countries to Mongolia? That is, should Mongolia, one of the least densely populated countries in the world, be assessed by the same standards as countries with more concentrated populations? Were the closings of schools and the reductions of staff justifiable in Mongolia? Did these closings of schools reduce access to education for children living in remote regions of the country? Some teachers feared the adoption of a market approach to education, but in an interview, the finance minister supported the idea, saying that private schools and standardized testing would foster greater accountability and efficiency in education.[141]

In December 2000, the ADB granted another $4.5 million for education.[142] It reported that the funds would be expended on textbooks, teacher training, and energy costs. Whether the administrators of the grant will focus on education or on such extraneous matters as privatization and reduction of costs will be worth watching. In any case, the money allocated in all the ADB loans has been a relatively minuscule amount. In the 1996–97 grant, a project of $4.5 million would be carried out over three years and $9 million over five years. The combined total adds up to $4.28 million a year, a tiny amount in comparison to the average of $250–330 million in annual grants and loans provided by the international donors. Education did not command the support that mining and energy did.

How have those in the education sector responded to the developments since the collapse of communism in 1990? College students have lobbied against high tuition and have complained about the reduction or complete elimination of living stipends, an entitlement of the communist era. One of their successes was a 1997 campaign to roll back a government-imposed increase in bus fares for students.[143] Their demonstrations and protests prompted the state to retreat and to restore reduced student fares. The MPRP government that came to power in July 2000 campaigned on a pledge of covering the tuition costs of college students who had limited means.[144] It has indeed allocated funds to assist an increasing number of needy college students with their tuition—by one account, doubling the number who received such aid from 1999 to 2002—but an unknown number of students still cannot afford school payments.[145]

In sum, education lacks the resources it commanded during the communist era, and the ensuing consequences are predictable. The elimination of government subsidies for boarding schools and the need to pay fees for their children's education have compelled many herders to pull their sons out of school, leading to a decrease in the rate of literacy. Poor salaries for educators have, on the one hand, led many to abandon teaching and, on the other hand, have prompted teacher strikes and demonstrations. Many school and university buildings require repairs and better maintenance. Old textbooks, often based on the Marxist paradigm, are still in use, and few new textbooks have been produced because of scant resources available to writers, publishers, and printing establishments. The number of vocational and technical institutes has declined throughout the 1990s and early 2000s, subverting efforts to retrain workers who lost their jobs with the closing of state enterprises. Imposition of fees has, in general, reduced access to education and has, in part, contributed to the high dropout rate for boys in the countryside.[146]

In late 2003, the government, facing elections in six months or so, began to allocate slightly more funds for education. It pledged to pay the expenses of dormitories, food, and school supplies for children of poor herders; with the help of donors, it provided computers for some schools;

it covered the tuition and some of the travel expenses of students from the countryside; and, with Japanese assistance, it pledged to rebuild twelve secondary schools, build five new schools, and repair some school desks and blackboards. Even if all these efforts come to fruition, schools will remain overcrowded, teachers poorly paid, and facilities not in good repair in much of the country.[147] For example, an official inspection by the state Professional Supervisory Board found that a majority of the kindergartens surveyed had dirty rooms and walls with cracks and had not required medical examinations of students—breeding grounds for infectious diseases, according to its report.[148]

DETERIORATION OF HEALTH STANDARDS

The advances in health during the communist era have also been eroded since 1990. Before the advent of communism in 1921, medicine was rudimentary and dispensed mostly by Buddhist monk-doctors or shamans, magicians, or fortune tellers. The arrival of the Russians and later the Soviet Union exposed the Mongolians to modern Western-style medicine. Tsarist Russian doctors stationed in their consulates in the capital city tended to the health needs of several thousand Mongolians, and a few Swedish medical missionaries cared for some Mongolians in the countryside. The first hospital was built in 1926, with help from the USSR. Some of the physicians were Russians, who trained Mongolian doctors, and by 1940, Mongolia had ten hospitals and 108 qualified physicians.[149] The post–World War II era witnessed such rapid development that by 1963 the country had ninety hospitals and 1,140 doctors. Despite the jump in population owing to the pronatal policy, the reservoir of physicians more than kept pace, and the number of doctors per 10,000 population rose from 5.2 to 27.9. Simultaneously, the number of auxiliary medical personnel, which included nurses, midwives, and feldshers (physicians' assistants), rose from 4,406 in 1960 to 18,674 in 1990, or from 40.5 to 88.8 per 10,000 population. Expenditures on health continued to rise, reaching 5.8 percent of GDP in 1991.[150]

The medical care was not on a par with that in Western industrialized countries, but it provided for rudimentary needs. Under the direction of the Ministry of Health, the medical system furnished basic services throughout the country. Feldshers offered outpatient care in the remote areas, while many *soums* had hospitals or, more accurately, clinics with up to five doctors each, qualified to undertake straightforward procedures. The state provided transport for patients who required a higher level of care that could be found only in the provincial centers or in Ulaanbaatar.[151]

In short, the health care system had problems and flaws, but it had certainly made a quantum leap forward under the communist regime. An ADB report, based upon an on-site visit in 1991, applauded the system, noting that "there is broad coverage and good access of the population to health services in Mongolia."

It is therefore startling to find this same report approving of a dramatic alteration of the system. It supported its "conversion from a system of free access to public health services to one that is priced and based on health insurance." The donors supported user fees and a reputedly more efficient system through the introduction of prices. The principle of free medical care would be abandoned in favor of a supposedly more effective use of resources. However, as of 1991, the ADB acknowledged that doctors were "not psychologically attuned to private practice and the concept of billing patients" and lacked marketing skills. Nor were patients used to paying for medical services. It did not mention that user fees might limit access to medical care, particularly for the increasingly large vulnerable segment of the population.[152]

The international donor agencies and their supporters in the new government criticized the health sector for its high doctor-to-patient ratios. Save the Children–UK responded, writing:

> However, with the country's opening up since 1990, it has been under criticism by Western free-market experts, for among other things, having doctor to population ratios (29: 10,000 in 1990, reduced to 25: 10,000 in 1998) which are even higher than in the United States. These ratios are viewed by critics as both economically inefficient and unsustainable. Such critics, however, appear to either ignore or underestimate the requirements of the unique nomadic and dispersed nature of the Mongol population. Senior Mongol health policy makers feel that a ratio (of doctors) per square kilometer is more relevant to their circumstances than a ratio which relates this to population size. This is because Mongolia is likely to have the same population dispersed over a 60 km. radius that the USA has in a one kilometer radius."[153]

Might this be another example of the lack of knowledge of Mongolia by some of the consultants employed by the international donor agencies? Yet, as of 2003, the ADB continued to urge reductions in staffing at hospitals and complained that too many people were sent to hospitals, and that patients spent too much time in them.[154]

The government implemented this policy throughout the 1990s, permitting it to reduce expenditures on health, which had constituted 5.8 percent of GDP in 1991 but declined to 3.8 percent in 1999. In 2001, the figure climbed to 4.3 percent, but only because GDP scarcely increased in 2001 and 2002.[155] Government expenditures on health per capita during this same period decreased by about 40 percent.[156] Privatization has not taken up the slack, except for the relatively tiny elite who can afford the cost of private physicians and drugs. Health insurance is gradually supplanting free health care, although the vulnerable groups would, in theory, have access to free care.

In practice, lack of state support has generated turbulence among health workers. Government salaries for physicians and medical personnel have decreased. The MPRP government that took power in 2000 affirmed the need for higher salaries and more money for health, but its pledges have not been entirely fulfilled.[157] Earlier, on February 28, 1997, 32,000 doctors and nurses held a one-day strike demanding higher salaries,[158] and in 1999, doctors who had not been paid for five months went on strike. The strikes would persist sporadically throughout the late 1990s and into the twenty-first century.

Medical personnel were also frustrated by the lack of equipment and medicines. They complained about eighty countryside ambulances that were more than ten years old and were often in disrepair, a vital drawback in a country where many herder families are scattered throughout the vast territory and require transport to secure medical care. Hospitals reported that they were short of surgical thread and medicines.[159] Various foreign donors on occasion provided such equipment. Denmark, for example, offered X-ray machines, the Japanese and the Rotary Club provided various types of medical equipment, and a Canadian mining executive donated $200,000 to fight the SARS outbreak of spring 2003. The Poverty Alleviation Program furnished thirty-five jeeps to countryside hospitals, and the ADB provided loans in part for medical equipment in sixty clinics to be set up principally in the countryside.[160] However, these grants and donations have been ad hoc and not comprehensive responses to the shortages. Confirmation of continuing shortages has repeatedly appeared in the press. Insufficient supplies have prompted medical personnel on occasion to employ used syringes, a considerable health hazard. The *UB Post* reported that a major hospital's only radiation therapy machine, which was nine years old and had been heavily used and badly maintained, had been out of order for three weeks, in part because replacement parts were unavailable. In the same month, the paper revealed that the dialysis machine in an Ulaanbaatar hospital had broken and attributed the deaths of six patients suffering from renal diseases to this. The only pediatric intensive care unit in the country, which cared for 850 children each year, reported that it had no respirators, few disposable gloves, and other basic equipment, compelling it to divert resources to a fund-raising campaign.[161] Moreover, there was always the gnawing problem of corruption, and it was alleged that "funds donated for health projects are [not] fully accounted for."[162]

It is no wonder that the elite sought medical treatment out of the country. In 2001, the prime minister went to the United States for treatment of an undisclosed ailment. According to several accounts, about 40,000 Mongolians annually traveled to Inner Mongolia or other parts of China for diagnoses, and one newspaper reported that "wealthy people select private hospitals for themselves."[163] The same account asserted that ADB support for a "structural adjustment" (i.e., reduction of health personnel) has contributed to declines in medical care.

Confronted with these obstacles, the Mongolian government, with foreign support, conceived of a new approach to medicine, a strategy that had actually much in its favor. The health system would now stress preventative care instead of reaction to already developed ailments or diseases. Public health and well-child campaigns would be the central focus, and the health care system would be decentralized, with additional resources provided to clinics and primary care and family doctors rather than to massive hospitals.[164] Such a policy would benefit the countryside, but implementation required moving doctors from Ulaanbaatar and other cities to remote regions, a Herculean task, since many physicians had settled in the capital. As of 2003, it seems that these reforms had not been properly implemented. "[M]any citizens have not been examined by their family doctors and say they do not know who their doctors are," it was noted. Furthermore, there was a serious "shortage of personnel treating children in rural areas."[165]

Government funding was limited and did not cover the total expenditures of health facilities. For example, its allocation to the Medical and Pedagogical Institute in Ulaanbaatar paid only for electricity, heating, and water.[166] Heat and transport consumed one-third of the government budget for health, leaving precious little funding for direct medical costs. Patients in hospitals had to pay fees for ambulances, blood tests, and physical examinations. They sometimes bought their own medicines and even their own bandages.[167] However, the privatization of many pharmacies, with scant government regulation, left patients with few guarantees about the quality of the medicines.

Lack of resources lay at the root of numerous problems. In the late 1990s, most Mongolians had dental problems, because they could not afford treatment, and many could not afford condoms to protect against venereal diseases and AIDS. Mental health hospitals had few medicines and scant supervision from trained psychiatrists.[168] The disabled organized protests complaining about the decline in facilities for them since 1990, and about a similar decline in employment opportunities in manufacturing and service industries.[169] Increased rates of unemployment were particularly devastating for the disabled, who were often the last to be hired and the first to be fired. A series of demonstrations by the blind in 2003 revealed the difficulties they faced. They complained that starting in 2000, the government required an annual certification of blindness in order to receive services and entitlements; many asserted that they had to pay what they considered to be bribes to doctors to receive such certifications. They also accused the government of not providing subsidies for housing and electricity and training for employment and of not encouraging employers to hire them.[170] Moreover, lack of government supervision of traditional medicine, which had revived and attracted more patients because of the decline and expense of modern medicine, has translated into poorly prepared and stored medicines and considerable quackery.[171]

The results of these cutbacks in health spending can readily be gleaned from health statistics. One telling note was that 39 percent of military recruits in 1997 were unqualified because of medical reasons. That is, many young adults in their prime, potential soldiers and frontier guards, were not in good health. Medical personnel found that many babies in the countryside were deficient in iodine, Vitamin D, and iron because of poor diets. Hepatitis and tuberculosis, two diseases that reflect both poverty and a decline in public health standards, have increased throughout the 1990s and early 2000s.[172] The incidences of cancer and cardiovascular diseases have increased, so that deaths per 100,000 people tripled between 1980 and 1997.[173] Gastrointestinal diseases have also spiraled upward. The stresses of the 1990s (unemployment, social disarray, etc.) may have contributed to the rise in these health problems.

Part of the decline may be owing to less concern for public health. Clean water has been less accessible both in the countryside and in Ulaanbaatar. Animals drink from wells meant for humans, leading to potential health hazards. Much of the water lacks important minerals, undermining its nutritive value. The government, with scant resources, was compelled to depend upon Japanese aid to increase the amount of water flowing to homes and businesses in Ulaanbaatar.[174]

Although the government has expressed interest in shifting its emphasis to primary and preventative care, it has not provided much of this. Nurses, whose number has declined since the fall of communism, lack the resources or the time for much preventative education. They can scarcely provide information on proper sanitation and cleanliness, leaving many Mongolians uninformed about the root causes of disease. "Environmental health concerns increasingly affect all Mongolians as pollution levels escalate and access to safe water and sanitation decline with increased urbanization and deteriorating infrastructure throughout the country," a UNDP report lamented in 2000.[175]

Public health deteriorated, particularly in the countryside. After a visit in May 2002, the director of public health programs for the Open Society Institute said that Mongolia had the worst public health sector of any of the formerly Soviet-dominated countries in which her foundation had offices. The virtual elimination of the previously free medical services provided by nurses and feldshers and the imposition of user fees left many herders with scant knowledge of and access to proper public health. Without much education about birth control, safe sex, and family planning, there was an upsurge in venereal disease and hepatitis.[176] Absent active public health campaigns, tobacco and alcohol consumption increased apace. The government, which relied on taxes on alcohol for much needed income, hesitated to mount campaigns against alcohol abuse. As a consequence, the number of vodka factories increased from 22 in 1990 to 183 in 1997, and the figure has continued to grow, although not as rapidly. Family networks and secure employment limited alcoholism during the communist era, but unemployment and social disarray from 1990 on were a recipe for alcohol abuse. According to police records, sobering-up stations admitted 100,000 cases per year.[177]

A native of the countryside who had moved to Ulaanbaatar testifies to the erosion of rural health services. Of her childhood in the communist era, she writes: "When I was a little girl I spent my summer vacations in Delgerkhangai, riding camels and horses, playing with lambs and kids, and eating delicious homemade yogurt. It was a wonderful place." On a recent visit, however, she found that the life of her relatives "today seems so much more strained—a struggle." Her brothers and sisters had to drive 400 kilometers to see a doctor; the one physician in Delgerkhangai treated toothaches and delivered babies, but more complicated cases required still another "bone-jarring" ride, because "not one specialist works" there.[178]

The decline in social, health, and education services may, in part, be attributed to the drive toward minimal government and to a reduced state budget. Postcommunist Mongolia, increasingly dependent for aid from international donors, is under considerable pressure to reduce expenditures. A distrust of government permeated the views of many of the international donors, whose representatives transmitted or at times imposed these attitudes on Mongolian officials. Under their scenario, the state would deliberately play a lesser role, particularly in the economy and in social services.

The state was deprived of resources and assets and faced reductions in income, including lower taxes, little or no tariff revenue, and fewer state enterprises. The revived MPRP government elected in July 2000 made some slight efforts to increase state revenues, focusing on taxes on herders, raising value-added taxes, reestablishment of some tariffs, and small increases in corporate and individual income taxes. Aside from revenue problems, the attitudes of high-ranking officials in the Democratic Union government (1996–2000) also impeded state efforts in the social sector. Prime Minister Enkhsaikhan asserted that economic policy was social policy—that is, economic changes and productivity were much more important than and dictated social policy.

It is no accident, then, that social problems intensified throughout the 1990s and early 2000s. The catalogue of social ills—unpaid doctors, nurses, and teachers, user fees deterring the poor from seeking medical services,[179] drastic increases in crime, an in-migration to Ulaanbaatar of herders who had lost their animals in 1999–2000 and 2000–2001, and pensioners with incomes eroded by the inflation of the early to mid 1990s—was predictable. According to the Economist Intelligence Unit, when the first Democratic Union government fell in April 1998, even members of its coalition criticized it "for not doing enough to help the poor and unemployed."[180]

The vast amount of foreign aid reaching Mongolia hardly made a dent in the intensifying social problems. Some aid was allocated to the social sector, but much of it appears to have either been siphoned off or not managed properly. In addition, much of the aid would be used reputedly to promote structural changes in government, which facilitated the development of a market economy, and to foster economic growth, particularly in the mineral and energy sectors.

LAND, AIR, AND WATER

Mongolian culture is inextricably linked with its environment. The herder Namkhainyambuu told me that Mongolians have a mystical sense of identification with their land and its flora and fauna. He was proud that much of Mongolian music and dance, literature, and even films and theater are imbued with references to Mongolian landscape and animals. The horse-headed fiddle is their most renowned musical instrument, and many Mongolian films capitalize on the spectacular and virtually empty landscape. Much of early Mongolian literature concerns the relation of man to animals, and many Mongolian cultural taboos relate to desecration of the environment. Naturally, as Namkhainyambuu himself represented, Mongolians' traditional dependence on pastureland and water reinforced the emphasis on cultural depictions of the environment.

The communist era did some damage to the environment. Industrialization, which included the construction of coal-burning power plants in Ulaanbaatar and open-pit coal mining in rural areas, contributed to air pollution and to damage of the land, and the communist state did not have a policy of "Nature protection."[1] Urbanization, population growth (encouraged by the state's pronatal policy), mining, tapping of energy supplies, and construction of railway and road networks also fostered environmental degradation.

According to Lkhagvasüren Nomin, an outstanding journalist descended from the old elite and a supporter of the democratic reformers, many encroachments on the environment also began in postcommunist times. She acknowledged that the new government had established a Ministry of Nature and the Environment, but noted that its small and relatively inexperienced staff has been prevented by inadequate funding from coping with the forces unleashed by the market economy.[2] Lack of resources has limited its ability to transmit information about conservation and to implement and enforce environmental regulations and laws.[3] Nomin, an urbanite who, like many Mongolians, enjoys a strong bond with the countryside, believes that some of the economic development of the postcommunist period has created major transgressions on the environment. On several hiking trips we took together, she attributed many environmental problems to commercialism and the desire for profit.[4]

A report conducted by an organization consulting for USAID confirms that the market economy has often fostered Mongolia's current environmental problems.[5] The two authors, David Craven and Molly Curtin, whom I met in Mongolia in the summer of 1998, were dedicated to the environmental cause, yet their report recommends privatization and "market-based mechanisms" as solutions for these problems. Ironically, they document that market considerations often precipitated environmental degradation. However, their report apparently needed to conform to USAID's market economy agenda. Their conclusions and recommendations often seem to be at variance with the rest of the report. The two authors show that "market-based mechanisms" persuaded herders to increase the number of goats, which had devastating effects on the grasslands, because they could earn more income from cashmere than from other animal products. "Market-based mechanisms" also contributed to overlogging (to supply the Chinese and Japanese demand for wood), hunting of deer for their antlers (sold at substantial profits to the Chinese), and rapid extraction of gold with scant efforts to reclaim the sites. To be sure, the communist government did not emphasize protection of the environment, but these three problems all originated in the postcommunist period and reflect "market-based mechanisms." The herders who increased the number of goats, the commercial and illegal loggers who ravaged the forests, and most of the gold-mining companies that damaged the land and the water supply sought to maximize short-term profits and scarcely considered the long-range outcome.

Craven and Curtin or, more likely, their employers view government deregulation as the solution for Mongolia's environment. Yet what emerges from the body of the report is the need for more funding for the Ministry of Nature and Environment, enabling its inspectors to better enforce the existing laws (a view to which Oyun, whose many interests and talents include mountain climbing, would subscribe). Craven and Curtin do not, however, explicitly call for more rangers to enforce environmental laws and protect the ecosystem, and their report reveals a lack of knowledge of Mongolian cultural patterns, which have traditionally emphasized collaboration in the pastoral economy rather than "market-based mechanisms," a concept that seems to have been tacked on to their recommendations in obedience to USAID's agenda.

Craven and Curtin identify land degradation as the central environmental problem. Because arable land is limited, human influences on the land are particularly threatening. Deep tilling of the soil in accordance with the communists' attempt to foster agriculture on state farms had led to erosion and some decline in production by 1990. However, the post-communist era, with farmers lacking funds for the purchase of fertilizer and chemical pesticides, has contributed to an even greater loss of soil fertility and to an increase in weeds and insects, all of which have caused a significant decline in agricultural production. Even more serious has been the overgrazing of pastureland that has accompanied the increase in the number of goats.

Mining also contributed to degradation of the land. Most of the viable mining operations are open-pit, and, as Craven and Curtin write, "according to law, all open pits must be reclaimed but that is not enforced."[6] Mining produces unattractive scars on the land and decreases the available pasture. In the communist period, coal, molybdenum, and copper mines constituted the greatest environmental hazards, but the damage was limited because a powerful government precluded much illegal mining by threatening harsh sanctions. The deliberate erosion of government authority in the postcommunist period has, however, permitted greater scope for illegal mining. Gold mining, which has witnessed perhaps the greatest percentage increase of any kind of mining, does not require exceptional equipment, facilitating the work of illegal miners, or "ninjas," who may number as many as 100,000.[7] One economist estimated that gold production increased fifteenfold from 1990 to 2002.[8] By 2002, 130 enterprises were mining gold.[9] The number of illegal operations is unknown. One gauge of these operations is that the government seized twenty-four kilograms of illegally mined gold in the first nine months of 2002.[10] By 2002, specialists at a conference convened by the UNDP concluded that "wildcat mining is running rampant."[11] As unemployment has increased, more and more people have attempted to eke out a living through gold mining.

Yet gold and other types of mining had negative consequences as well. Gold is, after all, a nonrenewable resource, and the dramatic increases in output could not be sustained and would lead to much more rapid depletion of deposits. To judge by the acceleration of complaints, gold miners were causing serious environmental problems. Their indiscriminate use of water led to the drying up of streams, rivers, and lakes. According to the Ministry of Nature and the Environment, gold mining and other industries have resulted in the drying up of 370 rivers and streams and 1,100 springs and lakes.[12] Fish were also poisoned, and nearby trees were parched. The report of a conference of gold-mining companies observed that "most small private companies working in the sector leave without doing the proper restoration." Some miners used mercury to extract the gold by evaporation and allowed it to drain into and pollute nearby bodies of water. One member of the Khural, noting the high number of accidents in mining and construction, accused the small mining companies and the illegal miners of ignoring safety standards, leading to an "unacceptable" number of deaths and injuries.[13] Despite these problems, the latest government plan envisions even greater dependence on mining. In accordance with its goal of 6 percent growth in GDP by 2004, the government projected that mining would by then constitute 21 percent of GNP and 54 percent of industrial production. By 2010 it will comprise 31 percent of GNP and 66 percent of industrial production.[14]

Other kinds of mining, as well as industries, have also contributed to environmental degradation. Coal, with its high ash content, produces considerable air pollution. The coal-fired power plants are inefficient. In addition, consumers cannot regulate the heat, and poor pipes leading to residences and businesses give rise to steam leaks, which also mar the environment.[15] Leather- and skin-processing plants, including a notorious one with Chinese owners, emit sulfate ammonium and other chemicals into the Tuul River, and unregulated industries producing toilet paper and shoes have also polluted many rivers.[16] The Ministry of Nature and the Environment has announced its intention to request that the Khural place the Tuul River, the main body of water near Ulaanbaatar, under special state protection, but Khural support is not guaranteed. In addition, a serious effort would entail the allocation of substantial funds to clean up the damage already inflicted on the river, but thus far this has not been proposed.[17]

In various trips throughout the country, I have observed the increased desertification owing to unregulated economic activities. Accompanying a crew to film a documentary about Mongolia, I saw the effects of unregulated cutting of trees, which are essential for preservation of water, and the potential for land degradation.[18] Many drivers crisscrossed and damaged the pastureland, which was also devastated by the numerous animals overgrazing near Ulaanbaatar or adjacent to the decreasing number of wells.

Despite a UNDP conference's declaration that "Mongolia's environment is threatened like never before,"[19] supervision and sanctions for deliberate degradation of land and water scarcely deter enterprises and individuals who pollute the environment. Fines imposed on gold miners are so minimal that sale of one ounce of gold more than compensates for them.[20] Moreover, the government often does not collect the fines.[21] The champions of the pure market mechanism among the international donor agencies and their Mongolian allies, with their support for limited government, a balanced budget, and austerity, have led the state to limit the enforcement of environmental laws by providing few resources to the Ministry of Nature and the Environment, which until recently had a budget of only about $75,000 a year.

Lack of sufficient resources has also impeded efforts to preserve protected areas. The government has designated about forty such areas, which include strictly protected areas, national conservation parks, nature reserves, and national and historical monuments. The state, in theory, limits access and the scope of activities in these areas and has added buffer zones for additional protection. However, reports indicate serious transgressions in the Great Gobi Strictly Protected Area, the earliest to be granted that designation and the largest, covering about 5,300,000 hectares of land, which is protected by only eight rangers.[22] Lacking cars or jeeps, the rangers travel on camels, limiting their mobility and their ability to police the territory assigned to them.[23] Illegal hunting, particularly of endangered species such as snow leopards, the Gobi bear, and Bactrian camels, illegal collection of a shrinking variety of herbs, and the felling of trees, including the valuable Saksaul, for firewood have been the result.[24] Still another threat to the environment is revealed in a January 8, 2004, *UB Post* headline: "Government Bid to Release Protected Land Squelched by Opposition." The government, without public discussion, sought to release 3 million square kilometers in the Gobi Strictly Protected Area, and only a coalition of a standing committee of the Khural, the World Wildlife Fund, and the UNDP prevented this from happening.[25]

Similar problems have plagued the Khövsgöl National Conservation Park, a protected area of great ecological significance. Virtually unregulated tourist camps along the shores of the Khövsgöl Lake have released wastewater into what was formerly a pristine body of water.[26] Tourists need to be educated about proper disposal of paper and waste, possible harm to plants and animals, and mechanized vehicles and their potential damage to land and air.[27] Yet again, the limited number of rangers can scarcely prevent tourists from harming the environment. Neither can they closely supervise the foreigners who pay considerable sums to hunt for rare species such as argali sheep and ibexes. The government expected to generate income from such "hunting tourism," but private hunting companies have garnered most of the profits.[28]

Christopher Finch, former executive director of the Mongolian Foundation for an Open Society, who had edited a UNDP study on the Mongolian environment, told me that Mongolia's forests, which cover only 11 percent of the country, are similarly threatened because of minimal regulations and protection.[29] State nurseries no longer provide seedlings for reforestation, and privatization has precluded rational forest management. Oyun, one of the most environmentally conscious members of the Khural, has reported that many private logging companies cut more trees than their licenses permit and often do not replant, and illegal loggers evade regulations. Aware of the market for lumber in China and Japan, these loggers clear-cut the trees, causing considerable damage in the forests.[30] The existence of small and private sawmills, whose mobility facilitates their efforts to avoid the authorities, exacerbates these difficulties.[31] Even the most revered areas have suffered from indiscriminate logging. The Bogd Khan mountains, which overlook Ulaanbaatar and have great spiritual significance for Mongolians, are increasingly denuded, and the insufficient number of rangers cannot police the forested areas.[32] Locusts and other insects damage and destroy many trees, and "no actions [have been] taken to alleviate the problems due to budgetary constraints."[33] Early in 2003, rangers estimated that they needed $90,000 to protect 10.3 million hectares of wooded areas from several particularly devastating insects, but curiously international donor agencies, which provided more than $300 million in annual aid to Mongolia, provided scant money for environmental protection.[34]

Lack of resources also often limits efforts at fire prevention and firefighting.[35] James Wingard, a consultant for U.S. and German philanthropic organizations that focus on fire prevention, attributed most fires to trespassers who were careless in lighting campfires, did not control sparks from stoves, or permitted vehicle exhausts to produce fires. He explained that without sufficient personnel, forest rangers can neither develop successful educational programs on proper behavior in forests nor travel throughout their territories to check on visitors. Thus fires continue to plague the country in spring and summer, with 385 in 1996 alone. Most firefighters have little equipment and protective clothing, because the government has devoted scant resources for these.[36]

Animals are another aspect of the threatened Mongolian environment. The postcommunist state designated "very rare species" (which could not be killed or trapped) and "rare species" (which could be hunted only with a special permit and fee), but such regulations have not been adequately enforced. The government-sponsored *Mongolian Red Book,* published in 1997, listed thirty endangered mammals, including the Gobi bear, reindeer, snow leopard, musk deer, and Bactrian camel, as well as thirty bird species.[37] Although numerous reports and popular media articles have been written about endangered species, the only successful preservation effort so far has been the reintroduction of Przewalski's horse at the Khustai Nuruu National Park, a 50,000-hectare reserve about 100 kilometers southwest of Ulaanbaatar.[38] Dutch environmentalists, who initiated the reintroduction, provided substantial funding for the park, which permitted the hiring of guards and rangers to protect this preserve, and in 2003, French environmentalists joined in this effort.

Other animals have not shared this unique kind of protection. For example, hunters have decimated the deer and antelope populations and have sold their antlers, sexual organs, and other body parts, mostly to Chinese who prize them for their reputed properties as sexual rejuvenators.[39] An animal census discovered that the deer population, which numbered 130,000 in 1989, had declined to 50,000.[40] The reindeer people of northern Mongolia, known as the Tsaatan, have suffered because of such depredations and lack of support from the government.[41] Similarly, muskrats and beaver have been poached for their supposed medicinal properties.[42] The proposed construction of a bridge to transport minerals to China would interfere with the traditional migration routes of antelopes through the region and would harm its unique flora and fauna.[43] Probably as critical, camel herds have decreased, because expertise in raising and breeding the beasts has declined and parts of their bodies can be sold at a profit to Chinese who attribute medical properties to them. The 1989 camel census counted about 558,000, but by 2002 this had fallen to 253,000.[44] The Mongolian government continues to export falcons, and the minister of nature and the environment has been accused of illegally selling them to Arab rulers at a rate far below the market price and pocketing the profits.[45]

U.S. advisors on the environment have stated that the Ministry of Nature and the Environment has neither the expertise nor the resources to protect the snow leopard.[46] Thus they were pleased that several snow leopards, Przewalski's horses, wild asses, and Gobi bears had been sent to breeding stations in Japan, although this policy exposed the Mongolian government's inability to protect and preserve its own animal population.[47] In 2003, the World Wildlife Fund pledged its technical expertise and a million dollars to save the reduced number of wild camels, still another indication of the Mongolian government's limited efforts in animal protection.[48] In addition to the profit motive, other threats to animals "include destruction of habitat areas, desertification, deforestation, competition from livestock (overgrazing), urbanization, interbreeding of wild and domestic species, eradication of natural predators, rodent pesticide application, declining water quality and quantity, wildlife trade, and illegal hunting."[49]

Oyun and foreign specialists on the environment concurred that many of these problems derive from the excesses of the market economy, from an emphasis on deregulation, and from a smaller government that does not have the resources and manpower to enforce environmental laws. The increase in the number of goats, the degradation of pasturelands, the poaching of animals to satisfy local and Chinese demand for animal parts, and the mining of gold and the lack of reclamation all derive from efforts to maximize profits. The studies commissioned by foreign agencies report these abuses and make recommendations about land degradation, air pollution, and declining water standards and inveigh against illegal logging, poaching of animals, and industrial discharge of heavy metals into the land and water. Yet they scarcely mention the Ministry of Nature and Environment's need for resources to enforce the laws; Oyun and a few other democratic reformers recognize that the limited funds at the ministry's disposal do not permit the hiring of enough guards and scientists.[50]

Without additional resources and a stronger government, the prospects for protection of the fragile Mongolian environment appear to be dim.[51] Dependence on deregulation and the market mechanism have so far permitted individuals and companies to poach animals and illegally cut trees and to engage in other activities that degrade the land, the water, and the air. Consultants can continue to issue descriptive reports about the parlous condition of the environment, but if they count on market mechanisms in a country where the rule of law is not firmly in place, it does not appear, judging from experience from 1990 to 2004, that their recommendations will be implemented. The Ministry of Nature and the Environment needs to be larger, not smaller, with adequate funds to employ more guards, rangers, and scientists for research and enforcement of environmental laws.

THE ARTS IN POSTCOMMUNIST MONGOLIA

The communist government did not value Mongolia's traditional artworks, and many statues, paintings, and textiles, as well as texts, were lost during the purges directed at Buddhism. The traditional arts were scorned, and those who preserved metalwork, banners, and other examples of decorative art were vulnerable to accusations of chauvinism and anticommunist sentiment. Ironically, Russian archeologists collected Mongolian art objects and shipped some of them back to the USSR, particularly to the Hermitage Museum in what was then Leningrad. Russian archeologists who excavated the ancient Mongolian capital of Khara Khorum brought back many of its treasures to the USSR.[52]

In 1924, the Mongolian government founded the Mongolian National Museum, whose collections included both natural history and Mongolian history and culture, and in 1971, a Museum of the Revolution, focusing on the communist era, was added. Ideological commentary on the National Museum's collection, which covered prehistory, costumes and jewelry, and Mongolian history up to the twentieth century, tended to derogate traditional Mongolian society and to classify the various artworks in Marxist terms—for example, describing objects as products of a feudal system. The Museum of the Revolution likewise, of course, portrayed the history of Mongolian communism in a positive light and avoided any criticism of the communist government.[53]

When I arrived in Mongolia in 1994 to examine objects that would be shown in an exhibition mounted at the Asian Art Museum in San Francisco, I found that the government no longer provided sufficient subsidies, compelling the museums to fend and raise money for themselves. The state allocated about 1.4 percent, or about $5.5 million, of its annual budget for all of art and culture, a paltry amount that, when divided among all cultural services, barely covered energy costs and some salaries.[54] "Meager funding provided by the state is not enough even to buy a good old snuff bottle," one journalist noted.[55] Most museums did not have the resources to enhance their collections. Museums also needed to raise much of their operating budgets themselves or they simply could not provide basic services. Dr. Sunduyn Idshinnorov, the former director of the National Museum of Mongolian History, which was created in May 1990 and comprised the old National Museum and the Museum of the Revolution, told me that the museum received only $50,000 annually from the government and had to earn income by leasing space in its building to NGOs such as Women for Social Progress, by selling a few catalogs, or by renting parts of its collection to foreign countries.[56] Idshinnorov was a historian of the older generation whose career had suffered because of ideology. He had been an enthusiastic proponent of festivities in 1962 to celebrate the eighth centenary of Chinggis Khan's birth, which was interpreted as Mongolian chauvinism by Moscow and the MPRP. He was thus relegated to a position as a lonely researcher in the Institute of History, where he remained until his appointment as director of the National Museum. A cautious man, he did not complain of the government's parsimonious treatment of the museum.

The Zanabazar Museum of Fine Arts, which houses collections of sculptures, paintings, and ivories, has loaned some of its precious objects to exhibitions organized in the West.[57] Other museums, such as the Theatre Museum, the Military Museum, the Victims of Political Repression Museum, and the Monastery Museum of the Choijin Lama are either forbidden to lend their objects abroad or have collections that have great indigenous significance but little attraction for foreigners.[58]

The repeated thefts of art objects since 1990 reveal the lack of resources available to museums. In 1997, several Buddhist statues were stolen from a monastery in Ulaanbaatar. Two years later, thieves purloined Buddhist statues from the Gandan, the most important Buddhist monastery in the country.[59] Even Erdenii Zuu, the site of the oldest Buddhist monastery in the country, suffered the loss of twenty-two objects, although most were subsequently recovered.[60] If thieves succeeded in purloining these extraordinarily precious artifacts from the most important monuments, it is not surprising that they could readily pilfer statues and paintings from provincial museums and monasteries.[61] As late as 2002, even after considerable publicity about efforts to guard the country's artistic heritage, museums and monasteries could not prevent major thefts. No wonder then that Dr. Idshinnorov observed that "it is about normal to lose things from Mongol museums."[62] Hardly any museums and monasteries had the funds to hire adequate security personnel. In addition, thieves plundered ancient grave sites and cemeteries—as many as 600 from 1995 to 2003, according to one account—and sold their ill-gotten booty.[63]

During on-site visits in 1997 and again in 2002 to produce reports for the Arts and Culture Program of the Mongolian Foundation for an Open Society, I discovered that climate and humidity controls in museums were often nonexistent. Most were overheated and poorly lit and had sagging floors. The installations were not well designed, and the museums had virtually no educational programs, although the Mongolian Foundation for an Open Society had provided money for a minimal Educational Center at the National History Museum.[64] Several other Western foundations had funded short-term seminars on preservation and conservation of art objects, but expertise could not be developed in such brief courses. Indeed, preservation of art objects did not substantially improve; a major water leak that damaged artworks in the Zanabazar Museum in 1997 confirms this deficiency.[65] Similarly, the State Library, with a collection of four million volumes and one of the largest collections of Tibetan manuscripts in the world, had little funding to protect the works in its care.[66] Having been escorted by the director of the Library, I can attest to water and insect damage. I saw precious seventeenth-century volumes of a Tibetan encyclopedia that were either waterlogged or infested with insects. I also noticed other damaged volumes as I wandered quickly through the stacks.

I met quite a number of painters, old and young, who have started to chart a new course in painting. They have established an umbrella organization known as the Union of Mongolian Artists, within which artists with common bonds have founded groups such as the Green Horse Society.[67] They can exhibit their works in the Mongolian Contemporary Art Center and the National Modern Art Gallery, both situated around Sükhbaatar Square. However, lack of state patronage and of a public with money to buy art objects prevent artists from devoting much time to art, because they need to work at other jobs to earn a living.[68] Nearly all the artists to whom I was introduced had either to find outside employment or to sell their art to tourists wandering around Ulaanbaatar, which, in some ways, was no different from the circumstances of Western artists. Limited contact with the outside world during the communist era and the current paucity of books on and reproductions of Western and world art and the lack of well-trained art historians and critics have affected artists. Many of the paintings I have seen are neither adventurous nor well executed and do not engage either with international trends in modern art or with the heritage of Mongolia. An International Cultural Exchange Society has set up a room with some Western art journals and books, which has attracted substantial crowds, but its founders recognize that it is inadequate and requires funding that has not been available in the private sector.[69]

Sculptors have faced an even more difficult time, except for those producing statues commemorating heroic or historical figures. Statues of the martyred leader Zorig, the World War II military hero Lkhagvasüren, and Chinggis Khan's wife Börte have received governmental and some private support, but most sculptors have had little or no state assistance. In addition, with the lack of sufficient numbers of wealthy patrons, sculptors have produced sketches but few actual works.[70]

The performing arts too have lost most of their state subsidies, subverting the quality of their work. With training offered by Russian ballet and opera masters in the communist period, the State Opera and Ballet offered creditable performances. However, the withdrawal of the Russians and the reductions in state support have resulted in lower standards.[71] The personnel of the State Opera and Ballet Theater have repeatedly criticized the cutbacks, and in 2001, the director of the theater contended that it could not survive without state subsidies.[72]

Sergelen, a trim, vivacious thirty-seven-year-old Russian-trained ballerina who now managed the Opera and Ballet Theater, escorted me around the theatrical complex and accompanied me to a number of performances. She lamented the impact of the reduction in state support on the theater. The building is scrupulously clean, but the seats are uncomfortable, with quite a number sagging or broken. The walls and ceiling need painting, the central curtain is threadbare, the costumes are clean but old, and the lighting facilities require updating. The building is handsome, but lack of funding has undermined its value as a site for dance and opera performances. Lack of rehearsal time and a paucity of good teachers result in performances in which the movements of the ballet dancers are often not synchronized, the opera singers sometimes overact to conceal the limits of their vocal range, and the modern dancers are athletic but frequently lack subtlety and grace.

Sergelen and other arts managers have attempted to cultivate the patronage of individuals and companies, including the local Mongolian agent for Christian Dior.[73] A Dutch businessman and a foreign mining company have also provided some funding, but state support is essential.[74] A flourishing performing arts sector requires state funding. The latest reports from government officials are not encouraging. As one official in the Ministry of Science, Technology, Education, and Culture acknowledged, "there is a big gap between the current amount received from the state and the amount required by state art and cultural organizations."[75]

Several of the leading national (and rural) performers have left the country, seeking opportunities elsewhere, and circus performers, in particular, have found employment in Western circuses. However, ordinary performers and directors of the circus have vehemently opposed state plans to privatize and eliminate subsidies for the national circus.[76]

The disappearance of state support has had a devastating effect on the cinema. As one foreign filmmaker observed, "[T]he once vibrant filmmaking industry of this vast and sparsely populated land has fractured and stalled . . . [and] it is financial constraints that have restricted Mongolia's filmmakers to a few sputtering efforts."[77] Under the tutelage of the USSR, Mongolians began to produce documentaries and feature films in the 1930s, and many important directors and actors were trained in Soviet film schools. Mongol Kino studio produced nearly all of these films, some of which were of high technical quality, although imbued with propaganda. The postcommunist era has witnessed the virtual end of Mongol Kino (except for its still good technical facilities), eliminating the most important source of funding for filmmakers.[78] The Mongolian Foundation for an Open Society, through its Arts and Culture program, has funded some documentaries, mostly dealing with issues of social justice—one on young children hauling heavily laden carts in Ulaanbaatar's Black Market in order to survive. It has also organized annual festivals since 1998, at which foreign and some local films have been screened. Individuals and a few corporations have supported a discrete number of low-budget feature films, and the television stations have commissioned a few films. However, financial constraints still plague filmmakers, and the number and quality of films fail to match the technical and artistic levels of the communist era, particularly from the 1940s to the 1960s.[79] One of the most prominent directors said, "[A]llowing for about 20 documentary films which are now made each year, there isn't any budget for art films." Even more distressed, he added, "[S]ince we cannot afford to make copies from a film as we used to, there is no way to show it to people in Mongolian nomadic society," leading to even further isolation for the people in the countryside.[80]

Music, which had received some state support, has faced similar financial problems. Throat singing (khoomii), long song singing, and the horse-headed fiddle (morin khuur), which produced the traditional folk music of Mongolia, often received subsidies in the communist era, and morin khuur orchestras, with singers in tow, survived the 1930s radical onslaught on traditional culture. The early 1990s proved to be more difficult, as the government offered less funding for such ensembles. Foreign fans helped to preserve the throat singing and morin khuur orchestras;[81] and Japanese, Korean, and Western producers and impresarios invited a few of the leading performers to give concerts abroad. Mongolian music drew audiences at ethnic festivals, as, for example, at the Silk Roads Festival organized in part by Yo-Yo Ma and by the Smithsonian Institution in Washington, D.C., in July 2002.[82] Yet, because popular taste in foreign countries is fickle, these ensembles cannot base their survival on occasional tours outside of Mongolia. Without state support, many of them may have to fold.

Even pop music confronts similar dilemmas. A UNDP-commissioned study by Peter Marsh, a graduate student in ethnomusicology at Indiana University, concluded that although businesses, specifically, bars, clubs, and purveyors of clothing and other goods to the children of the elite, seek to identify with and provide some funding for popular bands, the latter face considerable costs. Rents for sound equipment, concert halls, and musical instruments have skyrocketed over the past decade, and many groups have had to "stop working because they have no instruments."[83] Moreover, pirating of compact discs and lack of government enforcement of copyright laws have also impinged upon their incomes. The rural market for pop music cannot be tapped because "[s]tate funding for [countryside] tours dried up."[84] The rural population simply does not have the money to pay for tickets, making the bands almost totally dependent on Ulaanbaatar. The solutions that Marsh proposes, which are based on interviews with performers, envisage a stronger government. Although the musicians do not seek to "be associated with the government," they nonetheless suggest that the state should enforce copyright laws, provide a government-owned building as a concert hall, prod schools to include study and performance of rock music in their music curricula, and assist in promoting it in the countryside and in foreign countries. Those who protest the most about the government often seek a state that protects their rights (e.g., copyright) and offers them support and resources.

An Arts Council of Mongolia, an offshoot of the Arts and Culture program of the Mongolian Foundation for an Open Society, seeks to cope with these financial problems. A great boon to the arts when it was under the umbrella of the Mongolian Foundation, it is attempting not only to foster particular organizations and projects but also to train arts administrators. Recognizing that Mongolian art and cultural institutions lack skills in marketing and distribution, fund-raising, and contract negotiations, it hopes to promote the development of an MA program in arts administration at the Mongolian University of Arts and Culture.[85] This will be a long-term effort, as the professors themselves, including the director of the program, will require training. In addition, the Arts Council seeks to promote cultural tourism, cultural exchanges with other countries, arts festivals, and master classes. It also has announced plans to map the Buddhist temples that existed in precommunist Mongolia. To be sure, such measures are useful, and the Arts Council will probably succeed in obtaining some private funding for the arts. A few wealthy individuals and foundations could provide support for specific projects, but state support is crucial. A developing country such as Mongolia, with few wealthy individuals or foundations, cannot rely on private sources to subsidize arts and culture. The Arts Council and some of its U.S. advisors seek to transplant a U.S. philanthropic system for the arts into Mongolia, which may not be appropriate for the country.[86] They have succeeded, through art auctions, galas, and other activities, in raising some funds, but perhaps their most important activity may be lobbying for state funding and new tax laws.

"REVIVAL" OF RELIGION

Buddhism, the dominant religion of the Mongolians from the late sixteenth century to the early twentieth century, has revived somewhat after seven decades of a communist state hostile to its precepts and its leaders. However, it has not attained the status it had during the Qing dynasty's occupation of the country. The Qing court had supported the Mongolian Buddhist hierarchy, attempting to use Buddhism as a mechanism of control.[87] With such support, by 1900, the monasteries controlled at least one-fifth of the country's total wealth. Although they often provided the only schools and health care and served as repositories for artworks and books, they exploited laborers who worked for them, assisted Mongolian nobles in oppressing the larger population, and generally opposed secular learning. Thus the communists' attack on the Buddhist establishment in the late 1920s and 1930s did not create massive secular opposition. The state expropriated much of the property, including land, artworks, and animals, from the Buddhist monasteries, ordered the destruction of most of the monasteries, and sanctioned the killing of recalcitrant monks. A flourishing religious establishment numbering over 100,000 monks dwindled to fewer than 1,000 by the late 1980s. The avariciousness, obscurantism, and oppressiveness of the Buddhist hierarchy in its heyday had alienated many Mongolians and undermined potential support.[88]

The cessation of antireligious propaganda after 1990 has resulted in the reopening of some Buddhist monasteries, a slight increase in the number of young people assuming a religious vocation, and a rise in the total number of worshippers.[89] However, no massive support for the Buddhist religious organization has developed. The 1992 Constitution did not label Buddhism the state religion, and a Buddhist political party founded in the early 1990s gained few adherents.[90] Eight hundred young people have enrolled at the Religious Studies University at the Gandan monastery.[91] The monastery has also recruited several dozen six- and seven-year-olds for training. In 2001, one source estimated that 120 monasteries had reopened and that they had about 3,000 monks, a paltry number in comparison to precommunist times. A few nunneries, which attempted to help street children and schools, were founded in Ulaanbaatar, but the number of women attracted to such a religious vocation was limited.[92]

Accusations of unethical behavior and malfeasance against the Buddhist hierarchy also eroded support for the Buddhist religious organization. Some devout Buddhists complained that many monks and monasteries charged sizable sums for reciting prayers and for reading of the scriptures. In 1998, a group of monks sought audits of monasteries because of intimations of misuse of funds. In the same year, some monks accused the head of the Gandan, the largest monastery in the country, of nepotism and of squandering considerable sums for luxurious travel abroad.[93] Nomin, Oyun, and other democratic reformers have, in my estimation, strong religious views but are uneasy about the Buddhist hierarchy. Other criticisms have centered around excessive expenditures on statues and other artworks. The Gandan, for example, commissioned the erection of a huge statue known as the Megjid Janraisig. Two years later, the second largest Buddhist statue in the country was consecrated.[94] Some Mongolian democratic reformers found the cost of the statues and the rituals associated with their consecration unseemly, particularly in light of the high rate of poverty in the country. Nonetheless, Prime Minister Enkhbayar's own interest in Buddhism has resulted in the allocation of a small sum for restoration and repair of a few temples and monasteries.[95]

Despite this criticism and the resulting disaffection from some of the hierarchy's policies, the activities of foreigners contributed to the development of Buddhism in the country. The repeated trips of the Dalai Lama inspired the faithful. The Indian ambassador for almost a decade was a Buddhist incarnate who promoted the religion in Mongolia and built a temple and a monastery in Ulaanbaatar. Foreign Buddhist teachers arrived to propagate the religion, and one even lectured on television for a week about the Diamond Sutra.[96] In 2003, Buddhists founded a new television station in Ulaanbaatar; it is unclear whether Mongolians or foreigners are funding the station.[97]

Shamanism, the traditional religion of the Mongolians, also revived in the postcommunist era. The state banned shamanism in the communist period. Yet Mongolians I interviewed revealed that shamanic rituals were performed illegally.[98] Shamans survived and reemerged after 1990. In 1998, I, with a crowd of about fifty people, attended shamanic rituals on the banks of a river near the town of Mörön, and I witnessed other performances in other countryside locations. Travelers began to see offerings to the gods known as *ovoo*s, constructed of rocks, animal bones, money, bottles, and other objects, in sacred locations (e.g., the tops of hills) or strategically located sites. The Tsam masked dances, which convey both shamanic and Buddhist principles, also have begun to be revived at important festivals and celebrations. In addition, because physicians have begun to charge for their services, increasing numbers of the poor have been unable to consult with them and have instead turned to shamans for medical care.[99]

EXPLOSION OF MEDIA

The government dominated the media in the communist era. In 1957, it organized the Montsame News Agency to transmit national and international news to newspapers and radio stations.[100] *Unen* ("Truth"), a perfect copy of the USSR's *Pravda* ("Truth"), offered the MPRP's and the Council of Ministers' version of the news and had, by far, the largest circulation of any newspaper in the country, printing more than 100,000 copies a day by 1967 and an increasing number thereafter. Three other government newspapers supplemented *Unen*. A well-worked-out distribution system ensured that copies reached the countryside, bringing the official news all the way to the herders. Radio broadcasting originated in 1934, under the aegis of UB Radio, a government-operated station. By 1989, there were 444,000 radio outlets, with the government providing batteries at little or no cost to herders.[101] The state supplied the news to be broadcast on the radio. Similarly, the government provided news to television, which started to transmit in 1967, and by 1989, the total number of sets amounted to about 133,000.[102]

The postcommunist era witnessed an increase in outlets for the media. By the mid 1990s, 600 newspapers had registered with the Ministry of Justice, but most appeared only sporadically. In 2000, five daily newspapers divided up about 60 percent of sales. Those with the largest circulations were often funded by the government or by specific political parties. The vast majority of 160 newspapers printed in 2003 offered articles laced with violence, sex, and pornography. They also spread malicious gossip about officials, entertainers, and others in the public eye. According to Leah Kohlenberg, a sophisticated reporter who taught journalism in Mongolia for one year, journalistic standards were generally low.[103] Reporters used unattributed quotations, unsubstantiated rumors, and unverified facts in their articles and scarcely checked the accuracy of information they purveyed, facilitating government efforts to portray them as irresponsible.[104] Surveys of the population revealed that most considered government or political party newspapers more reliable than the independent ones. Investigative reporting and independent analysis of news were limited. *Il Tovchoo,* one of the few serious investigative and even muckraking newspapers, faced either harassment or lawsuits for its hard-hitting reporting.[105]

Radio transmission faced problems as well. New nongovernment broadcasting stations were founded—by 2002, there were thirty-five of them—but most were in Ulaanbaatar and did not take into account the needs of the countryside.[106] The stations in Ulaanbaatar, Darkhan, and Erdenet broadcast 90 to 140 hours a week, but most in the rural areas, except those funded by UNESCO and the Mongolian Foundation for an Open Society, transmitted programs only sporadically, with several limited to two hours a week. In addition, the central government supervised central radio and television, limiting access by dissenters and opponents to the state-operated broadcast media, and many observers considered the national media to be excessively supportive of the political party in power. Moreover, through most of the 1990s, many herders did not have the money to pay for batteries, and the disastrous winters from 1999 to 2001, which impoverished thousands, made matters worse. The government offered solar-powered radio receivers, but the $175 cost prevented their wide distribution.[107] The total number of radio sets decreased to 122,000 by 2001.[108]

The number of television stations increased to about 27 by 2002, but journalists generally avoided independent investigative reporting.[109] The availability of cable television and of foreign broadcasting corporations, including BBC, CNN, and Russian, Chinese, Japanese, Italian, and German stations, compensated somewhat, but only Mongolians in Ulaanbaatar and a few other cities had access to them, particularly the elite and highly educated groups. Similarly, Eagle TV, founded by the Among Foundation, a Christian missionary organization based in South Dakota, was accessible primarily to the citizens in the capital. However, it was the focus of much attention (until its suspension in 2003) because of its low-key Christian message and its strong support of U.S. policies.

Several nongovernmental organizations and one U.S. government agency have attempted to assist the Mongolian news media. DANIDA, the Danish aid organization, UNESCO, UNDP, and the European Union aid organization TACIS helped to found the Press Institute to educate journalists for a new, less authoritarian system and to build a printing plant so that journals would not depend exclusively on the government for paper and printing.[110] The institute offered training in investigative journalism, the shaping of articles, cultivating of numerous sources, and devising realistic business plans. Subsequently, its building became the site for press conferences with leading officials and housed computers, Internet facilities, and a library on the media. The Mongolian Foundation for an Open Society, with help from several experts from National Public Radio in the United States, sought to restore radio as a source of information and long-distance education, and USAID founded the *Gobi Business News* to provide herders with economic information.[111] However, one respected Mongolian journalist refers to the *Gobi Business News* as a "U.S.- government-sponsored free paper" that lacks media professionals, is controlled by the U.S. economic advisors in the country, purveys "propaganda for the market economy," and "teaches and preaches how the rural Mongols should live." She acknowledges that the paper offers some useful "business advice" to herders, although she resents the "U.S. government running a paper in another country, artificially making it the highest circulation periodical and distributing it for free."

The government scarcely promoted a new kind of journalism. Montsame was still the official news agency; all newspapers needed to register with the Ministry of Justice, and the Ministry of Infrastructure controlled access to licenses for electronic media. The Khural enacted a new Media Law,[112] but it consisted of one terse page, which many journalists did not conceive of as a ringing endorsement of free media. It was vague and did not provide complete protection for reporters. Journalists had wanted the law to provide almost absolute protection for reporters and to affirm the free flow of ideas and information and perhaps to restrict government subsidies for any specific newspaper. Dissidents and opponents of the successive governments have continued to complain about lack of fair access to the broadcast media, a problem that the various regimes have not entirely addressed. To be sure, the government has scarcely censored any media outlet.[113] In 2002, the MPRP government did close down three newspapers because of excessive sex and violence, not because of political issues.[114] The various governments since 1990 have, in isolated instances, detained and jailed journalists; the most recent incidents in 2002 were the jailing of a reporter for falsely stating a woman had contracted AIDS and the brief detentions of several journalists who attended and were reporting on a demonstration in opposition to the land privatization law.[115] However, they have generally respected freedom of the press.[116]

HUMAN RIGHTS

The governments' human rights record since 1990 is certainly better than in the communist era, although democratic reformers have some complaints. Even they acknowledge, however, that the smooth transitions from an MPRP government to a Democratic Union government in 1996 and then back to MPRP rule in 2000 are encouraging. They also admit that there have been no political prisoners or politically motivated disappearances or killings and few, if any, restrictions on freedom of speech or movement.[117] Finally, they concur that minority rights have generally been respected. The Kazakhs, Turkic Muslims who constitute about 5 percent of the population, have not been discriminated against, and they have not been compelled to abandon their language or cultural heritage.[118] However, Bayan-Ölgii *aimag,* where most of the Kazakhs reside, is one of the poorest areas in the country. As of 2003, few resources have been devoted to the economic development of the region, and the Kazakhs have had little representation in the government. Since 1990, some Kazakhs have migrated to Kazakhstan, but most remain in Mongolia. It remains to be seen whether positive political and economic support of the Kazakhs will succeed lack of overt discrimination against them.

In other areas, Oyun, the former Khural member Banzragchiin Delgermaa, a well-trained lawyer, and other advocates of human rights assert that the rule of law is not well established, and critics often question the system of justice. Rumors abound that judges favor relatives, members of the same political party, and natives of the same region as themselves and are not well versed in human rights, tend to uphold state rather than individual interests, often fail to respect individual property rights, and do not always mete out justice equitably.[119] Delgermaa also points out that the judiciary is relatively weak compared to the executive and legislative branches.[120] Both Oyun and Delgermaa also deplore abusive police treatment of the accused (including the use of torture) and horrendous prison conditions, which have resulted in a high incidence of deaths in prisons.[121] They have also documented cases of detainees being assaulted during interrogation.[122]

Noting that the 1992 Constitution emphasizes the social welfare obligations of the state, including guarantees of education, medical care, employment, a pension, and a clean environment for all citizens, activists have accused the various governments of not fulfilling their responsibilities. They have criticized the governments' increasing reliance on privatization for constitutionally mandated state tasks and have implied that the private sector cannot guarantee fine educational, medical, and social welfare facilities. Women's NGOs have pointed to domestic abuse and violence, discriminatory job loss, underrepresentation of women in government, and reduced spending on social welfare and education as human rights violations.[123]

A 2003 report from the National Human Rights Commission, which was vouched for by a senior consultant for the UN High Commission for Human Rights, documented such human rights abuses and added others. It focused on the mistreatment and torture of police detainees and prisoners, which resulted in serious injuries, malnutrition, and deaths, but also cited abuses by bureaucrats that led to delays in the judicial system and to corruption. It concluded that "all these facts [have] long [been made public], however nothing has been done to make changes." The commission also brought to light scandals involving medical care, particularly in the countryside. In one important province, the government allocated one-third of the budget for hospitals to the directors of the institutions, one-third to hospital workers, and one-third to the general revenues of the hospitals. Directors and managers pocketed some of the funds, turned down the heat in hospitals, reduced the number of meals that patients received, and limited the medications provided.[124] In addition, the commission documented illegal demands for fees at hospitals and schools for services that ought to have been provided free. Finally, it documented a panoply of social and economic ills that were not receiving sufficient attention—high rates of infant mortality, overcrowded schools, school dropouts, child labor, lack of consistent services for the disabled, inadequate medical equipment in rural areas, poor health, sanitation, and safety standards at workplaces, and trafficking in women. It emphasized the need for proactive measures for genuine implementation of the social welfare laws.[125]

MONGOLIAN HERITAGE

Soviet influence during the communist era challenged the traditional Mongolian heritage. For example, in 1941, the USSR coerced or cajoled the Mongolian government to adopt the Cyrillic alphabet and to discard the traditional Uyghur script for written Mongolian, separating the Mongolians, in part, from their cultural heritage. The USSR launched an even greater assault by encouraging a reevaluation of Chinggis Khan and the Mongolian empire. This new interpretation depicted the first unifier of the Mongolians as a rapacious plunderer who represented the feudal ruling classes and whose invasions retarded the development of the territories he and his troops had subjugated. Mongolian portrayals of Chinggis as a national hero and deification of the founder of the Mongolian empire were condemned.[126] Chinggis was thus "banished from Mongolia's consciousness and history books."[127]

The elimination of domination by the USSR in 1990 resulted in a ringing reaffirmation of the Mongolian heritage, which, however, began to fade as economic conditions worsened. For example, Mongolian museums claimed the Xiongnu (ca. third century B.C.E.–first century C.E.), Turks (fifth–eighth centuries C.E.), and Uyghurs (eighth–fifteenth centuries C.E.) as their ancestors, a historically dubious assertion, and exhibited the arts and crafts of these diverse peoples as part of the Mongolian heritage. Scholars and the general public rehabilitated Chinggis Khan and depicted him as a heroic figure and the father of the Mongolian empire and even an apostle of democracy, the latter an untenable portrait, which a few Westerners not conversant with Mongolian history accepted. Films, plays, symposia, and even popular songs dealt with his life and significance, paintings of him adorned Mongolian embassies abroad, and everything from vodka labels to paper money bore his supposed portrait.[128] Once this deification of Chinggis had become pervasive, the consolation it provided in difficult times was limited. Officials also announced grandiose plans to restore the use of the Uyghur script and to abandon the Cyrillic alphabet, but the practical difficulties, including expenses and greater separation from the rest of the world, dampened the original enthusiasm for this idea.[129] Revivals of the Naadam festivals, which include contests in the traditional Mongolian sports of wrestling, archery, and horseback riding, and of the elaborate celebrations of Tsagaan Sar, the Mongolian New Year, have been more successful.[130]

Such affirmations of Mongolian heritage are understandable at times of considerable stress and despair. Even intellectuals among the democratic reformers such as the journalist Nomin and the Khural members Oyun and Erdenebileg have shown great interest in the Mongolian past. Oyun writes that "she finds relief in reading the Dalai Lama's thoughts about compassion and the meaning of life"; Nomin has found solace in Buddhist and shamanic rituals. They and others have been fascinated by the lives and careers of Chinggis Khan, Khubilai Khan, and other renowned Mongolians and have taken great pleasure in the rituals associated with Naadam and Tsagaan Sar. It is difficult to predict how long these repeated reaffirmations will persist in the face of modern concerns and problems.

Chapter 8 | A NEW MONGOLIA IN A NEW WORLD

Much needed to be done after the transition from communism to democracy to link landlocked Mongolia more firmly to the outside world, and especially to establish good relations with the great powers. Proponents of a pure market system such as Davaadorjiin Ganbold and Prime Ministers Mendsaikhany Enkhsaikhan and Nambaryn Enkhbayar have tended to emphasize cooperation with the United States and the West,[1] while reformers such as Sanjaasürengiin Oyun, Hashbat Hulan, and Tömör-öchiryn Erdenebileg have supported a more balanced policy that stresses the need for contacts with the other countries of the so-called Third World and recognizes Mongolia's traditional relations with China and Russia. However, the withdrawal of Russian troops did not erase the historical antagonisms between the two peoples and governments, and a great deal remained to be negotiated.

MONGOLIA AND RUSSIA: RESTORING GOOD RELATIONS

One point of conflict between democratic Mongolia and Russia was the damage to the environment caused by the now abandoned Soviet military bases. In 1997, the Ministry of Nature and Environment conducted a survey of many of the 188 localities where Soviet forces had been stationed.[2] It found severe soil and plant damage, hidden foxholes and concealment of weapons, and destruction of animal species, not to mention water pollution. A quick appraisal of a site in the North Gobi that had reputedly been a base for 20,000 Soviet troops (perhaps an exaggerated number) revealed the environmental consequences of the Soviet encampments. After the closing of the base, its Mongolian neighbors razed and stripped many of the buildings, leaving behind piles of bricks and scrap metal, which littered the area. The water around the base had a brownish tint, perhaps a by-product of chemicals or other pollution introduced during military exercises.[3]

An even more contentious issue was the Mongolians' debt to Russia. According to the Russians, loans for construction projects, technical assistance, and general support for the services (roads, schools, hospitals, pensions, television, etc.) the Mongolians had enjoyed in the communist era amounted to $11 to 17 billion, depending on the source. Since Mongolia's GDP in 2003 hovered around $1 billion, payment of even the interest, not to mention the principal, on such a huge debt was unthinkable.[4] The Mongolians countered with evidence that Soviet control from the 1920s on had distorted the price mechanism in trade with the USSR. With the Mongolians limited to commerce with the Soviet bloc, prices for goods they supplied to their fellow communist countries had been artificially depressed. The USSR dictated the prices both of Mongolian commodities and of its own exports to Mongolia, which was thus compelled to sell its meat and animal products cheaply and to pay dearly for petroleum products and heavy machinery from the other communist states. In addition, from the 1960s on, the USSR and Eastern Europe had had exclusive access to Mongolia's copper, fluorspar, gold, and uranium deposits and often owned substantial stakes in Mongolian mining operations in the form of joint ventures, enabling them to obtain these resources at considerably less than world market prices. The Mongolians also insisted that they had legitimate claims to compensation for the environmental damage inflicted by Soviet troops in the quarter of a century or so during which they had been stationed in Mongolia, and that such Soviet obligations ought to be deducted from Mongolia's own debt.

During the early 1990s, the Russians demanded repayment of the entire debt, although by 2003, they seemed amenable to compromise. When Dashiin Byambasüren, the first prime minister to be chosen after the first election in Mongolian history, arrived in Moscow for consultations in September 1990, he met with a sharp rebuff in his efforts to reduce the debt. The Russians, however, made one concession: repayment of the debt would be postponed for ten years, but interest would continue to be charged from 1991 to 1995. In April 1996, Russian officials were said to believe that the debt could be handled without draconian impositions on the Mongolian economy. Yet during Russian Foreign Minister Yevgeny Primakov's visit to Mongolia in November 1996, the two sides failed to resolve the issue.[5] Suddenly, however, in February 1999, the Russian government began to move gradually toward a compromise. It instructed its Ministries of Roads and Communication, Finance, and Trade to cooperate with Mongolia in liquidating the debt incurred by the Mongolians in the construction of the Ulaanbaatar Railway. In return, the Russians would accept stock in the railway.

During his visit to Mongolia in November 2000, President Vladimir Putin seemed eager for compromise on the issue of debt. Yet in April 2002, the Mongolian press reported that the Russians put the debt at $11 billion, while the Mongolians offered payment of $300 to $400 million in the form of meat and potatoes.[6] The July 2003 visit of Prime Minister Enkhbayar to Russia seemed to be leading to an agreement, and in December 2003, the two sides finally made public the details of this compromise.[7] The Russians waived the debt in return for an immediate payment of $250 million from the Mongolian government, which issued bonds to cover part of the costs. Mongolian officials have, however, been reluctant to provide details about the monetary arrangements and other aspects of the agreement, which worries many Mongolians.[8] The controversial entrepreneur Robert M. Friedland, chairman of Ivanhoe Mines Ltd., a Canadian company engaged in exploiting gold and copper deposits at Oyu Tolgoi, in which it held a 100 percent stake, bought $50 million worth of these bonds, raising concerns about a possible quid pro quo.[9]

The attempted restoration of good relations with Russia may reflect the growing influence of China over Mongolia in the late 1990s and early 2000s. Mongolian and Russian concern about China's intentions in Mongolia may be spurring closer relations between the two countries. However, Russia continues to face its own economic crisis, and in addition, China has both the consumer goods and the sizable market that the Mongolians require. Russia and China themselves have sought improved relations, partly in response to what they perceive as the arrogance and activism of the United States. Trade has increased between these two previously hostile countries, and they have signed agreements renouncing the use of force against each other.

The decline in trade with Russia and the concomitant growth in commerce with China reflect the diminishing influence of Mongolia's former patron and the burgeoning impact of its southern neighbor. In 1989, more than 92 percent of Mongolia's trade turnover was with the USSR and the Soviet bloc, but by 1995, the comparable figure for Russia and Eastern Europe had slipped to 32 percent, and by 1998, it had declined to 25 percent. From 1996 to 1997, trade between the two decreased about 40 percent. On the other hand, trade turnover with China constituted about 1.5 percent of Mongolia's total in 1989, 14 percent in 1995, and 20 percent in 1998. By 1999, China had become Mongolia's largest trading partner. In 2002, Mongolia sent more than 42 percent of its exports to China and less than 10 percent to Russia. As of the same year, Russian goods constituted about 34 percent of its imports, but Chinese products were next with about 24 percent.[10] It seems likely that the percentage of imports from China will continue to grow.

Another problem that Russia and Mongolia have striven to resolve relates to law and order along their common borders, particularly along Mongolia's northwestern frontier with Tuva. In September 1995, the two sides signed an agreement to share information, to have counterparts with whom they could communicate, and to train Mongolian border officials in Russia. Their initial concern was rustling of animals along the Tuvan border, which provoked numerous complaints from Mongolian herders. Despite considerable discussions and some effort, the theft of animals persists, and in a notorious incident in January 2000, Tuvan rustlers killed two Mongolian herders. The two governments responded by demanding that a joint Russo-Mongolian border commission halt such incidents. However, the key issue was the lack of enough border guards, a state of affairs that emboldened criminals, and the question of funding for more patrols was not addressed.[11] Smuggling of drugs, cars, consumer goods, and weapons, and illegal importation of prostitutes and brides for sale across Mongolian territory, have not been brought under control. On the other hand, Mongolians have also been implicated in smuggling goods into Russia. In February 2000, the then acting president of Russia, Vladimir Putin, spoke at a meeting of Russian officials in Irkutsk and demanded that governors, customs officials, and the army pay greater attention to suppressing criminal activities along the border. The joint Russian-Mongolian border commission continues its activities, but without the necessary financial resources, and thus men and equipment, it cannot rein in abuses.[12]

Insufficient funds have also led to other difficulties that the Mongolians and the Russians have tried to untangle. For decades, power for several of the western provinces of Mongolia has derived from a link to the Siberian grid, but since the mid 1990s, financial problems have resulted in delays in payments to the energy suppliers. Prior to 1990, the Soviet government tolerated such delays, but Russian state and private companies now demand immediate payment. They have responded to late or no payments by cutting off power to the region, specifically, the provinces of Khovd, Uvs, and Bayan-Ölgii, or by threatening selective brownouts or electricity shortages. The Erdenet copper complex has not been immune from such power cutbacks. On two occasions in 1999, Russian officials failed to supply power because of arrears in Erdenet payments. In the previous year, delivery of petroleum for which the Mongolians had actually paid was delayed for quite some time.[13]

Mongolia and Russia have hatched several plans to cope with such uncertainty. However, the first, a joint Czech-Mongolian project to build a dam to provide hydroelectric power to the three western provinces, foundered because of apparent favoritism in the awarding of the contract, as well as questions concerning the flooding of archeological sites in the area. On April 30, 2000, Badarchyn Erdenebat, the publicity-seeking nouveau riche owner of a gold mine and other ancillary enterprises, who would be elected to the Khural in June that year, and who founded his own political party, started to construct a hydroelectric power station in another area to supply energy to the three provinces. He had neither received permission from the government nor conducted tests to assess the environmental impact of the station. At the time of writing, the state has suspended but not totally ruled out his clearly illegal operation.[14]

The Russian government's management of its partial ownership of the Erdenet copper enterprise also did not inspire confidence, although as late as of the present writing, the Mongolians still required Russian expertise. By 1999, Russian imports of copper had declined since 1990, but a much more critical issue was the manner in which the Russian government privatized 75 percent of its ownership of Erdenet. In 1994, it sold half of its 49 percent share and sought to sell another 25 percent for a grand total of $240,000, an extraordinary undervaluation of an enterprise that generated $1 million in profits annually. Early in 1999, Mongolia's Prime Minister Janlavyn Narantsatsralt, an ardent advocate of privatization, sent a letter to the Russian government sanctioning this somewhat suspicious sale and appeared to imply that he expected the Russians to do the same if and when the Mongolian government privatized its share of Erdenet. The Khural, which had not yet approved such a privatization, censured the prime minister for what it believed to be a breach of Mongolia's security interests, and he was compelled to resign. The previous year, the Russians had objected to the Mongolian government's dismissal of the Mongolian manager of Erdenet, who was accused of mismanagement and corruption (and, incidentally, of not fulfilling the state tax quota for the company). After six months, they finally acquiesced in the appointment of a new director. By 2003, Russian and Mongolian negotiators had met on three separate occasions to clarify ownership and rights in Erdenet, but no agreement had been reached.[15]

Still another economic rift that the Russians and the Mongolians attempted to overcome involved the Russian market for meat. Before 1990, Russia had been the main importer of Mongolian meat, consuming the equivalent of about two million animals annually, but financial problems in Russia, as well as the imposition of high freight prices and higher tariffs, had caused the Russian market for meat to diminish considerably. Late in 1999, a delegation from the Mongolian Ministry of Foreign Trade met with Russian counterparts in Moscow to eliminate tariff restrictions, reduce freight costs, and speed up shipment of meat through Russia. The Mongolian government also needed to dispel Russian apprehensions about the poor quality of meat from possibly diseased animals. Declines in the number of state veterinarians and high fees that deterred poor herders from using the services of private veterinarians heightened Russian fears. The Mongolians responded to these fears by proposing the construction of refrigerated slaughterhouses and meat-processing plants in three provinces adjacent to the Russian border, where Russian officials could presumably conduct inspections. They also emphasized better transport in refrigerated trains and better packaging in sending meat to the Russian market. By 2001, the Mongolians began to sell more meat, including horse meat, to Russia, although not nearly as much as in the heyday of their relationship with the USSR. An outbreak of hoof and mouth disease late in 2001, and again late in 2002, temporarily halted shipments of meat, but they were quickly restored.[16]

Despite all these difficulties, seventy years of Soviet influence had created links between Russia and Mongolia that have toned down some of the hostilities. Together with great animosity arising from its instigation of purges and repression, the USSR had a residue of good feeling because of its assistance in the establishment of the first Mongolian university, the first modern hospital, a social safety net, and construction of a basic transport system. In addition, many Mongolian leaders had been trained in the USSR, and indeed all the prominent figures among both the advocates of the pure market and the democratic reformers had been educated in Soviet or Eastern European universities or institutes. Moreover, evidence of Russian cultural influences in literature, the arts, cinema, and education are readily apparent. A few of the Russo-Mongolian joint ventures, such as the Ulaanbaatar Railway, the Erdenet copper complex, and Mongolrosvetmet (a nonferrous metals concern), are among the largest enterprises in the country. Russia provides 50 percent of Mongolia's electricity and much of its petroleum and remains its largest supplier of goods. Since 2000, Russian investment has increased somewhat, although not at the same rate as Chinese investment.[17] In 2003, a Russian company even purchased one of the country's largest coal mines.[18] At the same time, Mongolia seems to identify economically with Europe rather than with the Asian rice economies.[19]

Vladimir Putin's visit to Mongolia in 2000, the first such presidential trip in twenty-six years, and Prime Minister Enkhbayar's visit to Russia in July 2003 were the culmination of this effort to foster closer relations. President Putin pledged lower oil and energy prices, disaster relief, military cooperation, reductions in tariffs, greater cultural exchanges in theater and film, cooperation on livestock theft and other border issues, and construction of apartments in Ulaanbaatar for 340 families.[20] During Enkhbayar's visit, the Russians returned apartments that Russians had occupied in Ulaanbaatar, Erdenet, Darkhan, and other Mongolian cities and promised to promote tourism to Mongolia.

Restoration of friendlier Mongolian-Russian relations can also build on Mongolian public opinion's increasingly favorable image of their country's former patron, with which they attempted to establish more equitable associations than in the Soviet period. In a survey conducted in February 1996, 79 percent of Mongolians supported closer links with Russia, while only 35 percent opted for such ties with China. A seemingly minor observation offers telling evidence of the Mongolians' differing attitudes toward Russia and China. A report directed at consumers and retailers emphasized that Russian scales were more accurate and less easily altered than Chinese scales. It implied that the Chinese were dishonest and deliberately tampered with the scales for their own profit, while the Russians were more trustworthy. This same trust in the Russians may have prompted the 1994 restoration of cooperation between the Russian news agency Itar Tass and the Mongolian news agency Montsame, after a sharp break in 1991. Itar Tass pledged to share information at a low cost.[21]

The late 1990s nostalgia for a more stable time certainly played a role in improving Mongolian relations with Russia. Experiencing turbulence and a striking growth in poverty, the Mongolians perhaps idealized the Soviet period and thus sought to reaffirm ties with the Russians, associating them with better times.

In the late 1990s, an increasing number of official visits and other contacts between the two sides contributed to their greater cooperation. Mongolian parliamentary leaders, presidents, and foreign ministers have regularly traveled to Russia, which is among the first destinations for any newly elected or appointed major figure in the government. In March 2000, the Mongolian president was one of the first leaders to send a congratulatory message to the new Russian president, which proclaimed his wishes for even closer relations.[22]

Cultural and educational exchanges contributed to the growing closeness. From 1996 on, 75 Mongolian undergraduate students and 30 graduate students received fellowships from Russia each year, and in 2003, the Russians increased the number to 200 students. The fees for Mongolian students who paid for their own university education were reduced.[23] "Moscow Days," a festival of Russian films, theater, and art in Ulaanbaatar in October 2000, was an important step in the renewal of cultural contacts and continued with a "Days of Russian Culture" in Darkhan and Erdenet. In July 2003, an equivalent "Days of Mongolian Culture" was held in Moscow, St. Petersburg, and other cities in Russia. These events presaged extensive exchanges of theater and music. The resumption of cooperation in research on paleontology, geology, geophysics, history, and culture yields additional evidence of closer relations, as does the renewed popularity of Russian schools in Ulaanbaatar and other cities.[24]

Russian reaction to the disasters that afflicted Mongolian pastoralism from 1999 to 2002 also promoted more harmonious relations. The Russian government dispatched fodder, money, and veterinary assistance to the beleaguered herders and subsequently sent vaccines to combat hoof and mouth disease. In addition, it sent seeds to farmers hard hit by lack of Mongolian state support.[25]

MONGOLIA AND THE WEST

Pure market champions such as Ganbold and former prime ministers Enkhsaikhan, Tsakhiagiin Elbegdorj, and Rinchinnyamyn Amarjargal of the Democratic Union have supported closer links with Western countries. Several of them studied in or had been sent on study tours to the West. Amarjargal earned a graduate degree in economics in Great Britain, and after his unceremonious forced resignation as prime minister, Elbegdorj studied for an MA degree in the United States. Several of them formed strong relationships with some of the representatives of the international donor agencies and, as a result, were selected for study tours, granted scholarships for their children to study abroad, and received other benefits.

Oyun, Hulan, and the other democratic reformers were much more critical of the Western donor agencies and policies in Mongolia. They noted that the representatives of these agencies frequently threatened to suspend pledged aid if they did not get their way. While repeatedly emphasizing their desire to promote democratic institutions in Mongolia, these representatives sought to dictate policy by using the power of the purse. They attempted to capitalize on the leverage offered by the Mongolian need for aid to impose their own views.

As noted earlier, the democratic reformers criticized the speed and implementation of privatization, noting that it was "tainted by persistent accusations of corruption."[26] The privatization of small and large enterprises in the towns and cities, which the donor agencies encouraged, was rushed, resulting in inequitable outcomes. The haste with which privatization was carried out surely contributed to this.

In sum, the democratic reformers were concerned that the international donor agencies were seeking to advance a generic agenda in Mongolia. Oyun, in particular, believed that the agencies did not take into account Mongolia's unique circumstances and history. Mongolia was "in the words of the *Economist,* 'the star pupil of Western liberal economics . . . [and] meticulously following the instructions of international financial institutions, the country [had] liberalized its currency, trade and economy,'" and promoted privatization of state assets and elimination of subsidies, she noted. By encouraging a rigid application of pure market ideas, however, the "international financial institutions [helped to create] a sick economy." Oyun's flawless English permitted her to have numerous dialogues with Westerners, who, she notes, "are easily impressed by the many jeeps in the streets of Ulaanbaatar and the expensive houses that are being built in the capital's suburbs. In a country with per capita GDP of USD 450, however, these are not signs of a healthy . . . economy."[27] She concluded that rigid application of pure market principles had on occasion harmed Mongolia.

Mongol Amicale, the first U.S.-Mongolian joint venture, offers a specific example. A New York–based company, Amicale Industries, built a cashmere-processing factory in Mongolia in the early 1990s because of the considerable amount of raw cashmere available there—Mongolia is the second largest cashmere producer in the world—and its reputed quality. Its owner, Boris Shlomm, a successful, voluble, and crusty Russian-born and Yale-educated businessman with expertise in camel hair and cashmere products, started the factory with hopes of educating the herders about the importance of quality. He said that part of the appeal of setting up a factory was a ban on the export of raw cashmere, which was imposed in April 1994. Mongolian cashmere processors, including Amicale, could count on a ready supply of raw cashmere. However, under pressure from the ADB and the IMF, the Democratic Union government, which took power in 1996, rescinded the ban, offering Chinese and Inner Mongolian traders opportunities to buy the raw cashmere. The Mongolian government imposed a tax on the export of raw cashmere, but, Shlomm noted in an interview, Chinese and Inner Mongolian traders sought to evade this tax and often succeeded in doing so.[28] They frequently received subsidies and low-interest loans from the Chinese government to purchase the raw cashmere and had access to credit and to world markets. Similarly, Chinese cashmere processors had substantial government support. In addition, because China produced three times as much raw cashmere as Mongolia, it had considerable leverage in determining prices. Shlomm complained that Amicale, which had no government subsidies and encountered higher costs in transporting cashmere products to world or even Asian markets, confronted shortages of raw cashmere. In the winter of 1999 and spring of 2000, Chinese and Inner Mongolian traders offered substantially higher prices for raw cashmere, virtually cornering the market. Because Amicale could not compete with the heavily subsidized Chinese traders and processors, it suspended operations, laying off about a hundred employees. However, Shlomm has not given up; he has forcefully presented his case to Mongolian and American officials and representatives of the international donor agencies and at meetings of the Council on Foreign Relations and the Mongolia Society. Late in 2000, Amicale recommenced operations, but on a lesser scale.[29]

The application of pure market principles by the international donor agencies hobbled Amicale and failed to take into account the inequitable competition between it and the Chinese firms. The Mongolian cashmere-processing industry could not initially compete with the Chinese. It needed protection and access to domestic supplies of raw cashmere.[30] Amicale was a commercial operation abiding by the pure market, but the Chinese traders and processors had substantial state support and could be considered monopolies. Yet the international agencies did not distinguish between the two and encouraged the Mongolian government to persist in so-called free trade, which would harm this U.S.-Mongolian joint venture, a policy that Western investors would not find comforting. Oyun found the insistence on "free trade" by the international donors hypocritical. "Even now, the developed and supposedly free-market West annually spends USD 350 billion on agricultural subsidies," she noted. "Ironically, the very countries that push developing countries to open up markets themselves maintain trade barriers and import quotas when it suits them."[31] In any event, fears of such inconsistent government policies, enacted in this case at the behest of international donor agencies, may have deterred Western investment.

The foreign investors who have not been deterred have contributed funds for new enterprises or new technology. However, as of 2003, 70 percent of such investment has been lavished on geology and mining, and government regulations offer a five-year tax exemption for mining and processing of mineral resources. Canada has been the principal foreign investor in mining, and the 2002 discovery of gold and copper at Oyu Tolgoi prompted Ivanhoe Mines to invest even more funds, although the importance of this site remains uncertain.[32] Some foreign investment has resulted in an increase in U.S. imports from Mongolia.[33] However, as noted earlier, investment in local industry has been limited, partly because of the paucity of labor and of high transport costs. In addition, withdrawal of state support for small businesses and the elimination of most tariffs in May 1997 undermined the butter, milk, yogurt, leather, and shoe industries when cheaper goods from or transported via China undersold local products. The elimination of most tariffs translated into a 10 percent decline in revenues, and local industries were devastated. Foreign or even local investment has not thus far translated into a revival of local industry.[34]

Despite Mongolia's social and economic problems, Westerners, in particular Americans, saw the country as a great success story throughout the 1990s. They repeatedly referred to Mongolia as the first formerly communist state in Asia to opt for democracy and a market economy. Unlike China, which maintained an authoritarian political system while moving toward a market economy, Mongolia was undergoing so-called political and economic reforms simultaneously. During a whirlwind tour of Mongolia (lasting less than a day), U.S. Secretary of State Madeleine Albright said, "Here you are building economic and political democracy at the same time while still remaining true to your national heritage, culture, and values." An American official escorting Secretary Albright joyously reported: "This is definitely a feel-good stop. Mongolia is a staggering success story." However, a dissident Mongolian leader questioned this assessment, pointing out that "it is impossible for her to hear the views of the people."[35] He implied that most Mongolians had fared better economically with Soviet aid and the accompanying social safety net of pensions, welfare, and health benefits than with the austerity demanded by the IMF and the other international donor agencies.

Western donors, pleased with the reputed political successes in Mongolia, have continued to support Mongolians who espouse democracy and, in particular, the market economy. In 1998, they provided funds for an East Asian Women's Conference in Ulaanbaatar, supported foundations established by Democratic Union officials, and offered scholarships to Mongolians for study abroad. By the late 1990s, some Mongolians feared that foreign-educated students might not return to Mongolia, a brain drain that a small country could not afford. In addition, many unemployed laborers went abroad to seek work—about 30,000 to South Korea alone. Such potential emigration was not helpful to Mongolia, which required labor for economic development, although the money sent back by these workers was invaluable.[36]

On the other hand, greater openness to the outside world led to some beneficial results and more exposure to the West. Scientists and archeologists were among the first beneficiaries of such greater access. The American Museum of Natural History restored the paleontological and geological explorations of Mongolia that had been interrupted in 1925, and seismologists and astronomers set up equipment in the country to assist in scientific experiments. Michael Novacek, dean of science at the museum, has led the paleontological expeditions and has been impressed with the cooperation of his Mongolian colleagues and the Mongolian government. Archeologists from the United States collaborated with Mongolian specialists on study of rock painting sites in Bayan-Ölgii *aimag*, in research on possibly sacred burial sites of early pastoral nomadic cultures, and in excavations of Xiongnu tombs, while German and French archeologists explored the first Mongolian capital at Khara Khorum and other earlier remains throughout the country.[37]

Still another result has been increasing military cooperation between the West, principally the United States, and Mongolia. U.S. Department of Defense personnel have visited Mongolia; the Mongolian defense minister has been invited to conferences in Hawaii, and as of September 1999, a U.S. military attaché has been assigned to the U.S. Embassy in Ulaanbaatar. The commander in chief of U.S. Pacific Operations arrived in Ulaanbaatar in August 2000, a month after the reconstituted MPRP had regained power in parliamentary elections, presumably to ensure continued cooperation. Since then, several Mongolian commanders have been trained in Hawaii and in American military schools, Mongolia has collaborated in NATO civil defense exercises, and the United States has provided communications equipment for Mongolian border troops.[38] In 2003, the chief of staff of the Mongolian Armed Forces met with high-ranking military officials in Washington to discuss military cooperation.[39]

In the same year, Mongolia dispatched two troop contingents to help the United States in the occupation of Iraq, and, "according to foreign mining employees who work in the Gobi Desert," the Mongolian government appears to have allowed the installation of "electronic surveillance equipment to monitor North Korea and the Lop Nor nuclear testing site in China."[40] Oyun and others opposed the dispatch of Mongolian "peacekeeping" forces to Iraq, and "support for the war was not universally welcomed by all Mongolians."[41] Finally, the chair of the U.S. Joint Chiefs of Staff visited Mongolia in January 2004 to thank the government for its support in Iraq and to donate a million dollars for training of peacekeepers, with promises also to provide military equipment to the Mongolian army.[42] In off-the-record interviews with me, Chinese officials exhibited some anxiety about U.S. intentions in Mongolia. They inquired whether the United States sought to use Mongolia to foster rifts between Russia and China, or whether it intended merely to use Mongolia as a listening post.

Europe and Mongolia

European countries were less concerned with security issues than the United States. One of their objectives was to cope with the humanitarian problems faced by Mongolian society. European states have provided assistance through TACIS (Technical Assistance to the Confederation of Independent States) and other programs. The Italian government has sent food and medical aid to the several hundred reindeer families of Northern Mongolia; the Danish government, through DANIDA, has started training and education programs for street children and school dropouts and has provided fellowships for budding social workers; the United Kingdom has started educational programs for Mongolian physicians; Norway has helped to build straw-bale houses for the homeless; the French government has initiated projects to improve the response to emergencies, to train physicians, to assist regions affected by forest fires, to ensure the potability of the water and the quality of the air in Ulaanbaatar, and to upgrade water supplies in several rural locations; Sweden has offered assistance on tourism, vocational assistance, and information technology; and Spain has offered loans for improvement of the sewers in Ulaanbaatar.[43] All these countries have also supplied emergency assistance to herders afflicted by the disastrous winters from 1999 to 2002. European nongovernmental organizations have also contributed to such efforts. Save the Children–UK, has established summer camps, shelters, and training centers for street children, has founded a facility for mentally handicapped children, and has even provided trolleys for children compelled to haul sizable loads in the wholesale Black Market. Its executive directors have been imaginative and yet pragmatic in the programs they have undertaken to help street children. The Christina Noble Foundation has worked with homeless children, although an accusation that a guard employed by the foundation beat and starved children has tarnished its image.[44]

European governments also supplied tangible economic assistance. NORAD, the Norwegian Agency for International Development Cooperation, provided mentoring in agriculture and in the production of woolen garments. The Dutch offered assistance in training of veterinarians, study of climate, and dairy and poultry production. They also sought to restore the native Przewalski horse, which had become almost extinct, into its habitat. The French expanded the telephone network and provided help for hospitals. The Germans furnished low-credit loans to small businesses and to telecommunications companies, set up a waste-processing plant in Ulaanbaatar, offered loans for hydropower projects, and pledged financial support for a German Mongolian school in Ulaanbaatar. Finland has funded three meteorological stations, the Czech Republic has provided training in agriculture and in 2003 pledged $5.4 million in loans and grants from 2003 to 2007, and Luxembourg has initiated programs to train bankers.[45]

A few European consultants were sensitive to Mongolian desires to determine their own policies and programs. Unlike many of the representatives of the international donor agencies, a Danish educational consultant for DANIDA, which provided $800,000 to rural schools, said, "Neither foreign experts in education nor foreign fund providers are in a position to teach Mongolians how to change their educational system; it is up to Mongolians to decide since our cultural backgrounds are different. We just offered and shared our experience and knowledge with our Mongolian colleagues." This philosophy influenced not only Danish efforts in retraining teachers and in revising textbooks but also their establishment of a Press Institute to train journalists for a free media.[46]

Foreign study opportunities in Europe for Mongolian students were designed to develop skilled and knowledgeable leaders to foster this independence in a Mongolian way. Manchester University offered fellowships to Mongolians for study of economics. Hungary, Poland, and other countries formerly in the Soviet bloc provided similar support for Mongolian students in a variety of disciplines. Germany, which has had a long association with Mongolia, also offered fellowships for training in medicine and in the arts and sciences.[47] The opening of the French Embassy in Ulaanbaatar in October 1996 promised additional opportunities for Mongolians to pursue their studies in France, and the French have also opened a cultural center with a library and computer access.[48]

Such aid and cultural opportunities aside, economic relations with Mongolia's former communist allies in Europe have not increased dramatically. Distance and relatively poor transport have impeded trade, leaving the Czech Republic and Poland as the only significant players. Hungary and Bulgaria still have joint ventures with Mongolia that were established during the communist era, and in 2003, Ukraine attempted to regenerate previously vital commercial relations, signing an agreement to trade farm machinery, medicines, and chemicals for Mongolian fluorspar and animal products.[49]

Western Europeans have fostered economic relations with Mongolia, but not enough to be truly significant. The Swiss and Italians have sent spinning and knitting equipment to the Gobi Cashmere State Company. France has imported horse meat and has encouraged Mongolians to produce better packaging and transport for the meat. Italians have helped to process 500,000 hides annually. The German airline Lufthansa and MIAT, the Mongolian airline, have sporadically maintained flights from Frankfurt and Berlin to Ulaanbaatar.[50] Germany, with a $32 million turnover, and Italy, with about $12 million, are Mongolia's biggest Western European trading partners.[51]

MONGOLIA AND NORTHEAST ASIA

Both the democratic reformers and the champions of the market economy have approved of attempts to widen Mongolia's relations beyond the great powers. The market economy advocates would probably prefer an alliance with the West but recognize that their geographic position between Russia and China precludes that possibility. Thus they too have attempted to cultivate relations with nations in Asia to avert sole reliance on China or Russia.

Although the Western countries could act as a counterbalance to growing Russian or Chinese influence or possible encroachment, Mongolia's own region of Northeast Asia offered perhaps greater security, at least economically. Japanese and Koreans have traditionally felt strong bonds with the Mongolians and have shown great interest in the Mongolian empire. The Mongolians could capitalize on this reservoir of good feelings to promote their security and independence and to foster economic development.

Japan naturally had more resources with which to assist the Mongolians. In 1972, despite differing views about World War II reparations payments by the Japanese, Japan and Mongolia established diplomatic relations. However, it was only the 1990 collapse of one-party rule in Mongolia that set the stage for closer Mongolian-Japanese relations. During the enthronement of Emperor Akihito in November 1990, Mongolian President Punsalmaagiin Ochirbat met with Prime Minister Toshiki Kaifu, who in August 1991 paid an official visit to Mongolia, inaugurating a more rapid pace of interchanges. Japan was particularly interested in Mongolia's natural resources, and both the Japanese and the Mongolians recognized that improvements in Mongolia's infrastructure were required to better exploit these.

Japan's interests shaped the kind of assistance it offered to the Mongolians, although humanitarian considerations also played a role. Starting in 1991, Japan, which remains as of 2004 the largest donor of aid to Mongolia, provided specific grants for telecommunications, business management, the Gobi Cashmere Company, meat and iron processing, railroads, milk factories, road building, repair of heavy machinery, and coal mining. It also contributed funds to the Number Four Power Station in Ulaanbaatar to ensure a steady supply of energy to the city's inhabitants. Tokyo became the venue for the meetings of international donors until the summer of 1999, when a meeting was convened in Ulaanbaatar. In addition to economic interests, Japan was particularly concerned about political stability in Northeast Asia and believed that economic and political disruptions in Mongolia might undermine such stability. Japanese leaders repeatedly proclaimed their hopes that Mongolia would fit in and identify with East Asia rather than Eastern Europe and Russia, which they thought essential to ensure order.[52]

Yet beyond its economic and strategic objectives, Japan also provided substantial aid. From 1991 to 1996, Japan accounted for 65.6 percent of the foreign assistance offered by individual states, although by 1998, it supplied only 40 percent of the aid. The aid has taken the form of gifts of public buses, diesel power stations for the countryside, motorcycles and generators for rural hospitals, a crime laboratory for the police, and fertilizers, combines, and tractors for agricultural settlements. It has also entailed funding for the digging of new wells and other projects to ensure the safety and reliability of Ulaanbaatar's water supply, and construction of flour mills. Some of these efforts have not been successful. The Japanese provided diesel power generators to herders but did not offer training. Nor did they recognize that herders did not have the money for fuel and spare parts. The Japanese company producing the generators made money, but the herders were not helped. The Japanese government has also sent aid in times of crisis. During the devastating winters from 1999 to 2002, it dispatched funds for hay and for medical equipment for herders and their animals afflicted by the so-called *zud.* Japanese specialists have consulted with their Mongolian counterparts to produce master plans for tourism and to devise policies concerning preservation of historical and archeological sites.[53]

The Japanese International Cooperation Agency (JICA) has managed most of the Japanese aid programs. Projects it has supported include renovation of school buildings, teacher training, new railroad signals, training of health personnel, assistance with desertification and agriculture, providing fire-fighting equipment, help for the disabled, improving air quality in Ulaanbaatar, and equipment for blood transfusions.[54]

The Japanese have also promoted cultural and educational developments in relations with Mongolia. They have offered scholarships to Mongolians to study in Japanese universities, have supported Japanese-language training in Mongolia, and have established a Japanese-language primary school in Ulaanbaatar. The Japanese government has provided funds to assist school dropouts in order to prevent an increase in the number of street children. Specific government agencies have arranged Mongolian art exhibits and cultural days in Japan and have also mounted Japanese exhibits and performances in Mongolia. In 2002, the Japanese opened a cultural center in Ulaanbaatar with a library, conference rooms, language laboratory, and space for exhibits. The Mongolians responded to this substantial amount of aid by one gesture that the Japanese appreciated: they returned the remains of Japanese soldiers or prisoners of war in World War II who had died and been buried in Mongolia.[55]

As the 1990s came to an end, however, the Japanese became increasingly concerned about the efficacy of their economic aid to Mongolia. Some of the funds appear to have been misused or mismanaged, and it has been difficult to account for some of the money or to determine whether the aid reached the intended recipients. The Japanese government has demanded greater accountability, as have other international donors. Auditors and examiners started to arrive in Mongolia in 1999 to ascertain whether the aid had been properly used. Aid has persisted throughout the 1990s and the early twenty-first century, and trade between Japan and Mongolia has increased, but not at the rapid clip that had been expected. In fact, since 1997, trade with Japan has remained static, if not in actual decline. It increased from $17.4 million in 1990 to $58.8 million in 1992, but the figure for 2002 had decreased to $46 million.[56] China, Russia, and the United States had outstripped Japan in trade turnover, perhaps because of the problems with the Japanese economy. Yet Japan offered important economic benefits for Mongolia. Japanese tourists, who supplied badly needed foreign exchange, outnumbered visitors from any other country, and direct flights from Osaka to Ulaanbaatar are now available; until the late 1990s, Japanese consumers were a vital market for Mongolian cashmere products, and the Mongolians, seeking to find an alternative to Russia for their animal products, have been selling horse meat to Japan. Japan and China had become such sizable markets for Mongolian timber that the Mongolian government had to limit wood exports. Japan also offered employment, mostly manual labor and relatively low-paying service occupations, to unemployed Mongolian workers. In addition to supplying natural resources to Japan, Mongolia has tried to repay its benefactor by supporting Japan's bid to become a permanent member of the UN Security Council.[57]

Despite its aid programs and its trade turnover with Mongolia, Japan cannot compete with China and Russia in its economic dealings with Mongolia. Thus the hope of developing an East Asian alternative to Mongolia's two immediate neighbors has not been fulfilled. Investment in Mongolia, a key indication of interest in an economy, has hardly attracted Japanese entrepreneurs. From 1990 to 1999, five Japanese concerns invested $54 million in Mongolia, not a ringing endorsement of the economic potential of the country, and despite a quick flurry of investments in mining from 2000 to 2003, investment from Japan amounts to only 7 percent of the total.[58] Sumitomi, Itochu, and other major corporations have suggested that Mongolia offer discounts and incentives to promote investments, but it is too early to tell whether such policies will actually foster a rapid flow of Japanese capital into the country.[59]

South Korea and Mongolia have had greater connections in the 1990s, but such economic relations have not matched the extraordinary growth of those between Mongolia and China. Earlier, North Korea had been the second country in the world to establish diplomatic relations with the Mongolian People's Republic. From 1948 to 1990, the two states maintained cordial economic relations and cultural exchanges. However, the Mongolian government's recognition of South Korea in 1990 generated tensions with North Korea. The North Korean government has twice closed down its embassy in Ulaanbaatar because of disagreements with Mongolian policies. Nonetheless, relations have persisted, and Mongolia has served as an intermediary in contacts with North Korea, particularly concerning the latter's development of nuclear weapons.[60]

Since 1990, however, Mongolian governments have opted to focus on closer relations with South Korea, recognizing that its more robust economy had much more to offer. This policy paid off, and South Korea became the third largest investor in Mongolia between 1990 and 2002, providing capital for mining, construction, and telecommunications and information technology in particular. By 2002, South Korea was Mongolia's fourth most important trading partner, importing Mongolian meat and supplying 40 percent of the country's telephones at one point. Since 1997, Korean Air Lines and MIAT have provided direct air services from Seoul to Ulaanbaatar. However, unlike Japan and the United States, Korea has until recently offered scant economic assistance. From 1991 to 1999, it made $14 million in loans and gave $200,000–$300,000 in annual grants. In 2000, it pledged to increase its assistance to $3.1 million in grants and $19 million in loans. The Democratic Union government had sought additional aid from Korea in minerals and energy development, and such help appears, at least on a limited scale, to be forthcoming.[61] Korean and Mongolians have also initiated projects of cultural collaboration, particularly in archeology.[62]

Another tangible economic benefit from South Korea has been its importance as an outlet for unemployed Mongolians, but this has also created difficulties. As of 2004, 30,000 Mongols reputedly lived in South Korea, although only seven hundred are legally entitled to work in the country. According to one unofficial estimate, they send back $80 to $100 million dollars, which constitutes almost 10 percent of Mongolia's GDP. However, problems with these illegal workers have not been resolved. Mongolian officials have complained about the low salaries, industrial accidents, and the long hours demanded of Mongolian workers, not to mention employer seizure of passports and sexual abuse. They have negotiated labor contracts, specifying higher wages, maximum hours, and acceptable health and safety standards for Mongolian employees, but these apply only to the small minority of legal workers. Naturally, too, these workers would be the first to be dismissed in an economic decline, which is precisely what happened during the Asian economic crisis of the late 1990s. In 1998 alone, 3,000 Mongolian workers returned to Mongolia because of the South Korean economic downturn. Nonetheless, many Mongolian workers remain in South Korea, despite the lack of health insurance and social security.[63]

MONGOLIA AND CENTRAL ASIA

It would seem natural for Mongolia to identify and maintain closer relations with the newly established states of Central Asia. Many in Mongolia and Central Asia share a pastoral nomadic heritage, and both experienced Soviet rule or influence for about seventy years in the twentieth century. One major difference is that much of Central Asia converted to Islam, while most Mongolians are Buddhists. However, seven decades of communist rule weakened formal religions, reducing the possibility of religious conflicts and improving the chances of mutually beneficial relations. Mongolia shares a border with Muslim Kazakhstan, and Kazakhs constitute about 5 percent of the country's population, most of them living in the western province of Bayan-Ölgii.

Yet the turbulence in Central Asia in the 1990s and the early twenty-first century has precluded much contact except for Kazakhstan. Mongolia established diplomatic relations with Uzbekistan, Tajikistan, and Turkmenistan, but this formal relationship did not translate into any significant political involvement. For a time, a civil war raged in Tajikistan, and Uzbekistan and Turkmenistan, ruled by authoritarian rulers, had stalled economies. Surprisingly, Kyrgyzstan provided $1,170,000 of goods in trade and planned to assist in building an oil refinery, which was projected to provide 15 percent of Mongolia's needs. By 1999, Kyrgyzstan had invested $750,000 in Mongolia and air links had been negotiated. However, this scarcely made the two countries significant economic partners, and dramatic increases in their economic relationship seem unlikely.[64]

Kazakhstan is the only Central Asian country to have more than a perfunctory relationship with Mongolia, partly because of the latter country's Kazakh minority. Faced with an economic depression in Mongolia after the withdrawal of Soviet economic assistance, an estimated 39,000 Kazakhs left for Kazakhstan in 1991–92. Many were to be disappointed, as Kazakhstan had similar economic difficulties, including problems in the privatization process. Such problems prompted Mongolia's Prime Minister Puntsagiin Jasrai to make an official visit to Kazakhstan to negotiate better conditions for Kazakh émigrés. However, their economic situation did not improve, and many Kazakhs had returned to Mongolia by 1996. They came back to similarly unsettled conditions in Mongolia. A 1997 letter from Bayan-Ölgii to the prime minister of Mongolia pleaded for greater assistance from the central government, because every second family had a member with no employment and every third lived below the poverty line.[65]

Economic relations between Kazakhstan and Mongolia started promisingly, but progress has been disappointing. Kazakhstan's trade with Mongolia amounted to only $7.6 million in 2002.[66] Mongolia planned to exchange its copper for grain, flour, and oil, but by 1997, Kazakhstan had piled up a substantial debt to the Erdenet copper mines, exacerbating the financial problems of that vital enterprise. Reciprocal visits by the two countries' presidents in 1998 and 1999 produced pledges of cooperation, Kazakhstan agreeing to establish joint ventures in grain processing and woolen fabrics and processing in Mongolia, to trade for cashmere and meat and meat products, to pay its debts to Erdenet, and to provide oil for Mongolia.[67] Both sides have committed themselves to improving road and air links between them. By making the first official visit of his presidency a trip to Kazakhstan in March 1998, Natsagiin Bagabandi sought to emphasize the significance of the two countries' mutual relations. In any case, the effectiveness of these pledges remains to be seen.

MONGOLIA AND WEST ASIA

West Asia, the other mostly Islamic region with which Mongolia has begun to deal, is too far away to be of much significance to it. Yet several

West Asian countries have developed promising relationships with Mongolia, Turkey being the most important. Like the Turkic states of Central Asia, Turkey perceives itself as having historical links with Mongolia. Diplomatic relations were established in 1969, but the Turkish president's official visit in 1995 generated the first substantial joint cooperative efforts. Although trade and investment remained relatively insignificant as of 2004, Turkey has set up an embassy on the main thoroughfare of Ulaanbaatar, and one of its first ambassadors was very active in fostering cordial relations. By 1997, the two countries had agreed to air links between Istanbul and Ulaanbaatar, and Turkey provided scholarships for at least 300 Mongolian students and founded a Turkish Studies Center in Ulaanbaatar, which fostered knowledge of Turkey and of Islam and conducted research on ancient Turkic monuments in the Orkhon valley. In 2001, the Turkish International Cooperation Agency pledged to help in transportation, communications, irrigation, and education projects. After his official visit to Kazakhstan in March 1998, President Bagabandi went on to visit Turkey and Kuwait.[68]

Bagabandi's trip to Kuwait proved to be particularly productive. Shortly thereafter, the Kuwait Foundation offered loans for road building and for construction of a hydroelectric power plant (which is still in the planning stage as of 2004) in Gov-Altai province and of the so-called Millennium Road. Trade between the two countries doubled between 1997–98 and 1998–99, although the totals remained relatively insignificant. In addition, because Kuwait and several of the Arab lands, like Mongolia, have large desert regions, they could offer technical assistance concerning the Gobi desert.

The objectives of some of the authoritarian Arab regimes have resulted in difficulties and have led some Mongolians to question the advisability of overly close relations. They are concerned about incurring sizable debts to the more dictatorial Arab governments, fearing the favors these governments might want in return. The first seemingly minor controversy involved export of Mongolian falcons, whose numbers have declined over the past decade, to Kuwait, Saudi Arabia, and other Arab countries (see chapter 7). Recruitment by Arab states of Mongolian laborers may generate a second potential controversy. Some Arab states have, in the past, been accused of exploiting foreign workers and servants, which might trouble Mongolian officials as they notice more of their people accepting employment in these lands. On the other hand, specific tangible benefits have accrued to Mongolians in relationships with Arab countries. Egypt has provided scholarships for Mongolian students and has offered training for the Mongolian police, and has cooperated on desertification and mining. Starting in 1998, Jordan imported mutton from Mongolia, and the lamb-eating West Asian countries could offer a market for Mongolian animal products.[69]

Israel, the non-Islamic West Asian state, has offered assistance similar to that provided by the Arab countries. Establishing diplomatic relations with Mongolia in 1991, it started shortly thereafter to provide technical aid in agriculture, mining, tourism, and education. Israel's successes in fostering agriculture in the desert and in promoting tourism impressed the Mongolians, who sought to develop those sections of their own economy. Trying to facilitate relations, in 1995, Israel eliminated visa fees for Mongolians visiting the country for up to thirty days. Some jobless Mongolians capitalized on this provision to secure illegal employment. By 2000, Israeli authorities had to cope with increasing numbers of illegal workers from Mongolia and had to deny entry to several groups of Mongolians.[70] As of 2004, Israel's trade turnover with and investment in Mongolia were negligible, making it unlikely that relations between the two countries would be extraordinarily significant.

MONGOLIA AND SOUTHEAST ASIA

Mongolia's relations with Southeast Asia have borne some fruit, but, like its contacts with Europe and Central and West Asia, have hardly dislodged particularly China and secondarily Russia as its most important contacts. Mongolia sought and in 1998 was granted admission into the Association of Southeast Asian Nations. Democratic Union leaders, in particular, made official visits to foster trade and investment. President Ochirbat traveled to Indonesia, and Foreign Minister Nyam-Osoryn Tuya visited Thailand and Vietnam, stimulating the Vietnamese president to make the first official visit to Mongolia of a leader of that state in forty-five years.[71] Part of this Mongolian effort stemmed from a professed desire to emulate the economic successes of the so-called Tigers of Southeast Asia, particularly Singapore. One of the most prominent Democratic Union leaders noted that the Asian Tigers had emphasized economic policy and relegated social policy to a secondary position, counting on economic growth to reduce poverty and attendant social problems. He advocated Mongolian adoption of this model and its trickle-down theory. Thus Southeast Asia served as a convenient vehicle to support the pure market philosophy of many in the Democratic Union. Mongolia did enjoy an increase in trade with Southeast Asian countries, which by 1998–99 amounted to about $1.8 million each with Malaysia and Indonesia and $1.6 million with Thailand—modest amounts compared to the trade turnover with China—and it did receive some aid from Malaysia.[72] The visits of the Australian prime minister and the Indonesian president in 2003 presaged possible increases in trade.[73]

India and Mongolia have a special relationship, because they share certain cultural traits. Indian Buddhism, as filtered through Tibet, had been the dominant religion in Mongolia since the seventeenth century, and Mongolian Buddhists revered early Indian Buddhist leaders and sages. In more modern times, India was the first noncommunist state to recognize the Mongolian People's Republic. However, it did not establish an embassy until the 1990s, when it appointed a Buddhist, Kushok Bakula, who was believed to be a reincarnation of a Bodhisattva, as its ambassador. Bakula promoted any evidence of a Buddhist revival in Mongolia, and the Mongolian government allowed him considerable leverage, on which he capitalized to construct a sizable monastery in Ulaanbaatar in 1999. Illness caused him to depart in 2000, and he died in 2003. Although Buddhism had revived somewhat by the time of his death, it had not made the extraordinary strides it had achieved in Tibet. Neither had India's economic relationships with Mongolia become particularly significant. Total trade turnover between the two countries in 2002 amounted to a paltry $1 million (out of Mongolia's total trade of $1.2 billion), and India's investments came to only $3.5 million. President Bagabandi visited India early in 2001, hoping to obtain support from India in building a new airport, fostering information technology, and improving higher education. He received such assurances, and within a few months, forty Mongolian students left for advanced study in India.[74] A trip by Prime Minister Enkhbayar early in 2004 elicited similar pledges of assistance in livestock production, science, technology, and information technology, India's forte.[75]

With the support of both democratic reformers and champions of the pure market, officials have tried strenuously to expand Mongolia's relations with the outside world, but their efforts have not altered its continued economic reliance on Russia and, particularly, China for commerce and investment. As of 2002, trade turnover with these two neighbors constituted about 55 percent of Mongolia's international commerce. Investment from China and Hong Kong alone amounted to about 45 percent of total foreign investment. The international donor agencies have supplanted Russia as the main source of foreign aid, which gives them considerable economic leverage, and they have used such influence to foster specific political and economic policies. However, they have not succeeded in achieving an extraordinary increase in Western investment and trade with Mongolia. In fact, as we shall see, some of their market economy policies have facilitated China's developing economic relationship with Mongolia.

Chapter 9 | SINO-MONGOLIAN RELATIONS

By the early twenty-first century, to the dismay of some of the democratic reformers, China was playing an increasingly important role in Mongolia. They feared not only the authoritarian Chinese government but also economic dependence on China. A legacy of at least two thousand years of mistrust and intermittent confrontations and hostilities between the two societies has influenced contemporary Mongolia's relations with China. Qing dynasty rule over Mongolia embittered the Mongolians. Manchu and Chinese officials exploited them, and Chinese merchants capitalized on their country's political domination to enrich themselves at the expense of the Mongolians. Thus when the Chinese Revolution erupted in October 1911, the Mongolian nobility attempted to break away from China in December of the same year, but disunity prevented this. Subsequently, in 1921, the Mongolian People's Revolutionary Party took power, with Soviet assistance and guidance, if not domination, as noted earlier.

Yet almost a decade elapsed before the USSR could replace the Chinese as the dominant external stakeholder in Mongolia. A student of Mongolian affairs offers a graphic although perhaps exaggerated view of Chinese influence when he writes: "The Mongols depended on Chinese merchants for tea, Chinese peasants for farming, Chinese artisans for the building of monasteries and making of Buddhist artifacts, Chinese money-lenders for capital, and Chinese labor for hard work other than livestock herding." Estimates of the number of Chinese in the country, based on a sketchy census conducted in 1918, range from 100,000, out of a total population of approximately 675,000, to a more likely figure of about 25,000 to 30,000, with by far the largest number concentrated in the capital city. In 1925, four hundred Chinese firms operated in the country, while only fifty Russian firms had established a foothold.[1] However, the late 1920s and early 1930s witnessed a large-scale exodus of the Chinese from Mongolia, prompted by the Mongolians and their Soviet patrons. By 1932, the Chinese comprised about 10 percent of the industrial labor force as against 63 percent just three years earlier.

Even after the conclusion of World War II, the Chinese could not challenge the predominance of the USSR in Mongolia. They were forced to accept the Yalta agreements concluded by Joseph Stalin and Franklin D. Roosevelt in 1945, and acquiescing to U.S. pressure, Chiang Kai-shek agreed to a plebiscite for the Mongolians. The result was a foregone conclusion. On October 20, 1945, almost 100 percent of the Mongolian electorate reputedly opted for independence. In 1947, however, conflict between Chiang's forces and the Mongolians concerning territory along the Xinjiang-Mongolian border offered him a pretext to renounce the plebiscite.

The Chinese Communist victory in 1949 did not necessarily bode well for Sino-Mongolian relations. In his renowned interviews with the journalist Edgar Snow in the late 1930s, Mao Zedong had said that Mongolia would inevitably return to Chinese jurisdiction after the communist victory in China. Even more alarming had been the rapid communist move into Inner Mongolia in 1947 and its immediate incorporation as a so-called autonomous region within China.[2]

In 1952, the Mongolian head of state, Tsedenbal, appeared eager to restore relations with China, in part to avoid total dependence on the USSR. He traveled to Moscow, where he met with Stalin and Zhou Enlai and agreed to construction of a railroad from the Chinese border to Ulaanbaatar, which then linked up to the USSR, facilitating contact between all three countries. Having thus laid the foundation for increased relations, Tsedenbal went to Beijing within a few weeks to sign an agreement on economic and cultural cooperation. The two sides negotiated quite a number of agreements from 1953 to 1955, most of which concerned Chinese aid. This assistance, in the form of grants and loans, covered the costs for the construction of a paper mill, roads, bridges, apartment buildings, and a textile factory, among other projects.

Possibly as important as the monetary aid was the dispatch of Chinese workers. Mongolia suffered from a shortage of labor, which prevented the initiation of construction and infrastructure projects. China, conversely, had a surplus of workers with skills and experience that the Mongolians lacked. By the mid 1950s, about 10,000 Chinese workers had arrived in Mongolia to assist in the construction efforts envisioned in these agreements.

However, by 1957, the Sino-Soviet dispute had heated up and impinged upon Mongolia's relations with its two neighbors. Two considerations ultimately led Mongolia to favor the USSR. The Mongolians still recalled Qing domination over their land and feared annexation. They did not have similar concerns about the Russians, who had the vast territory of Siberia to populate and develop. A second distinction was that the USSR could offer much more aid than China could. Therefore, by 1965, nearly all the Chinese laborers had left Mongolia, necessitating even greater dependence on the USSR for economic development. And the Soviet leadership almost immediately provided the support the Mongolians required, pledging over six hundred million rubles in aid and to train Mongolians to perform the tasks previously undertaken by the ousted Chinese laborers. A few months later, the two parties negotiated a trade agreement favorable to the Mongolians. Even more important, the following year, the USSR and Mongolia signed a Treaty of Friendship, Cooperation, and Mutual Assistance, part of which entailed a Soviet guarantee of the territorial integrity of its neighbor. Troops from the USSR began to arrive almost immediately, and as the Sino-Soviet conflict intensified, tens of thousands of Soviet soldiers were stationed in Mongolia.[3]

The onset of the Chinese Cultural Revolution, particularly as it affected Inner Mongolia, generated even greater animosity between China and Mongolia. One target was the Inner Mongolian leader Ulanhu and the Mongolian nationalism that the Chinese accused him of representing. Violence erupted between Red Guards, mostly wandering bands of Chinese youths, and Mongolians, and eventually between the Chinese army and Mongolians. The government-controlled press in Mongolia published severe critiques of what Mongolians perceived to be China's oppressive policy in Inner Mongolia. Mongolian support for their kinsmen in Inner Mongolia persisted throughout the Cultural Revolution and inflamed tensions between Mongolia and China.

Meanwhile, the Chinese were concerned about the large number of Soviet troops stationed in Mongolia—probably as many as 100,000—and the close cooperation between the two countries, as evidenced by repeated exchanges of military delegations. China also accused the USSR of economic exploitation of Mongolia and its natural resources. According to Chinese reports, Soviet nostrums about "equality" and "mutual assistance" were designed to conceal their colonialist practice of purchasing livestock, wool, and minerals, Mongolia's most important resources, at reduced prices. Russian managers often controlled industrial enterprises and considered Russian, not Mongolian, interests in their decisions.

Charges and countercharges between Chinese and Mongolian leaders persisted until the early 1980s. The conclusion of the Cultural Revolution paved the way for attenuation of their conflicts. Improvements in the relations between the USSR and China also fostered closer contacts between China and Mongolia. The means by which relations were improved resembled the ping-pong diplomacy that marked the resumption of China's relations with the United States. Wrestling was the medium in this case, as a Mongolian wrestling team was invited in 1983 to put on demonstrations in Inner Mongolia and in Beijing. Later in the year, tourism between the two countries was restored, and border crossings were reopened. Commerce inevitably followed such freedom of movement. Even more significant was a 1984 speech by Hu Yaobang, general secretary of the Chinese Communist Party. Visiting Inner Mongolia, Hu spoke about the future of the region and of its links with Mongolia. He proclaimed that peaceful resolution of border disputes would foster commercial and cultural developments that would benefit both sides. The following year, China and Mongolia signed a five-year agreement to trade Mongolian minerals and livestock for Chinese petroleum products and trucks. As noted earlier, Mikhail Gorbachev's speech in Vladivostok on July 29, 1986, with its pledge to withdraw Soviet troops from Mongolia, set the stage not only for better relations between the USSR and China but also between Mongolia and China.

The three years after Gorbachev's speech witnessed a diverse array of contacts between China and Mongolia. Within weeks after the speech, the two countries signed a consular treaty. Later, delegations of scholars, writers, and trade union leaders, members of friendship committees and leaders of women's groups, and tours by acrobatic troupes and athletic teams followed one after another across the Sino-Mongolian border. Renewing scientific and technological cooperation after a twenty-year lapse, the two countries signed an agreement concerning joint projects on animal husbandry, energy, and light industry.[4]

Similarly, economic relations burgeoned. Trade volume in 1986 doubled compared to the previous year, with Mongolia providing paper products, carpets, used tires, and scrap metal in exchange for textiles, bricks, tiles, and consumer goods. By 1987, trade volume between Mongolia and Inner Mongolia alone amounted to $2.43 million, a sizable increase from the 1985 figure of $412,000. The sensitive issue of the recruitment of Chinese labor also came to the fore. The Mongolians certainly needed Chinese workers for the infrastructure and construction projects that they envisioned. The two sides had complementary needs. Mongolia required skilled labor, while China could profit from Mongolia's animal and mineral resources. Yet Mongolia still feared that these Chinese workers would be the first wave in an onslaught of Chinese who would migrate and overwhelm Mongolia, as they had done in Inner Mongolia. Nonetheless, they negotiated for Chinese workers to build a tourist center, a kindergarten, and tourist *gers* in Ulaanbaatar.[5]

Political and diplomatic interchanges between the two neighbors continued apace. Visits back and forth by highly ranked Chinese and Mongolian officials began to cement relations. In June 1987, the vice chair of the National People's Congress of China paid an official visit to Mongolia, the first parliamentary contact in twenty years. The following year, the first delegation of the Mongolian Khural since 1960 arrived in Beijing to meet Chinese legislators. In July 1989, the Chinese Communist Party and the MPRP restored ties. Tserenpiliin Gombosüren's trip was the first official visit to China by a Mongolian foreign minister in forty years, and his brief sojourn in Beijing resulted in a treaty that led to closer relations.

The new agreement permitted the Mongolians to open a consulate in Hohhot in Inner Mongolia, to eliminate visa requirements for Chinese and Mongolian citizens crossing their borders, to establish intergovernmental commissions on trade, science, and technical cooperation, and to lay the framework for additional cultural exchanges. Gombosüren also met with Chinese dignitaries, including President Yang Shangkun, who ended their audience by announcing that "China and Mongolia are equal." Later that year, the Chinese foreign minister, Qian Qichen, reciprocated with a visit to Mongolia to solidify relations between the two countries.[6]

POSTCOMMUNIST MONGOLIAN
ATTITUDES TOWARD CHINA

The year 1989 proved to be pivotal for Sino-Mongolian relations. In June, the Chinese authorities clamped down on protesting workers and students in and around Tiananmen Square in Beijing, reputedly killing several thousand people. Such repression imposed definite limits on dissidence. Yet these turbulent events did not impede Chinese contacts with Mongolia. In fact, in July, a delegation from the Chinese Communist Party arrived in Ulaanbaatar to negotiate with the MPRP, as if nothing had happened. Jambyn Batmünkh, the Mongolian head of state, went to meet with Gorbachev in Moscow to discuss the Mongolian response to the Tiananmen repression. They must have agreed to de-emphasize it, or at least not to let it interfere with Mongolia's relations with China.[7]

The official line of the Mongolian government over the past decade has been that China has abandoned efforts to expand into Mongolia. There is some merit to this view. With no menacing Soviet troops in Mongolia, China need not fear for the security of its borderlands. Continued turbulence in Russia, as well as a considerable defusing of Sino-Russian hostilities, has reduced Chinese anxieties and lessened the possibility of a Chinese policy of occupying Mongolia and attempting to use it as a buffer zone against a threat from the north. Naturally, if the West, particularly the United States, seeks to use Mongolia as a base for espionage or for other military purposes, the Chinese might react differently. However, they appear to have decided that seeking economic influence and potentially economic domination are better strategies than seeking to govern still another restive so-called national minorities area, which could be as troublesome as Tibet and Xinjiang have been.[8]

In interviews with architects and implementers of Mongolian foreign policy, I have found a professed lack of concern about Chinese economic leverage. In July 1998, when I met with Minister of External Relations Amarjargal, he asserted that he did not fear Chinese investment in land or in industrial or retail enterprises. A few days earlier, I had interviewed Jambaljamtsyn Od, the foreign policy advisor to Prime Minister Elbeg-dorj, who added that China offered a huge market for Mongolian products. Tümenbayariin Ragchaa, a member of the communist old guard who had traditionally identified with Soviet interests, also saw no threat posed by growing Chinese investment in the Mongolian economy.[9]

The democratic reformers appeared less sanguine about China's intentions, although they emphasized the need to learn about China and to develop a corps of China specialists. Many were alarmed by the growing Chinese influence, but they were realistic enough to educate their children to deal with it. The prominent pollster Luvsandendev Sumati was typical in his ambivalence. In his talks with me in the late 1990s, he repeatedly pointed to the overt and covert effects of what he perceived to be Chinese influence on the Mongolian economy and political life. Yet his son was fluent in Chinese and was earning his degree in a Chinese university, and his daughter was also studying in a Chinese university. Tömör-öchiryn Erdenebileg, who had studied Chinese language and civilization at university, expressed concern about Chinese intentions. Chuluuny Ganbold, the editor of the E-Mail Daily News, was worried about China, but his daughters studied in Chinese schools in Beijing.

The general Mongolian population appeared to concur in the judgments of the democratic reformers. In a survey conducted by the Sant Maral Foundation in February 1996, 79 percent of respondents expressed a desire for closer ties with Russia; 54 percent also opted for closer links with Japan; but only 35 percent supported such ties with China. Annual polls since then have reached the same results. As early as 1993, the Economist Intelligence Unit, in its survey of Mongolian economic developments, found that "many ordinary people express the traditional fear that the growing presence of Chinese, mainly small businessmen, in Mongolia could be a prelude to a Chinese takeover." Some Mongolians feared that cheap Chinese imports would subvert nascent industries, and that the Chinese, either on their own or through Mongolian agents, would buy majority shares in important enterprises on the Stock Exchange. By late 1997, "rumours that companies have been bought by Chinese individuals or companies [had] aroused some popular criticism."[10]

Despite these concerns, the various Mongolian governments since 1990 have persisted in a policy of maintaining good relations and seeking even closer contacts with China. In 1991, Punsalmaagin Ochirbat, the first president after the collapse of communism, went to China as his first official visit abroad. While in Beijing, he negotiated public health and environmental agreements. Later that same year, on his way back from Japan, he once again stopped over in China and met with Chinese President Yang Shangkun. In late summer of 1991, Yang Shangkun became the first Chinese president to visit Mongolia, and his trip resulted in tangible agreements, which started with a pledge not to interfere in each other's internal affairs and to seek mutually beneficial and peaceful relations. China permitted landlocked Mongolia use of the port of Tianjin from which to ship its exports. It also committed itself to a package of loans and aid and an increase in trade, air services, and cultural and scientific exchanges, while Mongolia committed itself to protecting Chinese investments in Mongolia.[11]

A stream of high-level visitors has continued, without interruption, since then, with some leading to tangible agreements, but most have been principally goodwill trips. Leaders of the MPRP and the Chinese Communist Party have exchanged delegations; Chinese and Mongolian military officials have visited each other, with one Chinese minister of defense arriving in Ulaanbaatar in June 1996 and another visiting the Mongolian capital in January 2000. Still another delegation of high-level Chinese military officials arrived in 2001. One pattern that emerges from these meetings is repeated assurances by the Mongolians, probably at the insistence of the Chinese, that they accept a one-China policy, with Taiwan simply regarded as a province of China.[12]

The visit of Chinese Premier Li Peng to Ulaanbaatar in April 1994 was probably one of the most important of these exchanges. Li signed a Treaty of Friendship and Cooperation meant to define Sino-Mongolian relations. The treaty recognized the independence, sovereignty, and territorial integrity of Mongolia and committed the two countries to policies of nonaggression, noninterference in each other's internal affairs, and peaceful coexistence. Each pledged not to join alliances directed at the other, and neither would allow their territories to be used by the troops of another country for an attack against the other. In addition to the treaty, China promised to respect Mongolia's nuclear free-status in return for yet another pledge that Mongolia acknowledged the existence of one China, although the Chinese conceded that Mongolia could maintain unofficial relations with Taiwan. With political issues resolved, the two countries then devised additional areas of scientific, educational, public health, cultural, and technological cooperation and agreed on means of improving postal and telecommunications facilities. They also increased commercial opportunities and pledged to cooperate on the use of water along their borders, and the Chinese provided a sizable loan for purchase of consumer goods and other Mongolian needs.

After Li's visit, President Ochirbat commented: "There are no unresolved issues of principle between Mongolia and China." In light of developments since then, his assessment was too rosy.[13]

Four and a half years later, Mongolian President Bagabandi met with Jiang Zemin, general secretary of the Chinese communist party, and Premier Zhu Rongji. The agreements they negotiated included the standard formulas: guarantee of Mongolian independence and territory; nonaggression and peaceful coexistence; and the one-China mantra. Once these formalities had been concluded, a slew of agreements and potential areas of cooperation were on the agenda. The two sides pledged to cooperate on serious violations along the borders, including illegal entry, smuggling, money laundering, and narcotics. The Chinese planned to assist Mongolia to build an oil refinery in Zuunbayan, with a capacity to process 500,000 tons annually, and to expand rail and road links between the two countries. China also pledged to supply Mongolia with petroleum and petroleum products, to grant loans, to promote tourism, and to cooperate in ensuring that trade goods exchanged between the two countries were of high quality. Scholarships for study at Chinese higher educational institutions would be available to Mongolian students, and Mongolians could receive treatment at Chinese hospitals at a discount. Both sides also supported exchanges in science, education, and athletics.[14]

Nonofficial contacts between Chinese and Mongol citizens accelerated from the beginning of the 1990s on. The variety of exchanges and delegations was remarkable. Mongolian Buddhists arrived in Inner Mongolia; a delegation from an association of the Mongolian disabled, leaders of the Mongolian Khural, representatives of the Mongolian Women's Federation, and reporters from the government newspaper *Ardyn Erkh* visited China.[15]

Such exchanges culminated in a professed reconciliation of Mongolian-Chinese security relations. Ravdan Bold, then secretary of the National Security Council (whose members included the president, the prime minister, and the chair of the Khural), the government body primarily responsible for the policies needed to guarantee Mongolia's security, and currently Mongolian ambassador to the United States, is a principal architect of Mongolia's defense and security strategy. Several years before he assumed his position, he had written: "Historically, Mongolia has viewed both neighbors' [i.e., China's and Russia's] policies on many political-strategic issues with caution and even apprehension. Today, historical lessons should certainly be taken into account, but we should not allow ourselves to be trapped by history as we formulate our national security policy." Bold and the other authors of the *Mongolian Defense White Paper*, issued by the Ministry of Defense in 1998, asserted that neither Russia nor China "is striving to exert dominant influence in Mongolia." They also documented the growing cooperation in military affairs between China and Mongolia and China's acceptance of Mongolia's neutrality and nuclear-free status. No doubt others might challenge Bold's description of China's intentions, but official Mongolian pronouncements endorsed this benevolent view of China's objectives in Northeast Asia. Joint military conferences, round-table talks, military exchanges, and Chinese grants for military equipment and for Chinese-language training for the Mongolian military indicate the growing links between the two countries.[16]

INCREASE IN SINO-MONGOLIAN ECONOMIC RELATIONS

Perhaps the most significant result of the agreements and exchanges was closer economic relations. Much of the impetus for such relations derived from interchanges between Mongolia and the Inner Mongolian Autonomous Region. The Mongolian government had established a consulate in Hohhot in Inner Mongolia as early as 1990. Border trade increased, and the town of Erlian on the Inner Mongolian side of the border flourished as a result of commerce. It even supplied electricity for Zamyn Üüd, the Mongolian town right across the border. Zamyn Üüd itself had benefited so much from commerce that it built a fifty-bed hotel.[17]

These legal and economic developments have translated into a tremendous increase in trade. A large number of Mongolians travel annually to China and Russia to buy food and other basic commodities, with most now going to China. From 1991 to 1996, Mongolia had a favorable balance of trade with China, but it has increasingly sent its raw materials for processing to its southern neighbor. China thus reaps the substantial additional value that accrues from processing and refining cashmere, copper, and other products it imports from Mongolia. In turn, the collapse of agriculture and of processing industries after the fall of the communist system compelled the Mongolians to seek flour, rice, and vegetables from China. With the elimination of customs duties on May 1, 1997, imports of Chinese flour increased. By 2004, two-thirds of Mongolia's flour and most of its sugar and rice were imported from China. Mongolia had been self-sufficient in flour during the communist era, and its dependence on imports for essential foods has been a stunning reversal. With limited supplies of wheat and other agricultural products, and with shortages of fuel, machinery, spare parts, and credit, many processing mills have closed.[18]

Mongolian trade with China has increased rapidly, in fact, more rapidly than with any other country. In 1989, the total turnover at current prices amounted to $24.1 million, but by 2002, it had climbed to $388.2 million. As of 2002, 42.1 percent of Mongolia's exports went to China, which outstripped all of Mongolia's other trading partners, and China provided 24.3 percent of Mongolia's imports. These figures do not include the apparently sizable amount of illegal trade and smuggling along the Sino-Mongolian frontier.[19]

Chinese loans and technical aid to Mongolia accelerated in the 1990s and early twenty-first century. The number of such technical advisors is difficult to ascertain. Statistics are fragmentary, perhaps because both the Mongolian and the Chinese governments may want to downplay the Chinese presence. One telling indication of the Chinese presence is that by 1999, 39.1 percent of the foreigners who received work permits were Chinese, the highest percentage for any nationality. Simultaneously, the

Chinese have been providing low-interest or interest-free loans for a hydroelectric power station, solar-powered generators, repair of bridges, construction of hospitals, and the building of a World Trade Center in Ulaanbaatar, among other projects.[20]

Chinese philanthropic assistance also fostered closer relations. During the Mongolian crisis following the collapse of communism, the Chinese sent substantial quantities of rice and other food aid. Such ad hoc help was formalized in a 1999 agreement in which the Chinese pledged assistance for disaster relief, and within the next three years, they abided by the agreement and provided grants for herders whose animals were afflicted with hoof and mouth disease.[21]

Chinese economic involvement was not limited to such generous aid but also included investment designed for profit. The pace of investment has quickened over the past five years. Moreover, rumors abound that Chinese investors have surreptitiously used Mongolian agents to bid for them in auctions privatizing Mongolian enterprises. The total of Chinese investments may thus be much higher than officially recognized. The Chinese will invest $120 million in an oil refinery in Nailakh,[22] and as of 2003, China had more than 600 businesses in Mongolia, the largest investments being in mining, construction, processing raw materials (including cashmere, skins, and hides), and knitting and sewing factories.[23] Late in the year, the Chinese ambassador to Mongolia cited tourism and information technology as other sectors for possible investment.[24]

In recognition of the growing importance of Chinese investors and owners, the Mongolian Chamber of Commerce organized a Mongolian-Chinese Economic and Business Council in July 1999 to facilitate and promote Chinese investment and to publicize Chinese accomplishments in economics, culture, and science. A second meeting of the Council in January 2000 provided a venue for Chinese investors to lobby for an elimination of the export tax on cashmere and for a reduction in the price of copper concentrate sent to China for refining.[25]

China also has a vital role in regional economic cooperation projects. Since the early 1990s, the UNDP and the individual governments have been touting the development of Northeast Asia as an integrated unit, with individual countries offering complementary assets. China and North Korea could supply cheap and abundant labor; Mongolia and Russia (from Siberia), mineral and natural resources; and Japan and South

Korea, capital and technical expertise. Not everyone is sanguine about the prospects of this proposition. One contrary view is that the relations between two of the areas, Siberia and Mongolia, are limited because Mongolia offers few attractive goods and little hard currency.[26]

China's cooperation is vital for Mongolia's participation in such regional plans. Since their gradual resumption of relations, the Chinese and Mongolians had been negotiating about the construction of a natural gas pipeline from Siberia to China, which seeks additional sources of energy as its economy continues to grow. They had planned to make the Kovyktinskoye fields accessible to China, and the shortest route traverses Mongolia, offering Mongolians opportunities to levy fees and to obtain a clean source of energy. In an interview with me, Baabar, one of the Democratic Union finance ministers, presented the pipeline as Mongolia's economic salvation. As of 2004, it appears, however, that the planned route will skirt Mongolia because the Chinese do not want the pipeline to traverse a different country on its route from Russia.[27]

Educational and cultural exchanges between China and Mongolia have increased, although not as rapidly as the increase in English and Russian studies in Mongolia. In 2002, Hohhot hosted "Ulaanbaatar Days," a festival of Mongolian art, music, and film. The Mongolians opened a Center for Chinese Studies to train China experts and assist Mongolian businessmen, and the Chinese government sent 77 students to Mongolia to study the Mongolian language. Still, the number of translators and interpreters was insufficient; by 2002, 600 joint ventures needed such services. By early 2003, 2,000 Mongolian students were studying Chinese at Mongolian universities.[28]

MONGOLIAN GRIEVANCES

Yet serious problems have persisted. Many of the Mongolian democratic reformers fear Chinese expansionism, a fear fueled by the appearance of unofficial Chinese publications portraying Mongolia as part of China. On the other hand, China is concerned about Mongolia stirring up the Mongolians of China into opposition.[29]

As noted earlier, the policies of the Western and international donors since 1990 have contributed to tensions by facilitating Chinese entrance into and growing domination over Mongolia and its economy. The elimination of barriers in trade that the IMF, the ADB, and other international organizations have all strenuously promoted has left Mongolia vulnerable to possible economic manipulation from China. As we saw in chapter 8, after a ban on exporting raw cashmere was rescinded at the insistence of the IMF, Mongolian cashmere processors and Mongol Amicale, the joint American-Mongolian cashmere processor, could no longer compete. One knowledgeable observer asserts, perhaps hyperbolically, that this change in policy has "turned [Mongolia] into a raw material warehouse for China."[30]

The IMF, adhering to its pure market philosophy, has responded to the crises faced by Mongolian cashmere processors by saying that companies that cannot pay the market price for raw cashmere should not be in production. Oyun objected strenuously to IMF policy, insisting that Mongolian cashmere-processing industries needed protection until they could compete with stronger neighbors.[31] In any event, the Mongolian processing companies do not currently have a sufficient supply of raw cashmere, because most is sold to the Chinese. As one newspaper put it, "If the situation continues . . . before long the domestic cashmere market will be dominated by Chinese dealers and Chinese might take over the world's cashmere market."[32] Similarly, Mongolian wool processors face the same competition from wealthier Chinese traders, who can afford to pay higher prices for the excellent quality of wool produced in Mongolia.[33]

The cashmere trade has not been the only economic issue that has provoked tensions. Echoing Sino-Mongolian trade under the Ming dynasty, complaints about the quality of products have repeatedly arisen. As early as 1994, Mongolians questioned whether many Chinese imports were safe and conducive to good health. The Mongolian press has frequently spoken of the poor food storage facilities used by Chinese traders, the sale of out-of-date merchandise, and the fact that many Chinese goods are infested with insects. One article claimed that inspectors found 3,000 insects in ten tons of imported Chinese flour, which then had to be destroyed. Another asserted that half the Chinese food arriving in Mongolia had been found to contain dangerously high levels of pesticides, including DDT. The 1996 Economist Intelligence Unit Country Report reported that many Mongolians believed that Chinese food had caused an outbreak of cholera.[34] Some of these accusations appear to reflect an age-old suspicion of and hostility toward the Chinese. Whether all these attributions are accurate is immaterial; more important is that many Mongolians believe such accounts.

Similar accusations have been leveled at other Chinese products. Newspaper articles, as well as officials, have advised Mongolian storekeepers and merchants not to use Chinese scales or balances because of their untrustworthiness. Five Chinese-built Yu-12 planes supplied in 1993 by a Harbin-based company, two of which had crashed by 1998, causing thirty-five deaths, were thought even more unreliable (although overloading and poor maintenance by inadequately trained Mongolian technicians may have been partly responsible for the disasters), and the Mongolians returned the remaining planes to China. No wonder that a Westerner traveling in Mongolia was told that "all things made in China are terrible."[35]

Illegal activities by Chinese citizens received much notice in the Mongolian press, contributing to a negative image in the public mind. Officials have captured numerous Chinese smuggling cars, alcohol, and narcotics into Mongolia. Chinese livestock rustlers and fishermen poaching in Mongolian waters have posed continual problems, and several Chinese have been caught smuggling out marmot pelts. Moreover, the authorities have repeatedly rounded up Chinese prostitutes and pimps, and on one occasion detained a group of Chinese who were escorting North Korean women traveling to China for marriage or prostitution. News reports of fights between Chinese and Mongolians have also occasionally appeared.[36]

According to Mongolian sources, a few Chinese have been brazenly taking advantage of their position to ravage Mongolian resources. They have encouraged illegal cutting of Mongolian timber, even in the sacred Bogd Khan Mountains, and have paid the desperate unemployed Mongolians who provided the wood only a third of the world price. Mongolian sources have also accused the Chinese of poaching deer antlers. Late in 1998, the government was compelled to ban deer exports and to impose severe limits on hunting, partly to curtail deer poaching. The Mongolian camel population has decreased partly because of the Chinese demand for camel meat and hooves. Chinese have been detained for illegally mining for gold and polluting nearby waters by indiscriminate dumping of mercury.[37] State authorities have also complained that Chinese-owned businesses in Mongolia did not pay taxes and that several produced illegal drugs. They arrested one Chinese owner for producing ephedrine in his factory rather than the medicines for which he had a license. In a random check of foreign, mostly Chinese, factories, the Mongolian authorities found that 80 percent violated labor laws or health and safety regulations. Several compelled laborers to work overtime and did not permit rest periods.[38] One Chinese manager of a knitting factory responded that Mongolian laborers did not work hard, were unsteady, and produced shoddy goods.[39]

Numerous noneconomic issues have also bedeviled Sino-Mongolian relations. In 1995 and 1996, the Mongolian government protested the testing of two nuclear weapons in Xinjiang, not far from the Mongolian border. It complained of the high levels of radiation these tests produced on Mongolian territory and expressed dismay at a purported Chinese plan to bury nuclear wastes near Mongolia. When China signed the Comprehensive Nuclear Test Ban Treaty late in 1996, these issues receded somewhat.[40]

Rumors of Chinese attempts to manipulate or to take advantage of Mongolia have been pervasive. As early as 1992, when the Chinese had barely established a presence in the country, several political parties accused the Chinese of seeking to annex Mongolia. The rumors had become so unsettling that Mongolian Prime Minister Dashiin Byambasüren was compelled to respond and avowed that China respected Mongolia's territorial integrity and would not intervene in Mongolia's domestic affairs. However, such allegations persisted. In 1998, a prominent newspaper reported that China surreptitiously interfered in Mongolia's internal affairs, usually through Mongolian agents. In early 1999, an op-ed essay in the *UB Post* mentioned rumors that the Chinese had plans for a coup d'état in Mongolia if the situation there became turbulent. One analyst pointed out that China provided funds to support the victorious Democratic Union in the June 1996 elections in order to undermine the MPRP and therefore Russian influence in Mongolia. Another asserted that a 1998 contribution of $20,000 to the Mongolian Social Democratic Party was an attempt to combat the MPRP.[41]

CHINESE GRIEVANCES

The Chinese have, in turn, been irritated with Mongolian policies, including support for Tibetan Buddhism. The Mongolians permitted the

Dalai Lama to visit Mongolia in 1979, 1982, and 1987. Although the government delayed his visits in 1991 and 1994 to prevent his arrival during state visits by President Yang Shangkun and Premier Li Peng, it granted him entry in each case about a month after the Chinese dignitaries had departed from Mongolia. In 2002, he arrived, via Japan, in Mongolia, irritating the Chinese who, for several days, halted train traffic between China and Mongolia in response. In addition, numerous *gers* and apartments display images of the Dalai Lama, and the inhabitants worship at shrines in honored places in their homes. The Chinese regard Tibet as an internal issue and bristle at any assistance or support for the Dalai Lama.[42]

They have been even more concerned about an Inner Mongolia-Mongolia link. Chinese officials remember that the Mongolian government denounced Chinese policy in Inner Mongolia during the Cultural Revolution. With the establishment of regular relations between China and Mongolia, Mongolian government criticism has been silenced. Nonetheless, demonstrations in Inner Mongolia have persisted.[43] For a time, Mongolians in Mongolia on occasion contributed to Chinese fears of external involvement in Inner Mongolia. In September 1993, for example, former Prime Minister Byambasüren, as head of the newly created Mongolian Development Support Foundation, organized a World Forum of Mongolians in Ulaanbaatar.

The Chinese viewed this meeting as an attempt to stir up Pan-Mongolian sentiments, which might lead to further disruptions in Inner Mongolia. However, as economic relations with China have developed, and as Mongolia has become increasingly dependent on China for trade and investment since the mid 1990s, calls for such forums of the world's Mongolians have diminished. Although Mongolia continues to have cultural and economic exchanges with Buryatia, Tuva, and Inner Mongolia, Mongolian leaders have scarcely alluded to Pan-Mongolianism, probably for fear of antagonizing the Chinese.

However, individual Mongolian nationals have reacted to the sporadic hard-line Chinese policies toward Inner Mongolia. In February 1996, Mongolian demonstrators, particularly from the Mongolian Students' Union, marched and paraded around the Chinese Embassy in Ulaanbaatar and eventually gave the officials at the embassy a petition calling for the release of numerous Mongolian nationalists who had been arrested in Inner Mongolia. A few Mongolians from Inner Mongolia had fled to Mongolia in the late 1980s and early 1990s, and they occasionally led protest marches in support of fellow nationalists in their homeland. The last protest to date occurred on June 4, 1999, which marked the tenth anniversary of the killings at Tiananmen. The demonstrators burned the Chinese flag near the Chinese Embassy in Ulaanbaatar and demanded justice for ethnic minorities, particularly fellow Mongolians, in China. However, the government itself recognizes its dependence on China. For example, in December 1998, President Bagabandi visited Inner Mongolia and stated that "he was impressed with China's efforts to protect the culture and education of the Mongolian minority."[44]

A potentially troublesome problem that has been resolved is Mongolia's relations with Taiwan. Three years after the fall of communism in Mongolia, Taiwan expressed interest in direct business links with, and official government visits to, Mongolia. By the following year, trade had developed. Mongolian government sources, however, yield few statistics on commerce with Taiwan. The State Statistical Bureau does not mention Taiwan separately in its list of Mongolia's trading partners. The Economist Intelligence Unit reports, however, that Mongolian trade with Taiwan, which amounted to $400,000 in 1994, climbed to $1.4 million in 1997. My interviews with Mongolian officials indicate that trade has increased since then. In December 1998, the government sent the former Mongolian ambassador to the United Nations, Luvsangiin Erdenechuluun, to Taiwan to foster economic relations, and he and his Taiwanese counterpart signed a memorandum promising to support trade and tourism and to establish representative offices in each other's lands. By 2004, Taiwan had set up twenty joint ventures, mostly in knitting and sewing and computers, had provided 150,000 tons of rice in relief (partly through the Taiwan branch of the relief agency World Vision),[45] had instructed three hundred Mongolian businessmen in management, had sent school supplies for children of low-income families, and had offered advanced Chinese-language training for language teachers from Mongolia. On the other hand, the United States suspended imports from a Taiwanese-owned factory in Mongolia because it employed child labor and compelled laborers to work fourteen-hour days. Despite such onerous demands on laborers, enterprises have been able to recruit about 3,000 to 4,000 Mongolian workers for their factories in Taiwan, and the number will no doubt increase.[46]

Additional evidence of growing contacts is an article in the Mongolian press reporting that the number of tourists from Taiwan has increased. In addition, the Mongolian and Tibetan Affairs Commission in Taiwan convened two scholarly conferences, one in May 1999 and another in August 2000, on Mongolian history and culture and on modern Mongolia. By 2002, each state had set up a consulate in the other's country.[47]

Ironically, neither country accepted the sovereignty of the other until 2002. Mongolia still endorses a one-China policy and officially considers Taiwan to be part of China. In 1998, it indicated that it would not support Taiwan's admission into the United Nations. On the other hand, Taiwan also considered Mongolia to be part of China until recently. In 2002, however, Taiwan recognized Mongolia as an independent country and removed it from maps of China.[48]

Some Mongolian problems with China have intensified as economic relations have accelerated, while others have actually diminished. Complaints about Chinese control over the cashmere industry, about adulterated or defective Chinese imports, about the growing number of both overt and covert Chinese investments and joint ventures, about Chinese smuggling of currency, narcotics, and animal products, about unfair competition by Chinese entrepreneurs in certain industries, and about interference in Mongolian politics have multiplied. On the other hand, controversy over Inner Mongolia has receded or at least has not reared up over the same time period. The day-to-day economic issues appear to have generated greater animosity, while the issues of seemingly greater import have dissipated. The former have been based upon and have been precipitated by the contacts between ordinary Chinese and Mongolians, and the long-term prognosis seems to be intensification of such enmity. Despite such tensions, Mongolia is becoming increasingly dependent on China for consumer goods and as a market for its raw materials.

THE FUTURE

Mongolia would appear to have an economy that could dovetail with that of China. Yet present trends foster a superior-inferior, not a complementary, relationship. Within a decade, China has gained considerable leverage over the Mongolian economy, and, judging from my visit in September 2003, the number of Chinese and Chinese-owned enterprises, including restaurants and retail stores, has increased dramatically. Numerous Mongolians believe that the recent opening of new stores in Ulaanbaatar is the result of Chinese or South Korean investment. In 1990, Chinese investments in and trade with Mongolia were minimal, but by 2003, China was by far the largest investor in Mongolia and its most important trade partner. Facing almost no customs duties, Chinese enterprises have flooded the market in Mongolia with cheap consumer goods and have thus undermined native Mongolian industries.[49] With the decline and collapse of such industries, Mongolia has been compelled to trade its raw materials for Chinese finished products. In addition, the lack of regulations on foreign capital has enabled the Chinese to buy quite a number of Mongolian enterprises. Pressure from international donors to privatize Mongolian organizations rapidly has provided an opportunity for Chinese individuals or companies overtly or covertly to bid for Mongolian industries and service enterprises. With such growing economic leverage, China would not need to occupy Mongolia to exert considerable influence on the country.[50]

China seems determined to play a leading role in Mongolia and indeed in all of Central Asia. As I wrote in an article in 2000, "[T]here are indications that China harbors aspirations of replacing Russia as the dominant economic force in Central Asia, thus placing Beijing in a better position to address its domestic security concerns."[51] The fact that the Chinese leader Hu Jintao's first foreign visit as the dominant force in his country was to Central Asia and Mongolia in May and June 2003 indicates the significance attached to the region by the Chinese authorities. In addition, Hu's pledge to provide $300 million in aid and loans for the construction of roads linking China and Mongolia and for improvements in infrastructure and mineral exploration and extraction offers the Chinese even greater access to Mongolia's natural resources, contributing to the colonial relationship.[52] Of potentially greater concern is the Chinese grant of a million dollars for coordination with the Mongolian Ministry of Defense. Will China seek to play a greater military role in Mongolia and thus have even greater political and economic leverage?[53]

If Mongolia seeks to avert Chinese domination, it would, for a time, seem prudent to place duties on some key foreign goods and to impose regulations on foreign capital and on foreign ownership of native enterprises. This policy, particularly tariffs on some products, would offer native industries breathing space to restore themselves and to elicit both state funding and indigenous bank credit (assuming that the current banking system is reformed and similarly restored). Controls on foreign capital and investment and on joint ventures would also offer protection from the vagaries of the rapid transfers of short-term capital. Mongolian enterprises cannot, on their own, compete with state-supported, monopolistic Chinese enterprises. An exclusive emphasis on privatization and a market economy will simply make Mongolia even more vulnerable to Chinese economic domination. With its own native industries, Mongolia could develop a more equitable economic relationship with China—a link that is not colonialist in appearance and that would seek to overcome the tensions that have frequently characterized their relations since the time of Chinggis Khan.

In 1990, for the first time in three hundred years, Mongolia had the opportunity to move toward independence and democracy. From 1691 to 1911, the Qing dynasty and Chinese merchants had imposed a harsh, oppressive rule on Mongolians, and from 1921 to 1990, the Soviet Union dominated the country. The collapse of the USSR offered the Mongolians a chance to chart their own course. Yet they needed temporary assistance to compensate for the changes in commerce, investment, and technical advice that ensued after the disruptions in the communist world.

The IMF, World Bank, ADB, USAID, and JICA, the Japanese International Cooperation Agency, as one observer noted, "rushed in to fill in all that empty space,"[1] and sought to foster democracy and a market economy, conflating the two and promoting free market shock therapy. In their ardent support for privatization, liberalization of prices and trade, minimal government, a balanced budget, and austerity, they occasionally impeded the Mongolians' efforts to achieve the independence and democracy they cherished.[2] By threatening not to supply already approved aid when they objected to specific Mongolian government policies, they undermined the Mongolians' small steps toward independence, which entails the ability to make one's own decisions, even if they are wrong. An even clearer example of the leverage of the international donors was that in 2002, the Khural delayed consideration of the following year's budget until the IMF representative returned to Mongolia. As one journalist noted, it appeared "that Mongolia had simply traded one form of dependence for another."[3] This evidence of the international agencies' influence not only impinged upon independence but also upon democracy. Many Mongolians, rightly or wrongly, believed that their own elected officials were relatively powerless. One foreign reporter who visited at the height of the presidential election of 2001 wrote: "I talked with other highly educated Mongolians who shared Sumati's apparent indifference to the outcome of the election. Some of them felt that, regardless of who won, the country's fortunes were largely in the hands of the three most influential foreign donors—the I.M.F., the World Bank, and the Asian Development Bank."[4] Even if this was not entirely true, the fact that so many Mongolian intellectuals share this view is telling and harms the democratic process.

Other foreign organizations have come perilously close to intervention in Mongolia's internal political affairs, perhaps also influencing the democratic process. The Konrad Adenauer Foundation directly and the International Republican Institute somewhat less directly played important roles in the victory of the Democratic Union in the 1996 elections, and the Democratic Union leaders attributed their success to the two organizations. As of 2004, the IRI continues its involvement and even commissioned a poll of the Mongolian electorate's political preferences nine or ten months before the next Khural election.[5]

Both the international donor agencies and the foreign political organizations have generally supported the Mongolian champions of a market economy rather than the democratic reformers. Many of the democratic reformers are no longer on the political scene. Zorig was murdered; the herder Namkhainyambuu has died; Nomin is studying abroad. Hulan was based in Russia for several years as the wife of the Mongolian ambassador. She returned to Mongolia in 2002 and ran for election to the 2004 Khural, but, as mentioned earlier, lost. Oyun remains in the Khural but is a lonely voice calling for accountability, transparency, and modified economic policies (diverging from the pure market economy approach), as well as opposing corruption.

The international agencies' repeated emphasis on economic growth has not been matched with a similar concern for equitable distribution of income and with social welfare. Their representatives did not devote as many resources and as much attention to the consequences—unemployment, poverty, crime, corruption, and growing disparities in income—of the policies they urged Mongolians to undertake. The gap between the rich and the poor continues to widen, partly because of the abuses associated with the privatization of public assets. The losers in this scramble, the 36 percent (and probably more, owing to the impact of the disastrous winters of 1999–2002 on herders) living below the poverty line, have scant guarantees of state support because of the austerity and the balanced budget policies championed by the international donors and Mongolian advocates of the market economy. Foreign philanthropic organiza-tions such as World Vision, Save the Children, and DANIDA have on occasion been forced to supplant the state in assisting with food security, abandoned children, and other problems associated with poverty. Well-meaning organizations such as the UNDP have also collaborated with the various governments to convene conferences, workshops, and symposia on herding, the environment, and other vital problems, but it is difficult to gauge the effectiveness of such meetings, particularly when these agencies periodically fund repeated meetings on the same subject.

To be sure, the donor agencies themselves have provided valuable philanthropic assistance to Mongolian education, health, and social welfare, but their objective of grafting a market economy onto Mongolia as quickly as possible has helped to foster such social problems. Privatization of the herds, which they championed, has not been a success, and the Mongolian government and the agencies themselves have been scrambling to promote herders' cooperatives to mitigate the risks in a herding economy.

The international donors' support for a weaker state has also had serious implications. Mongolian government protection of the environment and support of education, health, arts, and culture have all diminished (as is the case with many countries in the former Soviet bloc), with the predictable consequences of degradation of the land, air, and water, school dropouts, and damage to precious artworks and manuscripts. The drive for a weaker government is exemplified in the promotion of a gradual move toward privatization of the Mongolian version of Social Security. Although this remains a controversial policy in the United

States itself, American advisors representing the U.S. government proposed it in Mongolia. Ironically, the advisors who called for a minimal state received their own salaries, either directly or indirectly, from governments.

Some critics also question their repeated injunctions about private sector growth, with scant state involvement, as the optimal strategy for Mongolia and the other formerly communist states. They observe that a weak state cannot implement the rules of a market economy, including such basic guarantees as contracts, property rights and individual rights. Although the forms of democracy—free elections, transfer of power, and relative freedom of the press—have been followed in Mongolia, the increasing incidence of corruption and the mounting evidence of lack of economic democracy (growing disparity in incomes, limited access to education and health facilities and social welfare) could undermine the current political stability. Overwhelming one-party rule—in 1992 and again in the 2000 Khural elections, more than 90 percent of the winners were identified with the MPRP—limits dissent, and the minority Khural members have repeatedly complained about being denied an opportunity to speak at the beginning of the parliamentary term, about the limitations on open debates on critical issues such as land privatization, and about the general lack of transparency in government. However, the disunity among the leading politicians and political parties hampers the development of a viable opposition. For example, three political parties united to form an anti-MPRP coalition in 2002, but it is unclear whether their alliance will survive after their surprising success in the 2004 Khural elections. They represent entirely different interests and policies and may break up in the same way that the Democratic Union fragmented after its victory in the 1996 Khural elections.[6] The economic disarray and the lack of unity could give the communist old guard, with their authoritarian tradition, an opportunity to play a more important role in the future.

Finally, the policies promoted by the international donors and the supporters of the market economy in the Mongolian government have, paradoxically, facilitated economic links that overwhelmingly favor China. The eliminations of tariffs and of controls on foreign investment have permitted Chinese entrepreneurs and companies to acquire considerable leverage over the Mongolian economy. Such leverage may, in the future, translate into political influence and has already muted Mongolian government criticism of Chinese policy in Inner Mongolia and Tibet.

Despite these concerns, some of the representatives of the international donor agencies have brushed aside criticism and continue to make overly optimistic predictions about economic growth and reduction in poverty. They have repeatedly stated that economic growth is the solution to the problem of poverty and have denigrated economists who hold contrary, "pro-poor" views, such as Hafiz Pasha, who writes of "the need to place poverty reduction as the central objective of the process of development."[7] In fact, the rise in annual GDP was lackluster until 2002, and insufficient to reduce unemployment, and, perhaps as important, the unfavorable balance of trade is increasing and is approaching about 70 to 75 percent of the annual amount of foreign aid.[8] "The concern for pro-poor policies is the consequence of a deep rooted disillusionment with the development paradigm which placed exclusive emphasis on the pursuit of growth," Hafiz Pasha observes.[9]

There has been little serious debate and transparency about the activities of the international financial agencies in Mongolia. Many of their consultants know very little about Mongolia and merely recommend and apply general (some might say "cookie-cutter") pure market policies to the country, policies that have damaged Mongolia. Their proposals at times diverge from the political and economic consensus in their own countries, and many critics assert that the international financial organizations and the private contractors and consultants they employ ought to be much more accountable to and subject to oversight by the publics— in the West and in Mongolia—that they purport to represent. Some Mongolian critics have often wondered whether they represented the interests of Mongolia or of foreign groups or states. This was particularly the case when they urged the sale of the country's major power plant to an American energy firm accused of unethical, if not criminal, behavior and the sale of two successful banks to owners who had scant experience in operating such financial institutions. In addition, their policies have social implications and social costs, including the possibility of increased poverty, inadequate medical and educational facilities, and a frayed social safety net, especially because they promote privatization of education, medicine, and the rest of the social welfare sector.

Should the pure market model and economists alone determine the course of foreign assistance? Should Mongolians not be able to determine their own political and economic future? Wouldn't an informed discussion by a wide range of knowledgeable Mongolians and foreign experts be a better basis than an imported pure market agenda for charting a foreign aid and development program appropriate to Mongolia's needs and cultural heritage? As Oyun has aptly stated: "Mongolia is at a crossroads: will its government come up with *home-grown policies for economic development* [emphasis added] and introduce new, higher standards in the way it leads political, economic and social processes, or will it continue to slide on the path of imprudent policies and the weak rule of law?"[10]

NOTES

CHAPTER I

1. See Peck, "Chagi's Charge," 28–37, for a popular and charming account of the Naadam festival.

2. Becker, *Lost Country,* 44.

3. Erik Eckholm, "A Gentle Hero Dies, and Mongolia's Innocence, Too," *New York Times,* October 25, 1998, 3.

4. Krouchkin, *Mongolia,* 515; interviews, Tömör-öchiryn Erdene-bileg, May 9, 1994; Luvsandendev Sumati, Ulaanbaatar, August 14, 1997.

5. See Michael Kohn, "Democratic Leader S. Zorig Murdered," *Mongol Messenger,* October 7, 1998, 2; id., "Interest of Nation Is Priority One: S. Zorig," ibid., October 14, 1998, 2.

6. Sanjaasürengiin Oyun, e-mail to the author, February 4, 2004.

7. Interview, Hashbat Hulan, Ulaanbaatar, May 26, 1998.

8. Staisch and Prohl, *Dschingis,* 26.

9. One product of her employment as a researcher was a series of articles on developments in modern Mongolia. See, e.g., Hashbat Hulan, "Mongolia's Political Transformation: Observations and Comparisons," *Mongolian Journal of International Affairs* 1 (1994): 28–37.

10. Bulag, *Nationalism,* 86.

11. Interview, Hashbat Hulan, Ulaanbaatar, May 26, 1998.

12. Middleton, *Last Disco,* 180.

13. Two different views regarding the so-called satellite status of Mongolia may be found in Lattimore, *Nomads and Commissars,* 155–57, and Murphy, *Soviet Mongolia,* 180–206.

14. On the failures of collectivization in the early 1930s, see Bawden, *Modern History,* 304–11. For an MPRP interpretation of collectivization, see *History of the Mongolian People's Republic,* ed. and trans. Brown and Onon, 267–82. For a positive view of one collective, see Rosenberg, "Political Leadership." For less positive views, see Schmidt, *Mongolia in Transition,* 73–76, and Batbayar, *Zuuni Mongol,* 369–75.

15. Dashpurev and Soni, *Reign of Terror,* 42, 49, give higher figures for the numbers executed.

16. From an interview with his grandson Tömör-öchiryn Erdenebileg, Ulaanbaatar, June 21, 1998. Also see Rupen, *How Mongolia Is Really Ruled,* 79, 83.

17. Heaton, "Mongolia 1979," 81.

18. Sanders, "Restructuring and Openness," in Akiner, ed., *Mongolia,* 61.

19. Ibid., 67–68.

20. Jarrett, "Mongolia in 1987," 81.

21. Cultural exchanges were initiated almost immediately after diplomatic recognition. The International Relations and Exchanges Board developed programs to bring Mongolians to the United States and send American scholars and students to Mongolia.

22. Sanders, "Restructuring and Openness," in Akiner, ed., *Mongolia,* 70–71.

23. Sanders, "Mongolia in 1988," 47–48.

24. Rossabi, "Mongolia: A New Opening?" 279.

25. Based on interviews with Lkhagvasüren's granddaughter Lkhagvasüren Nomin, Ulaanbaatar, May 22, 1998. The most important battle against the Japanese is covered in great detail in Coox, *Nomonhan.*

26. For studies of earlier Mongolian relations with China, see Bartow, "Policy of the Mongolian People's Republic," and Kim, *Entwicklung der politischen Beziehungen.*

27. Sanders, "Mongolia in 1989," 62.

28. Ibid., 66.

29. Krouchkin, *Mongolia,* 446–47, 451–52.

30. Dasheeveg, *Muan-in Tuukhen Temdeglel,* 22–23.

31. Ackerman and DuVall, *A Force More Powerful,* p. 444.

32. Dasheeveg, *Muan-in Tuukhen Temdeglel,* 23–24.

33. On Qing rule in Mongolia, see Sanjdorj, *Manchu Chinese Colonial Rule,* and Rossabi, *China and Inner Asia,* 149–58.

34. Heaton, "Mongolia in 1990," 50–51.

35. Disunity had prevented Mongolians from asserting their independence after the collapse of the Qing dynasty in China in 1911. Without Soviet intercession in 1921, they might have not been able to create a separate country. See Bawden, *Modern History,* 187–237, and Ewing, *Between the Hammer and the Anvil?*

36. Dasheeveg, *Muan-in Tuukhen Temdeglel,* 24.

37. Staisch and Prohl, *Dschingis,* 29.

38. Ibid., 29.

39. Interview, Luvsandendev Sumati, Ulaanbaatar, May 19, 1998.

40. Dasheeveg, *Muan-in Tuukhen Temdeglel,* 34–36.

41. Ibid., 24–25.

42. Interviews, Hashbat Hulan, Ulaanbaatar, May 26, 1998; Tsakhiagiin Elbegdorj, Ulaanbaatar, May 12, 1994.

43. Becker and Prohl both wrongly state that January 21 was Lenin's birth date. Becker cannot be relied upon because the facts in the book are often incorrect.

44. Dasheeveg, *Muan-in Tuukhen Temdeglel,* 27.

45. For the attacks on Chinggis, see Rossabi, *China and Inner Asia,* 267–68, and Hyer, "Reevaluation of Chinggis," 696–98.

46. Staisch and Prohl, *Dschingis,* 29–30; interview, Bat-Erdenin Batbayar, Ulaanbaatar, January 7, 1997.

47. Becker, *Lost Country,* 45; interview, Oidov Enkhtuya, Ulaanbaatar, August 24, 1997.

48. Interview, Davaadorjiin Ganbold, Ulaanbaatar, January 8, 1997.

49. Dasheeveg, *Muan-in Tuukhen Temdeglel,* 28.

50. On Choibalsan city, see Doebler, "Cities," 54–55.

51. Dasheeveg, *Muan-in Tuukhen Temdeglel,* 27. No one knows who actually dismantled the statue. A decade later the statue had been found and set up in a nightclub. But many of the statues of Russian and Mongolian communists have been preserved in the storage rooms of the National Museum of History and the National Modern Art Gallery.

52. Becker, *Lost Country,* 45, makes this assertion.

53. Interview, Tömör-öchiryn Erdenebileg, Ulaanbaatar, May 9, 1994.

54. Krouchkin, *Mongolia,* 439–40 and 442–43, for short biographical sketches.

55. Dasheeveg, *Muan-in Tuukhen Temdeglel,* 33. On the events of March of 1990, see also Fritz, "Doppelte Transition in der Mongolei."

56. Interview, Luvsandendev Sumati, Ulaanbaatar, May 20, 1998.

57. To understand why ordinary people had difficulty in understanding the strike, see Severin, *In Search of Genghis Khan,* 221. See also Staisch and Prohl, *Dschingis,* 31.

58. Staisch and Prohl, *Dschingis,* 31. Ackerman and DuVall, *A Force More Powerful,* p. 448, yields this quote.

59. Dasheeveg, *Muan-in Tuukhen Temdeglel,* 34.

60. Interview, Lama Dambajav, Ulaanbaatar, May 14, 1994.

61. Interview, Demchigiin Molomjamts, Ulaanbaatar, May 19, 1998.

62. Staisch and Prohl, *Dschingis,* 31–32.

63. Dasheeveg, *Muan-in Tuukhen Temdeglel,* 35; interview, Dashiin Byambasüren, Ulaanbaatar, May 6, 1994.

64. Dasheeveg, *Muan-in Tuukhen Temdeglel,* 36.

65. Staisch and Prohl, *Dschingis,* 31.

66. Heaton, "Mongolia in 1990," 51.

67. Interview, Dashiin Byambasüren, Ulaanbaatar, May 6, 1994.

68. Heaton, "Mongolia in 1990," 51.

69. Staisch and Prohl, *Dschingis,* 35.

70. Dasheeveg, *Muan-in Tuukhen Temdeglel,* 36.

71. Staisch and Prohl, *Dschingis,* 36.

72. Interview, Punsalmagiin Ochirbat, Ulaanbaatar, May 15, 1994.

73. Heaton, "Mongolia in 1990," 51.

74. Michael Kohn, "Democratic Leader S. Zorig Murdered," *Mongol Messenger,* October 7, 1998.

75. Dasheeveg, *Muan-in Tuukhen Temdeglel,* 51–54.

76. Heaton, "Mongolia in 1990," 52.

77. Dasheeveg, *Muan-in Tuukhen Temdeglel,* 28.

78. Staisch and Prohl, *Dschingis,* 36–37; interviews, Sanjiin Bayar, Ulaanbaatar, August 18, 1997; Bat-Erdeniin Batbayar, Ulaanbaatar, January 7, 1997. See the translation of Baabar's rather uneven work entitled *Twentieth Century Mongolia.*

79. Dasheeveg, *Muan-in Tuukhen Temdeglel,* 48.

80. Staisch and Prohl, *Dschingis,* 38.

81. Interview, Gotoviin Akim, Ulaanbaatar, August 23, 1997.

82. Middleton, *Last Disco,* 7.

83. Severin, *In Search of Genghis Khan,* 13.

84. Interviews, Badamtariin Baldoo, Ulaanbaatar, May 18, 1998; Demichigiin Molomjamts, Ulaanbaatar, May 19, 1998.

CHAPTER 2

1. Interview, T. Erdenebileg, Ulaanbaatar, June 21, 1998.

2. Bawden, *Modern History,* 216–36.

3. Doebler, "Cities, Population Redistribution, and Urbanization," 57, 186–87; Neupert and Goldstein, *Urbanization,* 39.

4. Doebler, "Cities, Population Redistribution, and Urbanization," 70–76.

5. National University of Mongolia, *Information Network.*

6. Grivelet, "Reintroducing the Uighur-Mongolian Script," 49–50.

7. See Kiselev, *Drevnemongol'skie.*

8. Heaton, "Mongolia 1979," 82.

9. Interviews, T. Erdenebileg, Ulaanbaatar, June 21, 1998; H. Hulan, Ulaanbaatar, May 26, 1998.

10. Asian Development Bank, *Mongolia,* 20–21.

11. Ibid., 28–29.

12. Nixson and Walters, *Mongolian Economy,* 51; Asian Development Bank, *Mongolia,* 23.

13. Jarrett, "Mongolia in 1987," 84; Milne et al., *Mongolian People's Republic,* 6–8.

14. Asian Development Bank, *Mongolia,* 170.

15. Nixson and Walters, *Mongolian Economy,* 120.

16. Shapiro, "Reporter at Large," 48.

17. See, e.g., Aslund, *Building Capitalism.*

18. One assessment of such experimentation from 1990 to 2000 notes that "Mongolia became a playground for free-market ideologues. It was the place to try out every pet theory, says one foreign resident. 'And if things went wrong, only 2.4 million people [would get hurt].'" See Crowell and Meijdam, "Experience," 33.

19. Baker, *Politics of Diplomacy,* 6; telephone interview, James Baker, Houston, March 2, 1998.

20. Baker, *Politics of Diplomacy,* 6; telephone interview, James Baker, March 2, 1998; interview, M. Zober, August 26, 1997.

21. Milne et al., *Mongolian People's Republic,* 9–12.

22. The Nobel Prize–winning economist Joseph Stiglitz has been among the strongest critics of this approach. See his *Globalization.* His harshest and perhaps most hyperbolic criticism has been leveled at the IMF. The international financier George Soros has also been critical, asserting that foreign aid has often served the interests of the donors and that the projects sometimes are imported and do not reflect the indigenous needs of the country. See his *George Soros on Globalization,* as well as William Finegan, "After Seattle," *New Yorker,* April 7, 2000, 40–51, and Bob Arnot, "Western Economists and the Transition Process," in Hare, ed., *Systemic Change,* 219–20, who asserts, rightly or wrongly, that the advocates of the pure market economy were

unswerving in their belief in the correctness of their view. He adds: "Western economists have not been particularly modest with regard to proffering advice to the countries in transition." Believing that these transitions have not been smooth, he "suggests the need for humility in the advice they offer."

23. Interviews, W. Prohl, Ulaanbaatar, May 25, 1998; B. Delgermaa, Ulaanbaatar, July 10, 1998; Konrad Adenauer Foundation, "Political Education Academy"; see Prohl's account in his and Staisch's *Dschingis*.

24. The IRI often gives its Freedom Awards to prominent Republicans, such as Dick Cheney and Lynn Cheney. See Mayer, "Letter," 91.

25. Tomlinson, "Mongolia's Wild Ride," 195–97; MNA, September 26, 2002; Asia Foundation, "Mongolia: Highlights of Foundation Program," 2; interview, K. Hunter, Ulaanbaatar, August 25, 1997.

26. *UB Post*, April 22, 1997; personal observations at Mormon Church services, Ulaanbaatar, June–July, 1998; May, 1999; EDN, September 20, 1999, and August 7, 2000; *UB Post*, August 29, 2001.

27. *Mongol Messenger*, May 10, 1997; EDN, June 16, 1997, and February 13, 1998; Reuters (Mongolia), January 7, 1998.

28. Interviews, J. Beauclerk, Ulaanbaatar, August 22, 1997, and June 30, 1998; S. Christiansen, Ulaanbaatar, June 22 and 24, 1998; C. Finch, Ulaanbaatar, April 30, 1999; D. Gardner, Ulaanbaatar, June 12, 1998; MNA, October 23, 2002, and February 27, 2004. In 2004, World Vision, for example, provided 7,000 tons of rice in relief assistance. See MNA, January 16, 2004.

CHAPTER 3

1. Tomlinson, "Mongolia's Wild Ride," 196.

2. See Johnson, *MITI*, and Vogel, *Japan*, 53–96, for greater analysis of these policies. One distinguished economic historian also questioned these prescriptions, asserting that growth and escape

from poverty depended on government policies covering law, taxation, education, transport, intellectual property, regulation of international trade, and financial markets. See Skidelsky, "Mystery of Growth," 31.

3. Quotations from Asian Development Bank, *Mongolia,* 11, 25, and 30.

4. Quotations from ibid., 61.

5. The International Monetary Fund report noted: "The rationalization of the number of ministries in late 1990 is expected to lead to further cuts in administrative costs as additional workers are let go. While new job opportunities are expected to be generated by the private sector, the authorities are considering measures to ameliorate the impact on workers during the transition period" (IMF, *Mongolian People's Republic,* 30). The private sector could not, however, absorb many of the government workers who were "let go." Neither did the state have the "resources to ameliorate the impact on workers." Many simply joined the large number of unemployed and scarcely received much state support.

6. Quotations from Asian Development Bank, *Mongolia,* 67, 93.

7. Keith Griffin writes, for example: "Privatisation is essentially an ideological issue and is not necessary for the creation of a well-functioning market-guided economy. . . . Privatisation is concerned with the transfer of property rights. Such a transfer in itself implies neither an increase in efficiency nor an acceleration of growth nor the protection of those threatened by poverty" (Griffin, ed., *Poverty and the Transition,* 11–12). Cevdet Denizer and Alan Gelb write that "formally privatizing state property is really the easy part of reform. Making companies profitable and finding new jobs for dismissed workers is the real challenge" (Denizer and Gelb, "Privatization in Mongolia," 93). See also Nixson and Walters, "Transition," and interview, Terry Peach, Ulaanbaatar, May 11, 1999.

8. Griffin, ed., *Poverty and the Transition,* 14–20, offers an alternative to the ADB strategy.

9. Heaton, "Mongolia in 1991," 52. A few years later, Sachs would alter his views. However, his agenda for Mongolia remained the

same: (a) an investor-friendly government; (b) higher coal and oil prices and elimination of energy subsidies to consumers; (c) more frequent flights and increase in tourism; (d) better roads to China and Russia; (e) greater access to the Internet; (f) additional research and transmission of information on cashmere and animal husbandry; (g) a greater share of profits from mineral and oil concessions to foreigners; (h) improvement of skills in accounting, management, and finances; (i) more efficient banks and lower interest rates; (j) continuation of privatization. See Sachs, "Towards Economic Strategies."

10. Korsun and Murrell, "Politics and Economics of Mongolia's Privatization Program," 486.

11. See Nixson and Walters, "Transition"; interview, Terry Peach, Ulaanbaatar, May 11, 1999.

12. See Cooper, *Wealth and Poverty*, 13, 54; Fernandez-Giménez, "Landscape," 302, 322–23; Mearns, *Pastoral Institutions*, 15; Schmidt, *Mongolia*, 48–51; Bruun and Odgaard, eds., *Mongolia*, 67.

13. Korsun and Murrell, "Politics and Economics of Mongolia's Privatization Program," 484–85; EIU, *Mongolia*, 1st quar. 1993, 34.

14. Korsun and Murrell, "Politics and Economics of Mongolia's Privatization Program," 483.

15. Schmidt, *Mongolia in Transition*, 41.

16. Interview, Sanjaasürengiin Oyun, New York, April 13, 2003. Such a hasty transformation may have been suitable for several of the Eastern European countries, which had previously been exposed to a market system. However, it may not have been as sound for Mongolia, which had moved almost directly from pastoral nomadism to a command economy.

17. Korsun and Murrell, "Politics and Economics of Mongolia's Privatization Program," 483.

18. Nixson and Walters, *Mongolian Economy*, 143.

19. Sanjaasürengiin Oyun, "From the Year," 3.

20. Nixson and Walters, *Mongolian Economy*, 147.

21. Ibid., 80.

22. EIU, *Mongolia,* 3d quar. 1993, 41; Mongolia, National Statistical Office, *Mongolian Economy and Society in 1996,* 25.

23. Griffin, *Strategy for Poverty Reduction,* 5, indicates that government expenditures decreased more than 50 percent from 1990 to 1992.

24. Nicholas Kristof, "Mongols, Off Your Horses and Call Your Brokers," *New York Times,* July 8, 1992, A4.

25. Korsun, "Inside Ownership," 161–63.

26. Nixson and Walters, *Mongolian Economy,* 51.

27. In primary trading, the corporation sells securities. In secondary trading, one stockholder sells to another, and the corporation is not involved in this sale.

28. Tomlinson, "Mongolia's Wild Ride," 196.

29. EIU, *Mongolia,* 3d quar. 1993, 41–42; 4th quar. 1993, 37.

30. Hahm, *Development of the Private Sector,* 2, documents that the goods were available at highly inflated prices.

31. Ginsburg and Ganzorig, "Constitutional Reform," 150.

32. Sanders, "Parliament," 144–50 offers a concise summary of the organizational structure of the government.

33. Denizer and Gelb, "Privatization in Mongolia," 90.

34. Mongolia, Ministry of External Relations, *Foreign Policy Blue Book,* 70–71.

35. Bruun and Odgaard, eds., *Mongolia,* 30.

36. EIU, *Mongolia,* 3d quar. 1993, 38.

37. Ibid., 2d quar. 1993, 35.

38. Ibid.

39. Mongolia, National Statistical Office, *Mongolian Economy and Society in 1996,* 29.

40. EIU, *Mongolia,* 4th quar. 1993, 39.

41. Ibid., 4th quar. 1994, 41.

42. Ibid.

43. Ibid., 2d quar. 1995, 51; interview, G. Oestreicher, Ulaanbaatar, May 28, 1998.

44. See, e.g., Griffin, *Strategy for Poverty Reduction,* 16–18; EDN, January 6, 1998. EDN, the newspapers *Mongol Messenger* and *UB Post,* and the bulletins of the Montsame and Reuters (Mongolia) news agencies are so short that I do not provide page numbers in citations.

45. EIU, *Mongolia,* 4th quar. 1995, 51.

46. Ibid., 44–45.

47. *UB Post,* April 27, 2000.

48. Griffin, *Poverty and the Transition,* 15, writes that the banking problems derived from "an allocation of credit that responds to arbitrary political interference and personal private connections rather than to commercial criteria."

49. Quotations from EIU, *Mongolia,* 4th quar. 1995, 38; third quar. 1994, 38.

50. EIU, *Mongolia,* 4th quar. 1994, 41.

51. Interviews with Sanjaasürengiin Oyun, New York, April, 2003; Hashbat Hulan, Ulaanbaatar, May 26, 1998.

52. EIU, *Mongolia,* 3d quar. 1994, 48.

53. Ibid., 1st quar. 1995, 36; Malhotra, "Mongolia," 18. A few of the wealthy had considerable influence. Luvsandanvangiin Bold, reputed to be Mongolia's first millionaire, received permission to construct the tallest tower in Ulaanbaatar and to establish the Golomt Bank, with Portuguese assistance and funding. See EIU, *Mongolia,* 3d quar. 1995, 43; 4th quar. 1995, 48; and 3d quar. 1996, 3: 49–50.

54. Interview, T. Batbold, Ulaanbaatar, January 4, 1997; EIU, *Mongolia,* 3d quar. 1995, 49.

55. On these projects, see EIU, *Mongolia,* 1st quar. 1995, 46; 3d quar. 1995, 54; 1st quar. 1995, 49; 2d quar. 1996, 53. The ADB continues, as of 2004, to emphasize large-scale construction projects. In that year, it allocated $60 million for a new road. See MNA, February 5, 2004.

56. EIU, *Mongolia,* 3d quar. 1995, 43. The Mongolian government continues to provide preferential treatment to foreign investors. It waives taxes fully on foreign investment in infrastructure for ten years and 50 percent for five additional years, a policy that

cost about $8 million from 2000 to 2002. The question is how does one define "investment in infrastructure"? EDN, April 29, 2003.

57. Schran and Yu, *Mongolia,* 26–38, describes some of the opportunities and problems for foreign investment. On contracts, see EIU, *Mongolia,* 3d quar. 1996, 56.

58. On corruption, see the revealing and careful analysis by Quah, "National Anti-Corruption," a study funded by the UNDP, and also Sneath, "Reciprocity," 85–100, for a comparison between the gift-giving and nepotism of the Soviet era and the corruption of post-Soviet Mongolia. For a general discussion, see Morgan, *Corruption.*

59. Interviews, Luvsandendev Sumati, Ulaanbaatar, May 18, 1998; Hashbat Hulan, Ulaanbaatar, August 9, 1997; Sanjaasürengiin Oyun, New York, April 2003.

60. I have encountered innumerable links among the political, business, and media elites (brothers, in-laws, cousins, etc., in important positions and having considerable opportunities to assist each other). I refrain from citing examples because it would embarrass the people involved, many of whom are not guilty of nepotism.

61. EIU, *Mongolia,* 3d quar. 1994, 40; 3d quar. 1993, 38.

62. Staisch and Prohl, *Dschingis,* 89; EIU, *Mongolia,* 2d quar. 1995, 46–47.

63. EIU, *Mongolia,* 3d quar. 1996, 55.

64. EIU, *Mongolia,* 4th quar. 1994, 37.

65. Severinghaus, "Mongolia in 1994," 73; EIU, *Mongolia,* 4th quar. 1995, 39.

66. EIU, *Mongolia,* 4th quar. 1994, 41; 3d quar. 1995, 49; 3d quar. 1996, 45.

67. Interviews, T. Batbold, Ulaanbaatar, May 20, 1998; J. Od, Ulaanbaatar, June 23, 1998. I witnessed some of this blurring and these overly cozy relationships. The head of the Mongol Bank invited my wife and me to a day-long picnic hosted (and lavishly so) by the president of one of the largest gold-mining operations, who

sold most of his gold to and was supposed to be regulated by the Mongol Central Bank. We all enjoyed the extraordinary largesse of this larger-than-life president, but we could not help him. The head of the Mongol Central Bank could.

68. Ochirbat quoted in EIU, *Mongolia,* 2d quar. 1995, 45. On the Japanese government's attitude, see ibid., 3d quar. 1996, 55.

69. Sumati, "Public Perception."

70. EIU, *Mongolia,* 1st quar. 1996, 43.

71. See Collins and Nixson, "Managing the Implementation," 389–407. See Wedel, *Collision and Collusion,* for a critique of donors in Eastern Europe.

72. EIU, *Mongolia,* 1st quar. 1994, 40; Malhotra, "Mongolia," 15, writes: "These figures do not appear to be indicative of a bloated state bureaucracy that the minimalist state doctrine and missionary zeal would have us believe exists in Mongolia!"

73. International Monetary Fund, *Mongolia, 1996,* 7.

74. EIU, *Mongolia,* 1st quar. 1995, 36.

75. An anecdote I heard from several educated Mongolians says that Christopher Columbus was the first consultant. He had no idea where he was going, and when he got there, he couldn't understand anything. When he returned to Spain, he was able to raise funds for his next trips.

76. A vast array of these consultants' reports may be found in the libraries of the UNDP–Mongolia and the Mongolian Foundation for an Open Society; *UB Post,* September 8, 1998. "Through our bank loans, we are steering Mongolia just the way we want it," one British visitor wrote; Allen, *Edge,* 20.

77. Note the concern of Felix Rohatyn, a successful investment banker who was appointed U.S. ambassador to France: "I'm not sure it's a great idea to live like a colonial governor when you are representing the U.S."; *New York Times,* January 23, 2001.

78. Mongolia, Ministry of External Relations, *Foreign Policy Blue Book,* 70–71.

79. Interview, R. Ground, Ulaanbaatar, April 30, 1999; some of the ADB projects in the pre-1997 period are listed at www.Asian

DevBank.org/Projects/Mon/Monlist.html (accessed December 13, 1997).

80. *Mongol Messenger,* September 25, 2002: see analysis in San-jaasürengiin Oyun, *Monghol ornii.*

81. The primary and secondary educational systems did require international donor funding for energy (heating), facilities, and materials for schools and retraining for some teachers.

82. EIU, *Mongolia,* 1st quar. 1996, 51.

83. *UB Post,* August 21, 1996.

84. *Bulletin of Sant Maral Foundation* 1 (February 1996): 8.

85. See Prohl's fascinating account in Staisch and Prohl, *Dschingis.*

86. IRI, *Programming in Mongolia,* 1–3; "*Pre-Election Assessment,*" 17; and "Key Candidates," 2–5; *Mongol Messenger,* September 13, 2000. As noted later, the IMF and the World Bank, and the Mongolian government, would in at least two critical instances provide the Golomt Bank with opportunities for considerable financial gains, lending credence to cries of favoritism by the MPRP opposition. Only time will tell whether inappropriate considerations prompted these organizations and the government to choose the Golomt Bank for such lucrative assignments.

87. Elbegdorj is quoted in *IRI 1996 Annual Report,* 9; EDN, February 9, 1999, and September 29, 1999; MNA, August 18, 1998.

88. Rossabi, "Mongolia in the 1990s," 11, suggested as early as 1997 that the Democratic Union would break up: "the Democratic coalition forged in the 1996 elections may, in fact, not endure."

89. EIU, *Mongolia,* 3d quar. 1996, 44.

90. Ibid., 45.

91. Schmidt, *Mongolia in Transition,* 13.

92. Interviews, R. Gonchigdorj, Ulaanbaatar, January 9, 1997; Z. Enkhbold, Ulaanbaatar, January 8, 1997; D. Ganbold, Ulaanbaatar, January 8, 1997.

93. Malhotra, "Mongolia," 20.

94. Interviews, B. Batbayar, Ulaanbaatar, June 30, 1998; T. Batbold, Ulaanbaatar, January 4, 1997.

95. Bikales, "Capacity Building," 437.

96. On August 26, 1996, a copy of the prime minister's letter to donors reached the offices of the Open Society Institute in New York.

97. Tokyo Donors Meeting, "Infrastructure Development Paper," http://bvoice.com/mong.donor2.htm 1 (accessed November 2, 1997).

98. EIU, *Mongolia,* 4th quar. 1996, 46.

99. Ginsburg, "Mongolia in 1996," 62.

100. EIU, *Mongolia,* 4th quar. 1996, 49–50; *Mongol Messenger,* January 1, 1997.

101. *UB Post,* October 16, 1996.

102. EIU, *Mongolia,* 4th quar. 1996, 50.

103. Ibid., 1st quar. 1997, 53–54; *UB Post,* December 18, 1996; interview, G. Oestreicher, Ulaanbaatar, May 28, 1998.

104. Bikales, "Conquering Financial Freefall," 17.

105. *Mongol Messenger,* August 5, 1997.

106. *Mongol Messenger,* August 15, 1997; December 24, 1997.

107. *UB Post,* October 30, 1997.

108. *UB Post,* December 4, 1997.

109. EIU, *Mongolia,* 1st quar. 1997, 55; 4th quar. 1996, 55.

110. EDN, February 19, 1997.

111. EDN, March 3, 1997.

112. EDN, April 24, 1997.

113. For tax evasion by companies, see EDN, May 31, 1999.

114. EIU, *Mongolia,* 2d quar. 1997, 55, 53.

115. Sanjaasürengiin Oyun, "From the Year," 3.

116. *Mongol Messenger,* May 28, 1997.

117. EIU, *Mongolia,* 2d quar. 1997, 51. There were further inequities in the military. A military draft existed, but a payment to the government could avert service. See *Mongol Messenger,* March 6, 1997.

118. EIU, *Mongolia,* 2d quar. 1997, 51.

119.   Other establishments may have been added since my last visit to these ministries.

120.   Nate Thayer, "Pain before Gain," *Far Eastern Economic Review*, February 6, 1997, 48.

121.   EIU, *Mongolia*, 1st quar. 1997, 58.

122.   Ibid., 4th quar. 1996, 46.

123.   Interviews, G. Oestreicher, Ulaanbaatar, May 28, 1998; J. Unenbat, Ulaanbaatar, June 26–27, 1998.

124.   Interview, T. Batbold, Ulaanbaatar, August 21, 1997.

125.   *UB Post*, December 3, 1996; EIU, *Mongolia*, 2d quar. 1997, 57–58.

126.   *Mongol Messenger*, June 11, 1997.

127.   *Mongol Messenger*, June 6, 1997; December 24, 1997.

128.   Interview, D. South, Ulaanbaatar, May 4, 1999; *UB Post*, December 11, 1996.

129.   EIU, *Mongolia*, 3d quar. 1997, 43.

130.   EDN, December 10, 1996.

131.   EIU, *Mongolia*, 3d quar. 1996, 55.

132.   EDN, January 14, 1997.

133.   EIU, *Mongolia*, 2d quar. 1997, 50.

CHAPTER 4

1.   *UB Post*, November 24, 1998.

2.   *UB Post*, April 27, 2000; EDN, October 4, 1999; interview, R. Amarjargal, Ulaanbaatar, June 30, 1998.

3.   *Mongol Messenger*, August 4 and 11, 1999; EDN, July 6, 1999; on the IMF threat to withhold payments, see EDN, January 24, 2000; EDN, December 8, 1999; on the lack of job creation, see EDN, March 1, 1999.

4.   EDN, September 5, 1997, and June 15, 1999. An economist described these efforts as "misappropriation of State assets under the name of privatization." See *UB Post*, November 10, 1998.

5.   On Pickering, see EDN, October 27, 1999; Gore's letter: Reuters (Mongolia), October 27 and November 2, 1999, and *Mongol*

Messenger, November 3, 1999. See also EDN, November 1 and 22, 1999. AES is the largest independent power producer in the world, with total assets of almost $38.7 billion and 59,000 MW of electricity generation from 177 facilities in 33 countries. See www.aes.com/aes/index?page=home (accessed July 14, 2004).

6. EIU, *Mongolia,* 1st quar. 2000, 47.

7. An article about AES in the *Mongol Messenger,* one of the two English-language weeklies published in Mongolia, raised additional doubts in the minds of many Mongolians. The writer quoted a Greenpeace report, which noted that AES's "track record is a sordid one, filled with illegal dumping, toxic spills, and lawsuits covered by falsified reports and political schmoozing. In short, AES tried to buy, deceive, or sue communities to allow it to build and operate dirty unnecessary power plants that pollute neighborhoods and endanger the global environment" (*Mongol Messenger,* January 12, 2000). This severe indictment may have been overstated, but AES's involvement in the California energy crisis of 2001 raises concerns about the propriety of a company involved in such controversy assuming control of Ulaanbaatar's vital heating system. The U.S. Federal Regulatory Commission "accused two major companies [including AES] of taking plants out of service in order to push up prices for electricity sold from some of their plants" in California. John Emshwiller, "California Blame Game Yields No Score," *Wall Street Journal,* May 22, 2001, A14, and "AES Unit Is Subject of Review Involving California Electricity," ibid., June 6, 2002, A19. AES owned the plants and, without acknowledging guilt, repaid the state of California for what appeared to be excess profits. Yet a year earlier this was the company that the IMF and other international agencies lobbied for and proposed to purchase Mongolia's power plants. In 2003, still other negative news about AES became known. It defaulted on payments of $85 million and then $336 million to a Brazilian State Bank for the purchase of major power plants in São Paolo and was accused of involvement with the discredited and bankrupt energy trader Enron in illegal rigging of the bidding during the auction for sale of the plants. See Raymond Colitt, "AES Seeks Deal Over $1.2 bn Brazil

Debt," *Financial Times,* February 25, 2003, 15; on the illegal rigging, see Demetri Sevastopulo, "AES Colluded with Enron to
Rig Latin American Energy Auction," ibid., May 21, 2003, 1. I
happened to have been present when two consultants for a
USAID contractor proposed support for an AES bid to purchase
the Mongolian power plants. Such cooperation between a U.S.
government agency and an energy company that was controversial even then, and that has subsequently been accused of illegal
activities, may indicate a situation in which the representatives of
the international donors, and, in this case, the United States, on
occasion favored, even if inadvertently, the interests of their own
corporations rather than those of the recipients of foreign aid. As
of 2004, USAID and the ADB continue to press for privatization
and commercialization of the energy sector. See MNA, February
19 and 20, 2004.

8. *Mongolia This Week,* April 7–13, 2000; EDN, February 15, 2000;
EDN, May 31, 1999; *UB Post,* November 10, 1998; and MNA,
April 15, 1998. In the run-up to the 2004 Khural elections, the
government, without specifying its sources, claims to have created 145,000 new jobs, or 36,250 per year. Even if these are accurate figures, they fall below the government's own estimate of
the country's needs. See MNA, June 9, 2004. While on campaign, the prime minister, also touting these claims, which still
require verification, asserted that the government would add
45,000 new jobs per year over the next four years. See MNA,
May 21, 2004.

9. *Mongolia This Week,* June 2–8, 2000; EDN, September 22, 1998;
June 8, 1999; Bikales, et al., "Mongolian Informal Sector" argues
that the informal sector does pay taxes, an assertion challenged
by the other sources cited. Moreover, even if some individuals in
the informal sector paid taxes, could anyone in government
gauge how much income unmetered taxi operators and kiosk
owners generate? It would seem difficult to elicit the proper
amount of taxation from such informal sector operations.

10. EDN, November 15, 1999; *Mongol Messenger,* September 3, 1998;
Mongolia, National Statistical Office, *Mongolian Statistical Yearbook, 2002,* 119; EDN, August 31, 2000.

11.   EDN, October 13, 1999.

12.   Interview, R. Amarjargal, Ulaanbaatar, April 30, 1994.

13.   EDN, January 5, 2000; MNA, February 18, 1998.

14.   EDN, September 18, 1998, and November 13, 2002.

15.   *Mongol Messenger,* July 19, 1997.

16.   MNA, January 31, 2000; EDN, February 1, 2000.

17.   EDN, January 28, 2000; November 9, 1999; April 4, 1999.

18.   EIU, *Mongolia,* 3d quar. 1998, 44.

19.   Ibid., 39.

20.   Lawless, *Wild East,* 54.

21.   On the holiday weekend when the merger was proposed, I happened to have dinner with Hulan and her husband at a Korean restaurant in Ulaanbaatar. She had just learned about the merger and was clearly distressed by the way it had been done.

22.   EIU, *Mongolia,* 3d quar. 1998, 39.

23.   EIU, *Mongolia,* 1st quar. 1999, 49; *Mongol Messenger,* October 28, 1998; Xinhua, September 7, 1998.

24.   *Mongolia News,* November 1999, 10.

25.   *Mongol Messenger,* August 18, 1999; EDN, August 23, 2001, and September 13, 1999.

26.   *Mongol Messenger,* February 3, 1999; Mongolia, National Statistical Office, *Mongolian Statistical Yearbook, 1998,* 69, and ibid., *2000,* 96–97; EDN, April 30, 1999, and August 14, 1999.

27.   Joshua Kurlantzick, "Capitalism Leaves a Bitter Aftertaste for Mongolians," *Washington Times,* December 4, 1999, A6.

28.   An article by Richard Tomlinson in *Fortune* magazine.

29.   Bruun and Odgaard, *Mongolia,* 123.

30.   EDN, May 1, 2001, and August 27, 2001; *Mongol Messenger,* April 19, 2000; *UB Post,* September 8, 1997. Shortages of equipment contributed to their woes. The number of tractors had decreased from 11,500 in 1989 to 4,700 in 2000; grain harvesters from 2,500 to 1,100; tractor drills from 6,200 to 2,000; and ploughs from 2,200 to 1,100. With all these difficulties, wheat output shrank from 596,000 tons in 1990 to 138,000 in 2001; potatoes from 131,000 tons to 58,000; and fodder crops from

127,000 tons to 2,700. After a slight decline from 1990 to 1999, vegetable output witnessed a slight increase from 41,700 tons in 1990 to 44,500 in 2001. The lowest wheat output in thirty years was recorded in 1998, and 2001 registered even lower wheat production. To be sure, early snows on occasion damaged crops, but weather was less of a factor than the decline in state support for seeds, fuel, and equipment for a sector of the economy that was tenuous owing to the limited arable land in Mongolia. Banks did not take up the slack of providing loans to farmers for the purchase of seeds, fuel, and equipment. Thus, by the late 1990s, the country was no longer self-sufficient in grain, and by 2001, it imported 20,400 tons of potatoes (none imported in 1990), 99,200 tons of flour (27,700 in 1990), and 4,700 tons of garlic and onions (none in 1990). *Mongol Messenger,* December 9, 1998, and April 19, 2000; EDN, September 16, 1998, and March 22, 1999; Mongolia, National Statistical Office, *Mongolian Statistical Yearbook, 2000,* 183. By 2003, 40 percent to 60 percent of some vegetables and 70 percent of flour was imported. See EDN, April 30, 2003.

31. Mongolia, National Statistical Office, *Mongolian Statistical Yearbook, 2000,* 182; *UB Post,* August 20, 1998; EDN, October 15, 1999.

32. Reuters (Mongolia), June 23, 1999; EDN, June 8, 1999.

33. Xinhua (Mongolia), March 5, 1998; Lawless, *Wild East,* 54–55; *Mongol Messenger,* July 17, 1998, and February 22, 2000.

34. EDN, July 30, 1999. The WB continued to press for privatization of one of the state's most important assets—the copper factory in Erdenet; Xinhua (Mongolia), March 5, 1998.

35. Mongolia, National Statistical Office, *Mongolian Statistical Yearbook, 2000,* 157; on the agreement with China, see Reuters (Mongolia), December 11, 1998; EDN, March 22, 1999. EDN, April 16, 1998, reported a 200 percent increase in oil exploration. SOCO International plc is headquartered in the United Kingdom, and its stock is listed on the London Stock Exchange (see www.socointernational.co.uk/ [accessed July 14, 2004]) but the principals in Mongolia are Americans based in Houston.

36. SOCO invested about $85 million from the mid 1990s to 2003 and has produced about 400,000 barrels of oil, most of which was exported to China. The government has received a grand total of $1.2 million in taxes from SOCO over the decade, a negligible amount. See MNA, February 3, 2004.

37. Mongolia, National Statistical Office, *Mongolian Statistical Yearbook, 2000,* 183.

38. EDN, February 8, 1999.

39. *Mongol Messenger,* October 4, 1997; *UB Post,* February 19, 1997; Mongolia, National Statistical Office, *Mongolian Statistical Yearbook, 2002,* 177. Early in 2003, 5,000 residents signed a petition to the government, complaining that illegal gold miners had considerably reduced the flow of the major Onghi River and had damaged the surrounding lands. See MNA, April 16, 2003.

40. Dapice, *Mongolia,* analyzes the limited labor required in gold mining; EDN, February 23, 1999; on the IMF's plan, see *Mongol Messenger,* November 11, 1998.

41. *Mongol Messenger,* December 8, 1999, and January 20, 1999.

42. EDN, September 13, 1997; interview, William Honeychurch, Ulaanbaatar, May 31, 1998, on the archeological implications of this project.

43. MNA, March 10, 1999; *Mongol Messenger,* September 8, 1999; and EDN, October 5, 1999.

44. Mongolia, National Statistical Office, *Mongolian Statistical Yearbook, 2002,* 188; MNA, March 11, 2004; on the Mercedes-Benz dealership, see EDN, October 6, 2000.

45. Mongolia, National Statistical Office, *Mongolian Statistical Yearbook, 2000,* 171–72. In 2004, the ADB offered a rather limited loan of $1 million to foster information technology in rural areas; *UB Post,* April 29, 2004.

46. Sadoway, "Emerging Tourism Frictions"; Mongolia, National Statistical Office, *Mongolian Statistical Yearbook, 1998,* 56; ibid., *1999,* 158; ibid., *2001,* 215; *UB Post,* November 14, 2002; *Mongol Messenger,* November 19, 2003; MNA, January 16, March 19, May 21, and June 3, 2004. See EIU, "Income from Tourists Falls in the

First Seven Months" (November 1, 2003), http://db.eiu.com/ search_view.asp? Doc_id = DB1293115&action = go&topicid =MN&pubcod . . . (accessed January 24, 2004). The Mongolian and Russian governments have announced joint plans to develop Lakes Baikal and Khövsgöl for tourism, possibly one step in the right direction. See EIU, "A Tourist Area Is to Be Set up in Siberia" (November 1, 2003), http://db.eiu.com/ search_view.asp?doc_id = DB1293114&action = go&topicid = MN&pubcod . . . (accessed January 24, 2004).

47. Interview, Rinchinnyamyn Amarjargal, Ulaanbaatar, June 30, 1998.

48. UNDP, *Human Development Report: Mongolia, 2000*, 16. The Save the Children–UK report is Malhotra, "Mongolia."

49. George Soros to the BBC, at http://news.bbc.co.uk/1/hi/ business/740410.stm (accessed May 17, 2004). Quoted in *Mongolia This Week,* May 11–18, 2000.

50. An op-ed essay in *UB Post,* March 15, 2000, subscribed to this view and challenged the IMF's opposition to higher salaries for government employees.

51. The quotation is from *UB Post,* April 3, 2003; the survey is discussed in EDN, November 24, 1999; see also *UB Post,* December 8, 1999; Quah, "National Anti-Corruption."

52. EDN, March 17, 1999; November 6, 1997; May 25, 1998.

53. Lawless, *Wild East,* 30; Erik Eckholm, "A Gentle Hero Dies and Mongolia's Innocence, Too," *New York Times,* October 25, 1998, 3.

54. EDN, October 19, 1998, and February 4, 1998; on the NGO, see EDN, June 3, 1999.

55. On these incidents, see, in order, *Mongol Messenger,* January 20, 1999, and October 28, 1998; *Mongolia This Week,* April 14–20, 2000; EDN, January 20, 2000. Despite acknowledgement of the illegalities involved in such wheat sales, the United States used the same scheme in 2004 in still another contribution of wheat for relief purposes, reputedly with "better safeguards." See *UB Post,* February 12, 2004.

56. MNA, October 3, 1998; *UB Post,* October 3, 2002. Zorig's wife

was briefly detained—see EDN, March 11, 1999. His sister Oyun believes that he was killed because of fear that, as prime minister, he would initiate a campaign against corruption. (Interviews in April 2003 in New York.) This assassination is eerily reminiscent of the murder in July 1998 of General Lev Rokhlin (including the arrest and prosecution of his wife), who had criticized President Boris Yeltsin for "surrounding himself with brazenly corrupt advisers" (Cohen, *Failed Crusade*, 161–66). A statue of Zorig was erected in a central location in the capital—right across the street from the Central Post Office. A fictionalized film about his life and career has also been produced. See *UB Post*, January 8, 2004.

57.   EDN, June 28, 1998; interview, B. Broadwell, Ulaanbaatar, May 2, 1999. The "Politbarometer" survey conducted by the Sant Maral Foundation several times a year repeatedly reveals that more than 50 percent of the population has no confidence in the Khural. A typical study tour found former Prime Minister Elbegdorj, the favorite of many international organizations, in Estonia to study "banking reforms." See *Mongol Messenger*, September 1, 1999.

58.   EDN, March 17, 1999; Reuters (Mongolia), January 13, 1999; EIU, *Mongolia*, 1st quar. 1991, 55; the quotation is from Lawless, *Wild East*, 63.

59.   UNDP, *Mongolia Update, 1998*, 29: "It was revealed by the government that only five per cent of foreign aid is spent on the social sector." Reuters (Mongolia), June 14, 1999.

60.   *Mongol Messenger*, June 3, 1998, May 10, 2000.

61.   James Wolfensohn, "Opening Address by the President of the World Bank Group" (World Bank Annual Meeting, Washington, D.C., October 6, 1998), 25–32.

62.   *Mongol Messenger*, April 5, 2000, and February 22, 2000; on the UNDP's attitude, see "NGOs Play Large Role in Poverty Alleviation," *Blue Sky* 4 (March 1998): 1, which writes: "Giving credit to the poor and expecting that they utilize the funds successfully is not realistic."

63.   EIU, *Mongolia*, 1st quar. 1995, 36; 1st quar. 1997, 52; 2d

quar. 1998, 49; EDN, June 22, 1999; EIU, *Mongolia,* 1st quar. 1999, 44.

64. Ministry of External Relations, *Foreign Policy Blue Book,* 74; EDN, March 3, 1999; Reuters (Mongolia); June 23 and 24, 1999.

65. EDN, November 22, 1999; *UB Post,* August 4, 1998.

66. The sources of the quotations and citations here are, in order: *UB Post,* March 11, 2000; World Bank, *Mongolia: Participatory Living Standards Assessment,* 8–14; Reuters (Mongolia), August 19, 1998; EDN, March 15, 1999; Reuters (Mongolia), July 1, 2000; *UB Post,* July 28, 1998.

67. Ginsburg and Ganzorig, "When Courts and Politics Collide," 312; for a more comprehensive view of the Constitutional Court and its role in politics, see Ginsburg, *Judicial Review,* 158–205.

68. *UB Post,* October 22, 1997; Prohl and Staisch, *Dschingis,* 66–67; EDN, April 21 and 29, 1998.

69. *Mongol Messenger,* July 24, 1998.

70. EDN, January 31, 2000, and January 24, 2000.

71. EIU, *Mongolia,* 3d quar. 1993, 41; *Mongol Messenger,* March 3, 1999.

72. EDN, July 13, 2000; Gordon Laird, "Mongolia: Days of Loss," *Far Eastern Economic Review,* July 6, 2000, 81–83; Ian Johnson, "Mongolia's Democrats Lose Their Grip," *Wall Street Journal,* June 28, 2000, A14; see Craig Turk, "Mongolia Diarist: Red Dawn," July 31, 2000, 42 for an IRI view of the elections.

73. *Mongol Messenger,* October 17, 2001; EDN, February 19, 2002; March 21, 2002; April 25, 2002; June 19, 2002.

74. *UB Post,* July 5 and October 18, 2001. Ambassador Pamela Slutz, Ambassador Dinger's successor, reiterated the same official U.S. view that private-sector economic growth would reduce poverty, a policy that has not borne much fruit. As we shall note, the rate of poverty, as assessed by the World Bank in 1995, has not decreased as of 2004 and may, in fact, have inched upward. See a journalist's interview with Ambassador Slutz in *Mongol Mes-*

senger, January 28, 2004. In addition, despite the private sector's increasing percentage of GDP, a 2002 survey of residents of Ulaanbaatar and of the countryside, conducted by the Mongolian Chamber of Commerce found that they perceived that "during the last 3 years[s] the poverty has been increased noticeably." See National Chamber of Commerce and Industry, *White Paper,* 30.

75.   EDN, December 27, 2000, and June 11, 2002; *UB Post,* June 13, 2002; several newspaper accounts claimed that Gerald Metals and Banco Lugano intended to use the Trade and Development Bank for money laundering. It is impossible to verify this assertion. For the shareholders who are contesting the sale, see EDN, November 22, 2002; May 2, 2003, and September 12, 2003. The Barents group of McLean, Virginia, under a contract with USAID, was the principal advisor to the Mongolian government on privatization. I have been unable to find precise figures on the fees it has charged for its services. See *UB Post,* July 24, 2003.

76.   EDN, October 6, 2003; *Mongol Messenger,* October 29, 2003; *UB Post,* October 9, 2003.

77.   In July 2000, the Agricultural Bank had held $3 million in non-performing loans and faced possible collapse. The government turned to USAID for assistance. An American appointed by USAID as director of the bank wrote off the bad loans but expanded the bank's operations in the countryside rather than retrenching. Within two years, he increased deposits and loans but demanded significant collateral and cash flow before issuing loans; he also was aggressive in seizing pledged collateral. The ensuing default rate amounted to less than 1 percent. The problem with this strategy was that only the small minority of well-off herders or countryside dwellers had the collateral and cash to be eligible for loans; the vast majority did not have these resources. Thus although the Agricultural, or Khaan, Bank could be a successful model, it actually reached relatively few countryside dwellers. See David Murphy, "Mongolia's Bank Reform," *Far Eastern Economic Review,* July 18, 2002, 41; for a more posi-

tive assessment of the Bank, see James Brooke and Jargal Byam-basuren, "In Mongolia, a Tilt Toward a Free Market," *New York Times,* October 21, 2003, W1, W7. On the bank's continued growth after privatization, see EDN, November 7, 2003.

78. MNA, July 22, 2003; *UB Post,* October 24, 2003.

79. *UB Post,* December 25, 2003.

80. *UB Post,* November 28 and December 12, 2003; EDN, November 21, 2003.

81. *Mongol Messenger,* February 6, 2002; EDN, March 14 and August 16, 2002; *UB Post,* October 17, 2002. A British court found that the Mongolian government was not liable for Jargalsaikhan's default on his loan, but the Marubeni Corporation promised to appeal. See *Mongol Messenger,* March 17, 2004. Prosecutors were reportedly preparing a case against a former Minister of Finance who may have illegally offered the guarantees. See *UB Post,* April 3, 2003.

82. EDN, April 3, 2003.

83. *Mongol Messenger,* May 22, 2002; EDN, June 12 and 15, 2002.

84. EDN, November 28, 2000; MNA, November 14 and July 3, 2002. The brother of the president of MCS had been an important government official, and the company often hired former government officials. The fact that the office of the Permanent Representative of the ADB was in the MCS building perhaps helped to bolster their relations with the international donor agencies. See *Mongol Messenger,* May 9, 2001, and EDN, November 5, 2003. On the founding of MCS in 1993, see EDN, September 5, 2003.

85. *Mongol Messenger,* December 18, 2002; EDN, May 23, 2001; interview, S. Oyun, New York, April 2003; the number of shares traded on the Stock Exchange continues to decline. See MNA, May 15, 2003.

86. The result was that domestic investment increased by only 2.3 percent in 2002. See Mongolian National Chamber of Commerce and Industry, *White Paper,* 14.

87. EDN, December 15, 2000; January 16, 2001; March 12, 2001.

88. EDN, November 11, 2001; *Mongol Messenger,* December 18, 2002. Chinese companies were even outbidding Mongolian companies for the purchase of waste paper from printing plants for use in manufacturing toilet paper. Mongolian toilet paper companies thus did not have sufficient raw material. MNA, February 13, 2004; *Mongol Messenger,* February 18, 2004.

89. EDN, September 4, 2001, and October 17, 2000; *UB Post,* January 25, 2001. In an article, "Graduates Go to Waste," *UB Post,* May 15, 2003, estimated that only 25 percent of college graduates secured positions in their chosen fields.

90. *Mongol Messenger,* January 3, 2001; *UB Post,* January 25, 2001.

91. The Millennium Road passed through the province of Bayan-Ölgii, one of the poorest regions of the country, the homeland of the largest minority group in the region. Since the early 1990s, the Muslim Turkic-speaking Kazakh inhabitants of the region, who constituted about 5 percent of the country's total population, had received little investment or support.

92. EDN, May 9, 2002; May 14, 2002; June 11, 2002; interview, S. Oyun, New York, April 15, 2003; EDN, November 12, 2002. A government source estimates that expenses for the Millennium Road in 2002 amounted to about $22 million. See MNA, May 5, 2003. Complaints about inadequate maintenance of roads, including the important tourist road from Ulaanbaatar to the ancient capital at Khara Khorum, appear regularly in the press. See EDN, September 11, 2003: MNA, April 30 and June 7, 2004. One of the latest construction projects is the dismantling of the tombs of the communist leaders Sükhbaatar and Choibalsang and their replacement by a two-story building to be used as a reception hall for visiting dignitaries (and perhaps a statue of Chinggis Khan); EDN, April 22 19, 2003. The government also unveiled plans to build a new airport for Ulaanbaatar, still another expensive project that could lead to cost overruns and graft. See *Mongol Messenger,* May 26, 2004. Simultaneously, it planned to build a new airport in Ölgii, the capital of the *aimag* of Bayan-Ölgii. See MNA, June 14, 2004.

93. Bikales et al., "Mongolian Informal Sector."

94.   For example, a random check of ten hairdressing salons by a government agency found that only one followed proper hygienic procedures. The same agency also discovered unsanitary conditions in a large number of informal sector sites selling liquor. See MNA, February 4, 2004.

95.   EDN, November 29, 2002, discusses the question of food security in unregulated food shops and kiosks; *UB Post*, August 11, 1998, notes that 70 percent of kiosk owners had not undergone medical tests; EDN, October 14, 2002, discusses the sale of outdated medicines by unregulated drug stores; on the evasion of taxes, see *Mongolia This Week*, June 2–8, 2000, and EDN, November 5, 2001; EDN, October 21, 2002, discusses the World Bank survey; and see Anderson, "Introduction to Mongolia's Informal Sector," on the lack of health and social welfare benefits for workers in the informal sector. A recent study concluded that 240,000 to 270,000 people earned their income in the "shadow economy"; EDN, August 14, 2003.

96.   EDN, September 25 and December 25, 2003.

97.   EDN, October 6, October 13, and December 30, 2003; *Mongol Messenger*, January 7, 2004; MNA, March 23 and May 4, 2004.

98.   See Grainger, "Great Mongolian Gold Rush," 148–49; Vardi, "Promoter," 125–32; "Ivanhoe Mines," Reuters, Vancouver, December 23, 2003, www.reuters.com/newsArticle.jhtml?type =topNews7storyID = 4061 (accessed January 4, 2004); and "Ivanhoe Revises Its Estimates of Copper and Gold Deposits," EIU, November 1, 2003, http://db.eiu.com/search_view.asp? doc_id = DB1293109&action-go&topicid = MN&pubcod . . . (accessed January 24, 2004). Robert M. Friedland, chairman of Ivanhoe Mines, "first came to international attention in 1992 when cyanide-laced tailings washed out of the abandoned Summitville gold mine in Colorado, killing all aquatic life in the Alamosa River for 17 miles downstream. In the late 1980's, the mine was operated by Galactic Resources of Vancouver, and Mr. Friedland was Galactic's principal shareholder. . . . [U.S.] federal officials pursued him to pay for cleaning up the cyanide, and in 1996 they persuaded Canadian judges to freeze $152 mil-

lion of his assets. To settle the case, Mr. Friedland agreed to pay $27.75 million over 10 years," one of the largest fines ever imposed for damage to the U.S. environment. See James Brooke, "Mongolia Is Having a Mine Rush," *New York Times,* October 3, 2003, W7.

99. See "Ivanhoe Shares Plunge after Development Study," Reuters, Vancouver, February 2, 2004, www.reuters.com/newsArticle .jhtml?type = topNews&StoryID = 42266.

100. *Mongol Messenger,* November 30, 2002; *UB Post,* October 31, 2002.

101. EDN, April 14, 2001.

102. "In 2002 Mongolia made debt repayments of US$20m on the principal and US$10m in interest on credits received from donors in 1992–93," the Economist Intelligence Unit noted ("External Debt Is Being Repaid," EIU, February 1, 2003, http://db.eiu.com/search_view.asp?doc_id = DB1158483&action = go&hits = 25&search = &da [accessed January 24, 2004]). However, "[i]n the next few years there is a risk that Mongolia will default on its external debt-servicing obligations . . . [partly because of its] continued use of foreign debt to finance its fiscal and current-account deficits" ("External Sector," EIU, August 1, 2003, http://db.eiu.com/search_view.asp?doc_id = DB1248272 &action = go&hits = 25&search = &da [accessed January 24, 2004]).

103. *UB Post,* September 18, 2002.

104. EDN, February 8, 2002; February 12, 2001; August 28, 2001; November 20, 2001; and January 15, 2003; *UB Post,* December 19 and April 12, 2002.

105. For a caustic and somewhat hyperbolic view of the foreign residents, see one resident's view in *UB Post,* December 19, 2002. "Indian Restaurants Fighting It Out in Mongolia," Press Trust of India, July 24, 2001; Lawless, *Wild East,* 141.

106. EDN, October 2, 2001; October 11, 2001; and June 19, 2002. By the following year's donors' conference, several delegations "expressed some concern that earlier assistance had

neither reduced poverty nor promoted sustainable growth sufficiently" ("Donors Pledge US$335m in Aid for 2004," EIU February 19, 2004, http://db.eiu.com/search_view.asp?doc_id =DB1331198&action = go&hits = 25&search = &dat [accessed March 1, 2004]).

107. For this report, see Griffin, *Strategy for Poverty Reduction.*

108. EDN, December 14, 2000, and January 16, 2002; *UB Post,* May 2, 2002; quotations from *UB Post,* May 1, 2003.

109. *UB Post,* December 4, 2003. There are other examples of misuse of such funds. More than 60 percent of a loan by Golomt Bank to a company to build a tourist hotel was used to speculate in sugar. The same bank provided a $340,000 loan to another company for cashmere-processing machinery; the company used it instead to buy raw cashmere. See *Mongol Messenger,* October 22, 2003. According to the official MNA (May 20, 2004), even the UNDP faced these problems. Equipment that it had provided had been stolen, and anywhere from 25 to 62 percent of specific projects it initiated went to foreign consultants.

110. MNA, May 30, 2002. In 2003, VAT revenue increased 21.3 percent, while corporate income tax rates were reduced from 40 to 30 percent ("Taxes Are to Be Cut and Pensions Will Rise" and "Government Spending Is Kept under Control," EIU, February 19, 2004, http://db.eiu.com/search_view.asp?doc_id =DB1331192&action = go&topicid = MN&pubcode [accessed March 1, 2004]).

111. EDN, October 15, 2003.

112. EDN, July 18, 2002; February 5, 2001; and December 26, 2000; *Mongol Messenger,* January 30, 2002. Another proposed means for raising revenue was to deduct taxes from the bank accounts of laggard companies. However, critics suggested that such actions would not only undermine the banking system but also prompt enterprises to pay in cash, not in bank drafts. See Lkhagvasüren Nomin, "Mongolian Tax Collectors Get Tough," Eurasianet, May 26, 2002, www.eurasianet.org/departments/ business/articles/eav052602.shtml (accessed August 14, 2002).

113. EDN, March 19, 2002; *UB Post,* April 25, 2002; *Mongol Messen-*

ger, March 20, 2002; *UB Post,* June 14, 2001; EDN, September 25, 2001, and April 25, 2002.

114.   *UB Post,* March 7 and 14, 2002; EDN, September 5, 2002, and January 17, 2001; *Mongol Messenger,* March 15, 2001, and July 17, 2002; *UB Post,* May 20, 2002; EDN, January 30, 2003, on survey.

115.   Police official: EDN, June 6, 2001; Civil Will Party: *UB Post,* November 9, 2000.

116.   Khural members were required to reveal their incomes to a government agency, but only Oyun and one other member made their financial statements public. See MNA, February 3, 2004.

117.   *Mongol Messenger,* May 8, 2002; EDN, February 24, 2003; the article was in *UB Post,* December 19, 2002. The minister of social welfare and labor is under investigation for possible involvement in a scheme to defraud workers who paid substantial sums to a government-licensed firm that promised them employment in Japan. See *UB Post,* February 12, 2004, and "Hunger Strikers Demand Human Rights," EIU, February 19, 2004, http://db.eiu.com/search_view.asp?doc_id = DB1331183&action = go&topicid = MN&pubcode (accessed March 1, 2004). In March 2003, the UNDP conducted a seminar for officials on corruption. Several speakers suggested that "an independent anti-corruption body be set up" but the Minister of Justice said "that such a step was unnecessary." See "Corruption among Public Officials Is Highlighted," EIU, May 1, 2003, http:db.eiu.com/search_view.asp?doc_id = DB1209626&action = go&hits =25 &search = &da (accessed January 1, 2004).

118.   "City Mayor Seizes Land from Poor Families," www.liberty center.org.mn/family_land_seized.htm, July 2, 2003 (accessed September 14, 2003); see also MNA, January 16, 2003.

119.   EDN, September 19, 2003; see also September 17, 2003.

120.   EDN, October 7, 2003. The land privatization process started on May 1, 2003, and was scheduled to end by May 1, 2005, with 568,000 households receiving land. As of January 2004, only 20,000 households had been granted land. See MNA, January 8, 2004. Oyun and others attribute the slow pace to corruption and

red tape. See *Mongol Messenger,* January 21, 2004. Banks are increasingly involved in buying land at auctions—reputedly for space to construct new bank buildings. Could some of these purchases lead to land speculation? MNA, February 3, 2004. For additional details, see Rossabi, "Communist and Post-Communist Law and Private Land."

121. "Agricultural Workers Demonstrate against Land Laws," EIU, February 1, 2003, http://db.eiu.com/search_view.asp?doc_id =DB1158456&action = go&hits = 25&search = &da (accessed January 24, 2004). For an official government response to the fear that large companies would be able to buy much of the farmland, see Tsolmon Bold, "Mongolian Government Rebuts Charge that Privatization Law Is Discriminatory," Eurasianet, December 20, 2002, www.eurasianet.org/departments/rights/ articles/eav122002a.shtml (accessed May 18, 2004). The article merely asserts that the law is not discriminatory and does not rebut the central contention about large companies and the privatization process.

122. Alec Appelbaum, "Dissent over Land Reform May Portend Unrest in Mongolia," Eurasianet, December 21, 2002, www.eurasianet.org/departments/rights/articles/eav122002 .shtml (accessed January 11, 2003); "The Last Best Place," *Economist,* December 21, 2002, 60; *Mongol Messenger,* June 19, 2002; *UB Post,* November 28, 2002; Susan Lazorchick, "Rights Activists in Mongolia Raise Alarm after Government Crackdown on Demonstrators," Eurasianet, November 15, 2002, www.eurasianet.org/departments/rights/articles/eav11502.shtml (accessed November 26, 2002); Oyungerel Tsedevdamba, "Pro-Democracy Activists in Mongolia Worry About Potential Roll Back of Reforms," Eurasianet, November 22, 2002, www.eurasianet.org/departments/rights/articles/eav112202 .shtl (accessed November 26, 2002). Quotation from Lkhagvasüren Nomin, "Mongolian Protestors Call for a Referendum Before Land is Privatized," *Transitions Online,* June 30, 2002, www.eurasianet.org/departments/rights/articles/pp063002 .shtml (accessed November 10, 2002).

123. EDN, May 30, 2001; Sumati, "Politbarometer 17," October 2002, 2–3; *UB Post,* September 18, 2002.

124. On GDP, see Mongolia, National Statistical Office, *Mongolian Statistical Yearbook, 2001,* 86. A survey in the most important towns found unemployment hovering between 27 percent and 38 percent. See EDN, January 8, 2003. See also EDN, March 15, 2002, and September 26, 2001. EDN, September 2, 2002, reveals that the Khural was not providing sufficient funds for winter preparations. The frustrated chair's views are discussed in EDN, April 15, 2003.

125. For the volatility, which at times works in Mongolia's favor, but which could just as well work against Mongolia, see Bernard Simon, "Strikes Push Up Prices of Industrial Metals," *New York Times,* February 3, 2004, W1.

126. The unemployment figures are reported in MNA, February 3, 2004. See also MNA, February 4, 2004, and *Mongol Messenger,* January 21, 2004.

127. EDN, December 4, 2002; *UB Post,* June 20, 2002.

128. EDN, November 13, 2002; MNA, May 15, 2003. The trade imbalance has increased throughout 2003, according to "Imports Surge in the First Eight Months of 2003," EIU, November 1, 2003, db.eiu.com/search_view.asp?doc_id = DB1293112&action = go&topicid = MN&pubcod (accessed January 24, 2004). Such a striking imbalance is naturally worrisome, particularly in light of Mongolia's sizable foreign debt.

129. As of early 2002, its foreign debt amounted to about $930 million or the high ratio of about 90 percent of annual GDP.

130. Bikales et al., "Mongolian Informal Sector."

131. Early in 2004, the ADB proudly announced that the private sector, which accounted for 57 percent of GDP in 1996, now produced 80 percent of GDP. It did not mention that these statistics revealed a decline in state activities. See MNA, February 2, 2004.

132. EDN, May 1, 2002; *Mongol Messenger,* July 31, 2002.

133. *UB Post,* December 12, 2003; EDN, December 4, 2003; *Mongol Messenger,* October 15, 2003.

134. On the splits within the Democratic Party, see "Co-operation between Opposition Parties Limited," EIU, May 1, 2003, http://db.eiu.com?search_view.asp?doc_id = DB1209624& action =go &hits = 25&search = &da; "Domestic Politics," EIU, November 1, 2003, http://db.eiu.com/ search _view.asp?doc_id =DB1293084 &action = go&topicid = MN &pubcod; "The Opposition Disrupts the Opening of Parliament," EIU, November 1, 2003, http://db.eiu.com? search _view.asp? doc_id =DB1293091&action = go&topicid = MN &pubcod (all accessed January 24, 2004); and EDN, December 12, 2003.

135. *Mongol Messenger,* October 29, 2003.

136. "Ballots Re-examined as Mongolian Elections Hang in Balance," Channel News Asia International, www.Channelsasia.com/stories/afp-asiapacific/view/92721/1/.html, June 30, 2004 (accessed July 1, 2004).

137. "Mongolia: A Shock to the System," June 29, 2004, www.eurasianet.org/departments/insight/articles/pp62904.html, June 29, 2004 (accessed July 1, 2004).

CHAPTER 5

1. For a more detailed description of Qing rule in Mongolia, see my introduction to Namkhainyambuu, *Bounty,* and the sources cited there.

2. Bruun, "The Herding Household," in Bruun and Odgaard, eds., *Mongolia,* 68.

3. Sambuu, *Malchidatl;* Ruth Meserve has translated an earlier work of Sambuu's on horses. See Meserve, "Historical Perspective of Mongol Horse Training," 249–305.

4. See Namkhainyambuu, *Bounty,* for an English translation.

5. For a listing of some of these dissertations, see Shulman, *Doctoral Dissertations on China and Inner Asia,* 112–14.

6. Schmidt, *Mongolia in Transition,* 81.

7. *UB Post,* August 21, 1996. See Murphy, *Soviet Mongolia,* 58, on the disadvantages of "nomadic agriculture" in Mongolia.

8. Schmidt, *Mongolia in Transition*, 88.

9. Humphrey and Sneath, *End of Nomadism*, 295.

10. Goldstein and Beall, *Changing World*, 93.

11. Ibid., 95.

12. See Humphrey and Sneath, eds., *Culture and Environment in Inner Asia*, 1: 64–65, for a description of the impact of these problems in one location.

13. For one critique of this approach, see Sander Tideman, "The Shortcoming," in Akiner et al., *Sustainable Development*, 75–89. For another approach to foreign aid, see "It Is Important for Mongolia to Be Independent from Foreign Aid," *Blue Sky* 8 (August, 1998): 4.

14. Campi, "Nomadic Cultural Values," 92; for a slightly different view, see Fritz, "Doppelte Transition in der Mongolei," 100–104.

15. Bruun, "Herding Household," in Bruun and Odgaard, eds., *Mongolia*, 67.

16. Ibid., 82; for an example of the ensuing political problems, see Liao, " 'Min-chu,' " 85–94.

17. Goldstein and Beall, *Changing World*, 108.

18. Ibid., 108.

19. Schmidt, *Mongolia in Transition*, 50.

20. Ibid., 56; Tserendorjiin Gankhuyag, a member of the Khural with special interests in the pastoral economy, said in an interview I conducted on May 28, 1998, that 62 percent to 70 percent of the herding households had fewer than 100 animals. On Gankhuyag, see Staisch and Prohl, *Dschingis*, 49–50.

21. Mongolia, National Statistical Office, *Mongolian Statistical Yearbook, 2002*, 151.

22. Vladimir Graivoronsky, "Livestock Privatization in Mongolia: Some First Results," in Sharma, ed., *Mongolia*, 202. Graivoronsky estimates that as of 1995, only 10 percent of herding households produced for the market; the rest were "subsistence households." A fine analysis of the differences between the rich and the poor is in Fernandez-Giménez, "Landscapes, Livestock," 359–71.

23. Graivoronsky, "Livestock Privatization," 200; Mongolia, National Statistical Office, *Mongolian Statistical Yearbook, 2001,* 96.

24. Mearns, "Territoriality and Land Tenure," 95–98.

25. The government issued a Land Law in 1994 that granted leases to camp sites and other pastoral resources. The law was generally not well implemented and often favored the privileged. See Fernandez-Giménez and Batbuyan, "Law and Disorder."

26. EDN, April 25, 2003.

27. Naoko Ishii, "The Livestock Sector in Mongolia," in Sachs, *Towards Economic Strategies for Rapid Growth,* n.p.

28. Rosenberg, "Cultural Issues," 260; EDN, May 21, 1997; EDN, March 26, 1997, reported that most herders received few, if any, newspapers. The *Gobi Business News,* founded in June of 1999, seeks to provide information for herders. Under the auspices of the Open Society Institute, Mongolia, Mr. William Siemering is attempting to expand radio broadcasts aimed specifically at herders. He reported on his efforts at the annual meeting of the Association for Asian Studies in New York in March of 2003.

29. Craven and Curtin, *Environmental Profile,* v; EDN, August 8, 1997.

30. UNDP, *Human Development, 2003,* 25.

31. *UB Post,* February 24, 1999; interview with T. Batbold, Ulaanbaatar, August 21, 1997.

32. Interview with Bat-Erdeniyn Batbayar (Baabar), Ulaanbaatar, June 30, 1998; EDN, October 30, 1997.

33. MNA, January 9, 2004. The Russians repeatedly provided vaccinations when outbreaks of the disease erupted. A recent hoof and mouth epidemic originated with gazelles and spread to cattle. See MNA, February 16 and 19, 2004 and *Mongol Messenger,* February 18, 2004. EDN, December 6, 1996 reported that goat and camel meat was, on occasion, fraudulently sold as beef and lamb and that pork fat was sold as camel hump, a great delicacy.

34. Mongolia, National Statistical Office, *Mongolian Statistical Yearbook, 1997,* 141; EIU, *Mongolia,* 2d quar. 1998, 51.

35. Ishii, "Livestock Sector," in Sachs, *Towards Economic Strategies*

for *Rapid Growth,* n.p.; interview, Boris Shlomm, New York, April 9, 1998.

36. Mead, "Letter from Mongolia: The Crisis in Cashmere," 60.

37. *Mongol Messenger,* August 27, 1997.

38. For additional details, see Barbara Skapa and Ann Fenger Benwell, "Women and Poverty during the Transition," in Bruun and Odgaard, eds., *Mongolia in Transition,* 135–46; State Statistical Bureau, "Women and Children of Mongolia"; Kojima, "Women in Development, Mongolia"; UNICEF, "An Analysis of the Situation of Children and Women in Mongolia," among other reports.

39. Mongolia, National Statistical Office, *Mongolian Statistical Yearbook, 1997,* 133; ibid., *2001,* 129.

40. EDN, July 2, 1999.

41. Mongolia, National Statistical Office, *Mongolian Statistical Yearbook, 1999,* 214; *UB Post,* August 21, 1996; EDN, November 20, 1996.

42. Mongolia, National Statistical Office, *Mongolian Statistical Yearbook, 1997,* 219–21. Banzragchiin Delgermaa, "UN Supports Food Security," *Blue Sky* 9 (October–November 1998): 1, writes that "this year's [1998] harvest of 188,327 tonnes is the worst in four decades." For more on economic relations with China, see Wang, *Chiu-shih nien-tai Meng-ku,* 50–71.

43. MNA, February 9, 2004. The statistics for 2002 indicate continued decline in production in cereals, wheat, potatoes, and vegetables but with an increase in fodder. See Mongolian National Chamber of Commerce and Industry, *White Paper,* 19.

44. EDN, November 9, 1998; Mongolia, National Statistical Office, *Mongolian Statistical Yearbook, 2001,* 167–71.

45. The government has belatedly recognized the need for some state assistance for veterinary services. In 2003, it allocated about $4.4 million for "veterinary measures" to prevent diseases among the animals. It is not clear from the source whether these funds will cover the services of veterinarians or simply the administration of vaccinations; MNA, February 10, 2004.

46. MNA, June 27, 2003.

47. Suvendrini Kakuchi, "Economic Reforms Exact Heavier Price on Women," *Blue Sky* 8 (August 1998): 3. "Rural residents have less access to education, health care, information, jobs and other human development opportunities than their urban counterparts," notes UNDP, *Human Development, 2003 Report: Mongolia,* 24; and see also ibid., 27–32, on disparities in mortality rates and access to drinking water, newspapers, magazines, television, and telephones.

48. Interview with Dashiin Byambasüren, Ulaanbaatar, January 6, 1997.

49. Mongolia, National Statistical Office, *Mongolian Statistical Yearbook, 2001,* 83, 114.

50. Wu, *Mongolia: Financing Education,* 16–19.

51. *UB Post,* August 25, 1998.

52. EDN, August 25, 1997.

53. *UB Post,* May 6, 1997.

54. UNDP, "Development of Distance Education," ii.

55. Schmidt, *Mongolia in Transition,* 168.

56. See the works of Humphrey and Sneath, Fernandez-Giménez, and Müller for trenchant analyses of the need for regulation of land and water use rather than the total privatization advocated by some free-market advisors to the Mongolian government.

57. For the attitudes of other herders, see Jill Lawless, "Letter from Mongolia," *Guardian Weekly,* June 13, 1999, 8, quoting a herder she visited: "My parents firmly believe that the socialist time was much better than this. They remember it fondly. They say things like, 'All for one and one for all.' Now you have to rely completely on yourself." Tomlinson, "From Genghis Khan to Milton Friedman," 200, quotes another herder: "Compared with the socialist time, life is worse. Before we had a regular income. Now we have to depend on the animals."

58. John Gittings, "Starving Mongolia Teeters on the Edge," *Guardian Weekly,* March 23–30, 2000, 6. For more on the *zud*s, see Lkhagvasüren Nomin, "Mongolia: The Tail of a

Dragon," Eurasianet, February 26, 2001, www.eurasianet.org/departments/environment/articles/eav022601a.shtml (accessed April 14, 2001).

59. "The Last Best Place," *Economist,* December 21, 2002, 60.

60. Namkhainyambuu repeatedly warned about the dangers in conversations I had with him in the summers of 1998 and 1999.

61. EDN, April 23, 2002.

62. Mongolia, National Statistical Office, *Mongolian Statistical Yearbook, 2001,* 146.

63. Tomlinson, "From Genghis Khan to Milton Friedman," 200.

64. Tsendmaa Natsagdorj, "Improved Pastureland Management Can Lead to Greater Profit Potential," *Gobi Business News,* July–August, 2000, 2; Ian Johnson, "In Mongolia, a Storm Blows Untried Nomads Down Path to Disaster," *Wall Street Journal,* May 3, 2000, A1: "[In 1991] the government, following the advice of dozens of Western organizations, decided to privatize the national herd. . . . In one swoop, Mongolia abandoned the collective herding of the Soviet era and reverted to clan herding. . . . [Inexperienced herders] had no idea where to take their stock and were given no advice by the largely defunct agricultural-extension office [when the *zud* hit]."

65. "The Last Best Place," *Economist,* December 21, 2002, 59.

66. *Mongolia This Week,* March 24–30, 2000; *UB Post,* March 8, 2000; *Mongol Messenger,* December 12, 2001; EDN, August 29, 2001.

67. *Mongolia This Week,* March 31–April 6, 2000.

68. EDN, April 23 and November 6, 2001. UNDP and the World Bank have belatedly supported the establishment of cooperatives, and the government declared 2003 the year of cooperatives. It remains to be seen whether this effort will meet with success. The Konrad Adenauer Foundation initiated such an effort in 1998, but little was accomplished. The government and the donor agencies will need to devote considerable resources to foster a successful cooperative movement. See "Herding Cooperatives Are Encouraged," EIU, May 1, 2003, http://db

.eiu.com/search_view.asp?doc_id = DB1209647& action = go &hits = 25& search = &da (accessed January 14, 2004).

69.   MNA, May 5, 2003. The international donors and the government have initiated programs to repair wells, provide transportation and veterinary services, supply hay and fodder, and grant solar generators, but most are limited and do not compare with government services provided in the communist era. See *Mongol Messenger*, May 2004, and MNA, April 2, 22, and 27, May 3, 6, 14, and 24, and June 9, 2004.

70.   On the catastrophes, see EDN, August 23 and October 8, 2002; on the prime minister's plan, see David Murphy, "No Room for Nomads," *Far Eastern Economic Review*, May 31, 2001, 30–32; on the importance of mobility, Humphrey and Sneath, *End of Nomadism*.

71.   Staisch and Prohl, *Dschingis*, 56.

72.   EDN, September 12, 2003.

73.   MNA, January 16, 2004.

CHAPTER 6

1.   EDN, November 19, 1996.

2.   Lawless, *Wild East*, 48.

3.   Many would not tolerate any criticism, and they intimated that they had special and superior economic expertise. Two specialists who described the representatives of the donor agencies in Russia wrote that "those who criticized their policies were held to be ignorant of modern economic theory or not to have understood the policy alternatives they faced"; Silverman and Yanowitch, *New Rich*, 9. In my own dealings with several representatives of the donor agencies, I was surprised by their incredibly belligerent attitude toward any criticism of their policies in Mongolia.

4.   Nixson and Walters, "Transition to a Market Economy," 18. He echoed the views of the Nobel-prize winning economist Joseph Stiglitz, who concluded "that growth wasn't enough to lift the poor out of poverty—policy had to be actively tilted in their

favor." See Doug Henwood, "Stiglitz and the Limits of Reform," *Nation,* October 2, 2000, 20.

5.   Stephen Holmes, "Capitalist Russia: Lessons for the Liberal State," *Open Society News,* Spring 1998, 16–19, argues that the state's incapacity actually harms the public. Personal security, sanctity of contracts, environmental standards, and rules of ownership all require government and officials who are accountable. Holmes concludes that "to protect our freedom, we had better protect the legitimate political authority that enables and sustains it" (19).

6.   EDN, October 5, 2000.

7.   See International Labour Organization, *Macro Policies and Poverty Alleviation: Mongolia.*

8.   EDN, October 5 and 17, 2000.

9.   EIU, *Mongolia,* 1st quar. 1995, 36, refers to the "remorseless growth of inequality."

10. Oyun, "From the Year," 1.

11. EIU, *Mongolia,* 3d quar. 1994, 48.

12. Tsogt, "Mongolia in the Grip of Poverty," in Atal, ed., *Poverty in Transition,* quotations from 252, 242, and 246. Some economists have argued that a survey based on a capabilities approach (longevity, mobility, literacy) rather than income yields a more accurate portrait of the poor, and such a measurement would find an even higher rate of poverty. In 1995, the government, while emphasizing a definition of poverty based on income, also endorsed the concept of capabilities (or lack thereof) as a measure of poverty. It identified six groups prone to inordinate risk of falling into poverty, which included the disabled, female-headed households, the unemployed, the elderly, children with only one or no parent, and families with many children. These were not all poor but they had specific characteristics that made them vulnerable. A consultant to the World Bank justified the emphasis on vulnerable groups, writing that "it may not be the lack of income alone that is causing poverty." She noted that the number of workers and dependent children in the household, the health of its members, and the access of rural households to markets were

critical gauges. Food consumption was not a sufficient signifier of poverty. Other elements that impinged upon poverty included crime, alcohol abuse, and poor health based upon inadequate nutrition. See Harper, *Assessment of Vulnerable Groups,* 3.

13. EIU, *Mongolia,* 3d quar. 1994, 4; EDN, December 9, 1996.

14. *UB Post,* September 13, 2001.

15. *Mongol Messenger,* August 4, 1999; interview, S. Oyun, Ulaanbaatar, April 29, 1999.

16. EDN, September 8, 1997, and March 13, 1998; Avery, *Women,* 42.

17. UNDP, *Human Development Report, Mongolia, 1997,* 19; UN Development Fund for Women, *Women in Mongolia,* 26, writes that "average calorie intake per person per day was 2,621 calories in 1989, 1,963 calories in 1993, and 2,158 calories in 1998." The declines in fruits, eggs, and vegetables were particularly noticeable.

18. *Russia Today,* October 9, 1998; EDN, March 15, 2002.

19. EIU, *Mongolia,* 1st quar. 2000, 48.

20. Forum for International Development, *Review of the 1998 Mongolia Living Standards Measurement Survey.* See Mark Brenner, "Poverty in Mongolia," in Griffin, "Strategy for Poverty Reduction," 20–36, for an explanation of why the slightly different standards, which included two new *aimags* in the 1998 survey, do not challenge the findings that the poverty rate remained the same. Brenner also argues (28) that the 36.3 percent figure in 1995 and 35.6 percent in 1998 are measures of extreme poverty and that "a more accurate incidence of poverty [based on nonfood items as well] in Mongolia is 51.6 per cent for 1995 and 51.7 per cent in 1998."

21. A Khural member said that "the living standards of the poor are lower by 10–15 times compared to the wealthy"; *Mongol Messenger,* February 27, 2002.

22. World Vision, "Addressing Food Security"; interview, D. Gardner, Ulaanbaatar, June 12, 1998; *Mongol Messenger,* February 10, 1999. An earlier report, based on surveys of households in Ulaanbaatar, *aimag* centers, and rural districts in July–August 1997, found that these households spent 74 percent of their income on

food. Moreover, 32 percent of people had not consumed vegetable products and 14 percent had not eaten rice in the previous month. One in four children was undernourished, and 40 percent were anemic. See Carolyn MacDonald, "Nutrition and Food Security," 6, 7, 9, 18.

23. Mongolia, National Statistical Office, *Mongolian Statistical Yearbook, 2000,* 44; EDN, September 6, 1999. UN Development Fund for Women, *Women in Mongolia,* 43, notes: "The poorer the household, the higher the proportion of female-headed households."

24. EDN, August 18, 1998.

25. Interview, P. Marsh, Ulaanbaatar, June 1, 1998.

26. MNA, March 24, 2000; *Mongol Messenger,* October 18, 2000. One response to the 1998 survey on poverty reveals much about the foreign advisors who were staunch advocates of the market economy. Distressed by the findings that poverty had not been reduced and that aid from the international donors had not led to "an improvement in the well-being" of the population from 1995 to 1998, an agency that consulted for USAID commissioned a "poverty expert" to examine the 1998 survey, focusing on the rural poor. The "poverty expert" disputed the findings, noting that the 1998 survey increased the number of households surveyed and added two items to the consumption basket and two new *aimags* to the geographic scope. She argued that the survey revealed that those labeled "poor" in the 1998 study had more livestock and consumed more food than in 1995, and thus that the poverty head count was too high.

However, Mongolian and foreign specialists challenged her analysis. As noted in chapter 5, the increased size of the herds in the 1990s did not signify greater prosperity. Instead, it reflected both the inability to transport and market animals and the absence of *zud*s (i.e., disastrous winters affecting the herds) from 1990 to 1999. Numbers of livestock did not correlate with "improvements in well-being." The "poverty consultant" produced this analysis in April of 2000 when the first *zud* resulted in the loss of about three million of the thirty-three million animals, losses that were in part owing to the rapid privatization of the herds encouraged by international donors. By December 2002, the Mongolian livestock census had been reduced by about a third, from thirty-three to twenty-three million, which vitiated her argument about herd size and increased well-being. Indeed, if her analysis were accepted, then the poverty head count in 2002 would be much higher than in 1995 and in 1998.

Her argument that many herders in 1998 were no longer poor because they consumed more food than in 1995 has also been subject to criticism. First, the comparison was misleading, because in 1995 consumption of potatoes, vegetables, and fruits by the rural poor had reached its nadir. Thus the percentage increases she cited for 1998, although an improvement, did not signify a move out of poverty. The finding that as of 1998 "calorie intake has not yet reached the level it was before the transition [i.e., 1990]" may have belied her view that poverty had decreased (UN Development Fund for Women, *Women in Mongolia,* 26). Second, she did not consider that "expenditures may reflect a systematic depletion of assets (e.g. livestock) in an effort to sustain consumption levels. In the long term such strategies are likely to be unsustainable, and thus current per capita expenditure does not represent a measure of 'permanent income,' but rather a postponement of the permanent reduction of living standards" (see Brenner, "Poverty in Mongolia," in Griffin, "Strategy for Poverty Reduction" 24). That is, a temporary increase in food consumption may have been masking the poor herders' continued depletion of their assets (and may also have reflected some access to aid from charities). Third, her emphasis on food consumption tended to slight other measures of poverty—access to clean water, medical care, clothing (a vital consideration in the frigid Mongolian winters), education, and media. Finally, she omitted to mention that most of the vegetables, fruits, and potatoes the herders consumed in 1998 were imported, principally from China, a change from 1995 but also an indication of the decline of Mongolian agriculture and of ever-increasing dependence on food imports.

In short, here is another example of an international donor agency—in this case, a contractor for USAID—going to great lengths to justify its pure market policies and challenging any contrary evidence that questioned those policies.

27. *Mongol Messenger,* November 19, 2003; EDN, December 8, 2003.

28. *Mongol Messenger,* September 18, 2003. The ADB resident representative also asserted that private sector economic growth was required to reduce poverty. See *Mongol Messenger,* September 12, 2003. The World Bank initiated a four-year $88 million poverty alleviation program in 2004, still emphasizing private sector growth. See MNA, May 12, 2004.

29. Bruun, "Mongolian Nomadic Herders," 1–4; Pedersen, "Aspects of Every Day Life in Post-Socialist Mongolia." Unlike the anthropologists, many of the foreign consultants rarely ventured outside of Ulaanbaatar, except for brief holidays in tourist *ger* camps or at historic or artistic sites.

30. *UB Post,* November 14, 2003.

31. On the situation in one rural area, see Matthew Heller, "The View from Murun," *Blue Sky* 2 (January 1998); 3.

32. Mongolia, National Statistical Office, *Mongolian Statistical Year-book, 2000,* 88; MNA, March 24, 1999. Rural migration into Ulaanbaatar has accelerated since 2000. One knowledgeable observer estimates that Ulaanbaatar had a population of about one million by May 2003. Interview, S. Menon, New York, May 8, 2003.

33. According to one survey, 27.9 percent of the migrants said that they were moving to Ulaanbaatar because the local schools were so poor. See MNA, January 26, 2004.

34. Phil Zabriskie, "Under a Broken Sky," *Time Asia,* February 24, 2003, captures the herders' melancholy at having to abandon their profession, as well as the bleakness of their lives in the *ger* encampments in Ulaanbaatar. He also captures the mind-set of some of the consultants dispatched to Mongolia. Zabriskie points out that under the communist system, "there was fresh hay available when needed, and a truck came around regularly to carry hides, meat and milk to market. Veterinary services— which have now largely disappeared—were widely available." The World Bank consultant's response to this sorry state of

affairs is that it's difficult "to change the mind-set from 'I'm a receiver' to 'I have to do this myself.'" The consultant's comment seems to imply that the herder would have to provide veterinary services himself, to come up with a truck himself, and to produce hay himself, not to mention dig deep wells himself. How is a herder, by himself, supposed suddenly to produce a truck or a veterinarian or sufficient hay or wells—tasks that require either government involvement or establishment of cooperatives (and probably both)? The antigovernment attitudes of many of the consultants lead them to a defense of seemingly inappropriate pure market positions. See www.time.com /time/ asia/magazine/ article/0,13673,501030224-423564-2,00.html (accessed June 7, 2003).

35. See Steiner-Khamsi et al., "School-Related Migration in Mongolia," for discussions of school-year migrations including the purchase or rent of apartments for schoolchildren by herders. This option was limited to the small number of wealthy herders.

36. Migration into Ulaanbaatar has increased dramatically in 2003 because the government eliminated fees for moving into the city. EDN, December 16, 2003; MNA, December 24, 2003.

37. *Mongol Messenger,* October 28, 1998, and May 13, 2004; Craven and Curtin, *Environmental Profile,* p. 56. Finally, in 2004, the World Bank allocated funds for attempts to clean up the water in the *ger* districts. It remains to be seen how effective these efforts will be. See *Mongol Messenger,* May 5, 2004.

38. The World Bank provided $200,000 for the building of eight bathhouses in the *ger* districts, certainly a useful contribution, but not nearly sufficient to meet the need. See MNA, June 24, 2003.

39. For graphic descriptions and photos, see *Mongol Messenger,* October 28, 1998. Two Westerners offer a straightforward description of these *ger* areas in "My Mongolian Wish," *UB Post,* July 24, 2003: "The district is very crowded and there is no running water, heating, drainage, or proper waste disposal. There are no street lights and no public bath houses. The area has no community playgrounds, so the 13,542 children who live in the dis-

trict usually play in the streets littered with garbage, threatened by stray dogs and unpredictable traffic."

40. EDN, September 19 and November 23, 2000; February 21, 2003.

41. Laura Ryser, "Mongolia Discovers Field of Gold," *Blue Sky* 2 (January 1998): 3. I am grateful to Scott Christiansen, the resident director for the Adventist Development and Relief Agency in Mongolia, for spending an entire morning with me on June 24, 1998, to explain and inspect a typical straw-bale house. On earthquakes and housing, see EDN, August 23, 1999.

42. UNDP, *Human Development Report, 2000*, 37; EDN, March 12, 2001, and August 24, 2000. Plans for improvements in air quality stretch back to 1991. See UNDP, "Reduction of Atmospheric Pollution." A 2003 study rated Ulaanbaatar as the third most polluted city in Asia. See MNA, January 22, 2004.

43. *UB Post,* May 26, 1998; Xinhua (Mongolia), January 21, 1998; MNA, February 29, 2000. For the WHO adviser, see EDN, December 12, 2002; *Mongol Messenger,* December 18, 2002.

44. Even the micro-gardens required Japanese economic aid. See MNA, January 27, 2004. On the planting of trees, see "15,900 Trees Were Planted in Ulaanbaatar in One Day," *Blue Sky* 6 (May–June 1998): 1, and MNA, February 13, 2004. On the Green Revolution, see Ts. Maidar, "Combating Hunger." In an interview (June 2, 2003), Maidar lamented the government's allocation of very limited resources for this effort and expressed concern about how the funds were dispensed. Despite these efforts, the amount of green area per capita in the capital decreased from 9 square meters in the mid 1990s to 6.3 in 2004; MNA, February 10, 2004. The year 2003 witnessed an increase in agricultural production, but certainly not enough for Mongolia to be self-sufficient. See MNA, February 19, 2004.

45. EDN, August 24, 2000, and May 30, 2001. A report commissioned by the UNDP in 1997 uncovered an array of problems and hazards. The *ger* districts produced substantial amount of radioactive coal ash (which was difficult to reuse) and contended with irregular trash collection (if residents were not at home, the waste would not be collected), and the collection process was

dusty and unhealthy. Having no reliable collection system, poor families simply threw the trash in public spaces, creating unsightly and dangerous dumps. Some apartments had vertical chutes for garbage, which emptied into small rooms emitting unpleasant odors and were rarely emptied. Other apartments had large steel containers placed outside or between buildings. The larger ones were "emptied at intervals of two weeks, several weeks, or even longer." Finally, a few apartments had neither chutes nor containers and sought to dispose of their waste in containers owned by other buildings, generating hostility. Many industries, hospitals and clinics, schools, restaurants, hotels, and other establishments had no containers and left piles of sometimes hazardous materials in public spaces. Generally, neither individuals nor enterprises had the resources to consider recycling. With so much trash in containers and public spaces, it was no wonder that scavengers, mostly the homeless and street children, picked through the garbage, creating an even greater mess. For the report, see UNDP, "Solid Waste Management." See also "Life in a Trash World," a photo essay on the homeless scavengers in *UB Post*, February 28, 2002.

46. UNDP, *Human Development Report, 2000,* 39.

47. MNA, July 19, 1999. However, the government decided to spend considerable sums to restore and repair Sükhbaatar Square, the central square in the country; MNA, January 9, 2004, and EDN, November 4, 2003. Even street lighting in the city needs considerable investment; MNA, February 3, 2004.

48. *Mongolia This Week,* June 16–22, 2000; EDN, July 5, 2001; *UB Post,* November 9, 2002.

49. MNA, February 5, 2004.

50. See "Should Ulaanbaatar Be Drinking Dirty Water," *Mongol Messenger,* February 11, 2004, and B. Enkhsaikhan, "Authorities Abuzz over Upriver Water Pollution" *UB Post,* February 5, 2004. Without some restrictions on such luxury housing, World Bank grants to improve Ulaanbaatar's drinking water would face hurdles. See MNA, February 13, 2004, on a World Bank grant.

51. In a survey of two thousand kiosks, as much as 50 percent of the food was found to be contaminated with dysentery germs. See

EDN, November 21, 1997. Because the workers in the kiosks had only makeshift toilets and were not required to undergo medical tests as food handlers, the levels of potentially hazardous bacteria in the products they sold were high. See *UB Post,* August 11, 1998.

52. EDN, May 30, 2000, offers these figures.

53. MNA, October 9, 1998; *UB Post,* January 12, 2001; Christopher Wren, "U.N. Report Maps Hunger 'Hot Spots,'" *New York Times,* January 9, 2001, A8.

54. *Mongol Messenger,* April 19, 2000; EDN, May 10, 1999; *Mongolia This Week,* May 19–25, 2000. The *UB Post,* May 13, 2004, reported a shortage of seeds for planting. In addition, from 2000 to 2003, milk imports doubled and imports of milk products quintupled. See MNA, May 2, 2004.

55. On the Taiwan-owned factory, see Joseph Kahn, "Citing Child Labor, U.S. Bans Apparel from Mongolia Plant," *New York Times,* November 29, 2000, C6; EDN, November 11, 1997; *UB Post,* August 4, 1998; EDN, November 11, 1997.

56. EDN, July 29, 1999; November 5, 1998; and April 16, 1998; during the election campaigns of 2000, the MPRP promised an almost immediate doubling of wages, a promise it did not fulfill. See *Mongol Messenger,* September 26, 2001.

57. Bender, "Pension Reform in Mongolia," 7, 11; id., "Pension Reform: Managing the Transition," 13, 15, 18; id., "Individual Accounts," 8.

58. Critics have argued that such advocacy of controversial pure market programs points to a lack of accountability by some international donor agencies—that is, the agencies have views that are not necessarily shared by the public that provides much of their funding. Even *Business Week,* September 8, 2003, 24, certainly not a leftist journal, voiced criticism of the shift "from traditional defined-benefit plans to defined-contribution plans such as 401(k)s, which cap the company's liability and shift the risk to workers and retirees." It expressed concern that "corporate sponsors of [defined-contribution] pension plans have been systematically looting them." For a withering critique of efforts to privatize Social Security and other pension systems, see Stiglitz, *Roaring Nineties,* 192–98.

59. EDN, September 24, 1999, and October 23, 1998; *UB Post,* November 30, 1998; *Mongol Messenger,* October 25, 2000; EIU, *Mongolia,* 4th quar. 1998, 47–48.

60. *UB Post,* October 20, 1998; EDN, February 7, 2001.

61. EDN, October 27, 2003. See also EDN, November 25 and December 19, 2003; MNA, January 8, 2004.

62. Perhaps also with the 2004 elections in mind, the government suddenly allocated funds for the repair of some children's playgrounds, which had been allowed to deteriorate for more than a decade, in Ulaanbaatar. See MNA, January 22, 2004.

63. MNA, January 26, 2004.

64. MNA, December 17, 1998; *Mongol Messenger,* October 28, 1998.

65. MNA, April 9, 1999; *UB Post,* December 6, 1997. As of 2004, Mongolia had 184 vodka, 11 wine, 29 beer, and 18 spirits factories. See *UB Post,* May 6, 2004.

66. Interview, Sosormaa, Ulaanbaatar, June 2, 1998. As of June 2004, no law on domestic abuse has been enacted. See MNA, January 9, 2004.

67. Mongolia, National Statistical Office, *Mongolian Statistical Yearbook, 2001,* 261.

68. Amnesty International, "Mongolia: Prison Inmates Starve to Death"; EIU, *Mongolia,* 2d quar. 1995, 47; EDN, July 29 and August 28, 1999; *UB Post,* August 4, 1999; interview, B. Delgermaa, Ulaanbaatar, July 10, 1998. A high percentage of inmates were diagnosed with tuberculosis. See EDN, May 4, 1998. Conditions remained deplorable as of 2003. *UB Post,* November 21, 2003.

69. As the former resident representative of the UNDP writes, "[G]rowth is essential, but public policy is needed to ensure broad-based growth that includes the poor in these benefits and to translate growth into human development." UNDP, *Human Development, 2003,* iii.

70. Griffin, "Strategy for Poverty Reduction," 2.

71. U.S. ambassador quoted from *Mongol Messenger,* July 17, 2002. A recent study of East Asia has also questioned the strategy pro-

posed by the ambassador. The authors note: "The Asian financial crisis has also shown the limitations of an approach that relies exclusively on economic growth and social austerity measures. Thus, the IMF began to acknowledge the 'human dimension' of the crisis and the need for limited, short-term social programs to assist the unemployed and others who had been affected by the events of 1997." See Tang and Wong, eds., *Poverty Monitoring*, 7. As noted, the IMF has followed the same pattern in Mongolia. It continues to emphasize private sector growth and government austerity as means to alleviate poverty. It has finally joined the Poverty Alleviation Programme but has allocated few resources for this effort.

72. Griffin, "Strategy for Poverty Reduction," 96.

73. UNDP, *Human Development Report: Mongolia, 2003*, 48.

74. Ibid., 50.

75. Griffin's and the UNDP's analyses seem to have had little impact on the international financial organizations. Preliminary plans for the World Bank's strategy on poverty for 2004 to 2007 reflect the same policies that have not succeeded in the earlier poverty programs. They include macroeconomic stabilization (which the UNDP had criticized as overly rigid—and is, one might add, ironic in view of the sizable U.S. deficits during the present Bush administration), private sector development, fostering of infrastructure for private sector growth, facilitating of foreign direct investment, and poverty alleviation projects. See MNA, February 27, 2004.

76. Rossabi, "Khubilai Khan and the Women," 153–80.

77. For a socialist view of the position of women, see Dolgormaa, *Status of Women*, 2–3; Barbara Skapa and Ann Fenger Benwell, "Women and Poverty during the Transition" in Bruun and Odgaard, *Mongolia*, 136.

78. Kojima, "Women in Development," 4.

79. Barbara Skapa, "Mongolian Women and Poverty during the Transition," in Griffin, ed., *Poverty*, 93, gives the more plausible figure of 86 percent literacy by 1989. However, the latest study, United Nations Development Fund for Women, *Women in*

Mongolia, 28, cites a figure of 95 percent literacy at the end of the communist regime.

80. Kojima, "Women in Development," 5.

81. Mongolia, National Statistical Office, *Mongolian Statistical Yearbook, 1997,* 62.

82. Kojima, "Women in Development," 6.

83. See Cariceo, "Maternal Mortality," 106–11.

84. United Nations Development Fund for Women, *Women in Mongolia,* 24. I can offer anecdotal testimony to the decline of medical facilities in the countryside. In trips to rural areas in 1997, 1998, and 2000, herders approached me seeking medicines for ailing women in the household, one with apparently serious gastrointestinal problems. They had neither the transport nor the money to reach distant clinics or hospitals. Local clinics had closed, and feldshers were unavailable. The number of feldshers declined from 4,538 in 1990 to 2,340 in 2001; Mongolia, National Statistical Office, *Mongolian Statistical Yearbook, 1997,* 65, and *2001,* 247. However, even urbanites had limited access to medicines. Fulfilling the requests of Mongolian friends, I brought children's vitamins, cough syrups, and other nonprescription drugs on trips to Mongolia from 1997 to 2002.

85. Kojima, "Women in Development," 11; United Nations Development Fund for Women, *Women in Mongolia,* 24. Philanthropic organizations such as World Vision have attempted to set up programs to assist pregnant women and their children in the countryside. See MNA, July 22, 2003.

86. Mongolia, National Statistical Office, *Mongolian Statistical Yearbook, 2001,* 253.

87. The number of crèches decreased from 441 in 1990 to 14 with 156 sections by 2001. Crèches accommodated 21,600 children in 1990 but only 1,100 by 2001. Part of this decrease may be attributed to the declining birth rate, but most of it represented a reduction in the number of physical facilities. See Mongolia, National Statistical Office, *Mongolian Statistical Yearbook, 1997,* 90–91, and *2001,* 237.

88. See, e.g., *Mongol Messenger,* February 10, 1999.

89. United Nations Development Fund for Women, *Women in Mongolia,* 23.

90. Kojima, "Women in Development," 19.

91. Cooper, "*Wealth and Poverty,* 8, 56; Mongolia, National Statistical Office, *Mongolian Statistical Yearbook, 1996,* 14; *1997,* 36; *2002,* 48–49.

92. United Nations Development Fund for Women, *Women in Mongolia,* 22; Skapa, "Mongolian Women," in Griffin, ed., *Poverty,* 94; EDN, November 22, 1996.

93. United Nations Development Fund for Women, *Women in Mongolia,* 19. In 1990, there were 1,127; by 2001, only 650. However, the number of marriages declined from 17,968 in 1990 to 12,393 in 2001. See Mongolia, National Statistical Office, *Mongolian Statistical Yearbook, 2000,* 45, and *2001,* 48.

94. Kojima, "Women in Development," 33–34.

95. Avery, *Women,* 21, 42, 18–19, 147, 162, and 151.

96. Sumati, "Politbarometer: Survey of Women's Attitudes" (1999), 2–3.

97. Kojima, "Women in Development," 16–18.

98. Liberal Women's Brain Pool, *Women's Empowerment,* 40.

99. See Women's Information and Research Centre, *Economic Status* 2, 9; Robinson and Solongo, "Gender Dimension," 240. The Women's Information and Research Centre survey of areas in five representative *aimags* found that "women have . . . been the first to be ousted from the labour market, most affected by the undermining of the universal social protection system, and found themselves disempowered under the new rubrics of a democratic political model." Focusing on private sector employment, the area touted by the international donor agencies and the Mongolian advocates of the market economy, the survey discovered that many women working in this sector were on temporary contracts and had "far fewer entitlements." The private sector employers "[o]ften remove women's rights to maternity benefit, specified leave and equitable pay and treatment in the

workplace." See *Economic Status,* 2, 12. The minimal government championed by the market economy supporters could not enforce regulations about safety, health, and equitability, leaving many women workers vulnerable to the whims of their private sector employers. Women who were "accustomed to job security and full contractual rights and obligations in the labour force" found themselves without such social welfare guarantees in the marketplace. Another survey found that women faced "widespread sexual harassment at the workplace" and that "women do not complain through fear of losing a job and later risk getting their marriage dissolved." (United Nations Development Fund for Women, *Women in Mongolia,* 21.) A weak government offered scant assistance to women confronted with such harassment. Many sources contend that wealthy or well-connected women received the bulk of the credit offered through various governmental and international donor programs. It is difficult to gauge the extent of such favoritism.

100. Robinson and Solongo, "Gender Dimension," 240–44.

101. Cooper, "Wealth and Poverty," 8, 56.

102. EDN, January 15, 1998; November 22, 1996.

103. Interview, John Beauclerk, Ulaanbaatar, August 22, 1997. Many of the prostitutes misjudged the circumstances of their profession. Corrupt police officers demanded protection or, in some cases, abused them. Similarly, pimps skimmed off part of their earnings and, on occasion, battered them. Many of their Mongolian clients refused to wear condoms. One admittedly limited study found that only 9 percent of men initiated usage of condoms. The resulting rate of sexually transmitted diseases was high. By the late 1990s, an increasing number of the prostitutes were young girls. A preliminary study of this group in Ulaanbaatar yielded evidence of the familial and social deterioration of the postcommunist era. A significant percentage had been reared in single-parent homes. Of those who had not been, a large number accused stepfathers of sexual abuse and rape. Moreover, 30 percent were illiterate, a sizable number for a country that had had an extraordinarily high rate of literacy in

the communist era. Because two-thirds did not know how to or did not use condoms, pregnancies and abortions were common. Alcohol abuse and depression afflicted many of them, and 89 percent were heavy smokers. See Women's Information and Research Centre, "STD/HIV/AIDS," 6–7; Save the Children Fund, *Girl Children as Sex Workers*, 3–16. The sale of young girls to houses of prostitution in Macao and Korea has increased in the early years of the twenty-first century. See B. Oolun, "Human Trafficking on the Rise," *Mongol Messenger*, February 18, 2004. Some Mongolian girls and women were increasingly offered as part of the sex tourist industry. See *UB Post*, April 8, 2004.

104. A Korean national was deported from Mongolia after falsely tempting 400 women with arranged marriages to Japanese men and then selling them either into erotic dancing or prostitution in Japan. See MNA, February 2, 2004.

105. Michael Dorgan, "Nation's Transition to Capitalism Swells the Ranks of Misery," *Detroit Free Press*, December 22, 2000, 12.

106. Briller, "Mongolia," 26.

107. Conor O'Clery, "Dark Side of Mongolia," *Irish Times*, November 7, 1998, www.irish-times.com8 . . . es/paper/1998/1107/fea1 .html (accessed November 7, 1998).

108. Interview, John Beauclerk, August 22, 1997; Briller, "Mongolia," 31–32; MNA, September 18, 1997; Danish Mongolian Society, *Street Children;* in 2001, the World Bank finally allocated $443,000 for agencies dealing with street children. Through the good offices of John Beauclerk, the resident representative of Save the Children–UK, I visited the summer camp, which trained the children in farming as well as other skills, and a residence in Ulaanbaatar for children whom Save the Children had placed in jobs in the cashmere industry. I also visited the residential and educational facility established by the Danish Mongolian Society (in 1998). The efforts of both organizations are laudable, but their facilities can only accommodate a fraction of the total number of street children. Humanitarian organizations do not have the resources to deal with the children. Serious

efforts require government intervention, with possible financial support from the international donor agencies. The number of street children had apparently not been reduced significantly by early 2003, according to the French newsmagazine *L'Express* ("Oulan-Bator," 58–67). On World Vision's efforts, see MNA, January 20, 2004. Paul Bacon, a Western observer, wrote in "UB Street Children: A Growing Problem," *UB Post*, March 4, 2004: "Over the past decade, the Mongolian government has been less than dynamic in tackling the burgeoning situation in the streets of the capital city."

109. Confirmation of the roles of World Vision and Save the Children is found in articles in the official government news service. See MNA, January 26, 2004.

110. EDN, May 8, 1997.

111. Quotation from *UB Post*, December 18, 1996; *UB Post*, November 3, 1997; EDN, June 27, 1997.

112. Mongolia, National Statistical Office, *Mongolian Statistical Yearbook, 1997*, 96, 104, 83, and *2001*, 83, 114, 231.

113. United Nations Development Fund for Women, *Women in Mongolia*, 30.

114. Lkhagvasüren Nomin, "Mongolia's Universities: A Woman's World," February 3, 2002, Eurasianet; www.eurasianet.org/departments/culture/articles/pp020302.shtml (accessed July 20, 2002).; Mongolia, National Statistical Office, *Mongolian Statistical Yearbook, 2001*, 232.

115. On these organizations, see Gillespie, "New Civic Society"; Women for Social Progress, *Voter Education Center;* Skapa and Benwell, "Women and Poverty," in Bruun and Odgaard, eds., *Mongolia*, 141–44, and the various publications of the Women's Information and Research Centre and the Liberal Women's Brain Pool. Also based on interviews with O. Enkhtuya, Ulaanbaatar, May 10, 1994, August, 24, 1997; R. Burmaa, Ulaanbaatar, April 3, 1998; O. Oyuntsetseg, Ulaanbaatar, May 7, 1999; L. Nomin, Ulaanbaatar, May 8, 1999.

116. Liberal Women's Brain Pool, *Women's Empowerment*, 49. Yet a joint UNDP–Japanese government study concluded that "gen-

der issues were not well considered either by donors or the government." See *Mongol Messenger*, March 24, 2004.

117. Wu, *Mongolia: Financing Education*, 2–3; Spaulding, "Education System," summarizes the main features of the educational system in the communist and immediate postcommunist eras.

118. Mongolia, National Statistical Office, *Mongolian Statistical Yearbook, 2000*, 104.

119. EDN, March 4, 2002.

120. Mongolia, National Statistical Office, *Mongolian Statistical Yearbook, 2001*, 236; MNA, November 4, 1998.

121. MNA, March 30 and May 14, 1999; EDN, November 11, 1999.

122. EDN, March 3, 1997.

123. EIU, *Mongolia*, 2d quar. 1997, 51.

124. *Mongol Messenger*, February 10, 1997. Bat-Uul, one of the leaders of the democracy movement in 1990 and a member of the Khural from 1996 to 2000, but whose credibility has been increasingly eroded, suggested the sale of statues of Choibalsan and Lenin to raise revenue.

125. EIU, *Mongolia*, 3d quar. 1995, 43; EDN, April 4 and 7, 1996; EDN, March 30, 1999.

126. *Mongol Messenger*, December 11, 2000; EDN, December 12, 2000, and December 27, 2002; *UB Post*, May 10, 2001.

127. EDN, April 11, 2001; MNA, August 26, 1998. Parents often had to pay for repairs of chairs and desks and for repainting of classrooms. See EDN, May 27, 2003. A survey in 2003 found that only 3.1 percent of children had access to the Internet. See EDN, July 16, 2003.

128. Interview, D. Badarch, Ulaanbaatar, January 6, 1997; International Labour Organization, *Macro Policies and Poverty Alleviation: Mongolia*, 25.

129. Bruun et al., *Country Analysis: Mongolia*, 29; interview, R. Baterdene, Ulaanbaatar, May 27, 1998; as of late 2003, the dropout rate for boys continued to be high. See EDN, December 9, 2003.

130. Bruun et al., *Country Analysis: Mongolia*, 29.

131. Mongolia, National Statistical Office, *Mongolian Statistical Year-*

book, *2001,* 232; Bruun et al., *Country Analysis: Mongolia,* 30. In 2004, the government founded a Center for Vocational Training, but it was unclear whether it would support private or public schools. See MNA, April 2, 2004.

132.   The survey is reported in EDN, June 9, 2000; see also *Mongolia This Week,* June 2–8, 2000; quotation from the critic is in EDN, July 15, 2003.

133.   EDN, March 3, 1999.

134.   EDN, January 25, 1997; October 26, 1999; *Mongol Messenger,* September 8 and 15, 1999. A Ministry of Education inspection found that "in 2002, more than 90 students were admitted to the Medical University by paying 'donations' of over Tg [tugrik] 110 million." *Mongol Messenger,* August 20, 2003. One of the English-language newspapers reported that "rumours of bribery and corruption are rife at this time of year as parents scramble to ensure the best education for their children." See *UB Post,* May 27, 2004.

135.   EDN, June 11, 1999.

136.   As a professor at the New School University wrote in a letter to the *New York Times* (November 24, 2001), "It would be wiser to make a call for us to get our own house in order before we exhibit the hubris of trying to spread reforms in areas where we are so clearly failures ourselves." On the other hand, the Mongolian Foundation for an Open Society (Soros Foundations) also joined with ADB in setting up a Children's Book Palace (really a library) in 2003; the Asia Foundation provided 5,000 books to the Mongolian Technical University; the Nordic Development Fund purchased laboratories for some secondary schools; and the Korean government outfitted forty-nine schools with computers—all laudable assistance. See MNA, April 30 and May 5, 2003.

137.   MNA, July 1 and 17, 2003; EDN, August 12, 2003; according to MNA, July 18, 2003, in 2003, the government allocated 50 percent less than in 2002 for school repairs.

138.   ADB, *Education Sector,* 48, 52.

139.   See Spaulding, "Education System" and "Mongolian Human

Resource," among other studies produced by the University of Pittsburgh team. Also see EDN, February 4, 1997, on the ADB's effort to reduce the teacher-student ratio from 1 to 12 to 1 to 15.

140. ADB, *Country Economic Review, Mongolia, October, 1996,* 16.

141. Interview, P. Tsagaan, Ulaanbaatar, January 7, 1997.

142. *Mongol Messenger,* December 20, 2000; *Mongolia This Week,* June 23–29, 2000.

143. *UB Post,* February 4 and March 6, 1997; EDN, July 23, 1997.

144. EDN, October 5, 2000.

145. According to preliminary statistics reported in EDN, June 5, 2003.

146. EDN, March 26, 1999; *UB Post,* June 14, 2001.

147. MNA, January 14, 15, 19, 20, and 27, March 12, and May 10, 12, and 13, 2004.

148. MNA, January 27, 2004.

149. Bawden, *Modern History,* 380. Public health advocates emphasized better sanitation and hygiene. The incidence of infectious and parasitic disease declined. The tuberculosis rate fell from 104.8 per 10,000 population in 1960 to 7.5 in 1990. Dysentery was lowered from 79.9 per 10,000 population in 1960 to 8.8 in 1990, and syphilis fell from 27.5 per 10,000 to 3.1 in the same period.

150. ADB, *Mongolia,* 234–35.

151. Ibid., 121–24.

152. Ibid., 123, 124.

153. Malhotra, "Mongolia," 17.

154. *UB Post,* October 16, 2003.

155. As a UNDP survey reports, "In 1990, 70.0 percent of health sector financing came from the State. This fell to 54.0 percent in 2002." See UNDP, *Human Development, 2003,* 10.

156. Bruun et al., *Country Analysis: Mongolia,* 30; Mongolia, National Statistical Office, *Mongolian Statistical Yearbook, 2001,* 83, 114.

157. Reuters (Mongolia), August 25, 1999; *UB Post,* November 17, 1998; EDN, October 3, 2000.

158. EIU, *Mongolia,* 2d quar. 1997, 51, 54; see also EDN, February 3, 1997, and December 15, 1999.

159. MNA, April 6, 1999; EDN, August 13, 1997; *Mongol Messenger,* October 16, 1997.

160. EDN, December 21, 1999; November 18, 1999; and August 2, 1999; MNA, May 15 and June 5, 2003; April 27 and May 10, 2004.

161. *UB Post,* October 4 and 18, 2001; December 4, 2003. See also International Labour Organization, *Macro Policies and Poverty Alleviation: Mongolia,* 48–49.

162. *Mongolia This Week,* June 2–8, 2000.

163. EDN, August 27 and September 12, 2001; December 10, 2003. Part of every negotiation with China entails agreement to provide such medical care to Mongolians who have the means to travel to Hohhot or Beijing. See also EDN, July 29, 2003. In 2004, the Speaker of the Khural sought medical treatment in Japan. See MNA, April 6, 2004, and *Mongol Messenger,* April 7, 2004.

164. Interviews, H. Hulan, Ulaanbaatar, May 28, 1998; R. Ehrich, Ulaanbaatar, August 22, 1997; Dr. M. Frank, Ulaanbaatar, May 3, 1999; and Dr. R. Jackson, Napa, Calif. (telephone), March 31, 1998; Bruun et al., *Country Analysis: Mongolia,* 30; EDN, January 2, 2002.

165. *Mongol Messenger,* January 2, 2003; EDN, June 2, 2003. See also Bruun et al., *Country Analysis: Mongolia,* 30; *Mongol Messenger,* March 19, 2003.

166. MNA, August 26, 1998.

167. EDN, February 4, 1997.

168. *Mongol Messenger,* April 28 and November 10, 1999; *UB Post,* April 22, 1997.

169. EDN, October 6, 1997, and September 8, 1998.

170. *UB Post,* September 25 and October 24, 2003; EDN, October 17, 2003.

171. Rai, "Mongolian Traditional Medicine," 3–7.

172. EDN, November 24, 1997, and February 20, 1997. The government reported that 19.6 percent of children under the age of five

were stunted and underdeveloped owing to poor nutrition. See *UB Post*, May 6, 2004. On the increased incidence of hepatitis and tuberculosis, see Mongolia, National Statistical Office, *Mongolian Statistical Yearbook, 1997*, 71, and ibid., *2001*, 250; see also EDN, October 29, 1997; MNA, August 19, 1998; *UB Post*, August 7, 1997; EDN, March 4, 1998.

173. UNDP, *Human Development Report, 2000*, 20; Gupta, "Radiological and Oncological Facilities," 3–9.

174. MNA, October 27, 1999; *UB Post*, December 25, 1996. The incidences of both syphilis and gonorrhea tripled between 1992 and 2001. See Mongolia, National Statistical Office, *Mongolian Statistical Yearbook, 2001*, 250.

175. UNDP, *Human Development Report, 2000*, 20; *UB Post*, October 22, 1997.

176. EDN, December 5, 2000; *UB Post*, April 29, 1997; and Farkas et al., "Health Status," 1641–47. The decline in medical standards may also be gauged from a 2003 study that found that 42 percent of medical workers surveyed could not diagnose SARS. See MNA, February 4, 2004.

177. EDN, July 11, 1998; *UB Post*, December 6, 1997, and July 7, 1998; *Mongol Messenger*, November 11, 1997.

178. *UB Post*, September 27, 2001.

179. For example, the press reported on several cases of parents of hemophiliacs who could not afford the user fees for treatments. See *Mongol Messenger*, June 17, 1998.

180. EIU, *Mongolia*, 2d quar. 1998, 45.

CHAPTER 7

1. UNDP, *Biological Diversity in Mongolia*, 17.

2. Batjargal, "Environmental Policy," 30.

3. "There is much talk about nature protection but fewer deeds," EDN, August 25, 2003, noted.

4. Interview, Lkhagvasüren Nomin, Manzshir, May 26, 2002.

5. Craven and Curtin, *Environmental Profile of Mongolia*.

6. Ibid., 46.

7. *UB Post,* October 24, 2002, and October 31, 2003.

8. *UB Post,* September 18, 2002.

9. MNA, December 4, 2002.

10. EDN, May 3 and September 9, 2002; MNA, October 21, 2002; *Mongol Messenger,* May 8 and November 20, 2002.

11. *Mongol Messenger,* November 13, 2002.

12. EDN, December 22, 2003. "Water levels in many rivers in the northern belt have fallen to dangerously low levels because of industrial use, and many water courses are badly polluted as a result of gold mining," the Economist Intelligence Unit noted (http://db.eiu.com/search_view.asp?doc_id+DB1331200&action = go&hits = 25&search = &dat [accessed March 1, 2004]). Another report notes that the "growing shortage of water reserves also related to the growing number of companies engaged in gold exploitation" (*Mongol Messenger,* February 18, 2004). Yet the government counts on gold production for increases in GDP. See EIU, February 19, 2004.

13. *Mongol Messenger,* October 29, 2003.

14. EDN, October 10 and December 3, 2002; *UB Post,* September 18, 2002; EDN, October 24, 2002; and MNA, January 6, 2003. In one province alone, about 10,000 herders whose animals had been lost in the *zuds* dug for gold by hand and used considerable quantities of water (MNA, June 10, 2003). For more on gold mining and its impact, see *UB Post,* April 17 and August 14, 2003. On the lack of reclamation by gold mining companies, see EDN, July 16, 2003. "A recent inspection of 68 placer mines revealed that only three companies had complied with regulations," the Economist Intelligence Unit noted (http://db .eiu.com/search_view.asp?doc_id = DB1293108&action = go& hits = 25&search = &da [accessed January 24, 2004]).

15. Craven and Curtin, *Environmental Profile of Mongolia,* 39–40.

16. EDN, January 16 and July 24, 2003; *Mongolia This Week,* May 21, 2002; *Mongol Messenger,* September 10, 2003.

17. MNA, January 27, 2004.

18.   Batjargal, "Environmental Policy," 44.

19.   *Mongol Messenger,* November 13, 2002.

20.   *Mongol Messenger,* October 25, 2000. The World Wildlife Fund issued a report warning about increasing desertification. See MNA, April 20, 2004.

21.   *UB Post,* August 11, 1998.

22.   *Mongol Messenger,* November 26, 2002. For a recent threat, see "New Bridge Will Violate Strictly Protected Area," *UB Post,* August 21, 2003. In 2000, the total government allocation for "protection of nature" amounted to about $30,000 a year. It has increased since then, but not enough for the needs of the environment. See Mongolia, National Statistical Office, *Mongolian Statistical Yearbook, 2002,* 283.

23.   *UB Post,* November 10, 1999.

24.   *UB Post,* March 6, 2003. Only about thirty Gobi bears have survived. On the fate of the wild camels, see Hare, "Searching for the Wild Bactrian." On illegal hunting by jeep, see EDN, July 21, 2003.

25.   *UB Post,* January 8, 2004; *Mongol Messenger,* December 17, 2003.

26.   EDN, July 24, 2002. On the effort to protect this lake, see Scully, "Pristine Mongol Lake," and MNA, February 16, 2004; and on the damage already done to the lake, see MNA, July 23, 2003, and EDN, August 22, 2003.

27.   Sadoway, "Emerging Tourism Frictions," 6–10; MNA, April 28, 2002.

28.   Craven and Curtin, *Environmental Profile of Mongolia,* 36.

29.   MNA, September 29, 1998; *Mongolia This Week,* April 21–28, 2000.

30.   Interview, James Wingard, Ulaanbaatar, June 24, 1998.

31.   Craven and Curtin, *Environmental Profile of Mongolia,* 28.

32.   EDN, March 4, 1999; MNA, March 4, 1999; *UB Post,* August 29, 2002, and February 7, 2003.

33.   *UB Post,* April 3, 2003; EDN, January 19 and October 24, 2002. A $15,000 grant from the Korean government for reforestation of

500 hectares of land is useful, but clearly more needs to be done; EDN, April 25, 2003.

34. EDN, June 3, 2003. Some 70 percent of an important forest in Selenge Province has been devastated by fires and illegal logging. A Korean aid agency has promised some help in replanting, but the underlying problem of continued desecration of the forest has not been resolved. Of the 32,000 hectares destroyed in the Selenge Province, only 150 hectares have been replanted. See EDN, May 16, 2003 and *UB Post,* May 23, 2003. Lacking funds for insecticides, rangers cannot prevent insect damage. The latest study reveals that 80 percent of the land is plagued by such infestations. See also MNA, July 8, 2003.

35. Interview, James Wingard, Ulaanbaatar, June 24, 1998; *UB Post,* August 22, 2001. The Japanese government recently donated seventeen firefighting vehicles and some accessories, but much more equipment is required; MNA, April 25, 2003.

36. EIU, *Mongolia,* 3d quar. 1996, 52.

37. Ministry of Nature and the Environment, *Mongolian Red Book;* UNDP, *Biological Diversity,* 100–101; *Mongol Messenger,* April 9, 1997; "Mongolian Red Book Published," *Blue Sky* 1 (November, 1997): 2.

38. EDN, May 31, 2000. Even with this project, lack of enforcement of regulations and laws has fostered problems. The media have reported illegal hunting of these wild horses. See EDN, January 3, 2003.

39. UNDP, *Mongolia's Wild,* 38–39; EDN, March 4 and April 8, 1999; MNA, March 4, 1999. Environmentalists, including an American, Kirk Olson, were concerned that the Millennium Road would impede the migration of the antelope population in eastern Mongolia and would thus facilitate the efforts of poachers. See EDN, May 21, 2003; for Olson's views, see EDN, August 18, 2003.

40. EDN, May 13, 1998; December 1, 1999. For the declines in the number of red deer and antelopes, see *UB Post,* March 31 and April 8, 2004.

41. *Mongol Messenger,* April 2, 1997. Several Italian-supported proj-

ects have attempted to assist the reindeer people, but most remain in dire circumstances and the reindeer population continues to decline. The U.S. Embassy in Mongolia offered them $4,000 in material assistance in 2004. See MNA, June 4, 2004. The *Mongol Messenger*, July 2, 2003, writes that the reindeer people were holding their own, with some state support, until the onset of the market economy.

42. *UB Post,* February 15, 2001.

43. *Mongol Messenger,* August 27, 2003.

44. Mongolia, National Statistical Office, *Mongolian Statistical Yearbook, 1998,* 85; *2001,* 132.

45. Lawless, *Wild East,* 179–89. The Ministry of Environment, in justifying its policy of selling falcons to Arab rulers, claimed that Mongolia still had 16,500 falcons. The Academy of Sciences contradicted this claim and gave the number as 6,050. See MNA, May 15, 2003.

46. Larry Johnson, "Seattle Group Trying to Save Endangered Leopard," *Seattle Post Intelligencer,* November 19, 2001, 4. For more on snow leopard conservation, see McCarthy, "Ecology and Conservation of Snow Leopards." Pastoralists kill snow leopards to protect their herds, and poachers hunt them for trophy seekers.

47. *UB Post,* March 7, 2002.

48. EDN, October 21, 2003.

49. Craven and Curtin, *Environmental Profile of Mongolia,* 22. China has also become a market for illegally exported medical herbs. See EDN, August 29, 2003.

50. In late 2003, one member of the Khural severely criticized the ministry for its "inadequate system of monitoring environmental concerns." See *UB Post,* October 16, 2003.

51. Some environmentalists are more optimistic about conservation projects supported by Western conservation groups: see EDN, June 23 and 25 and July 21, 2003. The World Wildlife Fund (WWF) has pledged to conduct research and advise on the protection of land and animals. See *Mongol Messenger,* September 3, 2003. It too has been critical, noting that none of the political parties has placed environmental protection on its platform for

the 2004 Khural elections. See *Mongol Messenger*, March 31, 2004. It also criticized the government for not undertaking an environmental assessment before building a hydroelectric power station in Khovd province. See *Mongol Messenger*, May 12, 2004.

52. See Kiselev, *Drevnemongol'skie,* for some of these excavations.

53. See, e.g., National Museum of Mongolian History, *Guide.*

54. Mongolia, National Statistical Office, *Mongolian Statistical Yearbook, 2001,* 114. This figure is for the year 2000.

55. EDN, June 2, 2003.

56. See Rossabi, "Report for Arts and Culture Program of the Mongolian Foundation for Open Society (Soros Foundations)"; interviews, D. Enkhtsetseg, S. Idshinnorov, T. Markiw, S. Watterson, and T. Ariunaa, Ulaanbaatar, January 6–10, 2002. Objects from the National Museum were borrowed for the exhibition "Modern Mongolia" organized at the University of Pennsylvania Museum of Archaeology and Anthropology, 2001. Late in 2003, Dr. Idshinnorov died while on a working trip to Japan.

57. See Berger and Bartholomew et al., *Mongolia,* for the San Francisco exhibition, and Béguin and Dashbaldan, *Trésors de Mongolie,* catalogue of an exhibition at the Musée national des Arts asiatiques–Guimet in Paris (www.museeguimet.fr [accessed May 20, 2004]).

58. EDN, February 28, 2000; see Mayhew, *Mongolia,* 140–46; Sermier, *Mongolia,* pp. 134–44, for descriptions of these museums.

59. *Mongol Messenger,* August 6, 1997, and March 26, 1999.

60. EDN, July 15, 1997.

61. EDN, January 4, 2000.

62. *Mongol Messenger,* February 7, 2002; thieves have also tried to smuggle dinosaur bones out of the country. See *Mongol Messenger,* May 21, 2003.

63. *Mongol Messenger,* November 5, 2003.

64. Interviews, Watterson, Ulaanbaatar, January 8, 2002; T. Ariunaa, Ulaanbaatar, January 10, 2002.

65. EDN, July 30, 1997.

66. *Mongol Messenger,* April 14, 1999. A museum in Taiwan has

pledged to assist Mongolian museums on specific projects, but much more is needed. See EDN, July 30, 2003.

67. *Mongol Messenger,* September 16, 1998; interviews, E. Amarsaikhan, D. Batsukh, D. Enkhtsetseg, and M. Ravjir, Ulaanbaatar, January 9–14, 2002. See *Zurag* for one exhibition of Mongolian women artists, and Uranchimeg, *Union of Mongolian Artists,* for some of the latest works of Mongolian artists.

68. With UNESCO support, the government provided a small sum (less than $100,000) for the preservation of paintings and for recording of musical works from 2001 to 2003. MNA, February 2, 2004.

69. Interview, D. Batsukh, Ulaanbaatar, January 11, 2002. A recent exhibition of modern French art, mounted by the French Embassy, has helped to expose Mongolian artists to Western art. See MNA, July 15, 2003.

70. MNA, February 10, 2004. The sculptor Denzen Barsboldt has, on occasion, raised funds for his projects, including a monument to Mongolian history at the ancient capital of Khara Khorum. See MNA, February 6, 2004, and interview, Denzen Barsboldt, New York, January 3, 2004.

71. *UB Post,* September 25, 1996; interview, B. Sergelen, Ulaanbaatar, January 12, 2002.

72. EDN, June 21, 2001.

73. EDN, November 7, 2001. The Japanese have pledged to provide $400,000 for sound and light equipment for the state Academic Drama Theater. See EDN, August 22, 2003, and *Mongol Messenger,* August 27, 2003. A German group funded a production of *La Boheme.* See *UB Post,* March 18, 2004.

74. This well-meaning Dutch businessman has established the Mongolsaikhan Foundation to support the theater and has raised about $15,000 over three years. Naturally, any contributions are valuable, but a more concerted and cohesive state effort is required for the viability of the theater. See *Mongol Messenger,* January 14, 2004.

75. *UB Post,* June 12, 2003.

76. EDN, May 19, 2003, and *UB Post,* May 22, 2003. The latest

reports indicate that the government is intent on privatizing the circus. See *Mongol Messenger,* October 15, 2003. The government provides around $700,000 for all the theaters and ensembles in the country, or less than one-half of one percent of the state budget. See MNA, June 7, 2004.

77. Woodworth, "Letter," 38.

78. EDN, February 15, 2002, and October 31, 2003.

79. Sanders, *People's Republic,* 78.

80. Quotations from MNA, January 28, 2004. The film *Story of the Weeping Camel,* which received numerous awards in international festivals, was produced by Mongolians, but the funding derived from Germany. See *UB Post,* February 5, 2004.

81. See, e.g., the documentary *Genghis Blues.*

82. Adrienne Mong, "Yo-Yo Ma's Silk Road Project," *Persimmon* 3, no. 1 (Spring 2002): 82–85.

83. Marsh, *Mongolian Pop-Rock,* 26.

84. Ibid., 32.

85. Interview, D. Tsedev, Ulaanbaatar, January 13, 2002.

86. They have thus far raised $10,000 in donations from two Mongolian banks, and they have a dedicated group of supporters of Mongolian arts in the United States. However, viability requires the tapping of native sources, particularly the state, for funds. See *Mongol Messenger,* January 14, 2004, for the bank donations. They also seek funding from foundations and private citizens in America. See Arts Council of Mongolia, *Quarterly Newsletter,* Spring 2004, 1–3.

87. For analysis of the political and economic role of Mongolian Buddhism, see Moses, *Political Role,* Rossabi, *China and Inner Asia,* and Bawden, *Modern History.*

88. Bruun and Odgaard, eds., *Mongolia in Transition,* 35; Humphrey, "Rituals of Death," 60–61.

89. Barkmann, "Revival of Lamaism," 69–79; Juergensmeyer, *New Cold War,* 119–24.

90. Interview, Lama Dambajav, Khamba Lama, Ulaanbaatar, May 14, 1994.

91. *UB Post,* November 5, 1996.

92. Bareja-Starzynska and Havnevik, "Buddhism," 5–9.

93. EDN, February 13 and June 5, 1998. On the monasteries' money-making activities, see EDN, May 21, 2003.

94. *UB Post,* October 29, 1996; *Mongol Messenger,* January 14, 1998.

95. MNA, February 2, 2004.

96. EDN, July 19, 1999; MNA, May 12, 1999. I saw his television program but could not gauge whether the audience understood much of his lecture, although most of it was translated into Mongolian. On the new Buddhist television station, see EDN, May 28, 2003. Another Buddhist from the United States founded a Center for Preserving the Mahayana. See MNA, June 20, 2003. The owner of a Canadian mining company donated $108,000 for the restoration of a monastery in the South Gobi. See EDN, September 3, 2003. A profile of one of these foreign Buddhist teachers is in Sermier, *Mongolia,* 119.

97. In addition, former prime minister Enkhbayar was an advocate of Buddhism and visited some of the holy Buddhist sites in India and other Asian countries. See MNA, January 19, 2004.

98. Interview, Nomin, New York, May 25, 1997.

99. Merli, "Shamanism," 1–4; on recent Tsam performances, see EDN, August 28, 2003.

100. Sanders, *People's Republic,* 133.

101. Mongolia, National Statistical Office, *Mongolian Statistical Yearbook, 1996,* 101.

102. Sanders, *People's Republic,* 133.

103. Lutaa, "Mongolian Media," 6–14.

104. Leah Kohlenberg and Lkhagvasüren Nomin, "Mongolian Media Struggle to Define Their Rights and Responsibilities," Eurasianet, October 13, 2000, www.eurasianet.org/departments/rights/articles/eav101300.shtml (accessed January 4, 2001).

105. Interview, G. Akim, Ulaanbaatar, June 26, 1998.

106. Press Institute of Mongolia, *Monitoring Mongolian Media, 2002,* 8–62, offers the latest survey of media outlets. See also EDN, February 19, 2003.

107. EDN, October 22, 1999.

108. Mongolia, National Statistical Office, *Mongolian Statistical Yearbook, 2001,* 189.

109. EDN, February 19, 2003.

110. Interview, T. Enkhbat, Ulaanbaatar, May 27, 1998.

111. Interview, W. Siemering, Ulaanbaatar, July 2, 1998. See also Leighton Croft, "Public Radio Veterans Support Mongolian Independent Radio," Eurasianet, October 4, 2002, www .eurasianet.org/departments/culture/articles/eav100402a.shtml (accessed October 26, 2002).

112. *UB Post,* September 15, 1998.

113. *Mongol Messenger,* November 4, 1998.

114. EDN, October 8, 2000. On some of the censorship issues and for an informed view of the press, see Kohlenberg and Nomin, "Mongolian Media Struggle to Define Their Rights and Responsibilities."

115. EDN, February 18, 2003; *Mongol Messenger,* February 12, 2003.

116. Speeches, Oyungerel and Kohlenberg, Association for Asian Studies meetings, New York, March 28, 2003.

117. However, the murder of the Minister of Infrastructure Sanjaasürengiin Zorig on October 2, 1998, and the inability of the authorities to capture the culprits trouble many human rights activists, because his killing may have been politically motivated.

118. One Khural member asserted that about 80 percent of the Kazakhs did not speak Mongolian. See MNA, April 28, 2003.

119. Interview, B. Delgermaa, Ulaanbaatar, July 10, 1998. On corrupt judges, see also *Mongol Messenger,* April 9, 2003.

120. Ginsburg and Gombosuren, "When Courts and Politics Collide," 326.

121. See Amnesty International, "Mongolia," and U.S. State Department, "Mongolia: Country Report on Human Rights Practices, 1990–2001." A nongovernmental organization sued the government on behalf of family members of an accused person who died while being detained. The initial court ruling favored the government, but the case is currently on appeal. See *UB Post,* February 7, 2003.

122. EDN, February 4, 2002.

123. EDN, February 28, 2000.

124. *UB Post,* December 12, 2002.

125. See National Human Rights Commission of Mongolia, *Human Rights.*

126. For a preliminary consideration of these issues, see Kaplonski, "Creating National Identity," and id., "Evoking the Past."

127. See Campi, "Rise of Nationalism," 46–58.

128. There have been at least two "Legacy of Chinggis [or Genghis] Khan" exhibitions in the United States in the past decade, one at the Asian Art Museum in San Francisco and another at the Metropolitan Museum of Art in New York. In addition, two groups, one Japanese and one American, have attempted to find his tomb. See Becker, "Hunting for Genghis." One recent American museum exhibition depicted Chinggis as an apostle of democracy (one of the chapters in Sabloff, ed., *Modern Mongolia,* the catalogue for the exhibition, is entitled "Genghis Khan, Father of Mongolian Democracy"), a view criticized by several historians of traditional Mongolia; for another assessment, see Aubin, "La Mongolie," 305–26.

129. For the original euphoria, see Grivelet, "Reintroducing the Uighur-Mongolian Script," 49–60.

130. See Peck, "Chagi's Charge," 28–37.

CHAPTER 8

1. Enkhbayar was a member of the MPRP, but he pursued a pure market policy after 2000. He actively cultivated controversial entrepreneurs such as Bazarsadyn Jargalsaikhan of Buyan Cashmere and did not cement relations with democratic reformers, labor union leaders, or human rights activists. See MNA, July 23, 2003.

2. EDN, October 8, 1997. For a useful survey, see Tsedendambyn Batbayar, "Mongolian-Russian Relations in the Past Decade."

3. *Mongol Messenger,* July 24, 1998.

4. Sanders, "Foreign Relations," in Bruun and Odgaard, eds., *Mon-*

golia, 240; Mongolia, National Statistical Office, *Mongolian Statistical Yearbook, 2001,* 83.

5. EIU, *Mongolia,* 1st quar. 1997, 50.

6. MNA, February 3, 1999; *Mongol Messenger,* November 15, 2000; EDN, April 1, 2002.

7. *Mongol Messenger,* July 9, 2003; on the final settlement of the debt, see *Mongol Messenger,* January 7, 2004; MNA, January 9, 2004; and Itar-Tass, January 12, 2004, http://eurasianet.org/departments/qanda/articles/eavo11204.shtml (accessed January 13, 2004).

8. *Mongol Messenger,* January 21, 2004.

9. See www.ivanhoe-mines.com/s/TurquoiseHill.asp (accessed May 10, 2004), and Reuters, Vancouver, December 31, 2003, www.reuters.com/newsArticle.jhtml?type = topNews7storyID = 4061 (accessed January 4, 2004).; See also "Opposition Questions Hoopla around Forgiveness of Soviet-era Debt," *UB Post,* January 8, 2004.

10. Mongolia, National Statistical Office, *Mongolian Statistical Yearbook, 1998,* 139; *2002,* 204.

11. EIU, *Mongolia,* 4th quar. 1995, 41; EDN, March 3, 1998; December 3, 1998: February 24, 1999; January 20, 2000; July 23, 1997; and December 3, 1998; *UB Post,* November 17, 1999; MNA, March 15, 2000.

12. Itar-Tass, May 22, 1999; *Mongol Messenger,* March 3, 2000; EDN, April 18, 2001; *UB Post,* June 13, 2000.

13. EDN, September 18, 1998; *UB Post,* March 23, 1999, and August 4, 1999; MNA, September 27, 1999; *Mongol Messenger,* March 1, 2000.

14. The Russians have offered the construction of nuclear power stations as a third alternative for Mongolia's energy needs. Mongolian critics of this proposal have pointed both to the Chernobyl disaster as evidence of Russian carelessness and to Mongolia's vulnerability to earthquakes as reasons to reject this proffered technology. On the hydroelectric stations, see Reuters (Mongolia), November 4, 1997; *UB Post,* May 4, 2000; and *Mongol Mes-*

senger, May 10, 2000. On the nuclear power issue, see EDN, February 10 and 25, 2000, and *Mongolia This Week,* March 24–30, 2000.

15. Itar-Tass, February 23, 1999; MNA, July 19, 1999; *UB Post,* July 21, 1999; EIU, *Mongolia,* 3d quar. 1998, 42; 4th quar. 1998, 48; 1st quar. 2000, 55; EDN, November 24, 1998, and April 23, 2003. According to MNA, May 26, 2003, more meetings will be required to discuss the joint management of the Erdenet copper enterprises.

16. EDN, November 11, 1999; March 22, 1999; January 3, 2001; November 13, 2001; October 12, 2001; March 25, 2002; October 17, 2002; and November 8, 2002; *UB Post,* March 2, 1999, and June 23, 1998. Enkhbayar's visit in 2003 resulted in a Russian pledge to buy additional meat from Mongolia. See *UB Post,* July 3, 2003, and EDN, July 16, 2003. The Russians have also pledged to train Mongolian veterinarians. See *UB Post,* July 3, 2003. In addition, they were "willing to cut tariffs on [their] traditional imports of animal origin . . . though the cuts are unlikely to be as drastic as Mongolia would wish"; EIU, November 1, 2003, http://db.eiu.com/search_view.asp?doc_id = DB1293113&action = go&topicid = MN7pubcod (accessed January 24, 2004).

17. EDN, July 16, 2003; the Russians have also expressed interest in the Asgat silver mines. See *Mongol Messenger,* November 19, 2003. There is some concern about the supply of petroleum because Yukos, a Russian company whose executives are on bad terms with the Russian government (its former director is in prison), provides nearly all of Mongolia's needs. Will the current Russian government's disenchantment with Yukos pose problems for Mongolia? See EDN, October 3, 2003.

18. *Mongol Messenger,* October 2003.

19. Staisch and Prohl, *Dschingis,* 98; EDN, January 20, 1998; MNA, July 2, 2003; *UB Post,* July 3, 2003.

20. *Mongol Messenger,* November 15, 2000; EDN, November 23, 2000.

21. The poll was conducted by the Sant Maral Foundation. Also see EDN, January 8, 1999; EIU, *Mongolia,* 3d quar. 1994, 42.

22. EDN, November 19, 1997, and March 30, 2000; *Mongol Messenger,* May 5, 1999.

23. EDN, November 11, 2003.

24. EDN, April 6, 2001, and December 22, 2003; September 2, 2002; September 5, 2002; and April 23, 2003; *Mongol Messenger,* March 22, 2000, and November 19, 2003.

25. EDN, March 28, 2001; April 4, 2001; and May 14, 2001; *Mongol Messenger,* May 21, 2001. The two countries have also cooperated in plans for tourism around Lakes Baikal and Khövsgöl. See *Mongol Messenger,* August 27, 2003.

26. Korsun, "Inside Ownership," 42.

27. Oyun Sanjaasürengiin, "From the Year," 1.

28. Interview, Boris Shlomm, New York, April 9, 1998.

29. Ibid.; EIU, *Mongolia,* 2d quar. 1994, 44; *Mongolia This Week,* April 28–May 4, 2000.

30. The latest statistics confirm that most of the raw cashmere is exported: "only about 20% of the raw product finds its way into the domestic processing industry. Foreign direct investment in the sector is mainly in primary processing" ("Cashmere Production Is Growing," EIU, August 1, 2003, http://db.eiu.com/ search_view.asp?doc_id = DB1248296&action = go&hits = 25 &search = &da [accessed January 24, 2004]).

31. Oyun Sanjaasürengiin, "From the Year," 3.

32. It appears that China will also be investing in the Oyu Tolgoi mines. See EDN, July 30, 2003.

33. Mongolian National Chamber of Commerce and Industry, *White Paper,* 42.

34. *Mongol Messenger,* February 23, 2000; Ministry of External Relations, *Foreign Policy,* 76; *UB Post,* May 13 and August 7, 1997; EIU, *Mongolia,* 3d quar. 1997, 50; ADB, *Country Review: Mongolia,* 11; EDN, September 13, 1997, and April 11, 2002.

35. Telephone interview, Chase Untermeyer, February 17, 1998; Reuters (Mongolia), May 2, 1998; EIU, *Mongolia,* 2d quar. 1998, 48. On another rapid visit, U.S. Deputy Secretary of State Richard Armitage praised Mongolia for its "commitment to

democracy and a free market economy" (*Mongol Messenger,* February 11, 2004). Success in this respect was attributed in part to the commitment of both the reformers and moderates in the government to nonviolence during the 1989–90 protests against the one-party system, and to Mongolia's combined parliamentary-presidential system under the 1992 Constitution, which divided power between the president and the Khural, thus limiting the possibility of executive absolutism. The swift pace of privatization and so-called economic reforms in the period from 1990 to 1992 were held to have set Mongolia on an irreversible course toward a market economy, while rapid development of inclusive yet clearly distinctive political parties and of NGOs fostered representative institutions. The holders of such views cited the high rate of literacy—actually a product of the communist era—and reputed homogeneity of Mongolians as favorable portents for democracy. Mongolians supposedly also resisted authoritarianism and were receptive to democratic institutions because of their historical individualism as pastoral nomads. It was not noted that control by authoritarian princes and khans had been the general rule from the thirteenth century on. See Fish, "Mongolia," 138–40, for the views of one Western Sovietologist.

36. *Mongol Messenger,* July 24, 1998; MNA, August 18, 1998; EDN, March 3, 2000, and May 21, 2003; December 27, 1999, and September 21, 1999.

37. See Novacek, *Dinosaurs;* Olsen et al., "Paleolithic Field Investigations"; Devevianko and Olsen, *Archaeological Studies;* Jacobson and Meacham, "When Stones Speak"; Francis Allard, "Sacred Bones, Fields of Stone," *Earthwatch Journal,* October 2002, 12–15; EDN, January 14, 1997; on French excavations, see EDN, June 17, 2003. The Smithsonian's National Museum of Natural History has also collaborated with Mongolian researchers on a number of projects in archeology, ethnogeography, botany, and paleoecology. See Fitzhugh, "Smithsonian Researchers." The benefits also include tangible economic assistance from the United States. See MNA, May 7 and June 14, 2004.

38. One by-product of this training is Jargalsaikhan Mendee's M.A. thesis, "Democratic Civilian," which suggests Mongolian adoption of the U.S. model of civilian control of the military. See also MNA, May 31, 2004.

39. MNA, September 17, 1998; *Mongol Messenger,* August 28, 1997; October 6, 1999; and August 16, 2000; EDN, September 21, 1999; August 11, 2000; September 20, 2000; April 1, 2002; October 3, 2002; and April 23, 2003. By 2000, the United States was providing military assistance valued at $2.5 million a year. See Tsedendambyn Batbayar, "Mongolian-Russian Relations in the Past Decade," 964.

40. Quote from James Brooke, "Mongolians Return to Baghdad, This Time as Peacekeepers," *New York Times,* September 25, 2003, A10.

41. "The CW-RP Condemns Mongolia's Stance on Iraq," EIU, May 1, 2003, http://db.eiu.com/search_view.asp?doc_id = DB1209621 &action = go&hits = 25&search = &da (accessed January 24, 2004); *Mongol Messenger,* November 12, 2003.

42. MNA, January 12, 13, and 16, 2004; *UB Post,* October 31, 2003; January 15 and 21, 2004. President George W. Bush sent the Mongolian government a letter of gratitude for the dispatch of troops to Iraq. MNA, February 3, 2004.

43. *Mongol Messenger,* April 21, 1997; May 30, 1998; September 16, 1998; May 17, 2000; and March 27, 2002, and March 17, 2004; EIU, *Mongolia,* 4th quar. 1996, 48; (1997:2): 52; MNA, April 29, 2003; *UB Post,* November 15, 2001; October 24, 2003; and December 12, 2003; EDN, July 19, 2001; October 12, 2001; November 19, 2001; and April 16, 2003. Mongolia was covered by the TACIS programme from 1991 to 2003, but thereafter transferred to ALA, the European aid and development organization that focuses on Asia and Latin America, whereas TACIS focuses on the countries of the former USSR and Central Asia.

44. EIU, *Mongolia,* 1st quar. 1997, 60; *Mongol Messenger,* February 10, 1999, and October 15, 2004; *UB Post,* December 21, 2000; EDN, April 19, 2000; February 18, 2002.

45. *Mongol Messenger,* October 20, 1999, and October 15, 2003; *UB*

Post, October 11, 2001; MNA, October 21, 2002, and May 22, 2003; EDN, January 30, 1997, June 22, 1998; February 17, 1999; September 28, 1999; December 8, 1999; June 16, 2000; July 3, 2001; and October 23, 2002.

46. Quotation from EDN, June 8, 1999; January 30, 1997; and September 1, 2000; DANIDA, "Teachers"; id., "School Drop-out." See also MNA, June 18, 2003, on Norwegian aid with publishing and with textbooks.

47. See *Mongol Messenger,* February 4, 2004, for more on Mongolian students in Germany.

48. *UB Post,* May 19, 1998, and September 12, 1997; EDN, March 18, 1997, and October 12, 2000. See *Mongol Messenger,* May 28, 2003, on Polish scholarships for Mongolian university students.

49. Ministry of External Relations, *Foreign Policy,* 84–87; *Mongol Messenger,* May 16, 2001, reports that Poland reopened its embassy in Ulaanbaatar; *Mongol Messenger,* March 26, 2003; EDN, August 2, 2000, and April 3, 2003; Mongolia, National Statistical Office, *Mongolian Statistical Yearbook, 2001,* 196.

50. EIU, *Mongolia,* 4th quar. 1997, 44; *UB Post,* June 23, 1998, and May 26, 1998; EDN, January 8, 1998.

51. MNA, January 27, 2004; Mongolian National Chamber of Commerce and Industry, *White Paper,* 42–45. Germany has ten companies based in Mongolia; 1,200 Mongolians study in German universities, partly for the excellent training but also partly to the lack of tuition. Thirty thousand Mongolians are reputed to be fluent in German.

52. Tsedendambyn Batbayar, "Mongolia and Japan in 1945–1995," 176–78; Barkmann, "Mongolisch-japanische Beziehungen," 141–44; *UB Post,* August 7, 1997; EDN, July 8, 2003, and October 29, 2003.

53. Barkmann, "Mongolisch-japanische Beziehungen," 158; *UB Post,* February 28, 2002; November 14, 2002; December 11, 1996; November 22, 1996; and November 17, 1999; EDN, November 10, 1999; March 12, 2001; November 10, 2000; August 20, 2001; March 17, 2000, December 1, 2000; September 20, 1999; *Mongol Messenger,* December 15, 1999; December 20, 2002; EIU,

Mongolia, 4th quar. 1997, 46; 3d quar. 1996, 50, 55: MNA, February 11, 2004.

54.   Interview, K. Matsumoto, Ulaanbaatar, May 27, 2002; EDN, June 26, 2001; August 22, 2001; September 3, 2001; September 28, 2001; January 16, 2002; and November 15, 2001; *Mongol Messenger,* January 3, 2003, and May 4, 2004; November 7, 2001; and October 4, 2000; MNA, June 12 and June 20, 2003, and May 24, 2004.

55.   *UB Post,* May 18, 1999; *Mongol Messenger,* July 14, 1999, and December 17, 2003; MNA, May 21, 2003; EDN, July 29, 1999; April 3, 2000; and August 19, 1998. This reburial of Japanese soldiers brings to mind Michio Takeyama's novel *Harp of Burma,* trans. Howard Hibbett (Rutland, Vt.: Charles Tuttle, 1966).

56.   Mongolian National Chamber of Commerce and Industry, *White Paper,* 43–45.

57.   "The use of external aid by Mongolia has been criticized by Japan in particular. The symposium gave particular attention to use of foreign consultants, the cost of which was criticized" (EIU, *Mongolia,* 4th quar. 1997, 48). *Mongol Messenger,* October 25, 2000; Barkmann, "Mongolisch-japanische Beziehungen," 158; Mongolia, National Statistical Office, *Mongolian Statistical Yearbook, 2002,* 202; EDN, April 27, 2000, and May 12, 1997; MNA, January 4, 1999; EIU, *Mongolia,* 3d quar. 1998, 43.

58.   Ministry of External Relations, *Foreign Policy,* 88.

59.   *Mongol Messenger,* August 13, 2003.

60.   See "Relations with North Korea," EIU, November 1, 2003, http://db.eiu.com/search_view.asp?doc_id = DB1293086&action = go&topicid = MN&pubcod (accessed January 24, 2004).

61.   Ministry of External Relations, *Foreign Policy,* 88; EDN, June 19, 2002, and July 25, 2003. In 2003, partly as a result of the visit of the Mongolian prime minister, South Korea pledged to provide more assistance—helping, for example, with medical treatment and renovation of Ulaanbaatar's water supply and sewage system. See *Mongol Messenger,* December 3, 2003; EDN, December 17, 2003, and *UB Post,* December 12, 2003; November 11, 1999; October 19, 2000; May 7, 1997; and January 11–12, 2001; March

20, 2000; EIU, *Mongolia,* 4th quar. 1995, 51; *Mongolia This Week,* June 9–15, 2000; Mongolia, National Statistical Office, *Mongolian Statistical Yearbook, 2002,* 202.

62. *Mongol Messenger,* September 3, 2003.

63. *UB Post,* February 17, 1997, and December 12, 2002; MNA, April 15, 1998, and July 18, 2003; EDN, September 8, 1998, January 20, 1998, and July 18, 2003. For the latest on Mongolian workers in Korea, see Lkhagvasüren Nomin, "Mongolian Workers under New Management in Korea," Eurasianet, January 20, 2003; www.eurasianet.org/departments/business/articles/pp012003.shgtml (accessed March 16, 2003); and for an official report about the poor conditions for these workers in Korea, see National Human Rights Commission of Mongolia, *Human Rights,* 82–91. Kim Wang-Bae, "Migration of Foreign Workers into South Korea," 326, writes that such illegal workers in South Korea "suffer not only from delayed wage payments but also from extremely long hours." The number of Mongolian illegal workers has increased dramatically, even in the United States, and their contributions to the Mongolian economy have similarly increased. See *Mongol Messenger,* November 5, 2003, and EDN, November 20, 2003. Numerous abuses have been recorded. For example, a con man received $3,500 each from 124 people to find them employment in Japan and then simply disappeared. See MNA, February 12, 2004.

64. Mongolian National Chamber of Commerce and Industry, *White Paper,* 43–45.

65. Ministry of External Relations, *Foreign Policy,* 108; EDN, July 28, 2000; July 7, 2001; November 12, 1999; and February 20, 1997; EIU, *Mongolia,* 4th quar. 1997, 40; 1st quar 1995, 40; *UB Post,* August 21, 1996; see also Eitzen, "Kazakhstan," 1–9. For more on the Kazakhs, see Waugh's recent popular book *Hearing Birds Fly.*

66. Mongolian National Chamber of Commerce and Industry, *White Paper,* 43–45.

67. Ministry of External Relations, *Foreign Policy,* 86, 88; EIU, *Mongolia,* 1st quar. 1993, 33; EDN, May 30, 1997; March 6, 1998; and December 30, 2003; and November 23, 1999.

68. EIU, *Mongolia,* 4th quar. 1995, 43; EDN, May 7, 1997; March 6, 1998; and November 3, 1999; MNA, August 8, 2001.

69. *UB Post,* August 4, 1999; June 23, 2001; and November 24, 1998; MNA, October 27, 1999; *Mongol Messenger,* August 25, 1999; September 15, 1999; August 8, 2001; November 11, 1997; September 15, 1999; and December 8, 1999; EDN, October 9, 1997, and November 13, 1998; Lawless, *Wild East,* 179–89; Ministry of External Relations, *Foreign Policy,* 86; EIU, *Mongolia,* 1st quar. 1995, 47. In 2004, an Islamic Cultural Center was established in Ulaanbaatar. See MNA, April 5, 2004.

70. MNA, July 23, 1998; *Mongol Messenger,* December 3, 2003; *Jerusalem Post,* February 17, 2000.

71. By late 2003, Vietnam and Mongolia had only a $1.5 million trade turnover. See MNA, January 8, 2004. A 2004 visit by the Vietnamese president led to predictions of a trade turnover of $10 million by 2010 and to pledges of cooperation in science and education, among other fields. See MNA, May 25 and 27, 2004.

72. MNA, July 29, 1998; *Mongol Messenger,* June 3, 1998, and September 17, 1997; EDN, April 17, 2000, and September 9, 1997; *UB Post,* October 10, 2002; Ministry of External Relations, *Foreign Policy,* 86; EIU, *Mongolia,* 2d quar. 1997, 52.

73. EDN, May 30, 2003. Australia, which has been granted mining interests, has also provided assistance in human rights education, scholarships for attendance at Australian universities, capacity building for a market economy, better services for *ger* dwellers in Ulaanbaatar, and protection and preservation of wild horses. La Trobe University will also train Mongolian economists. See *Mongol Messenger,* June 11, 2003, and EDN, September 19 and December 16, 2003. During the Indonesian president's visit to Mongolia in 2003, the two sides agreed to an increase in trade and in cooperation in agriculture and veterinary medicine. MNA, June 11 and 20, 2003.

74. See Barkmann, "Revival of Lamaism," 69–79, and Lawless, *Wild East,* 196–97, for quotation; EDN, July 19, 1999, and April 13, 2001; *UB Post,* January 5, 2001; and Ministry of External Relations, *Foreign Policy,* 86, 88; Mongolia, National Statistical

Office, *Mongolian Statistical Yearbook, 2002,* 202. In 2003, India supplied aid in the form of medicines. See *Mongol Messenger,* October 15, 2003, and EDN, November 6, 2003.

75. MNA, January 14 and 16, 2004. The Indian ambassador to Mongolia noted that "trade and economic relations between our two countries are fairly weak." See *Mongol Messenger,* March 17, 2004.

CHAPTER 9

1. See Rupen, *Mongolian People's Republic,* 19; Doebler, "Cities, Population Redistribution, and Urbanization," 40–44, 63; Black, *Modernization,* 106; and Ma, *Chinese Agent,* 71. For more on early Sino-Mongolian relations (through the 1980s), see Rossabi, "New Mongolia," 64–67, and id., "Sino-Mongol Relations."

2. Snow, *Red Star over China,* 88–89, f. 1; Stein, *Challenge of Red China,* 442–43.

3. Green, "China and Mongolia," 1351; Kim Sun-ho, *Entwicklung,* 51.

4. FBIS, *China,* October 23, 1986, D2; December 11, 1986, D1; July 20, 1987, D1; October 113, 1989, 10; July 8, 1987, D12; March 21, 1989, 6; July 11, 1989, 11.

5. FBIS, *China,* March 16, 1987, D2; November 1, 1989, 9–11; Kenneth Jarrett, "Mongolia in 1987: Out from the Cold?" *Asian Survey* 28, no. 1 (January 1988): 80.

6. See FBIS, *China,* March 31, 1989, 2–3; March 13, 1987, D1; June 8, 1987, D5; November 29, 1988, 14–15; June 19, 1987, D1; June 22, 1987, D1; June 25, 1987, D2; September 13, 1988, 13; March 24, 1989, 4; March 30, 1989, 4–7; August 31, 1989, 6.

7. FBIS, *China,* July 27, 1989, 6; Alan Sanders, "Mongolia in 1989: Year of Adjustment," *Asian Survey* 30, no. 1 (January 1990): 63.

8. On the problems in Tibet and Xinjiang, see essays by Rossabi, Goldstein, Kapstein, Bovingdon, and Bachman in Rossabi, ed., *Governing China's Multiethnic Frontiers.*

9. Interviews, R. Amarjargal, Ulaanbaatar, June 30, 1998; J. Od, Ulaanbaatar, June 23, 1998; T. Ragchaa, Ulaanbaatar, June 18, 1998.

In a lecture sponsored by the Asia Society in New York City on April 19, 2000, the minister of external relations, N. Tuya, added that Chinese investment would facilitate the introduction of new technology into Mongolia. It remains to be seen whether Chinese and other foreign investment will be as beneficial as Mongolian leaders hope. Schwarz, "Security of Mongolia," 87; Bold, "Changing International Order and Mongolia's Security," 11–12.

10. EIU, *Mongolia,* 3d quar. 1993, 38; 4th quar. 1997, 41.

11. FBIS, *China,* April 23, 1990, 20; November 15, 1990, 17; April 1, 1991, 11; August 26, 1991, 13.

12. FBIS, *China,* February 4, 1991, 14–15; February 5, 1991, 12–13; April 16, 1991, 15; June 15, 1992, 15; March 18, 1996, 14–15; EDN, January 18, 2002, and November 30, 2001.

13. FBIS, *China,* May 2, 1994, 15; EIU, *Mongolia,* 3d quar. 1994, 41; Ministry of Defense, *Mongolian Defense White Paper,* 93, 95.

14. *UB Post,* December 15, 1998; *Mongol Messenger,* December 16, 1998; EDN, December 15, 1998; EIU, *Mongolia,* 1st quar. 1999, 47. As of 2003, the route of the natural gas pipeline will skirt around Mongolia, and the Tumen River project is still in abeyance. The Chinese foreign minister visited Mongolia in 2001 and promised assistance in finances and in time of natural disasters. See *UB Post,* July 5, 2001.

15. FBIS, *China,* February 9, 1990, 4; October 26, 1990, 22; November 16, 1990, 10; March 15, 1991, 13; March 8, 1993, 8; April 2, 1993, 4; January 26, 1993, 10.

16. Bold, "Changing International Order and Mongolia's Security," 12; Ministry of Defense, *Mongolian Defense White Paper,* 52; EIU, *Mongolia,* 1st quar. 1997, 51; 1st quar. 1998, 42. Ravdan Bold later became Mongolia's ambassador to the United States.

17. FBIS, *China,* July 11, 1990, 5–6; August 7, 1990, 5; March 30, 1992, 5; June 17, 1992, 14–15; June 21, 1994, 6; December 4, 1990, 14; July 8, 1991, 6–7; September 15, 1992, 12–13; January 11, 1991, 11; September 8, 1993, 15; EIU, *Mongolia,* 2d quar. 1997, 58, and Wang, *Chiu-shih,* 56–58.

18. EDN, September 29, 1997, and September 5, 1997; *Mongol Mes-*

senger, September 16, 1998; EIU, *Mongolia,* 3d quar. 1993, 47; Mongolia, National Statistical Office, *Mongolian Statistical Yearbook, 2001,* 202, 174. By 2003, trade had increased so dramatically that additional train service was required. See EDN, June 16, 2003.

19. Mongolia, National Statistical Office, *Mongolian Statistical Yearbook, 2002,* 202–5; EDN, February 24, 2003. Preliminary figures for 2003 indicate additional increases, with 46 percent of Mongolian exports going to China and 26.8 percent of imports derived from China; MNA, January 23, 2004. Chinese currency is increasingly being used in Mongolian towns along the Sino-Mongolian frontiers. See *UB Post,* February 26, 2004.

20. EDN, August 6, 1999; August 27, 1997; April 15, 1997; May 9, 2002; September 19, 2000; December 3, 2002; and June 26, 2002; EIU, *Mongolia,* 3d quar. 1996, 55; 2d quar. 1997, 59; FBIS, *China,* March 9, 1995, 8; MNA, January 20, 2004; *Mongol Messenger,* January 7, 2004. The Chinese even provided some tractors to the Mongolians. See *UB Post,* May 22, 2003. It is also reported that at least 1,200 Chinese laborers will work on the construction of the Millennium Road and that an unspecified number will assist in the renovation of Sükhbaatar Square. See EDN, May 29, 2003, and MNA, June 6, 2003. Helping to promote better relations, the Chinese also agreed at the Sino-Mongolian Economic, Trade, Scientific, and Technical Meeting of April 1997 and then at later meetings to postpone and reschedule the repayment of loans granted both in the 1950s and in the early 1990s.

21. FBIS, *China,* November 14, 1991, 16; February 18, 1992, 12; MNA, August 31, 1999; EIU, *Mongolia,* 2d quar. 1997, 59–60; EDN, May 29, 2000; May 3, 2001; and September 3, 2002.

22. FBIS, *China,* January 28, 1992, 12; EIU, *Mongolia,* 3d quar. 1999, 50; *Mongolia This Week,* June 9–15, 2000; *UB Post,* January 13, 2000; *Mongol Messenger,* January 19, 2000; EDN, February 11, 1998; June 12, 2000; February 25, 1999; November 9, 2001; April 12, 2000; and September 18, 2002.

23. EDN, June 3 and December 11, 2003; MNA, June 5, 2003, and June 14, 2004. China has also indicated that it will increase

the number of its banks in Mongolia. See MNA, February 26, 2003.

24. EDN, December 15, 2003; another important Chinese investment is in a liquefied combustible gas plant; MNA, February 4, 2004.

25. EDN, July 16, 1999; *UB Post,* January 19, 2002; *Mongol Messenger,* January 19, 2000.

26. For this view, see Admidin and Devaeva, "Economic Cooperation," 29–38.

27. Schran and Yu, *Mongolia,* 34–35; D. Narantuya, "Is the Pipeline a Dream?" *Mongolia This Week,* April 7–13, 2000. In an interview on June 30, 1998, in Ulaanbaatar, Finance Minister Bat-Erdeniin Batbayar (Baabar) referred to the pipeline as one of the most important solutions to Mongolia's financial problems. He omitted mention of the revival of national industries or any other policy over which the Mongolian government has greater control than the route of the pipeline. Sabine Tavernise, "Russia to Build Pipelines in the East," *New York Times,* February 11, 2003, W1, W7, reports that the pipeline will definitely avoid Mongolia. An even more elaborate plan entails the development of the Tumen River zone, which the UNDP has promoted. This grandiose project involves North Korea, Siberia, the Russian Far East, China, Japan, and Mongolia and is designed to tap the region's abundant mineral and natural resources, to develop light industry (hides, leather, meat, and fish processing), shipbuilding, petroleum, and tourism, to construct roads linking the interior with ports to the east, and to promote commerce among the participating countries. Tariffs would be removed or at least reduced, and a special economic zone would be created. Mongolia would benefit because of direct access to the sea, more sustained development of the natural resources in its northeast, and a larger market for its products (about 350 million people live in the Koreas, Inner Mongolia, Northeast China, the Russian Far East, and Japan). Cooperation among the six countries has so far proved elusive, because each, focusing on its own needs and interests, supports different versions of the project. Again, China

is central to this project, as the city of Tumen lies within the autonomous region of the province of Jilin. As late as July 1999, the Chinese leader Jiang Zemin pledged to include Mongolia in any Tumen river project. However, little has happened over the past five years. See Marton et al., "Northeast Asia," 8–33; Olsen, "Tumen Project," 53–73; Kolpakova, "Political Implications," and *UB Post,* July 26, 1999. Still another (possibly utopian?) project is a railroad that would link the Chinese port of Tianjin, Ulaanbaatar, Russia, and Finland. The planners project a time of ten days from Tianjin to Finland. See Dominic Whiting, "Asia-Europe Railway," Reuters, Bangkok, January 21, 2004, www.reuters.com/newsArticle.jhtml?type = topNews&storyID =4173458 (accessed January 21, 2004).

28. MNA, September 30, 2002, and October 3, 2002; *Mongol Messenger,* May 31, 2000; and *UB Post,* February 28, 2002; EDN, June 10, 2003.

29. EIU, *Mongolia,* 3d quar. 1993, 40. In 1993, a 1946 map showing Mongolia as part of China was printed in a book entitled *Wai Menggu duli neimu* (The secret story of Outer Mongolian independence), published in Beijing. China's Foreign Ministry responded to protests "with a statement reaffirming the official position that China has always respected Mongolian independence, and the publisher's license was revoked" (Tom Ginsburg, "Nationalism, Elites, and Mongolia's Rapid Transformation," in Kotkin and Elleman, eds., *Mongolia,* 252).

30. Quotation from EDN, June 9, 1999; see also EDN, June 12, 2000, and *Mongol Messenger,* March 22, 2000. Interview, Boris Shlomm, New York, April 9, 1998.

31. Sanjaasürengiin Oyun, "From the Year," 3.

32. *UB Post,* August 14, 2003.

33. EDN, September 19, 2003.

34. See Rossabi, "Ming China and Inner Asia," in Mote and Twitchett, eds., *Cambridge History of China,* 239–40; Serruys, *Sino-Mongolian Relations during the Ming;* FBIS, *China,* August 22, 1994, 8; on Mongolian attitudes to Chinese foods, see Bulag,

Nationalism, 200–211; EDN, December 25 and May 15, 1997; MNA, March 3, 1999; March 15, 1999; June 15, 1999; *UB Post,* November 26, 1996; EIU, *Mongolia,* 4th quar. 1996, 48.

35. Quotation from Man, *Gobi,* 16; MNA, August 3, 1998; *Mongol Messenger,* June 3 and 24, 1998; *UB Post,* July 21, 1998.

36. *Mongol Messenger,* May 10, 1997, and October 15, 2003; March 28, 1997; and November 26, 1997; *UB Post,* March 7, 2002; EDN, January 30, 1998; April 5, 1999; and August 14, 2000; MNA, November 30, 1998; EIU, *Mongolia,* 1st quar. 1994, 39. Chinese nationals were involved in the largest number of crimes (including smuggling, narcotics, prostitution, and predatory moneylending) committed by foreigners. See *UB Post,* February 12, 2004.

37. *Mongol Messenger,* August 27, 2003.

38. EIU, *Mongolia,* 2d quar. 1995, 56; 3d quar. 1997, 50; 4th quar. 1998, 55–56; EDN, November 23, 1999; July 29, 1997; April 23, 2002, and October 14, 2002; *Mongol Messenger,* February 2, 2000; April 14, 2002; and July 31, 2002; *UB Post,* February 16, 2000, and November 22, 2001.

39. EDN, September 24, 2003.

40. Sheldon Severinghaus, "Mongolia in 1995: Gearing Up For the 1996 Election," *Asian Survey* 36 (January 1996): 99; EIU, *Mongolia,* 3d quar. 1995, 47; J. Enkhsaikhan, "Statement to the United Nations," and id., "Mongolia's Nuclear-Weapon Free Status," 342–59.

41. FBIS, *China,* June 26, 1992, 5; EIU, *Mongolia,* 2d quar. 1998, 48; 4th quar. 1998, 48; *UB Post,* February 17, 1999; interview, L. Sumati, Ulaanbaatar, April 28, 1999.

42. Shapiro, "Reporter," 46; FBIS, *China,* August 26, 1991, 13; EIU, *Mongolia,* 3d quar. 1995, 46; EIU, *Mongolia,* 4th quar. 1993, 33; MNA, October 29, 2002; Barkmann, "Revival," 69–79; EDN, May 7, 1999; interview, Ch. Ganbold, Ulaanbaatar, April 29, 1999. In an interview on May 14, 1994, the Lama Dambajav, one of the leading figures in Mongolian Buddhism, emphasized that the Buddhists wished to steer clear of politics and that the Dalai

Lama's visits were of purely religious intent. The latest account of the intricate politics of the Tibet issue is Melvyn C. Goldstein, *The Snow Lion and the Dragon: China, Tibet, and the Dalai Lama* (Berkeley: University of California Press, 1997).

43. EIU, *Mongolia,* 2d quar. 1996, 49; Jankowiak, *Sex, Death, and Hierarchy,* 33–37.

44. FBIS, *China,* March 14, 1996; EDN, December 3, 1996; MNA, June 4, 1999; Reuters (Mongolia), June 4, 1999; EIU, *Mongolia,* 2d quar. 1996, 49; 1st quar. 1999, 47.

45. On World Vision, Taiwan's efforts, see MNA, February 6, 2004. In 2004, one of every four families in Darkhan, the second largest city in the country, received contributions of rice from World Vision.

46. EDN, August 1, 2003; *UB Post,* November 28, 2003. For additional donations of rice, see *UB Post,* January 15, 2004. Mongolia and Taiwan have also exchanged business delegations. See EDN, October 31, 2003. Early in 2004, the two governments announced plans to increase the quota of Mongolian workers (all of whom would receive special training to acclimate them to their new environment) permitted to work in Taiwan to about 7,000. The remittances of these overseas laborers (who work in South Korea, the United States, and, to a limited extent, West Asia) are increasingly important for the Mongolian economy. See MNA, January 22 and 27, 2004.

47. EIU, *Mongolia,* 4th quar. 1993, 35; 1st quar. 1999, 47–48; 1st quar. 1998, 50; 1st quar. 1999, 48; EDN, December 12, 2000; February 18, 2000; and January 4, 2000; Scholars from Mongolia, Great Britain, the United States, and Russia attended the sessions; on the increasing number of academic, cultural, and economic exchanges between Mongolia and Taiwan from 1992 to 1997, see Wang, *Chiu-shih,* 79–83, and for additional details on such exchanges after 1997, see MNA, June 18, 2003.

48. Xinhua, September 11, 1998; EDN, March 14, 2002; *UB Post,* October 10, 2002.

49. My wife and I rented furnished apartments in Ulaanbaatar in the summers of 1998, 1999, and 2000, and found that almost every

piece of furniture and artifact was manufactured abroad, mostly in China. We noticed that this was the case in all the apartments of Mongolian friends whom we visited.

50. The latest economic developments are not encouraging. "Is China Becoming 'Dangerously' Important in Mongolia's Foreign Trade," *Mongolia This Week*, May 26–June 1, 2000, notes that "for the first three months of this year . . . China has sucked up all 100 percent of the copper concentrate, the main export item of Mongolia. This is in addition to the total volume of raw cashmere, total volume of raw hides and skins on top of the 14 percent of the combed cashmere. . . . China's share of the total Mongolian exports was 83.5 percent. In addition, 100 percent of the rice, 99.6 percent of all vegetables, over 80 percent of fruits came from China in 1999. . . . The dependency now developing on China as a single export market and source of food is likely to prove . . . dangerous."

51. See Morris Rossabi, "China Seeks to Bolster Its Economic Profile in Central Asia" (August 14, 2000), www.eurasianet.org/departments/business/articles/eav081400.shtml (accessed May 22, 2004), and Ted Weihman, "China Making Diplomatic Push in Central Asia" (June 9, 2003), www.eurasianet.org/departments/business/articles/eav060903.shtml (accessed June 10, 2003). See also French, "China Moves toward Another West: Central Asia," 1. China is interested in constructing a pipeline to the oil fields in Kazakhstan and the leaders of that Central Asian state "desire to form broader economic and security ties with the world's most populous nation." Chinese investment in such a pipeline will depend upon protection and production guarantees. In addition, the Chinese consider "Central Asia a critical source of potential customers and a worrisome area for potential security threats," security threats from what they refer to as Uyghur separatists in the region of Xinjiang. Quotations from Ibragin Alibekov, "China Steps Up Presence in Kazakhstan Oilfields" (January 21, 2004), www.eurasianet.org/departments/business/articles/eav012104.shtml (accessed January 27, 2004).

52. *Mongol Messenger,* October 15 and November 12, 2003. A recent

study by the ADB seems to support a project that offers China greater access to eastern Mongolia's mineral resources while reputedly improving transport in the region. See ADB, *Strategic Development Outline.*

53.   EDN, October 24, 2003.

AFTERWORD

1.   Hessler, "Letter," 60. Cf. Stephen Cohen's assessment of the role of some of these agencies after the collapse of the USSR: "Globe-traveling economic shock therapists, from universities, think tanks, and official agencies, were particularly influential in shaping media opinion about post-Communist Russia. Unfortunately, most of them knew little about the country (except that it had an economy) and did not care, seemingly in a Marxist-like belief that their laws and prescriptions applied equally to all societies" (Cohen, *Failed Crusade,* 49–50).

2.   Naturally not all of the representatives of the international donors held these views, but these were the general views of the agencies.

3.   Hessler, "Letter," 64. The Cambridge anthropologist David Sneath adds that Mongolia moved from a status as a junior or younger brother of the USSR to a dependent of Western-led developmentalism. See Sneath, "Lost in the Post," 39–52.

4.   Hessler, "Letter," 64.

5.   EDN, August 26, 2003.

6.   EDN, August 28, 2003. The consequences of lack of unity among leading political figures and political parties may be observed in the breakup of the Democracy movement that had led to the collapse of communism in 1990, the proliferation of political parties from 1990 to 1996 (at least fifteen registered parties for a population of 2.4 million), the need for the international agencies to help forge the Democratic Union in 1996, the fragmentation of the ruling Democratic Union from 1996 to 2000 (leading to four different governments during that time),

the difficulties encountered by the Motherland Democratic Party in coalescing into an anti-MPRP coalition, and the present existence of five major political parties and a host of minor ones.

7. Hafiz Pasha, "Pro-Poor Policies" (paper submitted to the Fifth International Conference of New or Restored Democracies, 10–12 September, 2003, Ulaanbaatar), 1.

8. Total imports in the first seven months of 2003 amounted to $447.6 million and total exports only reached $278.4 million; *Mongol Messenger*, August 20, 2003. As noted earlier, most of the increase in GDP in 2002 and 2003 was in mining and construction, and few in Mongolia have benefited from this increase.

9. Pasha, "Pro-Poor Policies," 1.

10. Sanjaasürengiin Oyun, "From the Year," 3.

SELECT BIBLIOGRAPHY

Mongolian names are alphabetized in the following order: first name, comma, surname.

INTERVIEWS

I give the identification as of the time of the interview. Most of those interviewed currently have different positions. For example, as of this writing, Tsakhiagiin Elbegdorj is prime minister of Mongolia, and Luvsangiin Erdenechuluun is minister of foreign relations.

Akim, Gotovyn, editor-in-chief, *Il Tovchoo*, Ulaanbaatar, May 10, 1994; August 23, 1997; June 26, 1998.

Albright, Wendell, second secretary, U.S. Embassy in Mongolia, Ulaanbaatar, January 7, 1997; August 11, 1997; June 2, 1998.

Alimaa, Jigjiddorjin, vice director, Monenzyme Research and Production Association, Ulaanbaatar, May 4, 1999.

Altanchimeg, Delegchoimbol, UN Food and Population Program, Ulaanbaatar, May 30, 1998.

Altantsetseg, N., director, School of Foreign Service, National University of Mongolia, Ulaanbaatar, January 6–13, 2002.

Amarjargal, Rinchinnyamyn, minister for external relations, Ulaanbaatar, April 30, 1994; June 30, 1998.

Anderson, James, field coordinator, Institutional Reform and the Informal Sector at the University of Maryland, Ulaanbaatar, May 10, 1994.

Ariunaa, Tserenpil, executive director, Arts Council of Mongolia, Ulaanbaatar, and private correspondence, January 7–10, 2002; May 2002.

Ariungua, Natsagdorjyin, senior researcher, Center for International Studies, Mongolian Academy of Sciences, Ulaanbaatar, June 25, 1998.

Avery, Martha, director of publishing program, Open Society Institute, Ulaanbaatar, January 4, 1997; August 9 and 22, 1997.

Badarch, Dendevin, president, Mongolian Technical University, Ulaanbaatar, January 6, 1997.

Baker, James, former U.S. secretary of state, telephone interview, March 2, 1998.

Baldoo, Badamtariin, councilor, Mongolian Academy of Sciences, Ulaanbaatar, May 18, 1998.

Baljinnyam, Damdiny, co-president, International Women's Association of Mongolia, Ulaanbaatar, June 11, 1998.

Batbayar, Bat-Erdeniin (Baabar), M.P., Ulaanbaatar, January 7, 1997; minister of finance, June 30, 1998.

Batbayar, Tserendambyn, director, Institute of Oriental Studies, Academy of Sciences, Ulaanbaatar, June 6, 1998.

Batbold, Tserenpuntsag, senior economic advisor to the prime minister of Mongolia, Ulaanbaatar, January 4, 1997; August 21, 1997; director, Premier International, Inc., May 20, 1998.

Bat-erdene, Dashiin, vice president, Mongolian University of Arts and Culture, Ulaanbaatar, January 4, 2002.

Bat-erdene, Regsüren, state secretary, Ministry of Science, Technology, Education, and Culture, Ulaanbaatar, May 27, 1998.

Batsukh, Dash, executive director, International Cultural Exchange Society, Ulaanbaatar, January 7, 2002.

Bayar, Sanjiin, special assistant to the president of Mongolia, Ulaanbaatar, May 30, 1998.

Bayasakh, Khereid, director, School of Foreign Service, National University of Mongolia, Ulaanbaatar, September 14, 1994; August 23, 1997.

Beauclerk, John, programme coordinator, Save the Children–UK, Ulaanbaatar, August 22, 1997.

Bender, Christopher, pension reform advisor to the Mongolian government, Development Alternatives, Inc., Ulaanbaatar, June 11, 1998.

Bevis, Alan, advisor, Second Roads Development Project, government of Mongolia, Ulaanbaatar, May 18, 21, 1998.

Bikales, Bill, economic advisor to the Mongolian government, Development Alternatives, Inc., Ulaanbaatar, May 12, 1994; June 6, 26, 1998.

Bikales, Margaret Eliot, assistant curator, National Museum of Mongolian History, Ulaanbaatar, August 23, 26, 1997; May 22, 29, 1998.

Bikleare, John, coordinator, Danish-Mongolia Center, Ulaanbaatar, August 22, 1997.

Bira, Shagdaryn, secretary-general, International Association for Mongol Studies, Ulaanbaatar, January 7, 1997; August 21, 1997.

Bold, Luvsanvandan, chairman, union of Mongolian Artists, Ulaanbaatar, January 8, 2002.

Braae, Christel, research fellow, Nationalmuseet, Copenhagen, December 23, 1997.

Broadwell, Bradly, advisor, International Republican Institute, Mongolia, Ulaanbaatar, May 2, 1999.

Brown, Ian, English for Special Purposes Institute, Ulaanbaatar, January 6, 1997.

Burmaa, Radnaagiin, chair, Women for Social Progress, Ulaanbaatar, May 10, 1994; April 3, 1998.

Byambasüren, Dashiin, former prime minister of Mongolia, Ulaanbaatar, May 6, 1994; January 6, 1997.

Chachkine, Elsa, director, French Cultural Center, Ulaanbaatar, May 19, 2002.

Chadraa, Baataryn, president of the University of Technology, Ministry of Science and Education, president of the Mongolian Academy of Sciences and rector of the Ulaanbaatar University, New York and Ulaanbaatar, November 4, 1992; May 15, 1994; June 19, 1998.

Christiansen, Scott, country director, Adventist Development and Relief Agency in Mongolia, Ulaanbaatar, June 22, 24, 1998.

Chul Choi, Young, ambassador of the Republic of Korea to Mongolia, May 20, 2002.

Dambajav, Lama, Khamba Lama, Tashichoeling Monastery, Ulaanbaatar, May 14, 1994.

Dash-Yondon, Budragchaagin, advisor to the president of Mongolia on political affairs, New York, September 30, 1998.

Delgermaa, Banzragchiin, M.P., chair, Subcommittee on Human Rights, Ulaan-baatar, July 10, 1998.

Denzen, Barsboldt, New York, January 3, 2004.

Dolgormaa, Dr. Handbal, director of Binderya Clinic, Mongolian Traditional Medicine, Ulaanbaatar, June 11, 1998.

Driscoll, Ann, U.S. Information Agency, Mongolia, Ulaanbaatar, January 7, 1997; August 11, 1997.

Eckel, Gunter, rural financial system advisor, Agricultural Bank of Mongolia, Ulaanbaatar, June 23, 1998.

Ehrich, Rebecca, family nurse practitioner, Peace Corps, Mongolia, Ulaanbaatar, August 22, 1997.

Elbegdorj, Tsakhiagiin, chair, Mongolian Democratic Union; M.P., Ulaanbaatar, May 9, 1994.

Enkh-Amgalan, L., director, Interpress, Ulaanbaatar, May 18, 1998; May 5, 1999.

Enkhbat, Dangaasüren, CEO, Datacom Co., Ltd., Ulaanbaatar, May 9, 1994; January 6, 1997.

Enkhbat, Tsendiin, managing director, Press Institute of Mongolia, Ulaanbaatar, January 7, 1997; May 27, 1998.

Enkhbayar, Nambaryn, chair, Mongolian People's Revolutionary Party, Ulaan-baatar, August 21, 1997; June 8, 1998.

Enkhbold, Zandaakhuugiin, chair, Government of Mongolia State Property Committee, Ulaanbaatar, January 8, 1997.

Enkhsaikhan, director, Bizmo, Ulaanbaatar, May 6, 1999.

Enkhsaikhan, Jargalsaikhany, secretary, National Security Council; ambassador of Mongolia to the United Nations, Ulaanbaatar and New York, May 7, 1994; October 16, 1996; March 24, 1997.

Enkhtsetseg, D., director, Mongolian National Modern Art Gallery, Ulaan-baatar, January 9, 2002.

Enkhtuya, Oidov, chair, Liberal Women's Brain Pool; member of Parliament, Ulaanbaatar, May 10, 1994; January 7, 1997; August 24, 1997.

Erdenebat, Badarchyn, president, Erel Mining Company, Ulaanbaatar, June 27, 1998.

Erdenebileg, Tömör-öchiryn, M.P., Ulaanbaatar, May 9, 1994; June 21, 1998.

Erdenebulgan, L., director, National Opera House, Ulaanbaatar, August 23, 1997.

Erdenechuluun, Luvsangiin, ambassador of Mongolia to the United Nations; foreign policy advisor to the president of Mongolia, Ulaanbaatar, November 6, 1992; August 8, 1997; April 27, 1999.

Erdenejargal, Perenlei, executive director, Mongolian Development Foundation, and associate director, Open Society Institute, Ulaanbaatar, May 12–15, 1994; August 10, 1997.

Estes, Richard, professor of social work, University of Pennsylvania, Ulaanbaatar, January 6, 7, and 8, 1997.

Farkas, Otto, programme coordinator, World Vision Mongolia, Ulaanbaatar, June 19, 1998.

Finch, Christopher, executive director, Open Society Institute, Ulaanbaatar, April 30, 1999.

Frank, Dr. Michael, medical director, German Embassy to Mongolia, Ulaanbaatar, May 3, 1999.

Ganbold, Chuluuny, editor, E-mail News, Ulaanbaatar, May 10 and 12, 1994; January 7, 1997; August 14, 1997; June 25, 1998; April 29, 1999.

Ganbold, Davaadorjiin, chair, Mongolian National Democratic Party, M.P., Ulaanbaatar, January 8, 1997; August 16, 1997.

Gankhuyag, Minteg, director, Public Administration Reform Project, Ministry of Finance; advisor to the president, MCS Holding, Ulaanbaatar, May 27, 1998.

Gankhuyag, Tserendorjiin, M.P., Ulaanbaatar, May 28, 1998.

Gantsog, Tserensodnom, rector of the National University of Mongolia, Ulaanbaatar, January 4 and 9, 1997; May 26, 2002.

Gardner, Douglas, UN Development Programme resident representative in Mongolia, Ulaanbaatar, June 12, 1998.

Gilberg, Rolf, curator of ethnology, Nationalmuseet, Copenhagen, December 23, 1997.

Gonchigdorj, Randaasumbereliin, chair of Parliament, Ulaanbaatar, January 9, 1997.

Gorelik, Oleg, deputy director, CEU Privatization Project, Ulaanbaatar, August 26, 1997; June 26, 1998.

Ground, Richard Lynn, resident representative, World Bank, Ulaanbaatar, April 30, 1999.

Gungaa, Dashtseren, director, Fine Arts Museum, Mongolia, Ulaanbaatar, August 9, 1997.

Halasz, Irja, journalist, Reuters, Ulaanbaatar, May 11, 1997; June 30, 1998.

Haraguchi, Akisa, project advisor, Japan International Cooperation Agency, Ulaanbaatar, May 19, 2003.

Honeychurch, William, Ph.D. student in archeology, University of Michigan, Ulaanbaatar, May 31, 1998.

Hulan, Hashbat, M.P. and chair, Standing Committee on Social Policy, Ulaanbaatar, January 4, 1997; August 9, 1997; May 26, 28, 1998.

Hunter, Katherine, assistant representative, Asia Foundation in Mongolia, Ulaanbaatar, August 25, 1997; June 30, 1998.

Idshinnorov, Sunduyn, director, National Museum of Mongolian History, Ulaanbaatar, May 21, 1998.

Jackson, Dr. Rebecca, Napa, California, telephone interview, March 31, 1998.

Jargalsaikhan, Bazarsadyn, general director, Buyan Holdings, Ltd., Ulaanbaatar, May 6, 1999.

Khishigbayar, D., director, Cultural Heritage Center of Mongolia, Ulaanbaatar, January 10, 2002.

Kohlenberg, Leah, freelance journalist, Ulaanbaatar, May 8, 1999.

Laden, Amy, Interplast, telephone interview, March 30, 1998.

La Porta, Alphonse, U.S. ambassador to Mongolia, Ulaanbaatar, June 2, 1998; April 27, 1999.

Lawless, Jill, English editor, *UB Post,* Ulaanbaatar, June 8, 1998.

Lawrence, Fred, International Republican Institute, telephone interview, February 21, 1998.

Lerner, Kelly, architect and advisor on Straw Housing, Adventist Development and Relief Agency in Mongolia, Ulaanbaatar, June 24, 1998.

Lutaa, Badamkhand, coordinator, Media Program Coordinator, Open Society Institute, Ulaanbaatar, June 12, 1998.

Lynch, Maurice, Munh-Orgil, Idesh & Lynch, Ulaanbaatar, May 13, 1999.

Maidar, Ts., leader of Green Revolution movement, Ulaanbaatar, June 2, 2003.

Markiw, Theresa, public affairs officer, Mongolia, Ulaanbaatar, May 28, 2002.

Mash, Geserjav, film director, Ulaanbaatar, April 27, 1999.

McCracken, James, vice consul, economic and commercial officer, U.S. Embassy in Mongolia, Ulaanbaatar, January 7, 1997; August 11, 1997.

Manduhai, Buyandelger. Ph.D. student in anthropology, Harvard University, Ulaanbaatar, July 5, 1998.

Marsh, Peter, Ph.D. student, Department of Central Eurasian Studies, Indiana University, Ulaanbaatar, June 1, 1998.

Matsumoto, Kenji, resident representative, Japan International Cooperation Agency, Ulaanbaatar, May 27, 2002.

Mawson, Jacinda, 1997–98 Luce scholar, National Public Health Institute, Nutrition Research Centre, Ulaanbaatar, June 10, 1998.

Menon, Saraswathi, UN Development Programme resident representative in Mongolia, New York, May 8, 2003.

Molomjamts, Demchigiin, former minister of finance and chair of State Planning Committee, Ulaanbaatar, May 19, 1998.

Narangerel, Rinchingiin, M.P., Ulaanbaatar, January 14, 1997.

Natsagdorj, Shagdarjavun, president, Center for Chinggis Studies, Mongolian Academy of Sciences, Ulaanbaatar, June 25, 1998.

Nomin, Lkhagvasüren, journalist and translator, Ulaanbaatar, May 26, June 18, 1998; May 8, 1999; Manzshir, May 26, 2002.

Ochirbat, Punsalmagiin, president of Mongolia, Ulaanbaatar, May 15, 1994.

Od, Jambaljamtsyn, foreign policy advisor to the prime minister of Mongolia, Ulaanbaatar, June 23, 1998.

Odjargal, Jambaljamtsyn, president, MCS Holding Co., Ulaanbaatar, May 27, 1998.

Oestreicher, Geoffrey, International Monetary Fund representative in Mongolia, Ulaanbaatar, May 28, 1998; May 5, 1999.

Oyun, Sanjaasürengiin, M.P., Ulaanbaatar and New York, April 29, 1999; April 2003.

Oyunbayar, Namsrai, editor-in-chief, *UB Post,* Ulaanbaatar, January 6, 2002.

Oyuntsetseg, Oidov, executive director, Women's Information and Research Centre, Ulaanbaatar, June 19, 1998; May 7, 1999.

Peach, Terry, senior lecturer in economics, Manchester University, Ulaanbaatar, May 11, 1999.

Peck, Robert M., fellow, Academy of Natural Sciences, Philadelphia, Ulaanbaatar, April 15, 1997.

Prohl, Werner, representative in Mongolia, Konrad Adenauer Stiftung, Ulaanbaatar, May 25, 1998.

Ragchaa, Tümenbayariin, former minister of agriculture and former chair, Ministry for Planning, Ulaanbaatar, June 18, 1998.

Richardson, Gregory, project manager, Needs Analysis for the Mongolian Legal Sector, Ulaanbaatar, May 12, 1994.

Rinchin, Munkhdalain, chief, Scientific Research Centre of Political Repression, Ulaanbaatar, May 11, 1994, May 14, 1996.

Rips, Jill, AVCS International, Ulaanbaatar, May 28, 1998.

Sabloff, Paula, adjunct assistant professor of anthropology, University of Pennsylvania, Ulaanbaatar, June 21, 1998.

Sanchir, Namkhaitseren, Union of Mongolian Artists, Ulaanbaatar, August 9 and 21, 1997.

Saranchimeg, Shagdariin, director, English for Special Purposes Institute, Ulaanbaatar, January 6 and 9, 1997.

Serjee, Zhambaldorjiin, director, State Central Library, Mongolia, Ulaanbaatar, August 9, 1997.

Severinghaus, Sheldon, Mongolia representative, Asia Foundation, Ulaanbaatar, June 30, 1998.

Shlomm, Boris, president, Amicale Industries, New York, April 9, 1998.

Siemerling, William, special advisor on media, Open Society Institute, Ulaanbaatar, July 2, 1998.

Sodnom, Namsrain, president, Academy of Sciences, Mongolia, New York and Ulaanbaatar, November 4, 1992; May 14, 1997.

Sosormaa, director, Centre against Violence, Ulaanbaatar, June 2, 1998.

South, David, communications coordinator, UN Development Programme, Mongolia, Ulaanbaatar, May 4, 1999.

Spaulding, Professor Seth, School of Education, University of Pittsburgh, Ulaanbaatar, June 23, 1998.

Sumati, Luvsandendev, director, Sant Maral Research Center, Ulaanbaatar, January 4, 1997; August 14 and 16, 1997; May 17–18, 1998; April 28, 1999.

Tsagaan, Puntsagiin, minister of finance, Mongolia, Ulaanbaatar, January 7, 1997.

Tsedev, Dojoogiin, president, Mongolian University of Arts and Culture, Ulaanbaatar, January 4, 2002.

Ulziijargal, S., English language program coordinator, Open Society Institute, Ulaanbaatar, August 27, 1997.

Undarya, Tumursukh, board member, Women for Social Progress, Ulaanbaatar, August 23, 1997.

Unenbat, Jigjidiin, governor, Bank of Mongolia, Ulaanbaatar, June 26–27, 1998; April 26, 1999.

Untermeyer, Chase, head of public relations, Compaq, telephone interview, February 17, 1998.

Uranchimeg, D., director, Mongolian National Modern Art Gallery, Ulaanbaatar, August 9, 1997.

Urantsooj, G., Women's Information and Research Centre, Ulaanbaatar, May 25, 1998.

Webster, Mary Clark, director, Energy Group, International Resources Group, Ulaanbaatar, May 23–24, 1998.

Whitlock, Lynn, second secretary, U.S. Embassy in Mongolia, Ulaanbaatar, May 12, 1999.

Windham, Professor Douglas, School of Education, State University of New York at Albany, Ulaanbaatar, June 23, 1998.

Wingard, James, project coordinator, Integrated Fire Management, German Agency for Technical Cooperation, Ministry for Nature and Environment, Ulaanbaatar, June 24, 1998.

Zober, Mark, country director, Peace Corps, Mongolia, Ulaanbaatar, August 26, 1997.

BOOKS AND ARTICLES

Academy of Sciences, Mongolian People's Republic, ed. *Information Mongolia.* Oxford: Pergamon Press, 1990.

Admidin, Andrei, and Elena Devaeva. "Economic Cooperation of Russia's Far East and Northeast Asia." *Far Eastern Affairs* 1 (1999): 29–38.

Akiner, Shirin, ed. *Mongolia Today.* London: Kegan Paul, 1991.

Akiner, Shirin, Sander Tideman, and Jon Hay, eds. *Sustainable Development in Central Asia.* London: Curzon Press, 1998.

Allen, Benedict. *Edge of Blue Heaven: A Journey through Mongolia.* London: BBC, 1998.

Altay, Halifa. "A Journey to Mongolia." *Journal of Institute of Muslim Minority Affairs* 12, no. 1 (January 1991): 91–103.

Amnesty International. "Mongolia: Prison Inmates Starve to Death." Photocopy. London, April 1995.

Anderson, James. "An Introduction to Mongolia's Informal Sector." Photocopy. Ulaanbaatar: World Bank, April 1997.

———. "Reaction to Crisis, Response to Policy: An Analysis of the Size, Origins, and Character of Mongolia's Informal Sector." Photocopy. Ulaanbaatar: World Bank, July 1997.

Andrews-Speed, Philip, and Serge Vinogradov. "China's Involvement in Central Asian Petroleum," *Asian Survey* 40, no. 2 (March–April 2000): 377–97.

Arts Council of Mongolia. *Quarterly Newsletter.* Photocopy. Ulaanbaatar, Spring 2004.

Asian Development Bank. *Mongolia: A Centrally Planned Economy in Transition.* New York: Oxford University Press, 1992.

———. "ADB Project Profiles." Manila, 1996.

———. *Country Economic Review: Mongolia, October, 1996.* Ulaanbaatar, 1996.

———. *Country Economic Review: Mongolia, August, 1997.* Ulaanbaatar, 1997.

———. *Education Sector Development Program.* Ulaanbaatar, 1999.

———. *Strategic Development Outline for Economic Cooperation between the People's Republic of China and Mongolia.* Manila, 2002.

Aslund, Anders. *Building Capitalism: The Transformation of the Former Soviet Bloc*. Cambridge: Cambridge University Press, 2002.

Atwood, Christopher. "The East Mongolian Revolution and Chinese Communism." *Mongolian Studies* 15 (1992): 7–83.

———. "National Party and Local Politics in Ordos, Inner Mongolia (1926–1935)." *Journal of Asian History* 26, no. 1 (1992): 1–30.

Aubin, Françoise. "La Mongolie des premières années de l'après-communisme: La Popularization de passé national dans les mass media Mongols (1990–1995)." *Études mongoles et siberiennes* 27 (1996): 305–26.

———. "Interrogations sur les droits humains: Le Cas de la Mongolie post-communiste." In Thierry Marrès and Paul Servais, eds., *Droits humains et valeurs asiatiques*. Louvain-la-Neuve: Academia–Bruylant, 2002.

Avery, Martha. *Women of Mongolia*. Seattle: University of Washington Press, 1996.

Baasansuren, T. *The Parliament of Mongolia*. Ulaanbaatar, 1995.

Badarch, D., N. Batsukh, and S. Batmunkh. "The Impacts of Industrialization in Mongolia." In Badarch, D., Raymond Zilinskas, and Peter Balint, eds., *Mongolia Today: Science, Culture, Environment and Development*, 3–20. London: RoutledgeCurzon, 2003.

Badarch, D., Raymond Zilinskas, and Peter Balint, eds. *Mongolia Today: Science, Culture, Environment and Development*. London: RoutledgeCurzon, 2003.

Baker, James. *The Politics of Diplomacy: Revolution, War, and Peace, 1989–1992*. New York: G. P. Putnam's Sons, 1995.

Bandii, R., and D. Khishigbuyan. "School Dropouts in Mongolia." Photocopy. Ulaanbaatar: Institute for Educational Development, 1996.

Bareja-Starzynska, Agata, and Hanna Havnevik. "Buddhism in Present-Day Mongolia." Paper presented at an international workshop titled "Mongolians from Country to City," held at the Nordic Institute of Asian Studies (NIAS), Copenhagen, October 28–30, 1999.

Barkmann, Udo. "The Revival of Lamaism in Mongolia." *Central Asian Survey* 16, no. 1 (March 1997): 69–79.

———. "Die mongolisch-japanischen Beziehungen (1996–1998)—Die Mongolei zwischen Globalisierung und Regionalisierung." In M. Pohl, ed., *Japan 1998/99—Politik und Wirtschaft*, 129–59. Hamburg: Institut für Asienkunde, 1999.

———. *Geschichte der Mongolei oder die "Mongolische Frage"—Die Mongolen auf ihrem Weg zum eigenen Nationalstaat*. Bonn: Bouvier Verlag, 1999.

_____. *Die Beziehungen zwischen der Mongolei und der VR China (1952–1996)*. Hamburg: Institut für Asienkunde, 2000.

Bartow, Barry. "The Policy of the Mongolian People's Republic toward China, 1952–1973." Ph.D. diss., West Virginia University, 1974.

Batbayar, Bat-Erdeniin. *Zuuni Mongol*. Ulaanbaatar, 1996.

———. *Twentieth Century Mongolia*. Translated by D. Suhjargalmaa, S. Burenbayar, H. Hulan, and N. Tuya. Cambridge: White Horse Press, 1999.

Batbayar, Tsedendambyn. *Modern Mongolia: A Concise History*. Ulaanbaatar: Mongolian Center for Scientific and Technological Information, 1996.

———. "Mongolia and Japan in 1945–1995: A Half-Century Reconsidered." In Stephen Kotkin and Bruce Elleman, eds., *Mongolia in the Twentieth Century: Landlocked Cosmopolitan*. Armonk, N.Y.: M. E. Sharpe, 1999.

———. "Mongolian Perspectives on Northeast Asian Regional Development." In Tsuneo Akaha, ed., *Politics and Economics in Northeast Asia*. New York: St. Martin's Press, 1999.

———. "Stalin's Strategy in Mongolia, 1932–1936." *Mongolian Studies* 22 (1999): 1–17.

———. "Mongolian-Russian Relations in the Past Decade." *Asian Survey* 43, no. 6 (November–December 2003): 951–70.

Batjargal, Z. "Environmental Policy in Mongolia." In D. Badarch, Raymond Zilinskas, and Peter Balint, eds., *Mongolia Today: Science, Culture, Environment and Development*, 21–48. London: RoutledgeCurzon, 2003.

Bawden, Charles. *The Modern History of Mongolia*. New York: Praeger, 1968.

Bayar Batzorig, "New Environment for Military Ethics." http://nsa.navy.mil./publications/micewski/batzorig.htm. No longer accessible.

Bayarkhuu, D. *The Challenge of Globalization and the Shaping of the New World Order*. New Delhi: Rajiv Gandhi Institute for Contemporary Studies, 2000.

———. *Asia Pacific—A Region of Globalisation and Competition in the 21st Century*. New Delhi: Rajiv Gandhi Institute for Contemporary Studies, 2001.

Bayasakh, Kh., ed. *New World Order in Post-Cold War Era in Asia*. Ulaanbaatar: National University of Mongolia, 1996.

———. "A Brief Introduction to the International Project: Ancient Kharakhorum: New Development Area." Photocopy. Ulaanbaatar, 1997.

Bazagur, D., et al. *Territorial Organization of Mongolian Pastoral Livestock Husbandry in the Transition to a Market Economy*. Policy Alternatives for Livestock Development Research Report No. 1. Brighton: Institute of Development Studies, University of Sussex, January 1993.

Becker, Jason. *The Lost Country: Mongolia Revealed.* London: Hodder & Stoughton, 1992.

———. "Hunting for Genghis Khan." *South China Morning Post Postmagazine,* September 7, 1997, 14–18, 30.

Bedunah, D. J., and S. M. Schmidt. "Pastoralism and Protected Area Management in Mongolia's Gobi Gurvansaikhan National Park." *Development and Change* 35, no. 1 (2004): 141–65.

Béguin, Gilles, and Dorjiin Dashbaldan. *Trésors de Mongolie, XVIIe–XIXe siècles.* Catalogue of an exhibition at the Musée national des Arts asiatiques in Paris, November 26, 1993–March 14, 1994. Paris: Réunion des Musées nationaux, 1993.

Bender, Christopher. "Individual Accounts: A Briefing Paper for the Government of Mongolia." Photocopy. Ulaanbaatar: Economic Policy Support Project, June 1997.

———. "Pension Reform in Mongolia: Issues and Recommendations." Photocopy. Ulaanbaatar: Economic Policy Support Project, July 1997.

———. "Pension Reform: Managing the Transition." Photocopy. Ulaanbaatar: Working Group of the Standing Committee on Social Policy, Ikh Khural, October 1997.

———."Proposed Specifications of the New Pension System." Photocopy. Ulaanbaatar: Economic Policy Support Project, April 1998.

Berger, Patricia, and Terese Bartholomew, et al. *Mongolia: The Legacy of Chinggis Khan.* New York: Thames & Hudson, 1995.

Bikales, Bill. "Capacity Building in a Transition Country: Lessons from Mongolia." In Merilee S. Grindle, ed., *Getting Good Government: Capacity Building in the Public Sectors of Developing Countries,* 435–63. Cambridge, Mass.: Harvard University Press, 1997.

———. "Conquering Financial Freefall: Mongolia's Prescription for Ailing Asian Banks." *Developments: Development Alternatives, Inc.,* Winter 1997, 1, 16–17.

Bikales, Bill, et al. "The Mongolian Informal Sector: Survey Results and Analysis." MS. Ulaanbaatar: Development Alternatives, Inc., April 2000.

Black, Cyril, et al. *The Modernization of Inner Asia.* Armonk, N.Y.: M. E. Sharpe, 1991.

Boersma, Rudy. "Neonatal Care and Services at Somon, Aimag and City Hospital Level in Mongolia." Photocopy. Ulaanbaatar, 1994.

Bold, Ravdan. "The Changing International Order and Mongolia's Security." *Mongolian Journal of International Affairs* 1 (1994): 9–14.

———. *The Mongolia's* [sic] *Strategic View.* Ulaanbaatar: Institute for Strategic Studies, 1996.

"Bridge to Nowhere: Mongolia." *Economist,* January 31, 2004, 58–60.

Briller, Sherylyn. "Mongolia: Out in the Cold." *Natural History* 106, no. 6 (July–August, 1997): 24–33.

Bruun, Ole. "Mongolian Nomadic Herders Today: Fieldwork in Khotont Sum, Arhangai Aimag." Paper presented at an international workshop titled "Mongolians from Country to City," held at the Nordic Institute of Asian Studies (NIAS), Copenhagen, October 28–30, 1999.

Bruun, Ole, and Ole Odgaard, eds. *Mongolia in Transition.* London: Curzon Press, 1996.

Bruun, Ole, Per Ronnas, and Li Narangoa, *Country Analysis: Mongolia. Transition from the Second to the Third World?* Copenhagen: Nordic Institute of Asian Studies, December 1999.

Bulag, Uradyn. *Nationalism and Hybridity in Mongolia.* Oxford: Oxford University Press, 1998.

———. *The Mongols at China's Edge.* Lanham, Md.: Rowman & Littlefield, 2002.

Butler, W. E. "The Advocate in the Mongolian People's Republic." *Journal of the Anglo-Mongolian Society* 6, no. 2 (April 1980): 73–88.

———. *The Mongolian Legal System.* The Hague: Martinus Nijhoff, 1982.

Byambasüren, D. "New Conditions of Geo-Policy of Central Asia-Mongolia." Ulaanbaatar: Mongolian Development Foundation, 1996.

———. "Present Political Situation in Mongolia and Its Perspectives." Photocopy. Ulaanbaatar: Mongolian Development Foundation, 1996.

Campi, Alicia Jean. "The Political Relationship between the United States and Outer Mongolia, 1915–1927: The Kalgan Consular Records." Ph.D. diss., Indiana University, 1988.

———. "The Rise of Nationalism in the Mongolian People's Republic as Reflected in Language Reform, Religion, and the Cult of Chinggis Khan." *Central and Inner Asian Studies* 6 (1992): 46–58.

———. "Nomadic Cultural Values and Their Influence on Modernization." In Ole Bruun and Ole Odgaard, eds., *Mongolia in Transition,* 90–102. London: Curzon Press, 1996.

———. "The Unique Challenges Facing Mongolia As It Adapts Its Nomadic Socialist Economy to the Market System." *Mongolica* 7 (1996): 221–34.

Cariceo, Carmen Mercedes. "Maternal Mortality in Mongolia: Cultural and Institutional Factors." Master of social work thesis, York University, 1994.

Center against Violence [Ulaanbaatar]. "Report of the Activities, 1996–1997." Photocopy. 1997.

Chalmers, Neil. *Wheat Production in Mongolia.* Policy Alternatives for Livestock Development Research Report No. 7. Brighton: Institute of Development Studies, University of Sussex, May 1993.

Chia Ning. "The Li-fan Yuan in the Early Ch'ing Dynasty." Ph.D. diss., Johns Hopkins University, 1991.

Choijilsuren, L. *S. Zorigiin Ineevkhiilel* [Zorig's smile]. Ulaanbaatar, 1998.

Chua, Amy. *How Exporting Free Market Democracy Breeds Ethnic Hatred and Global Instability.* New York: Doubleday, 2002.

Cohen, Stephen. *Failed Crusade: America and the Tragedy of Post-Communist Russia.* Rev. ed. New York: Norton, 2001.

Collins, Paul, and Nixson, Frederick. "Managing the Implementation of 'Shock Therapy' in a Land-locked State: Mongolia's Transition from the Centrally Planned Economy." *Public Administration and Development* 13 (1993): 389–407.

Cooper, Louise. *Wealth and Poverty in the Mongolian Pastoral Economy.* Policy Alternatives for Livestock Development Research Report No. 11. Brighton: Institute of Development Studies, University of Sussex, May 1993.

Cooper, Louise, and Narangerel Gelezhamtsin. *Liberalisation of the Mongolian Pastoral Economy and Its Impact within the Household—A Case Study of Arhangai and Dornogobi Provinces.* Policy Alternatives for Livestock Development Research Report No. 8. Brighton: Institute of Development Studies, University of Sussex, May 1993.

Coox, Alvin. *Nomonhan: Japan against Russia, 1939.* 2 vols. Stanford, Calif.: Stanford University Press, 1985.

Corcega, Thelma. "Nursing Education and Practice." Photocopy. Ulaanbaatar: World Health Organization, 1996.

Corcoran-Nantes, Yvonne. *Women's Access to Microcredit in Mongolia.* Ulaanbaatar: Women's Information and Research Centre, 1999.

Craven, David, and Molly Curtin. *Environmental Profile of Mongolia.* Bethesda, Md.: Development Alternatives, Inc., 1998.

Crowell, Todd, and Anne Meijdam. "Experience Is What Counts." *Asiaweek,* July 14, 2000, 33.

DANIDA. "Nature Conservation through Development of Eco-Tourism." Photocopy. Ulaanbaatar, December 1993.

———. "School Drop-out in Mongolia: Survey, 1993." Ulaanbaatar, 1994.

———. "Special Education in Mongolia." Ulaanbaatar, 1994.

———. "Teachers in Mongolia: Survey, 1992–1993." Ulaanbaatar, 1994.

Danish Mongolian Society. *Street Children: Mongolia.* Ulaanbaatar, 1997.

Dapice, David. *Mongolia: Finding a Sustainable Growth Strategy.* Ulaanbaatar: UN Development Programme, April 1997.

Dasheeveg, Kh. *Muan-in Tuukhen Temdeglel (1989–1996)* [A historical account of the Mongolian National Democratic Party, 1989–1996]. Ulaanbaatar: Interpress, 1998.

Dashnyam, D. "Review of Developments in Biotechnology." In D. Badarch, Raymond Zilinskas, and Peter Balint, eds., *Mongolia Today: Science, Culture, Environment and Development,* 49–65. London: RoutledgeCurzon, 2003.

Dashpurev, D., and Soni, S. K. *Reign of Terror in Mongolia, 1920–1990.* New Delhi: South Asian Publishers, 1992.

Denizer, Cevdet, and Alan Gelb. "Privatization in Mongolia." In Vedat Millor, ed., *Changing Political Economies,* 67–96. Boulder, Colo.: Lynne Rienner, 1994.

Derevianko, A. P., and John Olson. *Archaeological Studies Carried Out by the Joint Russian-Mongolian-American Expedition in Mongolia in 1995.* Novosibirsk: Russian Academy of Sciences, Siberian Branch, Institute of Archaeology and Ethnography, 1996.

Doebler, Robert Kenneth. "Cities, Population Redistribution, and Urbanization in Mongolia." Ph.D. diss., Indiana University, 1994.

Dolgormaa, B., S. Zmambaga, and L. Ojungerel. *Status of Women: Mongolia.* Bangkok: UNESCO Principal Regional Office for Asia and the Pacific, 1990.

Dollar, David, and Lant Pritchett. *Assessing Aid: What Works, What Doesn't, and Why.* Oxford: Oxford University Press, 1998.

Dondog, L. "The Present Socio-Economic Situation in Mongolia." *Bulletin of the International Association for Mongol Studies* 2 (1994); 3 (1995): 16–23.

Dondog, L., et al. *Mongolia: Foreign Inverstment* [sic] *Trade and Tourism.* Huhhot: Inner Mongolia People's Publishing House, 1996.

Doodewaard, Margaret van. "Mongolia: Who Bridges the Digital Divide." *International Institute for Asian Studies Newsletter* 33 (March 2004): 11.

Douglas, William O., and Conger, Dean. "Journey to Outer Mongolia." *National Geographic* 121, no. 3 (March 1962): 289–345.

Economist Intelligence Unit. Reports on China and Mongolia. London, 1993–2004.

Edstrom, Jerker, et al. *Mongolian Pastoralism on Trek towards the Market.* Policy Alternatives for Livestock Development Research Report No. 10. Brighton: Institute of Development Studies, University of Sussex, May 1993.

Ehrich, Rebecca. "Suggestions on the Future Direction of Health Care Provision in Mongolia." Photocopy. Ulaanbaatar: Peace Corps, Mongolia, 1997.

Ehrke, Ron. "Mongolia: Broadcasting Development Assistance." Photocopy. Ulaanbaatar, July 1995.

Eitzen, Hilda. "Promises and Pitfalls: Case-by-Case Privatization in Kazakhstan." *Central Asia Monitor* 5 (1999): 1–9.

Elbegdorj, T. "Transition to Democracy: Lessons and Challenges, Mongolia Case." Paper presented to the International Civil Society Forum–2003, Ulaanbaatar, September 2003.

Enkhbat, A., et al. *Forests and Forest Management in Mongolia.* Bangkok: Food and Agriculture Organization of the United Nations, 1997.

Enkhbold, Z. "Mongolian Privatization Policy and Methods of Implementation." State Privatization Committee of Mongolia Report. Photocopy. Ulaanbaatar, September 1997.

Enkhsaikhan, J. "Statement at the General Assembly of the United Nations." Photocopy. New York: Mission of Mongolia to the United Nations, October 1996.

———. "Statement to the United Nations on Disarmament and Security Issues." Photocopy. New York: Mission of Mongolia to the United Nations, October 1996.

———. "Mongolia's Nuclear-Weapon-Free Status," *Asian Survey* 40, no. 2 (March–April, 2000): 342–59.

Erdenechuluun, L. *Mongolia's Strategic Options.* Ebenhausen: Europe–Northeast Asia Forum, September 1997.

Ewing, Thomas E. *Between the Hammer and the Anvil? Chinese and Russian Policies in Outer Mongolia, 1911–1921.* Indiana University Uralic and Altaic Series, vol. 138. Bloomington: Research Institute for Inner Asian Studies, Indiana University, 1980.

Fairbank, John K., ed. *The Cambridge History of China,* vol. 10: *Late Ch'ing, 1800–1911.* Part 1. Cambridge: Cambridge University Press, 1978.

Farkas, Otto, et al. "Health Status and Risk Factors of Seminomadic Pastoralists in Mongolia: A Geographical Approach." *Social Science Medicine* 44, no. 11 (1997): 1623–47.

———. "On the Multi-Sectoral Approach to Early Childhood Care and Development." Photocopy. Ulaanbaatar: World Vision, Mongolia, 1997.

Feldstein, Martin. "Asian Fallout: The IMF's Errors." *Foreign Affairs* 77, no. 2 (March–April, 1998): 20–33.

Fernandez-Giménez, Maria. "The Role of Ecological Perception in Indigenous Resource Management: A Case Study from the Mongolian Forest-Steppe." *Nomadic Peoples* 33 (1993): 31–46.

———. "Landscapes, Livestock, and Livelihoods: Social, Ecological, and Land-Use Change among the Nomadic Pastoralists of Mongolia." Ph.D. diss., University of California at Berkeley, 1997.

———. "Reconsidering the Role of Absentee Herd Owners: A View from Mongolia." *Human Ecology* 27, no. 1 (1999): 1–27.

———. "The Effects of Livestock Privatisation on Pastoral Land Use and Land Tenure in Post-Socialist Mongolia." *Nomadic Peoples* 5, no. 2 (2001): 49–66.

Fernandez-Giménez, Maria, and B. Batbuyan. "Law and Disorder in Mongolia: Local Implementation of Mongolia's Land Law." Paper presented at the Eighth Conference of the International Association for the Study of Common Property, Bloomington, Indiana, May–June 2000.

———. "Law and Disorder: Local Implementation of Mongolia's Land Law." *Development and Change* 35, no. 1 (2004): 141–65.

Fifty Years of People's Mongolia. Ulaanbaatar, 1971.

"Final Report on Pilot Study in Ulaanbaatar Mongolia Conducted by the National Team under Supervision of the United Nations Interregional Crime and Justice Research Institute, UNICRI." Photocopy. Ulaanbaatar, 1995.

Fish, M. Steven. "Mongolia: Democracy without Prerequisites." *Journal of Democracy* 9, no. 3 (July 1998): 127–41.

———. "The Inner Asian Anomaly: Mongolia's Democratization in Comparative Perspective." *Communist and Post-Communist Studies* 34 (2001): 323–38.

Fitzhugh, William. "Smithsonian Researchers Develop New Initiatives," *American Center for Mongolian Studies Update* 2, no. 1 (Fall 2003): 5.

Fletcher, Joseph. "The Mongols: Ecological and Social Perspectives," *Harvard Journal of Asiatic Studies* 46, no. 1 (1986): 11–50.

Forum for International Development Economics. *Review of the 1998 Mongolia Living Standards Measurement Survey.* Washington, D.C.: Forum for International Development Economics, 1999.

French, Howard. "China Moves toward Another West: Central Asia." *New York Times,* March 28, 2004, 1, 8.

Friters, Gerard. *Outer Mongolia and Its International Position.* Baltimore: Johns Hopkins Press, 1949.

Fritz, Verena Maria. "Doppelte Transition in der Mongolei unter dem Einfluss ausländischer Geber." Ph.D. diss., Hamburg University, 1998.

Futaki, Hiroshi. "The Role of District Centres in the Mongolian Semi-Nomadic Society." Paper presented at an international workshop titled "Mongolians from Country to City," held at the Nordic Institute of Asian Studies (NIAS), Copenhagen, October 28–30, 1999.

Garnett, Sherman. *Rapprochement or Rivalry? Russia-China Relations in a Changing Asia.* Washington, D.C.: Carnegie Endowment for International Peace, 2000.

Garrett, Laurie. *Betrayal of Trust: The Collapse of Global Public Health.* New York: Hyperion, 2000.

Gillespie, Judith. "The New Civic Society in the Information Age: A Comparative Analysis of Mongolian Models of Women's Empowerment." Paper presented at the Mongolia Society Annual Meeting, Washington, D.C., 1998.

Ginsburg, Tom. "Political Reform in Mongolia." *Asian Survey* 35, no. 5 (May 1995): 459–71.

———. "Mongolia in 1996." *Asian Survey* 37, no. 1 (January 1997): 60–64.

———. "Mongolia in 1997." *Asian Survey* 37, no. 1 (January 1998): 64–68.

———. *Judicial Review in New Democracies: Constitutional Courts in Asian Cases.* Cambridge: Cambridge University Press, 2003.

Ginsburg, Tom, and Gombosuren Ganzorig, "Constitutional Reform and Human Rights." In Ole Bruun and Ole Odgaard, eds., *Mongolia in Transition,* 147–64. London: Curzon Press, 1996.

———. "When Courts and Politics Collide: Mongolia's Constitutional Crisis." *Columbia Journal of Asian Law* 14, no. 2 (2001): 309–26.

Goldstein, Melvyn, and Cynthia Beall. *The Changing World of Mongolia's Nomads.* Berkeley: University of California Press, 1994.

Gombosuren, Urantsooj. *Political Participation of Women in Mongolia.* Seoul: Korean Institute for Women and Politics, February 9, 1999.

Goulden, Clyde, et al. "Recommendations for Establishment of an International Long-Term Ecological Research Program in Mongolia." Photocopy. Ulaanbaatar, 1996.

Goyal, Hari. "Development Perspective of Mongolia." *Bulletin of the International Association for Mongol Studies* 2 (1995): 16–35.

———. "A Development Perspective on Mongolia." *Asian Survey* 39, no. 4 (July–August, 1999): 633–655.

Grainger, David. "The Great Mongolian Gold Rush." *Fortune* 148, no. 13 (December 29, 2003): 158–62.

Grasslands and Grassland Sciences in Northern China: A Report of the Committee on *Scholarly Communication with the People's Republic of China, Office of International Affairs, National Research Council.* Washington, D.C.: National Academy Press, 1992.

Green, Elizabeth. "China and Mongolia: Recurring Trends and Prospects for Change." *Asian Survey* 26, no. 12 (December 1986): 1337–63.

Greider, William. "The Global Crisis Deepens: Now What?" *The Nation,* October 19, 1998, 11–16.

Griffin, Keith, ed. *Poverty and the Transition to a Market Economy in Mongolia.* London: Macmillan, 1995.

———. "A Strategy for Poverty Reduction in Mongolia." Photocopy. Ulaanbaatar: UNDP, Mongolia, July 2001.

Grivelet, Stéphane. "Reintroducing the Uighur-Mongolian Script in Mongolia Today." *Mongolian Studies* 18 (1995): 49–60.

Gupta, B. D. "Radiological and Oncological Facilities for Cancer." Photocopy. Ulaanbaatar: World Health Organization, 1995.

Haggard, M. T. "Mongolia: The Uneasy Buffer." *Asian Survey* 5, no. 1 (January 1965): 18–23.

———. "Mongolia: New Soviet Moves to Bolster Ruling Group." *Asian Survey* 6, no. 1 (January 1966): 13–17.

———. "Mongolia: The First Communist State in Asia." In Robert Scalapino, ed., *The Communist Revolution in Asia.* Englewood Cliffs, N.J.: Prentice-Hall, 1969.

Haghayeghi, Mehrdad. "Politics of Privatization in Kazakhstan." *Central Asian Survey* 16, no. 3 (September 1997): 321–36.

Hahm, Hongjoo. *The Development of the Private Sector in a Small Economy in Transition: The Case of Mongolia.* Washington, D.C.: World Bank, 1993.

Hammond, Thomas. "The Communist Takeover of Outer Mongolia: Model for Eastern Europe?" In Thomas Hammond, ed., *The Anatomy of Communist Takeovers,* 107–44. New Haven, Conn.: Yale University Press, 1975.

Hare, John. "Searching for the Wild Bactrian Camel." *Natural History,* May 2000, 74–83.

Hare, Paul, ed. *Systemic Change in Post-Communist Economies.* London: Macmillan, 1999.

Harper, Caroline. *An Assessment of Vulnerable Groups in Mongolia: Strategies for Social Policy Planning.* Washington, D.C.: World Bank, 1994.

Harrell, Stevan, ed. *Cultural Encounters on China's Ethnic Frontiers.* Seattle: University of Washington Press, 1995.

Hart, Joe. "Mongolia: 20th Year of Economic Planning." *Asian Survey* 8, no. 1 (January 1968): 21–28.

Haslund, Henning. *Men and Gods in Mongolia.* London: Kegan Paul, 1935.

Heaton, William. "Ulanfu: Sketch of a Mongolian Career Through Crisis." *Canada-Mongolia Review* 4, no. 1 (April 1978): 63–69.

———. "Mongolia 1979: Learning from Leading Experiences." *Asian Survey* 20, no. 1 (January 1980): 77–83.

———. "Mongolia in 1990." *Asian Survey* 31, no. 1 (January 1991): 50–56.

———. "Mongolia in 1991." *Asian Survey* 32, no. 1 (January 1992): 50–55.

Herrmann, Wilfried, ed. *Asia's Security Challenges.* Commack, N.Y.: Nova Science Publishers, 1998.

Hessler, Peter. "Letter from Mongolia." *New Yorker,* July 16, 2001, 58–65.

History of the Mongolian People's Republic. Translation by William Brown and Onon Urgunge of the Mongolian text edited by Bagaryn Shirendyb et al. Cambridge, Mass.: East Asian Research Center, Harvard University, 1976.

Hodder, Dick, et al. *Land-locked States of Africa and Asia.* London: Frank Cass, 1998.

Holmes, Stephen. "Capitalist Russia: Lessons for the Liberal State." *Open Society News,* Spring 1998, 16–19.

Humphrey, Caroline. "Pastoral Nomadism in Mongolia: The Role of Herdsmen's Cooperatives in the National Economy." *Development and Change* 9, no. 1 (January 1978): 133–60.

———. "Avgai Khad: Theft and Social Trust in Post-Communist Mongolia." *Anthropology Today* 9, no. 6 (December 1993): 13–16.

———. "Rituals of Death in Mongolia: Their Implications for Understanding the Mutual Constitution of Persons and Objects and Certain Concepts of Property." *Inner Asia* 1, no. 1 (1999): 59–86.

———. *The Unmaking of Soviet Life.* Ithaca, N.Y.: Cornell University Press, 2002.

Humphrey, Caroline, et al. "Attitudes to Nature in Mongolia and Tuva: A Preliminary Report." *Nomadic Peoples* 33 (1993): 51–61.

Humphrey, Caroline, and David Sneath. "Pastoralism and Institutional Change in Inner Asia: Comparative Perspectives from the Meccia Research Project." Photocopy. London: Pastoral Development Network, 1996.

———, eds. *Culture and Development in Inner Asia.* 2 vols. Cambridge: White Horse Press, 1996.

———. *The End of Nomadism: Society, State and the Environment in Inner Asia.* Durham, N.C.: Duke University Press, 1999.

Hunt, Michael. *The Genesis of Chinese Communist Foreign Policy.* New York: Columbia University Press, 1996.

Hyer, Paul. "The Reevaluation of Chinggis Khan: Its Role in the Sino-Soviet Dispute." *Asian Survey* 6, no. 12 (December 1966): 696–98.

———. "Modernizing Mongolia: Some Observations." *Mongolica* 5, no. 26 (1994): 382–93.

Institute for Strategic Studies. *Regional Security Issues and Mongolia.* Ulaanbaatar: T & U Printing Co., 1997.

Institute of Development Studies at the University of Sussex. *Transformation of a Pastoral Economy: A Local View from Arhangai and Dornogobi.* Policy Alternatives for Livestock Development Working Paper No. 2. Brighton: Institute of Development Studies, University of Sussex, August 1991.

———. *Liberalisation of the Mongolian Pastoral Livestock Economy: Policy Issues and Options.* Policy Alternatives for Livestock Development Working Paper No. 3. Brighton: Institute of Development Studies, University of Sussex, September 1991.

———. *Options for the Reform of Grazing Land Tenure in Mongolia.* Policy Alternatives for Livestock Development Policy Options Paper No. 1. Brighton: Institute of Development Studies, University of Sussex, September 1993.

International Labour Organization. "Report to the Government on the Actuarial and Financial Valuation of the Social Insurance Pensions Scheme." Photocopy. Geneva, 1994.

———. "Macro Policies and Poverty Alleviation: Mongolia." Photocopy. Bangkok, February 1997.

———. "Report on Child Labour Situation in Mongolia." Photocopy. Ulaanbaatar, May 1997.

International Monetary Fund. *The Mongolian People's Republic: Toward a Market Economy.* Washington, D.C., April 1991.

———. *Mongolia, 1996.* Washington, D.C., February 1996.

International Republican Institute. *A Decade of Democracy.* Washington, D.C., 1994.

———. *Key Candidates in Mongolia's Parliamentary Polls.* Washington, D.C., 1996.

———. *Pre-Election Assessment: 1996 Parliamentary Elections in the Republic of Mongolia, 1996.* Washington, D.C., 1996.

———. *Annual Report, 1996.* Washington, D.C., 1997.

———. *Mongolia: Political Situation Update & Presidential Election Briefing.* Washington, D.C., May 1997.

————. *Post-Election Analysis: Mongolia.* Washington, D.C., 1997.

————. *Programming in Mongolia, 1991–1998.* Washington, D.C., 1998.

Jacobson, Esther, and James Meacham. "When Stones Speak: Mapping and Mongolian Surface Archaeology." *Geo Info Systems* 8, no. 2 (February 1998): 14–22.

Jacobson, Harold, and Michel Oksenberg. *China's Participation in the IMF, the World Bank, and GATT.* Ann Arbor: University of Michigan Press, 1990.

Jagchid, Sechin. *Essays in Mongolian Studies.* Provo, Utah: David M. Kennedy Center for International Studies, Brigham Young University, 1988.

Jagchid, Sechin, and Paul Hyer. *Mongolia's Culture and Society.* Boulder, Colo.: Westview Press, 1979.

Jagchid, Sechin, and Van Jay Symons. *Peace, War, and Trade along the Great Wall.* Bloomington: Indiana University Press, 1989.

Jankowiak, William. *Sex, Death, and Hierarchy in a Chinese City.* New York: Columbia University Press, 1993.

Jargalsaikhan, Mendee. "The Democratic Civilian Control of the Mongolian Armed Forces: The State Ih Hural." M.A. thesis, Naval Postgraduate School, 2000.

Jarrett, Keith. "Mongolia in 1987." *Asian Survey* 28, no. 1 (January 1988): 78–85.

Johnson, Chalmers. *MITI and the Japanese Miracle.* Stanford, Calif.: Stanford University Press, 1982.

Johnson, Eric. "Mongolian Electronic Mass Media." Photocopy. Ulaanbaatar, July, 1996.

Johnston, Alastair Iain, and Robert Ross, eds. *Engaging China: The Management of an Emerging Power.* London: Routledge, 1999.

Jontsen, Matti. "Mongolian Police." Photocopy. UN Prevention and Criminal Justice Programme, 1993.

Juergensmeyer, Mark. *The New Cold War? Religious Nationalism Confronts the Secular State.* Berkeley: University of California Press, 1993.

Kaplonski, Christopher. "Collective Memory and Chingunjav's Rebellion." *History and Anthropology* 6, nos. 2–3 (1993): 235–59.

————. "Evoking the Past: Official and Unofficial Histories under State Socialism." Paper presented at the Oral History Association Conference, Philadelphia, October 1996.

————. "'For the Memory of the Hero Is His Second Life': Truth, History and Politics in Late Twentieth Century Mongolia." Ph.D. diss., Rutgers University, 1996.

————. "Creating National Identity in Socialist Mongolia." *Central Asian Survey* 17, no. 1 (1998): 35–49.

————. *Mongolia: Democracy on the Steppe*. London: RoutledgeCurzon, 2004. Not seen.

Kappagoda, Nihal. *The Asian Development Bank*. Boulder, Colo.: Lynne Rienner, 1995.

Kapstein, Ethan. *Governing the Global Economy: International Finance and the State*. Cambridge, Mass.: Harvard University Press, 1994.

————. *Sharing the Wealth: Workers and the World Economy*. New York: Norton, 1999.

Kemmerer, Frances, et al. "Institutional Strengthening in the Education Sector." Photocopy. Pittsburgh: University of Pittsburgh School of Education, 1997.

Khazanov, Anatoly. *Nomads and the Outside World*. London: Cambridge University Press, 1984.

Kim Icksoo. "Tumen River Area Development Program and the Prospects for Northeast Asian Economic Cooperation." *Asian Perspective* 19, no. 2 (Fall–Winter 1995): 75–102.

Kim Sun-ho. *Die Entwicklung der politischen Beziehungen zwischen der Mongolischen Volksrepublik und der Volksrepublik China (1952–1989)*. Hamburg: Institut für Asienkunde, 1992.

Kim Wang-Bae. "Migration of Foreign Workers into South Korea: From Periphery to Semi-Periphery in the Global Labor Market." *Asian Survey* 44, no. 2 (March–April 2004): 316–35.

Kiselev, S. V, ed. *Drevnemongol'skie goroda* [Ancient Mongolian cities]. Moscow: Nauka, 1965.

Klugman, Jeni, ed. *Poverty in Russia: Public Policy and Private Responses*. Washington, D.C.: Economic Development Institute of the World Bank, 1997.

Kojima, Yukiko. "Women in Development: Mongolia." Photocopy. Manila: Asian Development Bank, May 1995.

Kolpakova, Vera. "The Political Implications of Regional Cooperation in Northeast Asia: Russia's Changing Role in the Region, and the Potentials of the Tumen River." M.A. thesis, University of Arizona, 1993.

Konrad Adenauer Foundation, Mongolia. "Action Plan for the Development of Co-operatives in Mongolia." Photocopy. Ulaanbaatar, May 1998.

Korsun, Georges Gabay. "Inside Ownership, Internal Influence, and Enterprise Behavior: Evidence from the Mongolian Large Privatization." Ph.D. diss., University of Maryland, 1995.

Korsun, Georges, and Peter Murrell. "Politics and Economics of Mongolia's Privatization Program." *Asian Survey* 35, no. 5 (May 1995): 472–86.

Kotkin, Stephen, and Bruce Elleman, eds. *Mongolia in the Twentieth Century: Landlocked Cosmopolitan.* Armonk, N.Y.: M. E. Sharpe, 1999.

Kotzel, Uwe. *Die Mongolische Volksrepublik: Politik, Wirtschaft und Gesellschaft: Eine Auswahlbibliographie.* Hamburg: Deutsches Übersee-Institut, Übersee-Dokumentation, Referat Asien und Sudpazifik, 1993.

Krouchkin, Yuri. *Mongolia Encyclopedia.* Ulaanbaatar, 1998.

Lake, Joseph. "Frontier Embassy." *Foreign Service Journal,* December 1992, 35–38.

Lan Mei-hua. "The Mongolian Independence Movement of 1911: A Pan-Mongolian Endeavor." Ph.D. diss., Harvard University, 1996.

Lattimore, Owen. *Nationalism and Revolution in Mongolia.* New York: Oxford University Press, 1955.

———. *Nomads and Commissars: Mongolia Revisited.* New York: Oxford University Press, 1962.

Lawless, Jill. *Wild East: Travels in the New Mongolia.* Toronto: ECW Press, 2000.

Liao, Hollis. "Outer Mongolia's Expulsion of Ethnic Chinese and Its Relations with Communist China." *Issues and Studies* 19, no. 10 (1983): 67–81.

———. "Recent Political Reform in Mongolia." *Issues and Studies* 27, no. 6 (1991): 86–101.

Liao Shu-hsing [Liao, Hollis]. " 'Min-chu lien-meng' chu-cheng te Meng-ku cheng-fu—min-chu-hua te k'ao-yen" [The Mongolian government under the rule of the Democratic Coalition]. *Chung-kuo Ta-lu yen-chiu* 42, no. 3 (March 1999): 85–95.

Liberal Women's Brain Pool. *Women's Empowerment and Development.* Ulaanbaatar, 1998.

Lukin, Alexander. "Russia's Image of China and Russian-Chinese Relations." *East Asia* 17, no. 1 (Spring 1999): 5–39.

Lutaa, Badamkhand. "Mongolian Media in Transition: Problems and Challenges." In *Reflection: Media Studies Centre.* Ulaanbaatar, November 1994.

Ma, Ho-t'ien. *Chinese Agent in Mongolia.* Translated by John De Francis. Baltimore: Johns Hopkins Press, 1949.

Macdonald, A. M. "The Hydrogeology of Mongolia." Keyworth, Nottingham: British Geological Survey, 1995.

MacDonald, Carolyn. "Nutrition and Food Security Survey Report." Ulaanbaatar: World Vision Mongolia, October 1997.

Maidar, D. *Grafika Mongolii.* Moscow, 1988.

Maidar, Ts. "Combating Hunger in Mongolia Using Urban Agriculture." Ulaanbaatar: Poverty Alleviation Study Centre, 1996.

Malhotra, Kamal. "Mongolia: Initial Impressions and Suggestions." Ulaanbaatar: Save the Children–UK, Mongolia, May 1998.

Man, John. *Gobi: Tracking the Desert.* New Haven, Conn.: Yale University Press, 1999.

———. *Genghis Khan: Life, Death, and Resurrection.* London: Bantam Press, 2004.

Marsden, Philip. "The Weather in Mongolia." *Granta,* Fall 2003, 29–45.

Marsh, Peter. *Mongolian Pop-Rock Unleashed.* Ulaanbaatar: UN Development Programme, Mongolia, 1999.

Martelle, Scott. "Horse Race of a Different Color." *Los Angeles Times,* March 15, 1998.

Martin, Roger Philip. "An Economic Analysis of Alternative Grazing Institutions in a Transition Economy: Jargalant 'Suum' Mongolia." Ph.D. diss., Washington State University, 1995.

Marton, Andrew, Terry McGee, and Donald Paterson. "Northeast Asian Economic Cooperation and the Tumen River Area Development Project." *Pacific Affairs* 68, no. 1 (Spring 1995): 8–32.

Maslennikov, V. A. *Contemporary Mongolia.* Translated by David Montgomery. Occasional Papers No. 1. Bloomington, Ind.: Mongolia Society, 1964.

Matthiessen, Peter. *The Birds of Heaven.* New York: North Point Press, 2001.

Mayer, Jane. "Letter from Washington: Contract Sport." *New Yorker,* February 16 and 23, 2004, 80–91.

McCarthy, T. "Ecology and Conservation of Snow Leopards, Gobi Bears, and Wild Bactrian Camels in Mongolia." Ph.D. diss., University of Massachusetts, 2000.

McMillan, James. "Mongolia: The Economy in 1968." *Asian Survey* 9, no. 1 (January 1969): 23–28.

Mead, Rebecca. "Letter from Mongolia: The Crisis in Cashmere." *New Yorker,* February 1, 1999, 57–63.

Mearns, Robin. "Pastoralists, Patch Ecology and Perestroika: Understanding Potentials for Change in Mongolia." *Institute of Development Studies Bulletin* 22, no. 4 (1991): 25–33.

———. *Pastoral Institutions, Land Tenure and Land Policy Reform in Post-Socialist Mongolia.* Policy Alternatives for Livestock Development Research Report

No. 3. Brighton: Institute of Development Studies, University of Sussex, February 1993.

———. "Territoriality and Land Tenure Among Mongolian Pastoralists: Variation, Continuity and Change." *Nomadic Peoples* 33 (1993): 73–103.

———. "Community, Collective Action and Common Grazing: The Case of Post-Socialist Mongolia." *Journal of Development Studies* 32, no. 3 (February 1996): 297–339.

———. "Sustaining Livelihoods on Mongolia's Pastoral Commons—Insight from Participatory Poverty Assessment." *Development and Change* 35, no. 1 (2004): 107–39.

Merli, Laetitia. "Shamanism in Transition." Paper presented at an international workshop "Mongolians from Country to City," held at the Nordic Institute of Asian Studies (NIAS), Copenhagen, October 28–30, 1999.

Meserve, Ruth. "An Historical Perspective of Mongol Horse Training, Care, and Management: Selected Texts." Ph.D. diss., Indiana University, 1987.

Middleton, Nick. *The Last Disco in Outer Mongolia.* London: Orion Books, 1992.

Milivojevic´, Marko. *The Mongolian Revolution of 1990: Stability or Conflict in Inner Asia?* Conflict Studies 242. London: Research Institute for the Study of Conflict and Terrorism, June 1991.

Miller, Robert J. "A Selective Survey of Literature on Mongolia." *American Political Science Review* 46, no. 3 (September 1952): 849–66.

Milne, Elizabeth, et al. *The Mongolian People's Republic: Toward a Market Economy.* Washington, D.C.: International Monetary Fund, April 1991.

Mitchell, Michael. "Mongolia." In William Carpenter and David Wiencek, eds., *Asia Security Handbook, 2000,* 215–22. Armonk, N.Y: M. E. Sharpe, 2000.

Mongolia. *Consumer Protection Law of the Mongolian People's Republic.* Ulaanbaatar, 1991.

———. *Banking Law of Mongolia.* Ulaanbaatar, 1992.

———. *Personal Income Tax Law of Mongolia.* Ulaanbaatar, 1992.

———. *Labor Law of Mongolia.* Ulaanbaatar, 1993.

———. *Law on the Government of Mongolia.* Ulaanbaatar, 1993.

———. *Civil Code of Mongolia.* Ulaanbaatar, 1994.

———. *Law of Mongolia on Prohibiting Unfair Competition.* Ulaanbaatar, 1994.

———. *Law on the Constitutional Tsets (Court).* Ulaanbaatar, 1994.

———. *Cooperative Law of Mongolia.* Ulaanbaatar, 1995.

———. *Resolution of the State Great Hural Concept of National Security of Mon-*

golia; *Concept of Mongolia's Foreign Policy; The Fundamentals of the Military Doctrine of Mongolia.* Ulaanbaatar, 1995.

——— "Project and Technical Assistance Proposals, 1996–1998." Photocopy. Ulaanbaatar, 1996.

———. *Press Law of Mongolia.* Ulaanbaatar, 1998.

———. *Economic Growth Support and Poverty Reduction Strategy.* Ulaanbaatar, 2003.

———. Ministry of Defense. *Mongolian Defense White Paper, 1997–1998.* Ulaanbaatar, 1998.

———. *Defense White Paper.* Ulaanbaatar, 2001.

———. Ministry of External Relations. *Foreign Policy Blue Book.* Ulaanbaatar, 2000.

———. Ministry of Foreign Affairs. *Mongolia in the World.* Ulaanbaatar, 2002.

———. Ministry of Health. Centre for Health Statistics and Information. *Health Statistics of Mongolia, 1960–1992.* Ulaanbaatar, 1993.

———. Ministry of Nature and the Environment. *Mongolian Red Book.* Ulaanbaatar, 1996.

———. National Chamber of Commerce and Industry. *White Paper on Mongolian Economy and Foreign Trade.* Ulaanbaatar, 2003.

———. National Human Rights Commission. *Human Rights and Freedoms in Mongolia: Status Report, 2003.* Ulaanbaatar, 2003.

———. National Statistical Office [State Statistical Office before 1997]. "Women and Children of Mongolia." Photocopy. Ulaanbaatar, 1995.

———. *Mongolian Economy and Society in 1996.* Ulaanbaatar, 1997.

———. *Mongolian Statistical Yearbook.* 1997–2002. Ulaanbaatar, 1998–2003.

——— *Monthly Statistical Bulletin.* 1998–2004.

———. State Property Committee of Mongolia. "Introduction to the Mongolian State Property Committee." Ulaanbaatar, 1996.

Mongolia and Consulting Services Co. *Annual Report.* Ulaanbaatar, 1998.

Mongolia and Inner Asia Studies Unit, University of Cambridge. *Inner Asia: Occasional Papers* 1– (1996–2004).

Mongolian People's Revolutionary Party. Ulaanbaatar: Mongolian People's Revolutionary Party, February, 1997.

Morgan, Amanda. *Corruption: Causes, Consequences, and Policy Implications: A Literature Review.* Washington, D.C.: Asia Foundation, October 1998.

Moses, Larry. "Sino-Japanese Confrontation in Outer Mongolia: The Battle of Nomonhan–Khalkhin Gol." *Journal of Asian History* 1, no. 1 (1967): 64–85.

————. *The Political Role of Mongol Buddhism.* Indiana University Uralic and Altaic Series, vol. 133. Bloomington: Research Institute for Inner Asian Studies, Indiana University, 1977.

Müller, Franz-Volker. "New Nomads and Old Customs: General Effects of Privatisation in Rural Mongolia." *Nomadic Peoples* 36–37 (1995): 175–94.

Müller, Franz-Volker, and Bat-Ochir Bold. "On the Necessity of New Regulations for Pastoral Land Use in Mongolia." *Applied Geography and Development* 48 (1996): 29–51.

Murphy, George G. S. *Soviet Mongolia: A Study of the Oldest Political Satellite.* Berkeley: University of California Press, 1966.

Murrell, Peter. "Reform's Rhetoric-Realization Relationship: The Experience of Mongolia." In Kazimierz Poznanski, ed., *The Evolutionary Transition to Capitalism,* 79–96. Boulder, Colo.: Westview Press, 1995.

Murrell, Peter, et al. *The Culture of Policy Making in the Transition from Socialism: Price Policy in Mongolia.* College Park, Md.: Center for Institutional Reform and the Informal Sector, September 1992.

Nakahashi, Tetsuo. "New Trends in the Study of Modern Mongolian History: What Effect Have Political and Social Changes Had on Historical Research?" *Acta Asiatica* 76 (1999): 7–39.

Namjim, T. *The Economy of Mongolia: From Traditional Times to the Present.* Edited by William Rozycki. Bloomington, Ind.: Mongolia Society, 2000.

Namkhainyambuu, Tserendash. *Bounty from the Sheep: Autobiography of a Herdsman.* Translated by Mary Rossabi. Introduction by Morris Rossabi. Cambridge: White Horse Press, 2000. Originally published under the title *Khonini khishig.*

National Museum of Mongolian History. *A Guide to the Museums of Ulaanbaatar.* Ulaanbaatar, 1997.

National University of Mongolia. *Information Network.* Pamphlet. Photocopy. Ulaanbaatar, n.d.

Neupert, Ricardo, and Sidney Goldstein. *Urbanization and Population Redistribution in Mongolia.* Occasional Paper Series, Population Series 122. Honolulu: East-West Center, December 1994.

Nixson, Frederick, and Bernard Walters. "Administrative Reform and Economic Development in Mongolia, 1990–1997: A Critical Perspective." *Policy Studies Review* 16, no. 2 (Summer 1999): 147–74.

————. "The Transition to a Market Economy: Mongolia, 1990–1998." Unpublished paper.

————, eds. *The Mongolian Economy: A Manual of Applied Economics for a Country in Transition.* Northhampton, Mass.: Edward Elgar, 2000.

Njama, Bulgan, et al. "Preliminary Findings and Recommendations of the Feasibility Study for Wind and Solar Energy for Rural Areas in Mongolia." UN Development Programme, Ulaanbaatar, October 1, 1993.

Novacek, Michael. *Dinosaurs of the Flaming Cliffs.* New York: Doubleday, 1996.

Olsen, Edward. "The Tumen Project CBM: An American Strategic Critique." *Asian Perspective* 19, no. 2 (Fall–Winter 1995): 53–73.

Olsen, John, et al. "Paleolithic Field Investigations in Mongolia, 1995." Photocopy. University of Arizona, Tucson, 1995.

———. *Archaeological Studies Carried Out by the Joint Russian-Mongolian-American Expedition in Mongolia in 1995.* Novosibirsk: Russian Academy of Sciences, Siberian Branch, Institute of Archaeology and Ethnography, 1996.

Olson, Craig, et al. *Combating Corruption in Developing and Transitional Countries: A Guidelines Paper for USAID.* Bethesda, Md.: Development Alternatives, Inc., March, 1998.

Onon, Urgunge. *Mongolian Heroes of the Twentieth Century.* New York: AMS Press, 1976.

Onon, Urgunge, and Derek Pritchatt. *Asia's First Modern Revolution: Mongolia Proclaims Its Independence in 1911.* Leiden: E. J. Brill, 1989.

Open Society Institute. *Programs on Performing Arts, Publishing, Arts and Culture, English Language, Travel Grants, Health Care, Educational Advisement.* Ulaanbaatar, 1997–98.

———. "Social Science Curriculum," "Ethics Curriculum," "Knowledge about Society." Photocopies of typed reports. Ulaanbaatar, 1997–98.

———. *Directory of Mongolian NGOs.* Ulaanbaatar, 2003.

"Oulan-Bator: Misére en sous-sol," *L'Express International* 2689 (January 16–22, 2003): 58–67.

Ovorkhangai *Aimag.* Chancellery of the Governor. "Local Program of Action for the Development of Children by the Year 2000." Photocopy. Ulaanbaatar, 1993.

Oyun, Sanjaasüregiin. *Monghol ornii shinechleltiin khuu zaya* (The current political, social and economic situation in Mongolia and the fate of transition). Ulaanbaatar, 2002.

———. "From the Year of the White Horse to the Year of the Black Horse." *International Institute for Asian Studies Newsletter* 31 (July 2003): 1–3.

Paine, S. C. M. *Imperial Rivals: China, Russia, and Their Disputed Frontier.* Armonk, N.Y.: M. E. Sharpe, 1996.

Pasternak, Burton, and Janet Salaff. *Cowboys and Cultivators: The Chinese of Inner Mongolia.* Boulder, Colo.: Westview Press, 1993.

Peck, Robert. "Chagi's Charge." *Natural History* 107, no. 5 (June 1998): 28–37.

Pedersen, Morten. "Aspects of Every Day Life in Post-Socialist Rural Mongolia." Paper presented at an international workshop "Mongolians from Country to City," held at the Nordic Institute of Asian Studies (NIAS), Copenhagen, October 28–30, 1999.

Petrov, Victor. *Mongolia: A Profile.* London: Pall Mall Press, 1970.

"Politbarometer." See Sumati, Luvsandendev.

Political Education Academy. Ulaanbaatar, 1998.

Potkanski, Tomasz, and Slavoj Szynkiewicz. *The Social Context of Liberalisation of the Mongolian Pastoral Economy.* Policy Alternatives for Livestock Development Research Report No. 4. Brighton: Institute of Development Studies, University of Sussex, March 1993.

Pozdneyev, A. M. *Mongolia and the Mongols.* Translated by John Robert Shaw and Dale Plank. Indiana University Uralic and Altaic Series, vol. 61. Bloomington: Research Institute for Inner Asian Studies, Indiana University, 1971.

———. *Religion and Ritual in Society: Lamaist Buddhism in Late 19th-Century Mongolia.* Translated by Alo Raun and Linda Raun. Occasional Papers no. 10. Bloomington, Ind.: Mongolia Society, 1978.

Press Institute of Mongolia. *Mass Media Survey of Mongolia.* Ulaanbaatar, July, 1997.

———. *Monitoring Mongolian Media, 2000.* Ulaanbaatar, 2001.

———. *Monitoring Mongolian Media, 2002.* Ulaanbaatar, 2003.

Quah, Jon. "National Anti-Corruption Plan for Mongolia." Ulaanbaatar: UN Development Programme, Mongolia, 1998.

Rai, Mahatam. "Mongolian Traditional Medicine." Ulaanbaatar: World Health Organization, 1995.

Reconstruction Bank of Mongolia. *1997 Annual Report.* Ulaanbaatar: Interpress, 1998.

Riskin, Carl, and Azizur Rahman Khan. *Inequality and Poverty in China in the Age of Globalization.* New York: Oxford University Press, 2000.

Robinson, Bernadette, and Altai Solongo. "The Gender Dimension of Economic Transition in Mongolia." In Frederick Nixson and Bernard Walters, eds. *The Mongolian Economy: A Manual of Applied Economics for a Country in Transition,* 231–55. Northhampton, Mass.: Edward Elgar, 2000.

Robinson, David. "Politics, Force, and Ethnicity in Ming China: Mongols and the Abortive Coup of 1461." *Harvard Journal of Asiatic Studies* 59, no. 1 (June 1999): 79–124.

Rosenberg, Daniel. "Political Leadership in a Mongolian Nomadic Pastoralist Collective." Ph.D. diss., University of Minnesota, 1977.

———. "Cultural Issues in the Privatization of Mongolia's Pastoral Production." *Mongolica* 7 (1996): 251–62.

Ross, Jeffrey. "The Mongolian People's Republic as a Prototypical Case of a Comparative Politics of Communist Systems." *Canada-Mongolia Review* 4, no. 1 (April 1978): 1–15.

Rossabi, Morris. *China and Inner Asia.* London: Thames & Hudson, 1975.

———. "Khubilai Khan and the Women in his Family." In Wolfgang Bauer, ed., *Studia Sino-Mongolica: Festschrift für Herbert Franke,* 153–80. Wiesbaden: Franz Steiner Verlag, 1979.

———. *Khubilai Khan: His Life and Times.* Berkeley: University of California Press, 1988.

———. "Mongolia: A New Opening?" *Current History,* September 1992, 278–83.

———. "How the Sino-Russian Summit Plays on the Steppe." *Asian Wall Street Journal,* April 25, 1996.

———. "Mongolia Recovers a National Identity." *Asian Wall Street Journal,* May 29, 1996.

———. *Mongolia in the 1990s: From Commissars to Capitalists?* Open Society in Central Eurasia Occasional Papers Series no. 2. Ulaanbaatar: Open Society Institute, August 1997.

———. "The Ming and Inner Asia." In Frederick Mote and Denis Twitchett, eds., *Cambridge History of China,* vol. 8, pt. 2: *The Ming Dynasty, 1368–1644,* 221–71. Cambridge: Cambridge University Press, 1998.

———. "A New Mongolia in a New World." In *Mongolian Political and Economic Development during the Past Ten Years and Future Prospect,* 42–85. Taipei: Mongolian and Tibetan Affairs Commission, 2000.

———. "Sino-Mongolian Relations." Paper presented at Columbia University Faculty Seminar, October 2000.

———. "The Development of Mongol Identity in the Seventeenth and Eighteenth Centuries." In Leonard Blusse and Felipe Fernandez-Armesto, eds., *Shifting Communities and Identity Formation in Early Modern Asia,* 45–60. Leiden: Research School of Asian, African, and Amerindian Studies, Leiden University, 2003.

———. "Communist and Post-Communist Law and Private Land." In Wallace Johnson, ed., *Central Asian Law: An Historical Overview: A Festschrift in Cele-*

bration of Herbert Franke's 90th Birthday. Monograph Series. Lawrence, Kan.: Journal of Asian Legal History, 2004.

———, ed. *Governing China's Multiethnic Frontiers.* Seattle: University of Washington Press, 2004.

Rupen, Robert. "The Mongolian People's Republic and Sino-Soviet Competition." In A. Doak Barnett, ed., *Communist Strategies in Asia.* New York: Praeger, 1963.

———. *Mongols of the Twentieth Century.* Indiana University Uralic and Altaic Series, vol. 37, pts. 1 and 2. Bloomington: Research Institute for Inner Asian Studies, Indiana University, 1964.

———. *The Mongolian People's Republic.* Stanford, Calif.: Hoover Institution Press, 1966.

———. "The Mongolian People's Republic: The Slow Evolution." *Asian Survey* 7, no. 1 (1967): 16–20.

———. *How Mongolia Is Really Ruled: A Political History of the Mongolian People's Republic, 1900–1978.* Stanford, Calif.: Hoover Institution Press, 1979.

Russell, Nigel, and Soren Waast. "Non-Formal Distance Education for the Gobi Women Project." Ulaanbaatar: UNESCO, 1994.

Sabloff, Paula. ed., *Modern Mongolia: Reclaiming Genghis Khan.* Philadelphia: University of Pennsylvania Museum of Archaeology and Anthropology, 2001.

Sachs, Jeffrey, ed. *Towards Economic Strategies for Rapid Growth in Mongolia.* Cambridge, Mass.: Harvard Institute for International Development, September 1997.

Sachs, Jeffrey, and Andrew Warner. "Prospects for Rapid Economic Growth in Mongolia." Cambridge, Mass.: Harvard Institute for International Development, June 1997.

Sadoway, David. "Emerging Tourism Frictions with Mongolian Traditional Ecological Knowledge." Paper presented at an international workshop "Mongolians from Country to City," held at the Nordic Institute of Asian Studies (NIAS), Copenhagen, October 28–30, 1999.

Sambuu, Jamsrangyn. *Malchdad okh Zovlolgoo* [Advice to herders]. Ulaanbaatar: State Publishing House, 1956.

Sanders, A. J. K. *The People's Republic of Mongolia: A General Reference Guide.* London: Oxford University Press, 1968.

———. *Mongolia: Politics, Economics and Society.* London: Frances Pinter, 1987.

———. "Mongolia in 1988." *Asian Survey* 29, no. 1 (January 1989): 59–66.

———. "Mongolia in 1989." *Asian Survey* 30, no. 1 (January 1990): 59–66.

————. "Restructuring and Openness." In Shirin Akiner, ed., *Mongolia Today*. London: Kegan Paul, 1991.

————. "Foreign Relations and Foreign Policy." In Ole Bruun and Ole Odgaard, eds., *Mongolia in Transition*, 217–51. London: Curzon Press, 1996.

————. "Parliament in Mongolia." In Philip Norton, ed., *Parliaments in Asia*. London: Frank Cass, 1999.

Sanjdorj, M. *Manchu Chinese Colonial Rule in Northern Mongolia*. Translated by Urgunge Onon. New York: St. Martin's Press, 1980.

Sauer, Christina. "The Resurgence of Tradition in a Post-Communist Society: The Role of the Mongolian 'ger' as a Vehicle for the Maintenance of Ideology and Practice in the Diachronic Process of Mongolian Society." *Central Asiatic Journal* 45, no. 1 (2001): 63–127.

Save the Children Fund. *Girl Children as Sex Workers: Situation and Trends in Mongolia*. Ulaanbaatar, 1998.

Schmidt, Susanne. *Mongolia in Transition: The Impact of Privatization on Rural Life*. Saarbrücken: Verlag für Entwicklungspolitik, 1995.

School of Foreign Service, National University of Mongolia. Ulaanbaatar, 1998.

Schran, Peter, and George Yu, eds. *Mongolia and Northeast Asia: Economic Development and Regional Cooperation*. Urbana, Ill.: Center for East Asian & Pacific Studies, 1999.

Schwarz, Henry. *Bibliotheca Mongolica*. Bellingham: Western Washington University Program in East Asian Studies, 1978.

————. "The Security of Mongolia." *Mongolian Journal of International Affairs* 3 (1996): 77–87.

Scully, Malcolm. "The Struggle to Protect a Pristine Mongolian Lake." *Chronicle of Higher Education*, March 24, 2000, B12–B13.

Sen, Amartya. *Development as Freedom*. New York: Knopf, 1999.

Sermier, Claire. *Mongolia: Empire of the Steppes*. Hong Kong: Airphoto International, 2002.

Serruys, Henry. *Sino-Mongolian Relations during the Ming*, vol. 2: *The Tribute System and Diplomatic Missions (1400–1600)*. Brussels: Institut belge des hautes études chinoises, 1967.

Severin, Tim. *In Search of Genghis Khan*. New York: Atheneum, 1992.

Severinghaus, Sheldon. "Mongolia in 1994: Strengthening Democracy." *Asian Survey* 35, no. 1 (January 1995): 70–75.

————. "Mongolia in 1995: Gearing Up for the 1996 Elections." *Asian Survey* 36, no. 1 (January 1996): 95–99.

————. "Mongolia in 1998 and 1999: Past, Present, and Future at the New Millennium." *Asian Survey* 40, no. 1 (January–February 2000): 130–39.

Shapiro, Fred. "A Reporter at Large (Mongolia)." *New Yorker,* January 20, 1992, 39–58.

Sharma, R. C., ed. *Mongolia: Tryst with Change and Development.* New Delhi: Vision and Venture, 1997.

Shirendev, Bazaryn. *Through the Ocean Waves: The Autobiography of Bazaryn Shirendev.* Translated by Temujin Onon. Bellingham: Center for East Asian Studies, Western Washington University, 1997.

Shulman, Frank J. *Doctoral Dissertations on China and Inner Asia, 1976–1990: An Annotated Bibliography of Studies in Western Languages.* Westport, Conn.: Greenwood Press, 1998.

Silverman, Bertram, and Murray Yanowitch. *New Rich, New Poor, New Russia: Winners and Losers on the Russian Road to Capitalism.* Armonk, N.Y.: M. E. Sharpe, 1997.

Skidelsky, Robert. "The Mystery of Growth." *New York Review of Books* 50, no. 4 (March 13, 2003): 28–32.

Smith, Robert. "Mongolia: In the Soviet Camp." *Asian Survey* 10, no. 1 (January 1970): 25–29.

Sneath, David. "The Impact of the Cultural Revolution in China on the Mongolians of Inner Mongolia." *Modern Asian Studies* 28, no. 2 (1994): 409–30.

————. "The Institutional Frames for Pastoralism and the Decollectivisation of the Mongolian Pastoral Economy." Paper presented at an international workshop "Mongolians from Country to City," held at the Nordic Institute of Asian Studies (NIAS), Copenhagen, October 28–30, 1999.

————. *Changing Inner Mongolia.* Oxford: Oxford University Press, 2000.

————. "Reciprocity and Notions of Corruption in Contemporary Mongolia." *Mongolian Studies* 25 (2002): 85–100.

————. "Lost in the Post: Technologies of Imagination and the Soviet Legacy in Post-Socialist Mongolia." *Inner Asia* 5, no. 1 (2003): 39–52.

Snow, Edgar. *Red Star over China.* New York: Garden City Publishing Co., 1939.

Soros, George. *George Soros on Globalization.* New York: Public Affairs, 2002.

Spaulding, Seth, et al. "The Education System of Mongolia." Photocopy. Pittsburgh: School of Education, University of Pittsburgh, 1993.

————. "Mongolia Human Resource Development and Education Reform Project." Photocopy. Pittsburgh: School of Education, University of Pittsburgh, 1993.

Staisch, Peter, and Werner Prohl. *Dschingis Khan Lächelt: Die Mongolei auf dem Weg zur Demokratie.* Bonn: Bouvier Verlag, 1998.

Stein, Günther. *The Challenge of Red China.* New York: McGraw-Hill, 1945.

Steiner-Khamsi, Gita, Sengedorj Tumendelger, and Ines Stolpe. "School-Related Migration in Mongolia." Ulaanbaatar: Mongolian Foundation for an Open Society, 2003.

Stiglitz, Joseph E. *Globalization and Its Discontents.* New York: Norton, 2002.

———. *The Roaring Nineties: A New History of the World's Most Prosperous Decade.* New York: Norton, 2003.

Strickland, S. S. "Human Nutrition in Mongolia during Economic Liberalisation: Available Data and Key Research Issues." Policy Alternatives for Livestock Development Research Report No. 2. Brighton: Institute of Development Studies, University of Sussex, January 1993.

Strickland-Scott, Simon. "Urban and Rural Life in Post-Socialist Mongolia." *Mongolian Studies* 24 (2001): 7–40.

Sumati, Luvsandendev. "Mass Media in Election Campaign of 1996." Photocopy. Ulaanbaatar, 1996.

———. "NGO Performance." Photocopy. Ulaanbaatar, 1996.

———. "Sant Maral Foundation." Photocopy. Ulaanbaatar, 1996.

———. "Politbarometer." Photocopy. Ulaanbaatar, 1997–2004.

———. "Public Perception of Privatisation in Mongolia." Photocopy. Ulaanbaatar, April 1999.

———. "Policy Makers and Opinion Leaders' Perception of Privatisation in Mongolia." Photocopy. Ulaanbaatar, September 1999.

Szynkiewicz, Slawoj. "Mongolia's Nomads Build a New Society Again: Social Structures and Obligations on the Eve of the Private Economy." *Nomadic Peoples* 33 (1993): 163–72.

Tang Kwong-leung and Wong Chack-kie, eds. *Poverty Monitoring and Alleviation in East Asia.* New York: Nova Science Publishers, 2003.

Tang Shiping. "Economic Integration in Central Asia." *Asian Survey* 40, no. 2 (March–April, 2000): 360–76.

Theroux, Eugene, and Michael Moser. *Business Guide to Mongolia.* Hong Kong: Asia Information Associates, 1996.

Tokyo Donors' Meeting. "Infrastructure Development Paper," Photocopy. February 1996.

———. "Paper on National Poverty Alleviation Programme." Photocopy. February 1996.

Tomlinson, Richard. "From Genghis Khan to Milton Friedman: Mongolia's Wild Ride to Capitalism." *Fortune,* December 7, 1998, 192–200.

Tong Yanqi. *Transitions from State Socialism: Economic and Political Change in Hungary and China.* Lanham, Md.: Rowman & Littlefield, 1997.

Tsogt, Nyamsüren. "Mongolia in the Grip of Poverty." In Yogesh Atal, ed., *Poverty in Transition and Transition in Poverty,* 223–55. New York: Berghahn Books–UNESCO, 1999.

Tsolmon, S., et al. *Foreign Trade Survey of Mongolia.* Ulaanbaatar, June 1996.

Tumen, D. "Introduction to the Anthropological Study in Mongolia." Photocopy. Ulaanbaatar, 1996.

Undarya, Tumursukh. "Fighting Over the Interpretation of the Mongolian Woman in Mongolia: Post-Socialist Identity Construction Discourse." *East Asia* 19, no. 3 (Fall 2001): 119–46.

Unenbat, Jigjidiin. "Mongolia: Legal Reform for a Market Economy." In *Governance: Promoting Sound Development Management: Seminar in Fukuoka, Japan on 10 May, 1997,* 113–20. Manila: Asian Development Bank, 1997.

United Nations Children's Fund [UNICEF]. "An Analysis of the Situation of Children and Women in Mongolia." Ulaanbaatar: UNICEF, 1995.

———. *UNICEF Mongolia.* N.p., n.d.

United Nations Development Fund for Women. *Women in Mongolia: Mapping Progress under Transition.* Ulaanbaatar, 2001.

United Nations Development Programme [UNDP]. Mongolia. "Development of Renewable Energy Applications for Rural Energy Supply." Photocopy. Ulaanbaatar, 1991.

———. "Reduction of Atmospheric Pollution from the Burning of Coal: Proposed Programme Strategy, 1992–1996." Ulaanbaatar, 1991.

———. "Development of Distance Education for 'Education for All.'" Ulaanbaatar, 1993.

———. *Mongolia's Wild Heritage.* Ulaanbaatar, 1996.

———. *Blue Sky Bulletin,* November 1997–98. www.un-mongolia.mn/archives/bsb-mag (accessed April 28, 2004).

———. *Human Development Report, 1996.* New York: Oxford University Press, 1997.

———. *Human Development Report: Mongolia, 1997.* Ulaanbaatar, 1997.

———. "Mongolia Update." Photocopy. 1997–98.

———. "Mongolian NGO Capacity Survey to Support Sustainable Human Development." Ulaanbaatar, April 1997.

———. "Solid Waste Management Study in Ulaanbaatar." Ulaanbaatar, November 1997.

———. *Biological Diversity in Mongolia.* Ulaanbaatar, 1998.

———. *Mongolia Update, 1998.* Ulaanbaatar, 1998.

———. *United Nations System in Mongolia, 1998.* Ulaanbaatar, 1998.

———. *Human Development Report: Mongolia, 2000.* Ulaanbaatar, 2000.

———. *Human Development Report: Mongolia, 2003: Urban-Rural Disparities.* Ulaanbaatar, 2003.

———. *A Partnership for Progress.* Ulaanbaatar, n.d.

United States Agency for International Development [USAID]. "Country Strategic Plan for Mongolia, FY 1999–2003." Photocopy. Ulaanbaatar, September 1998.

United States. Department of State. *Mongolia: Country Report on Human Rights Practices.* Annual report. Various years. Washington, D.C., 1990–2001.

Uranchimeg, Ts. *Union of Mongolian Artists–2000.* Ulaanbaatar: Dino Publishing, 2000.

Vardi, Nathan. "The Promoter." *Forbes,* November 24, 2003, 125–32.

Vogel, Ezra. *Japan as Number One.* Cambridge, Mass.: Harvard University Press, 1979.

Vreeland, Herbert Harold. *Mongol Community and Kinship Structure.* New Haven, Conn.: Human Relations Area Files Press, 1954.

Wang Wei-fang. *Chiu-shih nien-tai Meng-ku yü Chung-kung te cheng-ching kuan-hsi* [Ninety years of political and economic relations between Outer Mongolia and China]. Taipei: Meng-Tsang wei-yuan-hui, 1998.

Waugh, Louisa. *Hearing Birds Fly: A Nomadic Year in Mongolia.* London: Abacus Books, 2003.

Wedel, Janine. *Collision and Collusion: The Strange Case of Western Aid to Eastern Europe, 1989–1998.* New York: St. Martin's Press, 1998.

———. "The Harvard Boys Do Russia." *The Nation,* June 1, 1998, 11–14.

Williams, Dee. "Alcohol Indulgence in a Mongolian Community of China." *Bulletin of Concerned Asian Scholars* 30, no. 1 (January–March, 1998): 13–22.

Williams, John. "Mass Media in Post-Revolution Mongolia." 1995. http://userpage.fu-berlin.de/~corff/im/Landeskunde/john.html (accessed May 5, 2004).

Women for Social Progress Movement. "Election-96: Post-Election Conference Report." Photocopy. Ulaanbaatar, 1996.

———. *Voter Education Centre.* Ulaanbaatar, 1998.

Women's Information and Research Centre. *Survey on Social Insurance Issues.* Ulaanbaatar, December 1996.

―――. *Information on Gender.* Ulaanbaatar, 1997.

―――. *The Economic Status of Mongolian Women in the Transition Period.* Ulaanbaatar, May 1998.

―――. *STD/HIV/AIDS Knowledge, Attitude, and Behavior among the High Risk Group People—Female Sex Workers / Prostitutes and Homosexuals.* Ulaanbaatar, 1998.

―――. *Survey on the Vulnerable Groups Income Generation Project.* Ulaanbaatar, 1998.

―――. *Directory of Women's Non-Governmental Organizations in Mongolia.* Ulaanbaatar, 1999.

Woo, Wing Thyee, Stephen Parker, and Jeffrey Sachs, eds. *Economies in Transition.* Cambridge, Mass.: MIT Press, 1997.

Woodworth, Jessica. "Letter from Ulaanbaatar." *Persimmon* 3, no. 1 (Spring 2002): 38–45.

World Bank. *Mongolia: Aide Mémoire.* Ulaanbaatar, March–April 1994.

―――. *Mongolia: Public Enterprise Review Halfway through Reforms.* Washington, D.C., November 1996.

―――. *1998 Annual Meetings of the Board of Governors—Summary Proceedings, Washington, D.C., October 6–8, 1998.* Washington, D.C., 1999.

―――. *Mongolia: Participatory Living Standards Assessment.* Ulaanbaatar, 2001.

―――. *Rural Development Strategy for Mongolia.* Ulaanbaatar, 2002.

World Vision, Mongolia. "Addressing Food Security in Mongolia." Ulaanbaatar, January 1998.

Wu, Kin Bing. *Mongolia: Financing Education During Economic Transition.* Washington, D.C.: World Bank, 1994.

Zurag: Women Artists of Mongolia. San Francisco: Asian Pacific Islander Cultural Center, 2001.

Zvigelskaia, Irina. *The Russian Policy Debate on Central Asia.* London: Royal Institute of International Affairs, 1995.

NEWS AGENCIES

Associated Press. Mongolia. 1996–2004.

E-Mail Daily News. Mongolia. 1996–2003.

Foreign Broadcast Information Service. People's Republic of China. 1975–95.

Itar-Tass. Mongolia. 1996–2004.

Montsame News Agency. Mongolia. 1996–2004.

Press Trust of India. 2001.

Reuters. Mongolia. 1990–2004.

Xinhua: Mongolia. 1996–2004.

MAGAZINES AND NEWSPAPERS

Asian Survey, 1965–2004.

Far Eastern Economic Review, 1990–2004.

Gobi Business News, 1999–2004.

Mongol Messenger, 1991–2004.

Mongolia Business Review, March–April 1995–1997.

[Political Education Academy, Ulaanbaatar] *Mongolia Insight,* 1996–2004.

Mongolia Monthly, 1995–97.

Mongolia News, 1997–2001.

Mongolia This Week, 2000–2002.

Mongolian Journal of International Affairs, 1994–2004.

[Arts Council of Mongolia] *Newsletter on Mongolian Arts,* 2003–4.

UB Post, 1996–2004.

World Affairs 184, no. 1 (2002).

ANNUAL REPORTS, ULAANBAATAR, 1997–2002

Almaas Mining

APU Spirit and Beverage

Baga Nuur Coal Mine

CAA Hotel

Devshil Trade

Erdenet Mining

Gobi Cashmere

Jargalant Mining

Makh Impex

MIAT Mongolian Airlines

Mongolrosvetmet Mining

Neft Petroleum Import Concern
Nukht Tourism
Office Building of the Ardyn Bank
Shoroon Ord Mining
Solongo Restaurant
Spirit Bal Buram
State Department Store
Zoos Goyol Jewelry

Full Mongolian names are indexed in the following order: first name, comma, surname.

Asian Development Bank (ADB)
(continued)
270n7, 273n45, 285n131,
340–41n52; analysis of planned
economy, 44–48; dictates of,
72–73; education and, 107,
310n136; free trade and, 45; health
and, 168–70; housing and, 106;
market economy and, 43–44, 238;
and poverty reduction, 92–93, 139,
297n28; taxes and, 45–46
Association for Asian Studies, 288n28
Association for the Disabled, 78
Association of Southeast Asian
Nations, 222
Australia: Mongolian relations with,
223, 332n73
Avery, Martha, 154–55
Azerbaijan, 86

Bactrian camel, 180–81
Bagabandi, Natsagiin, 32, 220–21,
223, 233, 242; on pensions, 146; as
president, 79, 81–82, 86, 98
Baker, James, visit to Mongolia,
36–37, 39
Bakula, Kushok, 223
Banco Lugane Commerciale, 97,
277n75
Bangladesh, 143
banking system: problems in, 51–52,
58, 83–85, 99, 110, 123, 134, 154,
263n48; scandals in, 73, 83–85, 91,
94
Barents, 277n75
Batbayar, Bat-Erdeniin ("Baabar"),
49, 67, 237; career of, 26; as minister of finance, 83, 336n27
Batbayar, S., on poverty program,
137

Batbold, Tserenpuntsag, market
economy and, 70, 77–78
Batmünkh, Jambyn, 22–23, 230;
reforms and, 7–9
Bat-Uul, Erdenii, 4, 5, 24, 309n124;
in Erdenet, 13–14; Mongolian
Democratic Party and, 17; hunger
strike and, 19, 21
Bayangol Hotel, 17
Bayan-Ölgii, 125, 195, 219–20,
279nn91,92; rock painting
in, 211
Beauclerk, John, 307n108
Beijing, 1, 7, 226, 228–32, 312n163
Bellamy, Carol, 137
Bodi International Group, 68
Bogd Khan mountains, 180–81,
239
Bold, Luvsanvandangiin, 68, 73,
263n53
Bold, Ravdan, 234, 334n16
Boshigt, Gongorjavyn, 19
Brazilian State Bank, 269n7
British Council, 160
British Embassy, 65
Bruun, Ole, on poverty, 139–40
Buddhism, 29, 30, 40, 114, 185,
190–92, 223, 233, 321nn96,97;
purges against, 183, 190
Bulgan, 87
Bulgaria, 214
Buryatia, 241
Buryat Mongolians, 3, 5
Bush, George W., 328n42
Buyan Cashmere Company, 98, 112,
323n1
Byambasüren, Dashiin, 5, 200–201,
241; on China, 240; demonstra-
tions and, 21; IMF and, 58; meet-
ing with James Baker, 37; pensions

and, 126; as prime minister, 28,
    48–49

California, 269n7
Cambodia, 143
Cambridge University, 49, 130
camels, decrease of, 182
Canada, mining, 209
cashmere, 77, 100, 123–24, 131,
    326n30
Center for Chinese Studies, 237
Center for Preserving the Mahayana,
    321n96
Center for Vocational Training,
    310n131
Central Asia, relations with, 221–22
Central Asian Bank, 73
Central Procurement Co-operative
    Union, 116–17
Centre against Violence, 147, 153–54
Cheney, Dick and Lynn, 259n24
Chernobyl, 324n14
Chiang Kai-shek, 226
child labor, 144
Children's Book Palace, 310n136
China, 134, 244; abuses, 238–40;
    Central Asia and, 244, 340n51;
    economic relations, 234–37,
    335nn19,20, 335n23, 336n24; mili-
    tary cooperation, 234; Mongolian
    food imports, 231; Mongolian rela-
    tions with, 225–44
Chinese workers, 227, 229
Chinggis Khan, 26, 29, 184, 186,
    197–98, 245, 279n92, 323n128
Choibalsan, Khorloogiin, 2, 6, 21,
    279n92; purges and, 9, 12; statue
    of, 17, 309n124
Choibalsan city, 17
Christian Democratic Party, 38

Christian missionaries, 41–42
Christiansen, Scott, 299n41
Christina Noble Foundation, 213
cinema, 187–88
circus performers, 187, 319n76
Civil Will Party, 104–5, 108, 112
"Club of Young Economists," 11
collectivization of herds, 31
Columbus, Christopher, 265n75
communications, 87–88
Comprehensive Nuclear Test Ban
    Treaty, 240
Constitutional Court, 94
Constitution of 1992, 51, 53–54, 152,
    191, 196, 327n35
consultants, 42, 64, 282n109;
    lifestyles of, 64–65
Contract with the Mongolian Voter,
    67–68
cooperatives, 129, 291n68
copper, 77, 86, 103
Corporate Income Tax Law, 45; eva-
    sion of, 57, 75, 81
corruption, 59–62, 82, 84, 89–91,
    102, 107–8, 163, 170, 283n117; in
    education, 110, 310n134; in
    Poverty Alleviation Program,
    137–38
Council of Ministers of MPRP, 105,
    192
Council of Mutual Economic Assis-
    tance (COMECON), 30
Council on Foreign Relations, 209
Craven, David, 176–77
crèches, 304n87
crime rate, 147
Cultural Revolution, 227–28, 241
Curtin, Molly, 176–77
Cyrillic alphabet, 33, 197–98
Czech Republic, 213–14

dachas, 143
Dalai Lama, 191–92, 241
DANIDA, 85, 212–13, 248; media
and, 194
Danish Mongolian Society,
307n108
Darkhan, 7, 26, 31, 100, 119, 193,
205–6, 339n45; strikes in, 20
"Days of Mongolian Culture," 206
"Days of Russian Culture," 206
deer, decrease of, 181–82
Defoe, Daniel, 119
Delgerkhangai, 173
Delgermaa, Banzragchiin, 196
Democratic Party, 107, 112
democratic reformers, program of,
26
Democratic Union, 71–73, 76–85,
88–91, 94–98, 107, 112–13, 133,
135, 137–38, 141, 159–60, 173–74,
195, 207–8, 211, 218, 222–23, 247,
249, 266n88, 341n6; founding
of, 67–69; tax policy and, 76, 81,
82
Denizer, Cevdet, 260n7
Denzen, Barsboldt, 319n70
desertification, 179
Diamond Sutra, 192
Dinger, John: privatization and, 96,
276n74; street children and,
157–58
disabled and medical care, 171
divorce, increase of, 153–54
domestic abuse, 147, 153–54, 173,
302n66
donor agencies, market economy
and, 37–38, 55, 64, 68, 99, 103
Dorligjav, Dambyn, 19, 32
Dornod, 17, 100

Dundgov, 56; uranium mining and,
86
Dutch, aid to Mongolia, 212–13

Eagle TV, 41, 194
East Asian Women's Conference, 210
Economist Intelligence Unit, 56, 58,
69, 81, 95, 135, 174, 231, 238, 242
education, 160–67; communism and,
160–61; decline of, 130, 161,
309n129
Egypt, relations with, 222
Elbegdorj, Tsakhiagiin, 4, 14, 25–26,
32, 38, 56, 108, 207, 231, 275n57;
dismissal as prime minister, 91,
94–95; IRI and, 68; as new prime
minister, 113
Enkhbaatar, Damdensürengiin, 19
Enkhbayar, Nambaryn, 83–84,
112–13, 199, 201, 205, 223; Buddhism and, 191, 321n97; herding
and, 129–30; as prime minister,
95–98, 100–101, 104, 323n1,
325n16
Enkhsaikhan, Mendsaikhany, 11, 25,
38, 81, 87, 138, 173–74, 199, 207;
critique of poverty program, 136;
as prime minister, 70, 71, 76–78;
privatization and, 74
Enron, 269n7
Environmental Protection Agency,
103
Erdenebat, Badarchyn, 95, 202
Erdenebileg, Tömör-öchiryn, 7, 19,
26, 31, 34–35, 62–63, 69, 90–91, 95,
111, 133, 198–99; and China, 30, 231
Erdenechuluun, Luvsangiin, 242
Erdenet, 32–34, 40, 50, 107, 193,
203–5, 325n15; reform and, 13; sale

Great Gobi Strictly Protected Area,
179–80
Green Horse Society, 186
Green Revolution, 129
Griffin, Keith, 136, 148–50; critique
of donors, 149–50; critique of privatization, 260n7, 303n75

Harbin, 239
Hawaii, 211
herding, 85, 89, 287n20, 297n34;
banks and, 123; cooperatives
and, 129, 291n68; education and,
124, 126, 158, 162–63, 166; government and, 122, 125–26, 128, 130;
hazards of, 117–19, 125–27; pensions and, 126; privatization of,
120–21, 131, 148, 291n68; Red
Cross and, 128; UNDP and, 128;
women and, 124; World Vision
International and, 128; *zuds* and,
127–28, 131;
Hermitage Museum, 33
Hohhot, 48, 229, 234, 237, 312n163
Hong Kong, 224
hoof and mouth disease, 123, 205,
207, 236, 288n33
housing scandals, 107
Hu Jintao, aid and loans, 244
Hulan, Hashbat, 7, 19, 28, 30, 32–34,
38, 49, 59–60, 74, 95, 111, 113, 199,
207, 247, 271n21; Committee on
Social Welfare and, 72; on corruption, 78, 90–91; early life and
career of, 4; on foreign aid, 62, 69;
reformers and, 5
Humphrey, Caroline, 130
Hungary, Mongolian relations with,
214

hunger strike, 18–23
hunting income, 180
Hu Yaobang, 228

IBEX, 60–61
Idshinnorov, Sunduyn, 184–85,
318n56
Il Tovchoo, 193
income inequality, 63, 85, 87, 89, 111,
121, 134, 136, 138
India, Mongolian relations with, 223,
332–33n74, 333n75
Indiana University, 189
Indonesia, Mongolian relations with,
134, 222–23, 332n73
industry, decline of, 85–86
infant mortality, 151–52
informal sector, 101–2; taxes and,
270n9; women and, 154
Inner Mongolia, 34, 100, 122, 130,
156, 170, 208–9, 226–29, 233,
241–42, 249–50
Inner Mongolian Autonomous
Region, 234
Institute for International Studies in
Education (University of Pittsburgh), 165
Institute of History, 184
interest rates, 57–58, 83, 99, 109–10
International Commission of Jurists,
53
International Cultural Exchange
Society, 186
International Donors' Conference,
106
International Human Rights Day
demonstrations, 1–2
International Labor Organization,
employment and, 134

International Monetary Fund (IMF), 37, 54, 58, 66, 70, 74, 89, 92, 99, 107, 139, 210, 246–47; cashmere and, 208; control and, 72–73, 81, 100, 103–5; critique of, 62–63, 260n5, 266n86, 269n7; free trade and, 238; gold tax and, 82; market economy and, 44; Most Valuable Companies and, 80, 90; Reconstruction Bank and, 83–84; workers and, 63

International Relations and Exchanges Board, 254n21

International Republican Institute (IRI), 39, 73; elections and, 67–69, 247; Freedom Awards and, 259n24; GDP estimates, 93; poverty and, 93, 106, 303n71

International Women's Day, 21

Internet, 88, 100

Iraq, Mongolian troops in, 212, 328n42

Irish Republican Army, 18

Irkutsk, 155, 203

Islamic Cultural Center, 332n69

Israel, Mongolian relations with, 222

Istanbul, 221

Italy, aid to Mongolia, 212, 214

Itar Tass, 206

Itochu, 217

Ivanhoe Mines, 103, 201, 210, 280n98

Japan: Mongolian relations with, 215–18: aid, 215, 319n73; investment, 217–18; trade, 217

Japanese International Cooperation Agency (JICA), 216, 246

Jargal, 117

Jargalsaikhan, Bazarsadyn, 95, 98, 112, 278n81, 323n1

Jasrai, Puntsagiin, 108, 112; Kazakhstan and, 220; as prime minister, 56–59; scandal and, 61

Jiang Zemin, 233, 337n27

Jilin, 336–37n27

Johnson, Don, 66

Jordan, Mongolian relations with, 222

justice system, 196

Kaifu Toshiki, 215

Kazakhs, 195–96, 219–20, 279n91, 322n118

Kazakhstan, 86, 195, 219–21, 340n51

Khalkha Mongolians, 5

Khara Khorum, 33, 183, 211, 279n92, 319n70

Khonini khishig, 114

Khonkh band, 2

khoomii (throat singing), 188

Khovd, 32, 40, 203, 318n51

Khövsgöl, 140; disturbances in, 24

Khövsgöl Lake, 180

Khövsgöl National Conservation Park, 180

Khrushchev, Nikita, virgin land policy and, 7

Khubilai Khan, 198

Khural, 18–19, 21, 23, 25–28, 38, 40, 50, 55, 67–69, 71–74, 76, 78, 82–84, 90–91, 94–96, 98, 103, 107–9, 111, 120, 130, 133, 137, 178–80, 195–96, 203–4, 229, 234, 246–47, 249, 270n8, 275n57, 283n116, 285n124, 309n124, 322n118, 327n35; deadlock in, 16; elections, 112–13; 318n51; speaker of, 79

Khustain Nuruu National Park, 181
kiosks and public health, 143,
    280n95, 300n51
Kohlenberg, Leah, 193
Konrad Adenauer Foundation: activi-
    ties, 38–39, 291n68; elections and,
    67, 247
Korean Air Lines, 218
Kovyktinskoye, 237
Kuwait, 221
Kuwait Foundation, 221
Kyrgyzstan, 219–20

LaTrobe University, 332n73
Land Law, 288n25
Leeds University, 4
Lenin, Nikolai, 6, 16; statue of, 17,
    309n124
Lenin Museum, 14
Liberal Women's Brain Pool, 159,
    308n115
Li Peng, visit to Mongolia, 232, 241
Living Standards Measurement Sur-
    vey, 136
Lkhagvasüren, Jamyangiin, 9–10;
    statue of, 186
Lop Nor, 212
Lufthansa, 214
Luxembourg, 213

Ma, Yo-Yo, 188
Macao, 307n103
Maidar, Ts., 299n44
Malaysia, Mongolian relations with,
    223
Manchester University, 49, 102, 133,
    136, 214
Mao Zedong, Mongolia and, 226
market economy, 25–26, 36, 75–76,
    110, 113, 142, 146, 182, 222–23, 246;

conflation with democracy, 246;
    critique of, 148–50, 154, 301n58;
    education and, 160–67; environ-
    ment and, 176, 179; herders and,
    122–23, 127–28, 131
Marsh, Peter, 189
Marubeni Corporation, 98, 278n81
maternal mortality, 151–52
maternity rest homes, 151–52
McCain, John, 39
MCS, 61, 99, 278n84
Mearns, Robin, 130
meat market, 123, 204, 325n16
Media Law, 195
Medical and Pedagogical Institute,
    171
medical care, 118; communist era
    and, 167–68; decline of, 125–26,
    131, 169–70, 312n163, 313nn174,176;
    market economy and, 167–73; pri-
    vatization of, 152
medical equipment, lack of, 169–70
Megjid Janraisig, 191
Merkuri market, 134
Metropolitan Museum of Art,
    323n128
MIAT, 77–78, 97–98, 214, 218
Middleton, Nick, 5, 28
Military Museum, 185
Millennium Road, 100–101, 103,
    279nn91,92, 335n20; herders and,
    129–30
mineral extraction, 57, 86, 89, 101–3,
    109, 177–78; environment and,
    316n39
Minerals Law, 82
Ming dynasty, 238
minimal government, 52, 57, 63, 71,
    75–77, 89, 143, 293n5; critique of,
    148–50; environment and, 176–83;

herding and, 122, 125–26, 128, 130; job creation, 134; pensions and, 146; poverty and, 138; social sector and, 132, 306n99
Ministry of Defense, 234, 244
Ministry of Education, 126
Ministry of Finance, 108
Ministry of Foreign Trade, 204
Ministry of Health, 107, 167
Ministry of Infrastructure, 195, 322n117
Ministry of Justice, 193, 195
Ministry of Nature and Environment, 142, 317n45; weakness of, 176–79, 182–83, 199
Ministry of Public Security, 18, 22
Ministry of Science, Technology, Education, and Culture, 187
Ministry of Social Welfare and Labor, 140
Minjin Hashbat, 4
Mohammed al-Fayad, 128
Molomjamts, Demchigiin, career and views of, 21
Monastery Museum of the Choijin Lama, 185
Mongol Amicale, 208–9, 238
Mongol Central Bank, 53, 55, 73–74, 83–84, 104, 265n67
Mongol Daatgal Bank, 73
Mongolia: China and, 9; name of, 54; United States and, 9
Mongolian Academy of Sciences, 4, 317n45
Mongolian and Tibetan Affairs Commission, 243
Mongolian Business Women's Federation, 158–59
Mongolian Chamber of Commerce, 236, 277n74

Mongolian-Chinese Economic and Business Council, 236
Mongolian Contemporary Art Center, 186
Mongolian Defense White Paper, 234
Mongolian Democratic Party, 5, 17, 26–27
Mongolian Democratic Union, 4, 18–20, 22–23; founding of, 11; program of, 11–15
Mongolian Development Support Foundation, 241
Mongolian Embassy, 163
Mongolian Employers' Confederation, 108
Mongolian Federation of Trade Unions, 144
Mongolian Foundation for an Open Society, 79, 159, 162, 180, 185, 189; education and, 164, 310n136; films and, 188; radio and, 193–94
Mongolian Free Labor Committee, 23
Mongolian Green Party, 23
Mongolian Journalists' Union, 15
Mongolian National Democratic Party (MNDP), 67–68, 83, 95
Mongolian National Museum, 184, 318n56
Mongolian National University, 17–18, 161
Mongolian New Socialist Party (Motherland), 95
Mongolian People's Revolutionary Party (MPRP), 1, 5, 7–8, 18, 24, 27–29, 49–50, 55–56, 67–69, 74, 77, 79, 81, 83–84, 96, 98–99, 108, 110, 113, 115, 117, 119, 134, 159–60, 169, 173, 184, 211, 225, 230, 232, 240, 249, 266n86, 301n56, 323n1,

Nomonhan, 10
Nordic Development Fund, 310n136
North Korea, 143, 212, 218
Norway, aid to Mongolia, 212–13
Norwegian Agency for International
    Development Cooperation
    (NORAD), 212–13
Novacek, Michael, 211
nuclear power, 324n14
Number 4 Power Station, 215
nursing schools, 152

Ochirbat, Punsalmaagiin, 23, 222,
    232–33; foreign aid and investment,
    54, 56, 59, 77; foreign advisors and,
    70–71; Japan and, 215; loss of elec-
    tion, 79; as president, 28
Od, Jambaljamtsyn, 61; on China,
    231
Odjargal, Jambaljamtsyn, 61–62
Ölgii, 279n92
Olson, Kirk, 316n39
Onghi River, 273n39
Open Society Institute, 288n28
Orkhon valley, 221
Osaka, 217
overgrazing, 119, 122, 124, 130, 177,
    179
*ovoo*s, 192
Oxford University, 148
Oyun, Sanjaasürengiin, 3, 26, 30,
    32–33, 36, 39, 49, 60, 63–65, 72,
    87, 113, 133, 160, 196, 198–99,
    207–9, 211, 247, 275n56, 283n116;
    Buddhism and, 191; coalition with
    Republican Party, 111–12; on con-
    sultants, 42; on corruption, 62; on
    economic policy, 137; on energy
    prices, 108–9; on environment,
    177, 180, 182–83; on foreign aid,

59, 104–5; free trade and, 75–76;
    on IMF policies, 238; on income
    inequality, 134; on indebtedness,
    92, 95, 104–5; in Khural, 91; on
    Mongolia's future, 251; on privati-
    zation, 51; on shock therapy, 47
Oyuntsetseg, Oidov, 154
Oyu Tolgoi (Turquoise Hill), 103,
    201, 210, 326n32

Pasha, Hafiz, 250
pawnshops, 58, 101–2
pensions, 145–48, 152–53, 301n58;
    defined benefits, 145–48; defined
    contributions, 145–48; herders
    and, 118; privatization of, 145
perestroika and glasnost, 2, 5, 7–8,
    11–12
Personal Income Tax Law, 45
Pickering, Thomas, 81
Poland, 214
Politburo, 19, 20–23
Political Academy, 38
poverty: attitudes toward, 135–36,
    148–50; culture of, 150; measure-
    ment of, 136, 293n12, 294n20,
    295n26; social dislocation and,
    147; in Ulaanbaatar, 140–44
Poverty Alleviation Program, 59,
    135–40, 149–50, 155, 303n71; health
    and, 169; inadequacy of, 135
poverty eradication, 92–94, 106
Pravda, 192
Press Institute, 194, 213
price liberalization, 52, 55, 62, 71–72,
    77
Primakov, Yevgeny, 201
private sector growth: critique of,
    136–40, 148–50; poverty and,
    132–36, 276n74, 297n28, 303n71

Tumen River, 334n14, 336n27
Turkey, relations with, 221
Turkish International Cooperation
    Agency, 221
Turkish Studies Center, 221
Turkmenistan, 86, 219
Turks, 197
Tuul river, 178–79
Tuva, 241
Tuya, Nyam-Osoryn, 160, 222, 334n9

"UB Days," 237
UB Post, 240
UB Radio, 192
UB Railway, 201, 205
Ukraine, 214
Ulaan, Chultemiin, 96; as deputy
    prime minister, 113; unemploy-
    ment and, 134
Ulaanbaatar, 2, 4–5, 13–15, 17, 25–26,
    32–35, 37, 39, 56, 60, 64–65, 75–76,
    81–82, 87–88, 91, 95, 101, 105–6,
    108, 119, 130–31, 133, 134–39, 155–57,
    159, 161–62, 168, 170–75, 179–81,
    185–86, 188–89, 191–94, 206–7,
    210–18, 221, 223, 226, 229–30, 232,
    236, 241–42, 244, 263n53, 271n21,
    279n92, 297n34, 300n50, 306n103,
    332nn69,73 339n49; air pollution
    and, 142, 178; apartments in, 141,
    205; population growth and, 122,
    297nn32,33, 298n36; poverty in,
    140–44, 277n74; sanitation and,
    142, 330n61; street children and,
    157–58, 216, 307n108; trash removal
    in, 142–43
Ulaanbaatar Hotel, 17, 157
Ulanhu, 227
unemployment, 77–78, 100, 102–3,
    109–10, 121, 133–34, 139, 285n124;
    women and, 153, 155

Unen, 8, 192
Unenbat, Jigjidiin, 83
UNESCO, 193–94, 319n68
Ungern-Sternberg, Roman Nikolaus
    Fyodorovich von, 31
UN High Commission for Human
    Rights, 196
UNICEF, 137
Union of Mongolian Artists, 186
Union of Mongolian Believers, 23
Union of Mongolian Students, 20
United Kingdom, 212
United Nations Development
    Programme, 37, 54, 102, 106,
    141–42, 148–50, 172, 189, 194,
    248, 282n109, 336n27; environ-
    ment and, 178–81, 299n45; herders
    and, 128, 291n68; Human Devel-
    opment Report and, 89–90;
    Northeast Asia and, 236–37; on
    poverty, 93, 135, 138, 303n75
United States, 134, 145–47; military
    cooperation with, 211
UN Security Council, 217
urbanization, 32
Urga, 31
U.S. Agency for International Devel-
    opment (USAID), 61–62, 65, 70,
    81, 92, 96, 101–2, 110, 145–46, 159,
    176–77, 194, 270n7, 277nn75,77,
    295n26
U.S. Embassy, 66, 211, 317n41
U.S. Federal Regulatory Commis-
    sion, 269n7
user fees, 107, 136, 166, 168, 174
Uvs, 32, 203
Uyghur script, 33
Uzbekistan, 219

Value Added Tax (VAT), 106–7, 136,
    282n110

Composition, printing and binding: Sheridan Books, Inc.
Cartographer: Bill Nelson
Text: 11/14 Adobe Garamond
Display: Gill Sans Book